MEDIEVAL ARCHITECTURE
AND ITS INTELLECTUAL
CONTEXT

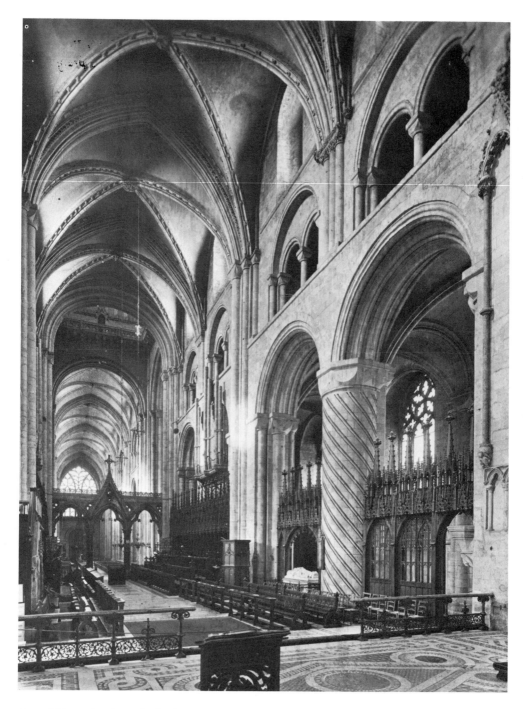

Frontispiece. Durham Cathedral, interior view of choir, looking west.

MEDIEVAL ARCHITECTURE
AND ITS INTELLECTUAL
CONTEXT

STUDIES IN HONOUR OF
PETER KIDSON

EDITED BY

ERIC FERNIE AND PAUL CROSSLEY

THE HAMBLEDON PRESS

LONDON   AND   RONCEVERTE

Published by The Hambledon Press, 1990

102 Gloucester Avenue, London NW1 8HX (U.K.)
309 Greenbrier Avenue, Ronceverte WV 24970 (U.S.A.)

ISBN 1 85285 034 5

British Library Cataloguing in Publication Data

Medieval Architecture and its Intellectual Context:
  Studies in Honour of Peter Kidson
    1. Europe. Architecture, Medieval – 300–1399
    I. Fernie, Eric   II. Crossley, Paul
    III. Kidson, Peter
    723

Library of Congress Cataloging-in-Publication Data

Medieval Architecture and its Intellectual Context:
  Studies in Honour of Peter Kidson
  Edited by Eric Fernie and Paul Crossley
    1. Architecture, Medieval – Themes, motives
    I. Kidson, Peter
    II. Fernie, E.C.   III. Crossley, Paul
    NA350.M43   1990
  723 – dc20   90-435663 CIP

Typeset by Ponting–Green Publishing Services, London
Printed on acid-free paper and bound in the U.K.
by Southampton Book Company, Southampton

Contents

Preface

This book consists of a collection of essays written as a mark of respect and affection for Peter Kidson as a teacher and as an architectural historian, on the occasion of his retirement from the Courtauld Institute. Contributors were approached either because they had been taught by him or had worked closely with him as colleagues. Over fifty people indicated that they wished to be associated with the project, and of the twenty-nine who submitted papers twenty-four are ex-pupils and five are colleagues.

No attempt was made to follow a plan or to encourage particular contributors to write on particular subjects, as is normal for *Festschriften*. While this has resulted in a diversity reflecting the varied interests of the recipient, it is equally worthy of note that the contributions are linked by at least one common concern: to see whatever is being discussed in the context of the thought of the time in which it was made. This is of course also one of the hallmarks of Peter Kidson's approach to the study of history and hence justifies the title of the book. To those contributors who have written on sculpture or painting, we would stress the 'and' in the title, arguing that the same intellectual concerns are evident in their essays as in the others, while invoking the no doubt self-interested claim that architecture is the mistress of the arts.

In producing the volume we have received invaluable help from a large number of people. First and foremost there are the contributors themselves, who accepted our various demands with equanimity and met our deadlines with punctuality (though one correspondent compared us unfavourably to the Electricity Board in our attitude towards late submissions). We would also like to record our special thanks to Martin Sheppard of Hambledon Press who could himself be taken for a pupil of the master, given the acuity and effort he has put into helping with the editing and seeing the volume through the press; to Sarah Pearson for all manner of assistance behind the scenes; to Jessica and Ivan Fernie for breaking the back of the keying-in; and to Jane Geddes and Robert Gibbs for advice on rendering compatible word-processed texts.

We gratefully acknowledge our debt to the following for permission to reproduce illustrations: Airfotos (54b); Ampliaciones y Reproducciones Mas (41a); Archives Photographiques, S.P.A.D.E.M. (52); Biblioteca Apostolica Vaticana (62, 67a–c); Bibliothèque Nationale, Paris (29a, 29b, 35a–38b); Church Commissioners (24e); Commissioners of Public Works, Ireland (50a, 50b); Courtauld Institute of Art (11b, 17, 19–20b, 28b, 28c, 30b, 31b, 32a, 33a–34b); English Heritage (14a, 15a, 15b, 16b); Marburg (63c); Munich Library (63b); National Monuments Record, London (18); Royal Commission on the Historical Monuments of England (frontispiece, 23a, 25a–27c); Salisbury Museum, 1, 2a, 2b); Sélestat Library (63a); Trinity College, Cambridge (13b); University of Lancaster Archaeological Unit (16d).

Those who wished to contribute an essay but were unable to are the following: Christie Arno; Joanna Cannon ('Petrarch, Pliny and Simone Martini'); Bridget Cherry ('Calculated Asymmetry? Late Medieval Church Towers in the London Area'); Reg Dodwell; Mary Dean ('W.H. Goodyear and the Theory of the Refinements of Gothic Cathedrals'); Julian Gardner ('The Back Panel of Christ Discovered in the Temple, by Simone Martini'); Virginia Glenn; Richard Halsey; John Higgitt ('*Tituli venusti*: the Role of Inscriptions in Anglo-Saxon Architecture'); Christopher Hohler; Deborah Kahn; John Lowden; Nigel Morgan ('The Proportions of the Page in English Thirteenth-Century Psalters'); Stephen Murray; Christopher Norton; Vivian Paul ('The Main Arcade Straight Bay Piers at Narbonne Cathedral: a Preliminary Assessment'); Hugh Richmond; Lyn Rodley; Veronica Sekules ('The Iconography of the Angel Choir Transformed'); Barry Singleton; Amanda Simpson; Jan van der Meulen ('The Original Location of the Sanctuary of Notre-Dame de Chartres'); and Frank Woodman.

It is hoped that their essays will be published individually with dedications to Peter Kidson.

Paul Crossley   Eric Fernie
Manchester   Edinburgh

April 1990

List of Contributors

Jean Bony	University of California at Berkeley
Alan Borg	Imperial War Museum
Allan M. Brodie	Royal Commission on Historical Monuments
T.H. Cocke	Darwin College, Cambridge
Nicola Coldstream	Macmillan Dictionary of Art
Paul Crossley	Manchester University
Jane Cunningham	Courtauld Institute
Peter Draper	Birkbeck College
Peter Fergusson	Wellesley College
Eric Fernie	University of Edinburgh
Richard Gem	Council for the Care of Churches
Robert Gibbs	University of Glasgow
Lindy Grant	Courtauld Institute
M.F. Hearn	University of Pittsburgh
T.A. Heslop	University of East Anglia
Virginia Jansen	University of California at Santa Cruz
Walter Leedy	Cleveland State University
Andrew Martindale	University of East Anglia
J. Philip McAleer	Technical University of Nova Scotia
Lesley Milner	Newcastle-upon-Tyne
Richard K. Morris	University of Warwick
Kathryn Morrison	Royal Commission on Historical Monuments
Anne Prache	University of Paris IV
Barbara Robertson	Organiser, Courtauld Summer Schools
Roger Stalley	Trinity College, Dublin
Anat Tcherikover	University of Haifa
Christopher Welander	London
Christopher Wilson	Queen Mary and Westfield College
George Zarnecki	Courtauld Institute

Introduction

Although he would be the last to acknowledge it, Peter Kidson is arguably the most influential historian of medieval architecture of his generation in the English-speaking world. Few scholars in his field have remained untouched by his special, and very personal, power to illuminate the broadest areas of medieval architectural history. In his hands medieval buildings have become much more intelligible as central achievements of the medieval mind. These essays, from ex-pupils and friends, are presented to him as a mark of respect and affection for a distinguished scholar and an outstanding teacher.

Peter Kidson was born in York in 1925, virtually in the shadow of the Minster. His fascination with Gothic architecture began in early childhood, for his home was only about a mile from the cathedral, and some of his earliest and most vivid memories were of that gigantic structure. In 1933 his parents moved to Kent, and from 1936 he attended Dartford Grammar School, leaving in 1941 with a School Certificate that included the top mark in Geography for the whole of England. It was in Geography that he gained an exhibition (turned into a scholarship) to Selwyn College in Cambridge in 1943, only to be almost immediately conscripted into the Royal Navy. In 1946 he returned to Cambridge where he took the history Tripos Part 1 in 1948 and got a first and then switched to Moral Sciences, graduating in 1950. He arrived at the Courtauld Institute later the same year, and has been there ever since.

His first two terms at the Institute were spent at the feet of Johannes Wilde, but it was the Middle Ages which really attracted him. At that time Peter attended lectures on French and English Gothic architecture given by Jean Bony at the French Institute. But the most important influence on him came from his tutor Christopher Hohler who introduced him to the values of erudite irreverence, and first kindled his interest in Gothic proportion by setting him an essay on the Milan controversy. He graduated in 1952 with first class honours, despite the fact that he had only finished half the examination paper. What he had written was so brilliant that the examiners (influenced by the confident percipience of Nikolaus Pevsner) were prepared to ignore such a single-minded disregard of the rubric. With the three-year support of a Graham Robertson research scholarship Peter began his doctorate, under the supervision of Geoffrey Webb, on *Systems of Measurement and Proportion in Early Medieval Architecture.* He gained his Ph.D. in 1956 with a thesis which was awarded an informal distinction by the examiners (no official distinctions being allowed). Though never published, the thesis commanded the admiration of scholars as distinguished as Jean Bony (who examined it), Rudolf Wittkower, and Robert Branner. In the meantime, in 1955, he had joined the staff of the Conway Library under George Zarnecki, who was always to give him encouragement and support.

In 1958 he published his first book, *Sculpture at Chartres*, still the most lucid presentation of that intricate iconography, and, at the same time, a refreshing revision of the canonical pronouncements of the great Emile Mâle. In 1959 he was appointed Conway Librarian, and in 1961 was elected a Fellow of the Society of Antiquaries. A year later he published what may be his most influential contribution to the study of English medieval architecture in his chapters in the *History of English Architecture.* Here, for the first time, English Romanesque and Gothic were analysed not in terms of antiquarian detail or 'interior space', but as the history of a series of architectural problems the solutions to which precipitated the emergence of new styles. Through most of the 1960s he dazzled a whole generation of students at the universities of Cambridge and East Anglia with the brilliance of his teaching. In 1967 he was made a full Lecturer at the Institute, and in 1971 was promoted to the post of Reader. His *Medieval World*, published in 1967, gave him the opportunity and the pleasure of applying his flair for speculation and synthesis across a thousand years of history. It was a *tour de force*, and it established his reputation as one of the few historians in his field able to tackle the broadest issues of medieval architecture. No one but Peter Kidson could have completely rewritten the chapters on Gothic for the latest edition of Bannister Fletcher's *A History of Architecture* with such magisterial ease and clarity. His more specialised articles reveal the same breadth of vision: from twelfth-century Tewkesbury to St George's Chapel Windsor, from St Hugh's Choir at Lincoln to the Master of Naumburg, from William of Sens and the factions at Canterbury, to his recent three-pronged attack on the most cherished beliefs of Erwin Panofsky, Otto von Simson, and Sumner Crosby about Suger's St-Denis.

All these studies display a range of rare and inimitable qualities: an elegance of expression that comes, not from some rhetorical formula, but from the strength and clarity of the thought itself; a sensitivity to formal values allied to a deep understanding of the particular historical forces which impinged on the meaning and shape of the architecture; and, perhaps most strikingly, a disciplined grasp of detail combined with an extraordinary gift for connection and synthesis. Virtually single-handed, Peter Kidson has taken the study of medieval architecture in this country onto a new level of intellectual sophistication. Alongside the study of the great churches of the Middle Ages as objects of antiquarian interest and analysis, he has introduced the rigorous and demanding worlds of medieval theology, history, and mathematics. It is a tribute to his influence that most of those practising medieval architectural history in Britain today take these high standards for granted.

Peter dislikes the public display of honours (he has refused an invitation to appear in *Who's Who*), but it would do both him and us a disservice if we were to ignore his record here. In 1972 he was Visiting Professor at the University of Victoria in British Columbia. In 1977 he was honoured with the appointment of Royal Commissioner, and from 1985 to 1987 was Chairman of the Commission's Architectural Committee. In 1982 he was elected President of the British Archaeological Association. In 1986 he was Rhind Lecturer for the Society of Antiquaries of Scotland, and in the same year he began his membership of the British Academy Committee for post-graduate awards in the humanities. Perhaps the most significant tribute to his international reputation was the invitation, in 1980, to deliver the Mellon Lectures at the National Gallery in Washington. His theme was a vastly expanded version of his doctoral thesis. Since then those lectures have been rewritten as a monumental study of systems of proportion and measurement in western architecture, from Periclean Athens to the Rayonnant of Louis IX. The book, soon to be published, promises to provide definitive answers to the most fundamental problems of classical and medieval architecture. In 1988, in recognition of a career of great distinction, he was awarded a Personal Chair in London University.

In the final analysis, it is as a teacher that Peter Kidson may have exercised his deepest and most lasting influence on the discipline of architectural history. He has never cast himself in the role of an instructor or guru; he hates missions and manifestos; he has scant respect for those who confuse education with the acquisition of knowledge. Stimulating and attentive to his students, he inspires their affection and respect. He conducts his classes as a conversation, relaxed, but at the same time demandingly intelligent. We never trod the well-worn highways, and he could open up the broadest intellectual perspective from the smallest archaeological detail, transforming dull collections of data into illuminating experiences of what really happened. Like one of his own intellectual mentors, R.G. Collingwood, he inspired us 'to re-enact the past in our own minds'; and like all great teachers he showed his pupils what really mattered in education: a love of speculation, argument and originality that they would continue to value long after most of them had forgotten whatever they had learned about medieval architecture. To many of those privileged to be taught by him he passed on something of his own Socratic delight in the unorthodox and the intellectually subversive. In the ever-colder climate of Higher Education in contemporary Britain Peter Kidson's example of courtesy, warmth and civilised

intelligence will remind us (to adapt a phrase of the elderly Kant) that
'Das Gefuehl fuer Humanitaet hat uns noch nicht verlassen'.

Peter Kidson

Bibliography of Peter Kidson

'The Gothic Vision': Review of Otto von Simson, *The Gothic Cathedral: The Origins of Gothic Architecture and the Medieval Concept of Order,* London and New York, *Times Literary Supplement* (August 17 1956), p. 486.

Sculpture at Chartres (with Ursula Pariser), London 1958 (reprinted 1974).

A History of English Architecture (with Peter Murray), London 1962 (revised edition 1965).

Contributions to 'Gothic Art' in *Encyclopedia of World Art,* vi, London 1962, ed. Massimo Pallotino *et al.,* pp. 499–510, 555–58, 587, 615–18.

The Gothic World, London 1967 (reprinted in *Landmarks in Western Art,* edited by Bernard S. Myers, New York 1985, pp. 279–438).

'Canterbury Cathedral: The Gothic Choir', *Antiquaries Journal,* 126 (1969), pp. 244–46.

'Vault', in *Encyclopedia Britannica,* 15th edition, Chicago 1974.

Contributions to *The Oxford Companion to Art,* edited by Harold Osborne, Oxford 1970, including articles on Backsteingotik; Bourges Cathedral; Chapter House; Chartres Cathedral; Jean and Pierre de Chelles; Decorated Style; Early English Style; Fibonacci Series; Gothic; Master of Naumburg; Pierre de Montreuil; Norman Style; Notre-Dame, Paris; Noyon Cathedral; Jean d'Orbais; Parler; Perpendicular Style; Reims Cathedral; Rayonnant Style; Sondergotik; Villard de Honnecourt.

'The Architecture of St George's Chapel, Windsor', in *The St George's Chapel Quincentenary Handbook,* Windsor 1975, pp. 29–39.

'The Sub-Roman Style': Review of Hans Erich Kubach, *Romanesque Architecture,* New York 1975, *Times Literary Supplement* (March 18 1977), p. 323.

Lincoln: St Hugh's Choir and Transepts, Courtauld Illustrated Archives, 1/3, 1977 (editor).

Review of Jan van der Meulen, *Notre-Dame de Chartres: Die vorromanische Ostanlage,* Berlin 1975, *Journal of the British Archaeological Association,* 130 (1977), pp. 168–70.

Lincoln: Gothic West Front, Nave and Chapter House, Courtauld
   Illustrated Archives, 1/5, 1978 (editor).

Review of François Bucher, *Architector: The Lodge Books and Sketchbooks of Medieval Architects*, New York 1979, *Journal of the Society of
   Architectural Historians*, 40 (1981), pp. 329–33.

'Architecture and City Planning' and 'The Figural Arts', in *The Legacy
   of Greece: A Reappraisal*, edited by M.I. Finlay, Oxford 1981, pp. 376–
   428.

Review of John Harvey, *The Perpendicular Style, 1330–1485*, London
   1978, *Antiquaries Journal*, 62 (1982), pp. 167–68.

Review of Jean Bony, *The English Decorated Style: Gothic Architecture
   Transformed, 1250–1350*, Oxford 1979, *Burlington Magazine*, 126
   (September 1984), pp. 570–71.

'St. Hugh's Choir', in *Medieval Art and Architecture at Lincoln Cathedral*
   (British Archaeological Association Conference Transactions for 1982),
   Leeds 1986, pp. 29–42.

Review of Jan van der Meulen and Jürgen Hohmeyer, *Chartres: Biographie
   der Kathedrale*, Köln 1984, *Journal of the British Archaeological Association*, 139 (1986), pp. 164–67.

'Gothic' in Sir Bannister Fletcher's *A History of Architecture*, 19th
   edition, edited by John Musgrove, London 1987, pp. 387–523.

'Panofsky, Suger and St Denis', *Journal of the Warburg and Courtauld
   Institutes*, 50 (1987), pp. 1–17.

'A Note on Naumburg', in *Romanesque and Gothic: Essays for George
   Zarnecki*, Woodbridge 1987, pp. 143–46.

Articles in *Macmillans Dictionary of Art* on Bourges Cathedral; Chartres
   Cathedral; Durham Cathedral; Gothic; Lincoln Cathedral; Proportion
   in Western Medieval Architecture; Suger of St Denis; Vitruvius in the
   Middle Ages (forthcoming).

'A Metrological Investigation', *Journal of the Warburg and Courtauld
   Institutes*, 53 (1990) (forthcoming).

Chapter on Art and Architecture, 1050–1250, in *The New Cambridge
   Medieval History*, 4, part 1 (*c.* 1024–1198), edited by David Luscombe
   and Jonathan Riley-Smith (forthcoming).

Systems of Measurement and Proportion in Early Medieval Architecture
   (forthcoming).

List of Illustrations

Tables

1

Some Medieval War Memorials

Alan Borg

Like all exceptional teachers, Peter Kidson has the ability to enthuse his students and to stimulate intellectual curiosity. It is not, therefore, especially surprising that this former student now devotes himself to the field of twentieth-century warfare, a subject which appears remote from the contemplation of Gothic architecture. The way in which I passed from medieval monasteries to modern military hardware is not the present concern, but I hope that I bring the Courtauld Institute disciplines, as taught in the 1960s, to my current calling. There are perhaps some reciprocal benefits as well and this essay springs from a study I had undertaken of the war memorials of the twentieth century.[1]

It seemed to me decidedly odd that, at least at first glance, the Middle Ages was one of the few periods of history not to have war memorials. The present century, with its two World Wars, has of course seen the high point (in numerical terms) of war memorial construction; in Britain alone virtually every village has its memorial, and in towns and cities they exist in multiplicity. Before this, the Boer and Crimean wars had produced a substantial crop of memorials, and the habit of building monuments to military victories can be traced back the Renaissance revival of classical forms and ideas. In antiquity, the most ancient of human monuments include memorials to war; the commemoration of victory was one reason why the Egyptians raised obelisks, and was the main reason why, centuries later, the Romans transported them to Rome and Constantinople, where they remain as symbols of imperial triumph. The Greeks erected the Mound at Marathon and built the Parthenon as memorials, while the Romans created triumphal arches, trophies, and victory columns. Monuments of every shape and kind commemorating war can be found in the ancient world, yet all this seems to have come to an end with the onset of the proverbially Dark Ages. It was only the conscious revival of classical forms during the Renaissance that led to the renewal of interest in memorials to war, so beginning the process which provided the essentially classical vocabulary of memorial forms that have been used in the twentieth century. In this story, the Middle Ages appears as a complete

---

[1] To be published in book form in 1990.

blank, the more unexpected for the fact that our medieval ancestors can hardly be said to have shown any distaste for the practice of war itself.

This was a first impression and, like many first impressions, it contains a certain element of truth, but closer scrutiny revealed that the idea of the war memorial did survive in the Middle Ages, in a variety of traditional forms. One of the most interesting examples of this survival is recorded by Geoffrey of Monmouth as his explanation for the building of Stonehenge.[2] He tells how King Aurelius Ambrosius, whose reign is set in the fifth century at the time Hengist and Horsa arrived in Britain, decided to build a national memorial in memory of his countrymen who were massacred near Salisbury by Hengist. The king collected carpenters and masons from all over the land and ordered them to build a monument of a new form that would commemorate the fallen. However, these craftsmen failed to come up with any ideas and so Tremorinus, Archbishop of the City of the Legions, suggested that Merlin might provide a solution. Once summoned, the magician proposed that the Giant's Ring on Mount Killarus in Ireland should be transported to Britain and re-erected as the national memorial. This was achieved, not without considerable difficulty and danger, and the ring was subsequently used as a royal necropolis and acquired its current name of Stonehenge.

This story has always been of considerable interest to prehistorians, since it appears to embody the folk memory of the movement of the stones from a distant site in the west to their present location – and this of course accords with modern geological opinion.[3] It is, however, equally interesting for its evidence of the survival of the memorial traditions associated with circular structures. Battle burial mounds themselves tend to be round and built memorials often followed this form. The mausolea of famous men like Augustus or Hadrian were round, and there are a number of military round memorials such as the great trophy monument of Adamklissi in Romania.[4] Stonehenge is perhaps more akin to Greek colonnaded *tholoi*, like that at Delphi, and although there is no question of precise parallels it seems virtually certain that a memory of such classical prototypes lies, however distantly, behind Geoffrey of Monmouth's story. It is also of more than passing interest to note that the type was revived in the twentieth century and used by Ninian Comper for the Welsh National Memorial in Cardiff, and by Charlton Bradshaw for the memorial to the missing at Ploegsteert.[5]

---

[2] *Historia Regum Britanniae*, available in many editions and most easily accessible in the translation by Lewis Thorpe, *The History of the Kings of Britain*, London, 1966, pp. 195–99.

[3] See Stuart Piggott, 'The Stonehenge Story', *Antiquity*, 15, 1941, pp. 305–19.

[4] A.V. Radulescu, *The Triumphal Monument Tropaeum Trajani at Adamklissi* (The Museum of National History and Archaeology), Constanta, n.d.

[5] In this context one might also cite the memorial to Indian troops at Neuve Chapelle, designed by Sir Herbert Baker.

The fact that Geoffrey of Monmouth records this story about Stone-henge suggests that it was, in all probability, how the monument was regarded in the Middle Ages. He relates another that preserves a different aspect of the memorial tradition.[6] This tells how Cadwallo, father of Cadwallader, was embalmed and his body placed within a bronze statue of himself on horseback, which had been set up on the West Gate of London as a memorial to his victory at the battle of Hedfield.[7] This monument does not survive (and may be entirely imaginary) but it recalls the classical practice of setting up equestrian figures of victorious commanders. There is some slight evidence for the continuation of this tradition into the Middle Ages; Justinian set up an equestrian figure of himself in Constantinople [8] and Charlemagne transported an equestrian bronze statue, supposedly that of Theodoric, from Ravenna to Aachen in 801. This may have been the inspiration for the well-known small bronze equestrian figure which is frequently identified as Charlemagne on horse-back.[9] However, public equestrian statues were virtually unknown in the west before the Renaissance condottiere revived the idea in thirteenth-century Italy, although the various medieval 'Constantine' figures were of course an aberrant strand of this tradition. It has been strongly argued that the most famous of medieval equestrians, the Bamberg Rider, is in fact a Constantine figure although alternative interpretations range from Alexander the Great to Parzival.[10]

It was equally uncommon in the Middle Ages to mark the site of a battle with a memorial. A possible exception is a stone found in North-ampton in 1823, bearing an inscription that was given in the *Gentleman's Magazine* as:

> Hic locus est iste incursu quo corruit hostis
> Quo cum certeret vincere victus erat

The author suggests these lines may have been penned by some monastic or scholarly person to mark the spot where the Danes or the North-umbrians were repulsed in an attack on Northampton in 1010 or 1064. The epigraphy indicates that the stone is of much later date and it may also be that it concerns a spritual rather than an actual battle. The fact that the stone was found on the edge of a churchyard might lend

---

[6] Thorpe, op. cit., p. 280.

[7] The date and a description of the battle comes from Bede, *Ecclesiastical History*, Bk 2, ch. 20.

[8] It is possible that the well-known medallion showing Justinian on horseback preceded by a figure of Victory may preserve a record of this statue. See C. Morrisson, *Catalogue des monnaies byzantines de la Bibliothèque Nationale*, Paris, 1970, I, p. 69.

[9] P. Lasko, *Ars Sacra*, London, 1972, pp. 18–19.

[10] J. Adhémar, *Influences antiques dans l'art du moyen-âge français*, London, 1939. On the identification of the Bamberg Rider see especially J. Traeger, 'Der Bamberger Reiter in neuer Sicht', *Zeitschrift fuer Kunstgeschichte*, 33, 1970, pp. 1–20.

support to the latter interpretation and so its identification as a war memorial is far from certain.[11]

A more certain memorial is found on the field of Crécy, where a plain but ancient cross traditionally marks the spot where John of Bohemia was killed.[12] Although set on a modern base, there seems no reason to doubt the story that this was erected as a memorial to the king who fell in the battle of 1346. However, the best known medieval battlefield memorial is that created by William the Conqueror after his victory at Hastings. Battle Abbey marks the site of the Norman victory and, according to the abbey chronicle, was the result of a vow which William made before the battle.[13] Not only was the abbey to be a thank offering for victory but it is specifically stated that it was to be in memory of those who fell in the fight; again, there seems no reason to doubt the tradition that the high altar was located at the spot on which Harold was killed.

Another foundation with a similar intent was the abbey and hospital established at Roncesvalles in the second quarter of the twelfth century.[14] This was of course retrospective commemoration and connected with the rapid development of the pilgrimage to Santiago, but the church was sited over what was believed to be the rock which Roland split with his sword Durendal. One legend also stated that Roland and his companions were buried here, although there were several rival locations,[15] and there are post-medieval accounts of the ossuary chapel decorated with paintings of the various battles fought at the Roncesvalles pass. The church also contained several items said to be associated with Roland, including his horn, stirrups, battle axes, and sword.

Such memorial foundations continued a long tradition in the establishment of religious buildings. The memorial aspect of the Parthenon has already been alluded to, and it has even been suggested that its sculpted frieze contained 192 figures in commemoration of the precise number of Greek soldiers who fell at Marathon.[16] The whole acropolis at Pergamon was essentially a vast war memorial, but especially apposite for the Middle Ages was the memorial forum built by Augustus in Rome,

[11] See *The Gentleman's Magazine*, March, 1848, p. 248. The inscription was also partially published in Wetton's *Guide-Book to Northampton and its Vicinity* , 1849, and the stone survives in the Central Museum, Northampton. I am most grateful to John Cherry for drawing my attention to this.

[12] For a study of the battle and John of Bohemia's role in it see G.F. Beltz, 'An Inquiry into the Existing Narratives of the Battle of Cressy,' *Archaeologia*, 28, 1840, pp. 171–92.

[13] *The Chronicle of Battle Abbey*, ed. & trans. E. Searle, Oxford, 1980.

[14] V. and H. Hell, *The Great Pilgrimage of the Middle Ages*, London, 1964, pp. 165–66 and *Bulletin Monumental*, 95, 1936, pp. 114–15.

[15] R. Lejeune amd J. Stiennon, *La Legende de Roland dans l'art du Moyen Age*, Brussels, 1966 (2 vols).

[16] J. Boardman, 'The Parthenon Frieze: Another View', *Festschrift fuer Frank Brommer*, Mainz, 1977, pp. 39ff.

with the Temple of Mars at its centre.[17] Preserved in this were the imperial standards that had been lost to the Parthians by Crassus in 53 BC and recovered by Augustus in 20 BC. Ovid records that on entering this forum the first thing one saw was an array of weapons captured by Roman soldiers from all parts of the empire. Actual examples of this practice survive, such as the bronze helmet dedicated to Zeus at Olympia by Hiero, tyrant of Syracuse, which was captured from the Etruscans during a battle in the bay of Naples in 474 BC.[18] It is inscribed with the words 'Hiero son of Deinomenes and the Syracusans (dedicated) to Zeus (spoils) from Cumae'. A particularly impressive variation on this idea must have been the monument erected after the sea battle of Actium in 31 BC at Nikopolis (near Preveza, western Greece). Here Octavian set up a row of captured bronze rams from enemy galleys, arranged in a long line on a terrace, like the lines of captured cannon seen in many modern western arsenals.[19]

This tradition of displaying weapons as a memorial was transmitted to the Middle Ages, as Roncesvalles suggests. Joan of Arc revealed in her examination of 17 March 1431, that after she had been wounded near Pari, in September 1429, she made an offering of a complete suit of white armour and a sword, which she had won in battle.[20] Similarly, in 1328, after the battle of Cassel, Philippe VI presented arms and armour to Notre-Dame in Paris and perhaps also to Chartres. The suit of armour which is still preserved at Chartres is traditionally said to have been the gift of Philippe le Bel after the battle of Mons-en-Pouille in 1304, but it is in fact of a later date.[21] One of the most extraordinary survivals of this kind is the large series of armours from the Franciscan monastery of Santa Maria delle Grazie near Mantua, which were set up on wooden figures in the church and were traditionally believed to be from the battle of Marignano in 1515.[22] Such collections of trophy arms were doubtless much more common than the sparse survivals suggest, and the non-Christian continuation of the tradition is witnessed by the large

---

[17] S. Walker and A. Burnett, *The Image of Augustus*, pp. 29–32.

[18] M. Finley, *A History of Ancient Sicily to the Arab Conquest*, London, 1968, p. 195.

[19] See *Archaeology*, 41, 5, pp. 28–35.

[20] J. Quicherat, *Procès de condamnation et de réhabilitation de Jeanne d'Arc dite La Pucelle*, Paris, 1841–49, 5 vols, 1, p. 179. The text indicates that this was a common custom for those who had been wounded: 'Interrogata qualia arma obtulit in ecclesia Sancti-Dionysii in Francia: respondit quod obtulit album harnesium, gallice *un blanc harnoys*, integrum, tale sicut uni homini armorum congruit, cum uno ense quem lucrata est coram villa Parisiensi. Interrogata ad quem finem eadem arma obtulit: respondit quod hoc fuit ex devotione, sicut consuetum est apud homines armorum quando sunt laesi; et quia fuerat leasa coram villa Parisiensi, obtulit ea Sancti Dionysio, propter hoc quod est clamor Franciae'.

[21] F.H. Cripps-Day, 'The Armour at Chartres,' *Connoisseur*, 110, 1942, pp. 91–95.

[22] J.G. Mann, 'The Sanctuary of the Madonna delle Grazie, with Notes on Italian Armour of the 15th century,' *Archaeologia*, 80, 1930, pp. 117–42 and 'A Further Account ...', *Archaeologia*, 87, 1938, pp. 311–52.

number of western medieval swords that were captured and stored in Turkish and Arab arsenals. These survive in many collections and normally carry arabic inscriptions on the blade.[23]

Very often the arms displayed in churches were those of a deceased hero, rather than trophies captured from the enemy. The helmet, shield, and sword displayed above Henry V's tomb in Westminster Abbey are supposedly those used by the king at Agincourt. The arms of the Black Prince are hung above his tomb in Canterbury and the idea of the knight returning his weapons to God lies behind the very common medieval practice of setting up funerary helms in churches.[24]

To return to the building of churches as memorials, it would seem that many foundations may have had a commemorative element. In most instances this is only one of many reasons for a new establishment and the memorial purpose may be implied rather than stated. However, in some cases it is explicit, as in the Late Gothic church of San Juan de los Reyes in Toledo, built by Ferdinand and Isabella to mark their victory over the king of Portugal at the battle of Toro.[25] This, like the mausolea-memorials of antiquity, was also intended to act as the royal necropolis, although the Catholic monarchs were eventually buried far away in Granada. San Juan also illustrates another ancient memorial practice, related to the *ex-voto* trophies, for the exterior walls of the church are hung with the chains of prisoners, said to be those of Christian slaves who had been freed from Moorish captivity. This idea goes back at least to the 5th century BC, for Herodotus records seeing chains hanging round the temple of Athene in Tegea that came from the Lacedaemonians defeated in battle.[26]

Probably the most impressive memorial foundation since antiquity was Philip II's palace and monastery of the Escorial. This was founded, like Battle Abbey, in fulfilment of a vow made before the battle of St Quentin in 1559.[27] The motif and the action may have been similar to William the Conqueror's at Hastings, but the imposing result has more in common with some state memorials of the twentieth century than with those of the eleventh. It is instructive and not a little depressing to find that the closest parallel for the Escorial, physically, spiritually, and geographically is General Franco's great national memorial in the Valle de los Caidos, whose centrepiece is a huge and gaunt underground basilica.[28]

---

[23] A.R. Dufty, *European Swords and Daggers in the Tower of London*, London, 1972, p. 15.

[24] J.G. Mann, *The Funeral Achievements of Edward, The Black Prince*, London, 1951.

[25] H. Lynch, *Toledo*, (Medieval Towns series), London, 1898.

[26] *The Histories*, trans. A. de Selincourt, London, 1954, p. 66.

[27] *Palacios y Museos del Patrimonio Nacional*, Madrid, 1970.

[28] *Monument National de la Sainte Croix de la Vallee des Morts*, Madrid, 1974.

The twentieth century has produced plenty of parallels for the medieval practice of building churches as memorials. Most are Gothic rather than Romanesque in style and a large number are public school chapels.[29] The First World War had a disastrous effect on the ranks of ex-public school boys and many schools saw a new or enlarged chapel as the ideal form of memorial. Others opted for more practical forms of building, such as new libraries, classrooms, or dormitories; sports pavilions were also popular. Some of this memorial architecture is of notable quality, most especially Sir Giles Gilbert Scott's chapel for Charterhouse, consecrated in 1927, which is derived from the cathedral of Albi. Scott also completed the nave of Downside Abbey as a school memorial, this time in an elegant High Gothic style of the latest Ile-de-France fashion. These school memorial chapels await a proper study and my intention here is merely to draw attention to the type. We should also add the form of the memorial cloister, also popular with schools, the finest example of which is certainly Sir Herbert Baker's design for Winchester, which moved Kipling to write: 'I think, indeed I know that so far as my own experience goes, it is incomparably the best of all war memorials.'[30] However, for the purposes of this short essay there is one modern monument in medieval style which is still more interesting. This is the Eleanor Cross at Sledmere in North Yorkshire, erected by Sir Tatton Sykes in 1899 in a careful and accurate medieval style. After the First World War the octagonal base was embellished with a series of brasses to form the memorial to the Yorkshire Regiment. These brasses were directly based on medieval examples; in some cases, as in the figure of Captain Edward Bagshawe, we have a direct copy of a particular example (in this case the famous Septvans brass at Chartham in Kent) supplied with a portrait head of the soldier commemorated; in others the figure is shown in modern military dress but in medieval pose. These must be among the latest memorial brass figures to have been made in Britain and provide a suitable termination to this brief and incomplete survey of the various types of medieval war memorial.

---

[29] C. Kernot, *British Public School War Memorials*, London, 1927.
[30] Quoted by Herbert Baker in his autobiography, *Architecture and Personalities*, London, 1944, p. 97.

2

The First Romanesque Cathedral at Old Salisbury

Richard Gem

Among the earliest ecclesiastical buildings undertaken following the Norman Conquest was the new cathedral of Salisbury (Old Sarum), a hill-top site to which the former bishopric of Sherborne was transferred *c.* 1075.[1] The prelate responsible for the move was Bishop Herman, one of the surviving appointees of King Edward; but he died in 1078 and left the building project to be brought to completion under his successor Bishop Osmund, chancellor of King William. The cathedral was dedicated in 1092, but a few days after the ceremony a violent storm destroyed the roof of the cathedral tower and loosened much masonry.[2] Remodelling of the fabric took place in the twelfth century, especially under Bishop Roger, but in the early thirteenth century the see was transferred again to New Salisbury and the Romanesque building was progressively demolished.

Evidence for the original structure first came to light again with the archaeological excavations conducted by St John Hope (principle director), Hawley (site director) and Montgomerie (surveyor and draughtsman) in the years immediately preceding the First World War. The advent of the war in 1914 and Hope's death in 1919 interrupted any proper publication of the excavations that may have been intended, and the discoveries now have to be interpreted from a variety of unsatisfactory sources. These sources comprise: Hawley's field diaries;[3] the annual interim reports delivered as lectures to the Society of Antiquaries;[4] Montgomerie's plan of the excavated structures;[5] and various photographs and slides.[6]

The interpretation of the building that has generally prevailed, however, is not that of Hope and his colleagues, but that put forward by Clapham

---

[1] William of Malmesbury, *Gesta Pontificum*, ed. N.E.S.A. Hamilton, Rolls Series. 52, 1870, pp. 182–83. Royal Commission on Historical Monuments, *The City of Salisbury*, I, London, 1980.

[2] William of Malmesbury, *Gesta Regum*, ed. W. Stubbs (Rolls Series. 90, 1887–89), p. 375.

[3] Preserved in the Salisbury Museum.

[4] Published in *Proc. Soc. Antiq.*, 25, 1912–13, pp. 93–104; 26, 1913–14, pp. 100–19.

[5] Preserved in the Salisbury Museum.

[6] In the Salisbury Museum and in the Library of the Society of Antiquaries.

in 1934 and 1947.[7] Even the more recent publication by the Royal Commission on Historical Monuments has tended to follow Clapham on some points, despite the fact that the authors of this did make use of many of the original sources. It may seem of value, therefore, to set out again some of the evidence for the eleventh-century building and, having done this, to seek to place it in its context within the corpus of Anglo-Norman Romanesque.

Of the plan of the eastern termination of the building there can be little doubt, for the remains of it were fully described by Hawley and Hope, and there also survive photographs of the excavated features (Plate 2a, b). There was a foundation wall of flint and mortar, about 2.1 m (6 feet 11 inches) thick, for a main apse; against the west face of which was a foundation for an altar or a bishop's throne.[8] Of the terminations of the presbytery aisles, however, the plan is uncertain. Hope says that they were 'square ended outside but probably apsidal within',[9] while Montgomerie suggests on his plan (Plate 1) that they were rectangular inside as well as out: probably there was no evidence for the form of the inner face.

Of the superstructure of the eastern arm it is clear that nothing survived, for Hope pointed out that it had 'all been demolished and nothing was left save foundation':[10] so it does not seem possible to determine whether the lateral walls of the presbytery were solid, or whether they opened through arcades to the aisles. Clapham theorised that there were solid walls extending westward as far as the mid-line of the transepts, and he further deduced from this that there was no crossing: but these suppositions seem to be based on no more than a misreading of the excavators' plans. Probably Clapham used as a basis for his observations the plan published in the *Proceedings of the Society of Antiquaries*;[11] but this plan, in order to make it suitable for publication at a small scale, had been much simplified, and was therefore liable to misinterpretation. The primary source, however, must be Montgomerie's plan; which is much less ambiguous and allows a more accurate interpretation.

The *Proceedings* plan used only one convention, stippling, to show all parts of the eleventh-century work, and consequently sought to avoid confusion by stopping the line of the presbytery *foundation* walls a little short of the partly eleventh-century piers of the *superstructure* that stood in line with the west wall of the transepts: otherwise the two would have run into one another. The manuscript plan, on the other hand, uses two

[7] A.W. Clapham, *English Romanesque Architecture after the Conquest*, Oxford, 1934, p. 22; idem., 'Old Sarum Cathedral', *Archaeological Journal*, 104, 1947, p. 142.

[8] Field Diary, 1913, p. 5; *Proc. Soc. Antiq.*, 26, p. 103.

[9] Ibid.

[10] Ibid.

[11] Clapham, op. cit., 1934, p. 22, n. 3.

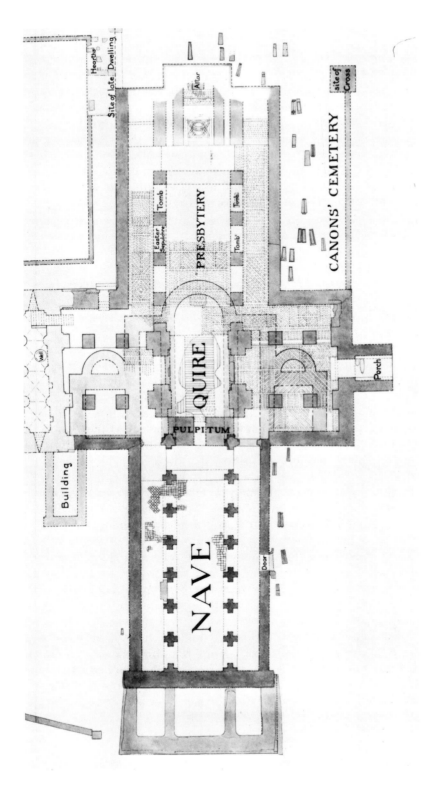

1 Salisbury Cathedral, detail from plan of excavations of 1912-24 by D. Montgomerie.

separate colours and is able thus to show the foundations running right up to and underlying the two piers. In any case, Montgomerie indicates the edges of the foundation walls with feint, broken lines, which stand in contrast with other elements in the plan, and it may be wondered whether any very clear traces of them were found: even if they were, it is fairly certain that they belonged to no more than the foundations, and foundations are commonly continued as sleeper walls across the crossings of building of this period. The evidence such as it is, therefore, for the presbytery and transept area would not preclude a regular crossing arrangement. Hope indeed bears this out: first, in his report he stated that there was 'a tower over the crossing';[12] secondly, in a slide prepared for his lecture he showed a reconstructed plan of the eleventh-century building in which there was precisely a regular crossing.[13]

The information from the excavations concerning the transepts themselves is comprised by photographs (Plate 2b), a few references in Hawley's diaries and in the published report, and the plans.[14] Each transept arm projected beyond the aisles for a depth about equal to its width from east to west; while opening off the east side of each was a shallow, apsidal chapel. There is no evidence suggesting the existence of galleries occupying the transept arms and these seem unlikely.

The most significant feature of the design of the building as seen by some commentators is the supposed existence of towers rising over the transept arms. These were first proposed by Clapham on the grounds that the transept walls when compared with those of the nave, as shown on the published plan in *Proceedings*, were considerably thicker.[15] However, reference to Montgomerie's plan shows that the walls of the eastern arm generally are shown at the greater width, and this represents the *foundation* level. In the nave the walls are shown thinner, and this represents the *wall superstructure* above foundation level. In the case of the transepts the walls are shown generally at foundation level, but on the west side of the north transept the upstanding wall is shown as being of the thinner dimension, comparable to the nave walls. There is no reference in Hawley's diaries or Hope's lectures to transept towers (indeed, Hope's belief in a crossing tower would preclude them): Clapham's theory again, therefore, seems based on a misunderstanding of the evidence.

Turning to the nave, the excavators' plans suggest that parts of the easternmost piers, in line with the west walls of the transepts, survived embedded in twelfth-century work from the time of Bishop Roger's remodelling. West of these original crossing piers were a further six piers on either side defining a nave of seven bays. The piers were apparently carried on continuous sleeper walls, parts of which were discovered

[12] *Proc. Soc. Antiq.*, 26, p. 103.
[13] Society of Antiquaries, collection no. 1550.
[14] Field Diary, 1913, pp. 10, 17.
[15] Clapham, op. cit., 1934, p. 142.

where they had not been robbed out.[16] These foundation sleepers would represent a continuation of the foundations discovered in the eastern arm and shown on the plans, although there is a slight change of axis west of the crossing. At one point in his diary Hawley suggests that all the piers that stood upon the sleeper walls had been robbed out:[17] however, Montgomerie in his plan included piers the length of the nave.

In 1972 the author visited the site while work was being carried out by the Department of the Environment, Ancient Monuments Division, for laying out in the turf the plan of the cathedral. The work was being executed by labourers on the basis of an office plan (based on Hope's) and no associated archaeological recording was in hand. The concreting of the eastern arm and transepts had already been completed, but at the east end of the nave what the workmen had uncovered of the archaeologically significant levels was still exposed. This included the western responds of the pair of piers in line with the west wall of the transepts, the footings of the next pair of piers to the west on either side, and the footing of a further pier on the south side only. In addition there were visible areas of flooring and the arrangement of steps leading up to the pulpitum.

Not enough was exposed of the easternmost piers to reveal clearly their eleventh- and twelfth-century development. Some ashlars remained *in situ*, however, on the west respond of the south pier, and these could be interpreted as indicating a respond that corresponded in width to the nave piers further west. The ashlars were arranged in plain rectangular steps, but it was not clear whether they were eleventh- or twelfth-century.

The nave piers further west were represented by their flint and mortar footings, standing slightly proud of the twelfth-century stone-flagged floor: on these footings would have stood the ashlar plinth courses of the piers, and the mortar bedding for these plinth stones remained visible. The footings may be interpreted as preserving the actual outline of the pier plinths (rather than merely their cores) because the twelfth-century floor was bedded up against them. The central of the three piers on the south side was planned by the author and Laurence Keen and can be seen to be of fairly regular cruciform shape (Plate 3b). The Inspector for the Department told me that no evidence had been encountered of the sleeper wall recorded in the earlier excavations.

In the aisles the original plans of Hope's excavations give no suggestion of any responds against the wall, and none were traced in the 1972 work.[18] Neither do any traces survive of external buttressing to the walls. The core of the south aisle wall itself does survive in its lowest parts, with some of its ashlar stones: the absence of any evidence of buttresses or responds probably points to their actual absence.

---

[16] Field Diary, 1913, pp. 49–50.

[17] Ibid., p. 45.

[18] I wish to thank Mr Beric Morley for this information.

2a Salisbury Cathedral, excavation of main presbytery apse, looking east, 1913.

2b Salisbury Cathedral, excavation of south transept apse, looking south, 1913.

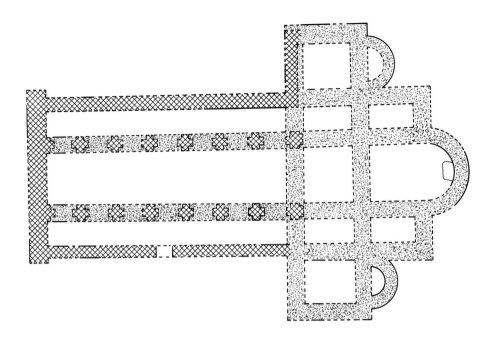

3a Salisbury Cathedral, plan c. 1075-92, from excavated evidence. Stippling
indicates foundation; hatching indicates superstructure.

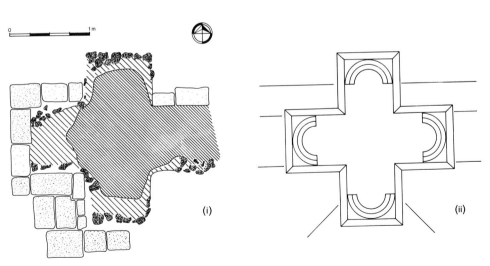

3b Salisbury Cathedral, plan of first pier west of the crossing in the south nave
arcade, c. 1075-92. (i) excavated evidence, surveyed 1972 by R.D.H. Gem and
L.J. Keen. Cross-hatching indicates mortar; dark stippling indicates flints;
lighter stippling indicates twelfth-century flagstones. (ii) Hypothetical
reconstruction of original pier plan.

At the west end of the church the nave and aisles are shown in Montgomerie's plan as ending in a plain wall running north and south, without any provision for west towers. However, this wall is shown projecting beyond the line of the aisles, and this may suggest the presence of features such as vices or turrets at these points. When the facade was remodelled in the twelfth century, the width of the new western block was defined by these short spur walls and an alternative explanation, therefore, might be that when the foundations of the west wall of the nave were laid it was already envisaged that western towers might be added in a secondary phase (as indeed they were).

Reconstruction and Discussion of the Eleventh-Century Church

From the archaeological evidence it is not possible to make a complete reconstruction of the eleventh-century church, but enough is apparent to make at least a partial reconstruction (Plate 3a) and comparisons. In overall dimensions the building measured only about 56 m (185 feet) internally from the apse to the west front; 18.5 m (61 feet) internally across the nave and aisles; and 36 m (118 feet) across the transepts.

The *east arm* terminated in an apse the same width as the main vessel and was flanked by aisles. It is not known whether there were arcades open between the main vessel and the aisles, or whether the aisles terminated in enclosed apses.

Further west lay the *crossing* of the church which was of normal plan, and which in elevation was probably surmounted by a tower. It is difficult to see where else was located the tower whose roof blew down in 1092. To either side of the crossing were projecting *transepts*, each with an eastern apsidal chapel. There is no evidence for galleries in the transepts: if they had contained galleries carried in the usual way on two bays of vaulting, these bays would have been of awkward dimensions. It is preferable to see the transepts, therefore, as open their full height from the pavement to the roof without galleries. The choir in the twelfth-century cathedral was located in the new crossing that was formed one bay east of the original crossing. The eleventh-century choir must have been located further west, in the original crossing and extending somewhat into the nave: in which case the original line of the pulpitum is likely to have been further west also.

We are in a position to say rather more on the subject of the *nave* than the parts further east. The key is provided by the plan of the piers indicated by the plinth footings: these seem to have carried unusually proportioned piers, with a cruciform core and an attached half column on each face (Plate 3b). North and south the pier measured was not more than 2.17 m (7 feet 2 inches), while the respond on the west face was not more than 85 cm (2 feet 9 inches) wide and may have been only 77 cm (2 feet 6 inches). These dimensions suggest that the walls carried by the piers may have been rather thin, and lead to some doubt as to whether there was a full gallery above the aisles, though the presence of a gallery cannot be conclusively ruled out on these grounds. In the aisles, the absence of any responds or buttresses indicates either groin vaults without transverse arches or, perhaps less likely, open wooden roofs: but it also suggests that the outer walls were relatively low and were not carried up into a gallery level. On balance, therefore, it is suggested that the lateral roofs leant-to immediately above the aisle storey, and that any openings above the main arcades looked only into the aisle roofs and not into a full gallery.

The simple cruciform piers are not a standard form in major English Romanesque buildings, but they do find a parallel at La-Trinité, Caen.[19] In the Norman building it may be seen, moreover, how this type of slender pier could be employed to carry a wall of reasonable thickness: the east and west responds of the piers supported only the inner order of the arcades; an outer order was carried on the dosseret of the half-column towards the nave. La-Trinité also shows the feature of nave piers with a projecting element towards the aisle but no corresponding responds on the aisle walls, the aisles being covered by groin vaults without transverse arches, as suggested here for Salisbury.

The overall size of Salisbury as by far the smallest of the Romanesque cathedrals built in England following the Norman Conquest, combined with the suggestion that features of its design looked to the tradition in which stood La Trinité, Caen, lead to the design being seen as something of a backwater in the history of Anglo-Norman Romanesque. It was an unambitious project in an obsolescent style that stood in contrast to the majority of the other Anglo-Norman cathedrals, which took as their base line the scale and style of Lanfranc's buildings at Christ Church, Canterbury, and St-Etienne, Caen, buildings which had created and established the High Romanesque style in Normandy and England. Salisbury was still essentially an Early Romanesque design: but it is precisely because of this that it is of interest, for it shows the presence of earlier concepts alongside the more dynamic ones introduced at the Conquest.

Perhaps the key to understanding the building is the first patron, Bishop Herman, who had been established in England through much of the reign of Edward the Confessor. Although he was himself by origin a Lotharingian, he represented the old Anglo-Saxon order, and his new cathedral at Salisbury was little larger than his former one at Sherborne (if the theory is accepted that the mid eleventh-century rebuilding of Sherborne underlies the present church).[20] His bishopric had ample

[19] M. Baylé, *La Trinité de Caen* (Bibliothèque de la Société Française d'Archéologie), 10, Geneva, 1979.

[20] R.D.H. Gem, 'Documentary Evidence for the Early History of the Buildings of Sherborne Cathedral', *Archaeological Journal*, 132, 1975, pp. 105–107

resources to undertake a major rebuilding on the scale of other Anglo-Norman cathedrals, but clearly he was not interested in a project of this type. Perhaps we see in Salisbury a representative of the direction that Romanesque architecture in England might have taken without the revolution in concepts of architectural patronage brought about by the Norman Conquest.

3

The Stonework Planning of the First Durham Master

Jean Bony

The historical position of Durham cathedral and the very nature of its invention have given rise to so much unwitting mythmaking, and our own perception of the conditions of architectural production in that period is so uncertain, that the time seems to have come now to re-examine, in the most meticulous detail, all the material signs of work procedures and of modes of thinking that can be read from the texture itself of the fabric. For the simplest of observations may reveal, though their implications, unsuspected approaches to construction, as well as mental attitudes or cultural backgrounds, which may all ask for further probing. By making us aware of unfamiliar aspects of the process of creation, such investigations are likely to provide some of the elements needed for a better assessment of what Durham actually meant in its time and of what could, with some validity, be said to constitute its novelty and its significance.

As a first move in that direction, this essay will consider the stonework of the initial stage in the construction of the cathedral, a period of very short duration but of critical importance, since it set the tone for what was to become the testing ground for a succession of unpredictable developments.

The chronology of the works and the extent and duration of the major campaigns of construction have been established by John Bilson [1] on such solid bases that there is nothing significant to be added.[2] In the 'First Great Campaign of Construction', as Bilson has called it, which lasted from August 1093 to September 1104, were completed the whole east arm, the crossing (with enough of the two easternmost bays of the nave to ensure its stability), the south transept in its entirety and the north transept up to gallery level. That constituted an ensemble large

---

[1] This chronology was presented already in John Bilson, 'The Beginnings of Gothic Architecture, II, Norman Vaulting in England', *Journal of the Royal Institute of British Architects*, 3rd series, 6, 1899, pp. 289–319; it was further refined in, Idem.,'Durham Cathedral: the Chronology of its Vaults', *Archaeological Journal*, 79, 1922, pp. 101–60.

[2] No valid re-evaluation of the chronology of Durham cathedral has so far been presented.

enough to be put into service as the new cathedral in September 1104.[3]

Bilson was not interested in defining exactly the successive stages within that major campaign of eleven years, but at least three stages can be recognised. The initial one consisted only of the peripheral walls of the east arm together with the three pairs of detached piers in the choir area and the east walls (meaning the aisle walls) of the two transepts.[4] It did not include the east piers of the crossing or the piers which support the main eastern elevation of the transept.

The limits of the first stage in building operations can be identified from the type of plinths used inside and outside that easternmost part of the work: for the plinths change in their profile or in their level in the north-east and south-east corners of the transept, indicating at those points the beginning of a second stage of work (Plate 4a). As the main arcade and *a fortiori* the aisle vaults of the choir could not be built without the existence of the east piers of the crossing, it is obvious that this first stage of work could have been of only short duration. Given the speed at which Durham was built and the enormous means at the bishop's disposal, it is likely not to have lasted even two years. The central structure of the choir was probably taken no higher than the top of the column capitals, and the outer walls of this eastern ensemble (including the main apse) must have been raised only to about the same height, stopping short of the zone of the aisle vaults.

Although this first stage represented just a start, it involved a considerable amount of masonry work, in which all the essential features of the design were already registered; and it is therefore possible to analyse on the mere basis of this very first section the specific character of the fabric and the principles that were applied in its construction.

The Masonry Work

The stonework at Durham is perfectly Romanesque in nature, conforming to the type which had been used for more than fifty years in the great buildings of the northern half of France, of Normandy in particular, and which had been spreading in the last twenty years not only to England in

---

[3] This inauguration was marked by the translation of the remains of St Cuthbert to the apse of the new building on August 29, 1104.

[4] The liturgical choir, where the stalls of the monks constituting the cathedral priory were situated, occupied originally the crossing area and part of the bays adjoining it to the east and to the west: see Arnold W. Klukas,'The Architectural Implications of the *Decreta Lanfranci*', *Anglo-Norman Studies, Proceedings of the Battle Conference 1983*, 6, Woodbridge, 1984, pp. 136–71 (plan p. 164); but from the second half of the 13th century the choir was transferred entirely to the east of the crossing. In view of that present position of the choir proper and for the simplicity of presentation, it has been decided in this essay to apply the term choir (or choir area) conventionally to the totality of the east arm of the Romanesque cathedral.

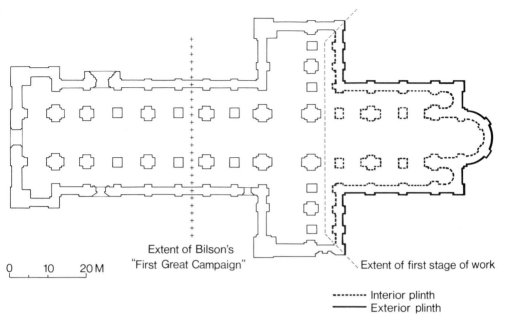

Extent of Bilson's "First Great Campaign"

Extent of first stage of work

0 10 20 M

-------- Interior plinth
———— Exterior plinth

4a Durham Cathedral, schematic plan showing extent of first stage of construction.

4b Durham Cathedral, interior wall arcading in choir aisle bays.

5a Durham Cathedral, exterior wall arcading on south side of choir bays.

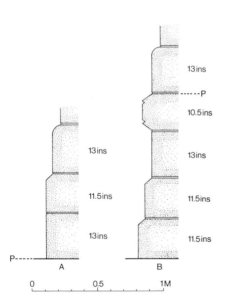

13 ins

- - - - - P

10.5 ins

13 ins   13 ins

11.5 ins   11.5 ins

13 ins   11.5 ins

P - - - -

A   B

0   0.5   1M

5b Durham Cathedral, plinth profiles
in first stage of work;
(i) Interior plinth; (ii) Exterior plinth.
(P: pavement level in the choir aisle)

5c Durham Cathedral, exterior plinth at
contact of choir and north transept.

the wake of the Conquest, but also southwards, along the great pilgrimage roads. It is a masonry of fine sandstone ashlar, with joints of very strong mortar about 1.5 cm (.67 inches) thick. In the areas of normal walling and in all the piers of compound type, the courses vary in height between 21 and 40 cm (8 and 16 inches), the great majority of the courses ranging between 24 and 35 cm (2.5 inches on either side of 1 foot). This is very close to the norms of stone production that can be observed at Winchester cathedral, where work had started in 1079, or in the late eleventh-century buildings of Normandy.

The Durham stonework is exceptionally elaborate in the detail of its execution. All the peripheral walls of the building have been designed and built with a dado of arcading, both on the inside and on the outside (Plate 4b). Interior wall arcadings can be found at all periods since late Antiquity, and they were becoming common in the 1080s, particularly in the areas north of the Loire. On the other hand, exterior arcadings at ground level were very unusual, being found at that date only on the outside of a few apses: St-Nicolas at Caen, *c.* 1080–85 is the earliest remaining example, although the apse of St-Etienne in the same city (begun *c.* 1066–67) may well have been the prototype.[5] At Durham this exterior arcading is exceptionally deep and large, normally two arches of two orders per bay, which means that wooden centrings had to be employed already at that low level of construction all along the walls (Plate 5a). Low level arcadings also meant that courses of set height recur more frequently at given levels, being needed for the bases and for the capitals and abaci of the shafts supporting the arches; and these courses of set height are continued horizontally into the wall panels, responds and buttresses. So that changes of height in the coursing should not be viewed, at Durham, as marking interruptions in the process of construction: they indicate only that the wall was reaching a height at which a fixed horizontal level (such as an impost or a string-course) had been set in the design.

The Plinthwork

Even more demanding in terms of course height were the plinths that run at the base of the walls (Plate 5b). Inside, walls and piers have plinths of a fairly simple type, composed of three courses above the level of the pavement: first a course 33 cm (13 inches) high, now reduced to 28 cm (11 inches) through the raising of the pavement level; then a course of blocks of 29 cm (11.5 inches), with their upper edge chamfered; and above that another course of 33 cm (13 inches), out of which are carved the bases of the shafts or columns supported by the plinth. This

---

[5] If so, the original apse of Lincoln Cathedral, which is the English building closest to St-Etienne in its details of execution, would be likely to have had already a low level exterior arcading.

makes a consistent sequence of three courses of set height (two of 33 cm (13 inches), one of 29 cm (11.5 inches) at the base of all the walls and under all the piers in that first-built section of the work (Plates 4b and 6a)

Outside, the plinth is taller and more refined in its profile. It is made up of five courses of pre-set height (Plate 5c). First come, just above the foundations, two successive courses of 29 cm (11.5 inches) chamfered at the top, like the 11.5-inch course of the interior. Next comes a plain course, of 33 cm (13 inches); then a thinner course, 26.5 cm (10.5 inches) only in height, but remarkable by its 7 cm (2.75 inches) projection in a tablet-like profile, which draws a firm horizontal line at the base of the whole structure; and above that comes yet another course of 33 cm (13 inches), which serves at the base course for the outer wall arcade. In total that makes for the whole plinthwork (interior and exterior) three series of chamfered courses of 29 cm (11.5 inches), four of plain rectangular-cut courses of 33 cm (13 inches), and, for the outside plinth only, one course of 26.5 cm (10.5 inches) shaped like a powerful string-course.

As the laying down of the plinths was the first act in the construction of the cathedral above foundation level, this importance given by the designer to the plinthwork means that a considerable amount of blocks cut to a set height had had to be ordered from the quarries before construction could start and be brought on the site in advance for the masons to arrange them in the required sequences before passing to the mounting of the wall arcades and eventually of the more usual ashlar masonry.[6] To get an idea of the quantities involved, one has only to measure the overall length of the exterior and interior plinths all along the extent of this initial stage of work, i.e. from the north-east angle of the transept, around the whole east arm of the church (with its original apses as revealed by the excavations of 1895), to the south-east angle of the south transept arm.[7] The length of the outer plinth proves to have been in the order of 130 metres (426 feet 6 inches); and the interior plinth, which had to follow the deep curves of the apses, and has to be supplemented by the plinths of the three pairs of piers of the choir, can be evaluated at about 200 m (656 feet). A sampling having indicated that the blocks used in the plinthwork average in length 80 to 85 cm (31.5 to 33.5 inches), one comes to a total, for that preliminary order of stone cut to set heights, of some 850 blocks of 33 cm (13 inches), some 600 chamfered blocks of 29 cm (11.5 inches), and about 180 of the 26.5 cm (10.5 inch) type: in all, an order of well over 1500 blocks of specified height, in addition to what must also have been needed in the matter of current walling material in more variable heights.

[6] The importance given to the plinthwork is a well known characteristic of Anglo-Saxon architecture both before and after the Conquest, Repton being probably the earliest example preserved.

[7] On the excavations of 1895, see John Bilson, 'On the Recent Discoveries at the East End of the Cathedral Church of Durham', *Archaeological Journal*, 53, 1896, pp. 1–18.

The Pierwork

Impressive as it is numerically, in respect of the mass involved, the planning of the plinthwork was simple and cannot in any way be compared with the degree of sophistication of the calculations implied by the designing and execution of the two pairs of great columnar piers of the choir area (Frontispiece). These represent an extraordinary achievement in terms of stonework planning; and the procedures that had to be followed to produce them, so demanding in technical skills, were to be repeated with slight variations in the transept, built in the second stage of the works, and were to set the basic rules for the somewhat later and simpler pier variations of the nave. Two very specific and unusual elements gave its complexity to the designing of that first series of columnar-type piers: one is the spiral patterning incised on the cylindrical part of the piers, and the other the merging in those piers of two principles of shaping, for they are not fully circular in plan, one third of the circle, on the aisle side, being replaced by a respond of the compound pier type (Plate 6a).[8]

The problem of the incised patterning is solved, in the Durham choir, with the greatest mathematical elegance. Until then, patterned piers were nearly all monolithic columns, which could be carved as a single unit, in the manner of a statue, and with no particular snags once the design had been carefully set. When columns with incised patterns were built in drums, as was attempted at Christchurch, Canterbury, in part of the undercroft to the enlarged dormitory building of the 1080s, the difficulty of making the pattern incised on one drum run smoothly into the lines of carving of its neighbours became painfully evident. The Durham master, for his much larger piers, which had to be built of multiple courses of normal ashlar masonry, found the perfect solution by linking the patterning of the piers to the joint alternate pattern of the blocks [9] in the stonework and by designing a type of block diagonally incised at such an angle that, with an exact mounting, the incision would be continued automatically from one course to the next.

The actual formula that produces the spiral pattern in the piers of the Durham choir is merely the repetition, joint alternate fashion, of twenty-seven courses of rigorously identical blocks 25 cm (9.75 inches) high and 42.5 cm (16.75 inches) long, all carrying the same diagonal incision, cut

---

[8] The origin of the spiral pier and its symbolic meaning will not be discussed here. On these aspects of the question, see Eric Fernie, 'The Spiral Piers of Durham Cathedral', *Medieval Art and Architecture at Durham Cathedral*, The British Archaeological Association Conference Transactions, 1980, pp. 49–58.

[9] On this point see Jean Bony, 'Durham et la tradition saxonne', *Etudes d'art médiéval offertes à Louis Grodecki* (S.M. Crosby, A. Chastel, A. Prache et A. Chatelet, eds.), Paris, 1981, pp. 79–92.

at the same angle and to the same profile (Plate 6b).[10] There are nine such carved and incised blocks in each odd number course, these courses ending in a vertical joint at the contact with the respond part of the pier; and, in the even number courses, eight blocks of that type, plus, at both ends, two half blocks of that curved shape, which become rectangular in their second half to merge into the profile of the pilasters of the respond. The designing and execution was impeccable. Nothing of the kind had been attempted before in medieval architecture: no previous example can be found of masonry work conceived and executed as the high precision assemblage of blocks cut in advance in such a way as to be not only interchangeable but reversible (a fine piece of template designing). In fact this was only carrying to its logical extreme the type of stonework introduced into England from the continent; yet significantly it was the problem raised by the patterning of columnar piers that made the designer of Durham convert the visual surface regularity of Romanesque masonry into absolute mathematical regularity.

This first Durham master, who clearly was English, purely Saxon in sensibility, especially in his sense of plastic and linear values, but no less clearly Norman-trained and enjoying to the full the new Romanesqueness, more Norman even than any Norman in his use of exterior dado arcades, gave in those piers the most decisive demonstration that he could outdo all continental builders in the handling of ashlar masonry.[11] Producing there a virtuoso performance in rationalised stonework, he placed himself far ahead of all would-be competitors, technically at the apex of the most advanced modernity.

A well-hidden showpiece of that virtuosity was the way in which he designed the bonding blocks which, on alternate courses (the even number courses, as has just been seen), must, according to the rules of sound masonry, bind together the two parts of those columnar piers, their cylindrical section and their respond section. For these bonding blocks, which start as half-blocks of the standard curved type on slightly over 21 cm (8.75 inches), have to continue, in their second section, as blocks of plain rectangular cut, 34 cm (13.5 inches) in length and set at an exactly calculated obtuse angle in relation to their curved section, to be in the right alignment for the respond (Plate 7a). No approximation was acceptable here; and an absolutely accurate template of that unusual composite shape had to be established and strictly followed by the stone cutters for that paradoxical junction of two forms to look perfectly normal and pass unnoticed.

---

[10] When applied as here to blocks with a curved surface or to their templates, the term length in all this article will mean the length of the developed arc to which the block has been cut.

[11] Joint alternate coursing means that, in a masonry composed of blocks all of the same size, the vertical joints of one course are placed exactly above the middle of the blocks of the preceding course.

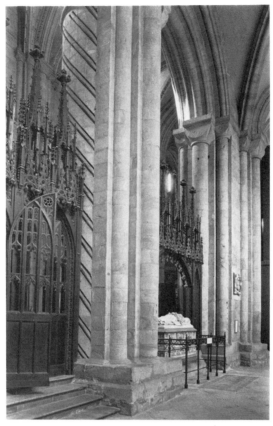

6a Durham Cathedral, easternmost columnar pier of choir on north side, seen
from the aisle.

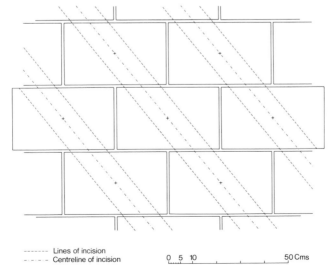

------- Lines of incision
- - - - Centreline of incision

0 5 10   50 Cms

6b Durham Cathedral, pattern of arrangement of incised blocks in columnar
piers of choir.

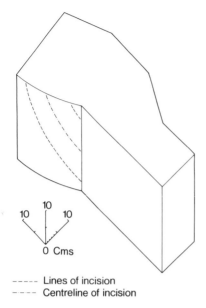

7a Durham Catheral, diagram of a bonding block in columnar piers of choir.

7b Durham Cathedral, analysis of the plan of a columnar pier in choir.

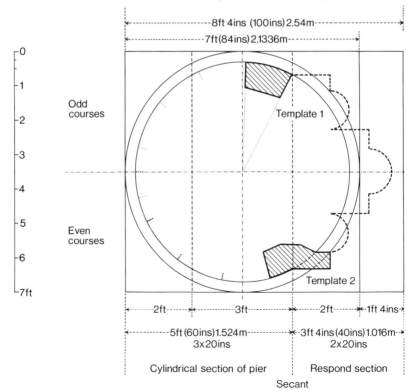

Each of those incised choir piers required, for the construction of its cylindrical core alone, a specified number of stone blocks cut with the highest precision to two different templates; and while, for each pier, twenty-six blocks only were needed of the complex bonding type (two for each of the thirteen even number courses), the masons had to be provided with as many as 230 of the standard 16.75 inch long curved type (14 x 9 for the odd number courses, plus 13 x 8 for the even number courses). As this first stage of work included four such piers, the quarries had to deliver within short limits of time a total of 920 blocks of the standard curved type, and 104 of the complex half-curved half-rectangular type, all impeccably sized and cut to templates.

This calculation accounts only for the rounded part of the pier. The respond part required in addition its own series of blocks to be shaped into the shafted and pilastered elements of which responds are composed. Examined on the spot (as far as the original mortar joints can be reliably recognised) this respond section seems to be composed, in all four piers, of seven blocks in the odd number courses and five only in the even number courses, in which the bonding blocks form already the outer pilasters. This would mean, for each pier, a further requirement of probably 163 blocks of various shapes, which are unlikely to have been more than roughly cut at the quarry, being carved in their finished form on the building site, but had necessarily to be all of the fixed height of 25 cm (9.75 inches) to agree with the strict coursing of the piers of which they were to become a part. The total amount of those respond type blocks for the four choir piers could then be tentatively evaluated at approximately 652 additional blocks of that semi-finished type, to be brought to the building yard at the same time as the high precision series described above, before the construction of the piers could begin.

These figures in the end become rather tiresome, although they are more or less unavoidable in any such listing of standardised units. Yet the implications of that state of affairs are not without interest. That the quarries were able to face such demanding specifications shows the high degree of competence achieved in the 1090s by the stone cutters of the Durham area.[12] More remarkable still and more significant in terms of

---

[12] In the first twenty years following the Conquest, ecclesiastical buildings of some importance had not been numerous in Northern England: at Durham itself Bishop Walcher had begun between 1072 and 1080 the construction of an ensemble of monastic buildings; but the programmes of repair and enlargement on the old sites of Jarrow and Monkwearmouth seem to have proceeded very slowly. The only new foundation of significance and requiring fine ashlar work, Tynemouth Priory, was begun only *c.* 1089. On the other hand masons and quarries must have been kept busy by the works of fortification needed for the defence of the northern frontier of the kingdom, the most important of which were the royal castles of Durham, founded in 1072, and of Newcastle, founded 1080. Richmond Castle, in northern Yorkshire, was another early stone castle. Castle building being always urgent work, the quarries must have developed the means of facing demands for the rapid production of large amounts of stone.

the mental training it pre-supposed is the amount of calculation and of advance designing carried to the minutest details of execution,which had had to be performed by the Durham master, with an unfailing decisiveness, to be able to order from the quarries those large series of perfectly shaped blocks that were so rapidly needed on the building site. It is easy for us now to observe and register on the spot the size and shape of the stone blocks and the rigour of their mounting. But how had the rules been set for that prefabrication and that assembling? Why twenty-seven courses in the piers? Why the height of 25 cm (9.75 inches)? Why that length of 42.5 cm (16.75 inches) for the standard type of curved and incised blocks? How had the templates been designed that dictated the work of the stone cutters?

This arithmetical and geometrical aspect of the designing is not so difficult to reconstruct. The height of the blocks and the number of the courses were obviously commanded in the end by the proportioning of the stories in the general design of the elevation. For the main arcade story up to tribune floor level to reach the height that had been ascribed to it, i.e. 12.471 m (40 feet 11 inches), the column-like body of the piers between base and capital had to be roughly 7 m (23 feet) tall, but slight variations were admissible and the eventual division of that height into twenty-seven courses of 25 cm (9.75 inches) resulted from the interaction of some other factors.[13]

An odd number of courses was necessary to give the proper bonding on alternate courses between the two parts of the pier (column-like core and respond); and twenty-seven courses of 25 cm (9.75 inches), plus the thickness of the joints, which averages one centimetre in the horizontal joints, comes to a total only 3.5 cm short of seven metres. The height of the blocks seems on the other hand to have been finally dependent on their length, for the solution to the problem of patterning had consisted in the creation of a type of incised block in which height and length were interdependent; and the length of the blocks was determined (as we shall see) by the geometric construction along which the plan of these dual shaped piers had been arrived at. The solution adopted for the combination in one pier of two different pier forms seems therefore to hold the key to the whole sequence of precise calculations that we find reflected in the stonework of those Durham choir piers.

Geometry of the Pier Plan

Once the architect of Durham had judged that the springers of the rib-vaults of the aisles could not be crowded onto the abacus of a column capital and that they would have to be supported on applied responds of

---

[13] The figures given here are based on Peter Kidson, *Systems of Measurement and Proportions used in Medieval Cathedrals*, Ph.D. Dissertation, London University, 1956.

the compound type, next to be decided was the point of junction between the two pier forms. A segment of the cylinder constituting the core of the pier would have to be sliced off, on the aisle side, to provide the flat vertical surface against which the wide three shaft respond could be applied. But in what precise position should the secant be placed?

Accurate plans of the columnar-type piers of the Durham choir show that the plinths on which they rest form in plan a rectangle of 2.13 by 2.54 m (7 feet by 8 feet 4 inches, or 84 by 100 inches), 2.13 m (7 feet) being their east-west dimension and 2.54 m (8 feet 4 inches) their north-south dimension.[14] They also show that the point where the two pier forms meet is situated at the distance of 1.52 m (5 feet, or 60 inches) from the choir face of the plinth. This position indicates a simple geometric construction, which must have been performed by drawing, on any tracing floor or tracing board, a full scale plan of the top surface of the plinth (Plate 7b).

First had to be drawn a 2.13 m (7 by 7 foot) square; and, inscribed within it, two concentric circles: the first one, tangent to the sides of the square and with a radius therefore of 1.06 m (3 feet 6 inches), giving the circumference of the base of the pier; and the second, with a radius of only 98 cm (3 feet 2.5 inches), shorter by 9 cm (3.5 inches) because this was the projection that had been decided for the base, giving the actual volume of the full cylindrical core of the pier. The next step was to draw a line cutting the square and its inscribed circles at the distance of 1.52 m (5 feet) from the side of the square which was to face the central space of the choir. This line cut off from the square a 61 cm (2 foot) length (a 2 to 5 relationship with the rest of the square) and at the same time it automatically also cut from the circumferences of the two inscribed circles two concentric arcs. The length of the chord subtending the arc of the smaller circle (the circle corresponding to the solid body of the round pier) gave the width available for the application of the respond on the aisle side of the pier. Then, in a third step, in order to provide a proper support for the bulk of that respond (which was to receive the three ribs of the projected aisle vaults), the 61 cm (2 feet) of plinth cut off by the secant line were extended to a length of 1.02 m (3 feet 4 inches, or 40 inches), so as to place the respond section of the plinth in a 2 to 3 relationship with the 1.52 m (5 foot) section supporting the

[14] Robert W. Billings, *Architectural Illustrations and Description of the Cathedral Church at Durham*, London, 1843, gives on plate LXA a measured plan of the northernmost pier of the south transept, which is similar to the piers of the choir, the only difference being that the plinth of that pier is reduced in its dimensions by one inch in relation to the choir piers: its width is 2.12 m (6 feet 11 inches) as against 2.13 m (7 feet) in the choir, as indicated in Billings in plate II.

cylindrical core of the pier.[15]

It was that geometric construction and that principle of proportioning which, by determining the precise placing of the points of junction between the two pier forms, made possible the fixing of the length and shape the blocks should have and the finalising of the design of the stonework in the piers. The establishment of the templates represented the last step in that computation and its final product. The points of contact between the two component parts of the pier now being fixed, what remained of the core became measurable and its circumference could be divided by whatever number of blocks would give a manageable size for the masons to execute the work of stone cutting, shaping to template and finally incising to pattern; and the building shows that the designer decided upon nine blocks (three sectors of three blocks), with the result that, once the width of the mortar joints had been taken into account, the length of these standard blocks turned out to be 42.5 m (16.75 inches).[16] The curve of the blocks was already given by the circle of which their length represented a sector (of about 25 degrees); and the angle at which their end surfaces were to be cut simply followed the radii of that circle. The template for the blocks could thus be cut with absolute precision in all its elements from the tracing floor.

Similarly the second template, so odd in shape, that was to be used for the bonding blocks on alternate courses, could also be copied directly from the same tracing floor: it was just a matter of following the lines inscribed, in the course of the preceding operations, on either side of the point of contact between the round pier core and the straight-sided respond pilaster. From these lines could then be read the form of the template: a first section curved, on a length of just over 21 cm (8.4 inches), i.e. half the length of the standard curved block; and a second section straight and just over 34 cm (13.5 inches) long, the measurement set in the respond design for the outer pilaster.

The whole design of this pier plan and of the templates it implied must have been settled very rapidly by so expert a designer as was clearly this first Durham master. After that, the calculations in height and

[15] It will be noted that these measurements make sense only in standard English feet and inches. This would seem to confirm that the English foot was already in use in the late eleventh century (see also E.C. Fernie, 'Anglo-Saxon Lengths: the 'Northern' System, the Perch and the Foot', *Archaeological Journal*, 142, 1985, pp. 246–254). This system of measurement, used in the small scale calculations, was combined at Durham, as shown by Peter Kidson (see n. 13 above), with another system, based on the toise of 1.42 m (4 feet 8 inches), for the large scale design of plan and elevation. The combined use of these two systems seems confirmed by the recurrence at Durham of a measurement of 2.13 m (7 feet), which is 1.5 toise and therefore the meeting point of the two systems.

[16] The vertical joints, which are not compressed by the weight of the blocks, are a little thicker than the horizontal joints: they average 1.3 cm (.5 inches), while the horizontal joints average 1 cm (.4 inches). For the meaning of the term length in this paragraph and in the following one, see note 10 above.

setting of the formula of the spiral patterning (which had to be established by tracing on the developed surface of the cylinder) could go ahead in all surety on the bases of the rigorous planning carried out at ground level.

Once this sequence of essentially simple but precise operations had been completed and fully coordinated the master could proceed to evaluate the quantities of stone required for the initial stage of work. Only then could he calculate exact numbers and place his order for two series of custom blocks (920 of the standard curved type and 108 of the composite bonding type) that had to be supplied for these first two pairs of complex columnar-type piers. The extent and accuracy of the planning required by its highly refined design placed Durham on a level of sophistication that was to remain unequalled for a long time.

There must seem to be in this essay an element of overkill, in its repetitious insistence on numbers. Yet it must be recognised that, as soon as we start examining its masonry closely, the building demonstrates that it could never had been started, not even conceived, without methods of advanced planning so unexpected in their elaboration that they force us to revise our current ideas on building yard practice in the Romanesque age. This stonework therefore becomes an essential new document on the intellectual history of the late eleventh century in that it enables us to come to some realisation of the nature of the mind that produced the design of Durham cathedral and that directed at least the early stages of its construction.

Obviously the designer who could handle with ease all these material issues was no common builder. But the date at which all this was taking place is the crucial element that gives a very special significance to what this man did and what his actions implied. His methods of serialisation and rationalisation, the evidence of his mathematical training, the urge he clearly felt for an absolute accuracy in the work of his teams as in the operations of his own mind place him as one of the identifiable fore-runners of that great mental shift of the early twelfth century. This (as we have recently been reminded) should not be viewed as a 'Renaissance' (so ambiguous and restrictive a term) but as a first Age of Enlightenment, affecting all aspects of culture in the western world.[17]

The spectacular achievements to which are attached the names of such men as Adelard of Bath in the scientific field or Pierre Abelard in matters of logic and ethics, came only some twenty five or thirty years later. But the movement had started before the end of the eleventh century, and not only with the jurists of Pavia, for the capture of Toledo and the conquest of Sicily had just given westerners access to the whole

---

[17] Charles M. Radding, *A World Made by Men: Cognition and Society, 400–1200*, Chapel Hill, 1985 (pp. 151 and 256 for the use of the term Enlightenment).

range of Hellenistic and Arabic science. In the generation of the 1090s, an exact contemporary of the master of Durham, like him working in England, was the other forerunner of the new science, Walcher of Malvern. In 1092 (probably the very year when the plans of Durham were elaborated) Walcher was measuring with the highest precision, by means of a Toledan astrolabe, an eclipse of the moon, to establish differences of longitude and cosmological time.[18]

Certainly Durham, situated so far to the north, seems very much out of the way. In fact it is not so surprising to find there, at that date, a remarkable manifestation, not to say manifesto, of avant-garde thinking: for the bishop who commissioned the cathedral, William of Saint-Calais, had just spent three years in exile at the ducal court of Rouen, as one of Robert Curthose's most trusted advisers, from 1088 to 1091; and there is every likelihood that his architect was part of his retinue. Arriving in Rouen in 1088 must have been an unusually stimulating experience: Toledo, reconquered three years before, had become the centre of attraction towards which scholars from all over western Europe were beginning to converge, to consult the treasure of scientific and philosophical manuscripts kept in the *armarium* of the former Great Mosque, now the cathedral. Norman scholars had doubtless been there already. Normandy was also, and more directly, involved in another no less momentous enterprise, the conquest of Sicily, by then almost complete; news was coming back of the wonderful richness of the libraries which had been found at Syracuse, captured two years before. Bishops were soon to be appointed to the new Sicilian sees and among those who were eventually chosen (he became Bishop of Syracuse in 1105 and must have been before that well known in the circles of Rouen) was that famous Norman arithmetician, Guillelmus R., who, we are told, had been the master of two royal clerks responsible, under Henry I, for the establishment of the accounting system of the English Exchequer.[19]

We can only have the most uncertain and hypothetical notion of what was happening in Rouen in those years; we cannot even say with any certainty that the designer of Durham was actually there and still less whom he could have met and how far he could have travelled outside Normandy between 1088 and 1091; but it looks very much as if the latest advances in the mathematical sciences had been directly responsible for the mastery in computation and planning that we find registered in the stonework of Durham cathedral. To read in clear this rare and precious testimony on the intellectual conjuncture of the 1090s, all that is needed is a bit of decoding.

[18] Dorothee Metlitzki, *The Matter of Araby in Medieval England*, New Haven, 1977, pp. 16–18.

[19] Michael T. Clanchy, *From Memory to Written Record: England 1066–1307*, London, 1979, pp. 108–10 and 235.

4

Como and the Book of Durrow

George Zarnecki

Reset in the courtyard of the Museo Civico at Como in Lombardy is a
modest but important marble Romanesque doorway (Plate 8) from the
demolished local church of Santa Margherita, originally Santa Maria
Antiqua.[1] The importance of this doorway lies in its innovative design,
unusual decoration and early date, all of which place it in the forefront
of a series of doorways known as the Lombard Porch. Such a porch
usually involves a projection in front of a doorway in the form of a pair
of free-standing columns resting on the backs of lions or on the shoulders of atlantes, the columns themselves supporting impressive arches or
canopies, as, for instance, at Piacenza, where there are three such
porches in front of the facade of the cathedral.[2]

The Santa Margherita doorway is, in comparison, small, its columns,
although free-standing, are very near the jambs of the doorway and they
do not carry the gabled roof of the porch but merely the middle of the
three carved arches. However, here, in embrio, is the Lombard Porch
and because it is only in a tentative, experimental stage in its evolution,
it gives some useful clues on the sources of its design.

In fully developed Lombard porches the lions or atlantes are placed
facing the faithful entering the church and are perpendicular to the
facade. The lions of the Santa Margherita doorway, on the other hand,
are parallel to the facade and face each other as if guarding the entrance.
Somewhat similar lions were used in the eleventh century in Apulia.
They supported the seats of bishops' thrones at Montesantangelo and
Siponto;[3] in the celebrated throne in San Nicola at Bari, a pair of lions
serve to support the footstool.[4] Similar lions were at times used in place

[1] For the bibliography on this church, see. O. Zastrow, *Scultura Carolingia e Romanica nel
Comasco: Inventario Territoriale*, Como, 1979, 2nd ed., pp. 40–41.

[2] *Il Duomo di Piacenza (1122–1972)*, Atti del Convegno di studi storici in occasione dell'
850 anniversario della fondazione della Cattedrale di Piacenza, Piacenza, 1975, p. 28.

[3] P. Belli d'Elia (edit.), *Alle sorgente del Romanico. Puglia XI secolo*, Bari, 1975, p. 31 (cat.
no. 43) and p. 64 (cat. no. 74).

[4] The throne, traditionally dated to 1098, is now considered, in my view wrongly, as a
work made between 1166 and 1170; see P. Belli d'Elia, 'La cattedra dell' abate Elia.
Precisazioni sul romanico pugliese', *Bollettino d'Arte*, 59, 1974, pp. 1–17.

of capitals.[5] It was only from *c.* 1105 that lions served to support the columns of doorways in Apulia (the Porta dei Leoni, San Nicola at Bari [6] in clear imitation of their earlier use in local church furniture.[7] The Como lions (Plate 9b) differ in one important respect from those in Apulia, namely that they hold between their forelegs other animals, either their young, or more likely, their prey. Lions, griffins and other imaginary beasts are frequently shown in later Lombard Porches with their prey as at Como, as if to emphasise their fierceness in their role as guardians.

Arthur Kingsley Porter claimed that the idea of employing lions in doorways was due to the architect of Modena Cathedral, Lanfranco, who, taking advantage of the two Roman lions newly excavated in Modena employed them in the doorway of the cathedral.[8] 'Few architectural motives ever invented have so profoundly influenced later art as did Lanfranco's Lombard porch carried on the backs of lions. From this time onward the Lombard porch became a characteristic feature of the north Italian style.' Unfortunately for this theory of the great American scholar, the Modena lions were incorporated into the porch not at the beginning of the twelfth century by Lanfranco but in the second half, when the facade of the cathedral was considerably altered and, thus, the origin of the Lombard Porch had nothing to do with Modena.[9]

A much more convincing claim was made by Emile Mâle when he linked the doorways of northern Italy with Assyrian art through the intermediary of illuminated Syriac manuscripts, which in turn, influenced Carolingian illuminations in which the motif of animals supporting

[5] T. Garton, *Early Romanesque Sculpture in Apulia*, New York and London, 1984, pp. 72ff.

[6] F. Schettini, *La Basilica di San Nicola di Bari*, Bari, 1967, pp. 72ff., fig. 140.

[7] Of the two marble lions, as yet unpublished, in the abbey museum at Montecassino, at least one served to support a column, for it has a round flat disc on its back. It was probably part of some church furniture in the building consecrated in 1071. Two doorways of the abbey were recorded in prints published in 1733 and they certainly had no lions and no columns but flat jambs decorated with classical-inspired motifs. Some fragments of them survive. For the prints of the doorways, see: V. Pace, 'Campania XI secolo: Tradizione e innovazioni in una terra normanna', *Romanico padano, Romanico europeo*, A.C. Quintavale (ed.), Parma, 1977, p. 226, fig. 1, and p. 227, fig. 3.

Two more early examples of lions supporting columns, but now out of their original context, from the cathedral at Mazara in Sicily, founded in 1093, are now in the local Museo Civico. In addition, there are also two elephants comparable to those supporting the archbishop's throne at Canosa. For the sculpture at Mazara, see V. Scuderi, *Arte Medievale nel Trapanese*, Trapani, 1978, pp. 13–15, figs 5–7, and for the Canosa throne see A. Grabar, 'Trônes épiscopaux du XIe et XIIe siècle en Italie méridionale', *Wallraf-Richartz Jahrbuch*, 16, 1954, pp. 8ff., figs. 2 and 3.

[8] A.K. Porter, *Lombard Architecture*, New Haven, London and Oxford, 1917, p. 151.

[9] F. Rebecchi, 'Il reimpiego di materiale antico nel Duomo di Modena', *Lanfranco e Wiligelmo: Il Duomo di Modena*, Modena, 1984, p. 344; also S. Stocchi, *Emilie romane*, La-Pierre-qui-Vire, 1984, p. 259. The belief that Modena started the fashion for columns supported by lions still has its adherents, e.g. F. de la Breteque, 'Les lions porteurs de colonnes', *Le Moyen Age: Revue d'Histoire et de Philologie*, Ser. 4, 34, 1979, p. 227.

8   Como, Museo Civico, doorway from Santa Margherita.

9a Doorway from Santa Margherita, detail.

9b Doorway from Santa Margherita, detai

10a Como, Sant' Abondio, west doorway, detail.

10b Saintes, Musée Archéologique, Roman relief.

columns is frequently found.[10] After an exhaustive study of the theme of lions as guardians and bearers, R.A. Jairazbhoy came to the same conclusion, namely that lions of Romanesque porches in Italy 'were in every instance anticipated by the art of the Ancient East'.[11] He believes that the lions flanking the doorway of Salerno Cathedral are the earliest instance of the motif in Italy.[12] In fact, there are two doorways with lions in Salerno Cathedral, both dating to between 1080 and 1085,[13] but they do not support columns and are merely placed on either side of the entrance to the atrium and then again to the church itself as crouching guardians. Like the lions at Como (unknown to Jairazbhoy) they are parallel to the facade, each pair facing each other. But here the similarity ends. The naturalism of the Salerno lions suggests some Roman model for them, while the bulky bodies of the Como lions, on which the legs, the tufts of the manes and other features are defined by shallow, incised grooves and the flat surfaces have strong outlines, betray no such connections.

The Santa Margherita doorway is not complete but three of its arches survive in fairly good condition (Plate 9a). They consist of a roll-moulded arch between two flat ones, an arrangement which was to be developed further in Sant' Ambrogio in Milan, in several churches in Pavia and elsewhere in Lombardy and beyond.[14]

The inner arch at Como is carved only on its main face, and the soffit is plain. At the apex is a human face from whose mouth emerge two-stranded bands forming six regular units of interlace, separated from each other by a narrow, plain space. This arrangement has good precedents in northern Italian art of the eighth century, for example in the sculpture of the ciborium in San Giorgio at Valpolicella (Verona) [15] and in miniature painting, for instance the Homilies of St Gregory at Vercelli (Biblioteca Capitulare, MS CXLVIII, 7v, 8 and 9).[16] The middle arch of the Como doorway is carved with a spiral of cable ornament alternating with a simple running scroll. These two arches, and especially the latter, have a close parallel in the doorway and the windows of the presbytery and the apse of Sant' Abondio at Como (Plate 10a), so much so that it is generally

[10] E. Mâle, *L'Art religieux du XIIe siècle en France: Etude sur l'origine de l'iconographie du Moyen Age*, Paris, 1922, p. 41.

[11] A. Jairazbhoy, *Oriental Influences in Western Art*, Bombay etc., 1965, p. 279.

[12] Ibid., p. 278.

[13] Pace, op. cit., p. 227.

[14] G. de Francovich, 'La corrente comasca nella scultura romanica europea: Gli inizi', *Revista del Reale Instituto d'Archeologia e Storia dell'Arte*, Roma, 1936, pp. 267–305. Part 2, 'La diffusione', 1937–38, pp. 47–129. See also an important recent study by A. Tcherikover, 'Romanesque Sculpted Archivolts in Western France: Forms and Techniques', *Arte Medievale*, 2nd series, 3, 1989, pp. 49ff., and especially pp. 61–66, where she discusses influences from Lombardy.

[15] E. Arslan, *La pittura e la scultura veronese dal secolo VIII al secolo XIII*, Milano, 1943, pp. 1–25, pl. 4.

[16] J. Hubert, J. Porcher, W.F. Volbach, *Europe in the Dark Ages*, London, 1969, p. 143, pls. 121, 162–163.

accepted that the same team of sculptors was at work in both churches.[17]

The history of Sant' Abondio is a little better documented than that of Santa Margherita.[18] This former cathedral of Como became a Benedictine monastery in 1013. The church as it stands today was consecrated by Urban II in 1095 on his way to France to preach the crusade. Such papal ceremonies are not reliable for dating purposes and there are good reasons to believe that, in this case, the church was completed some years earlier. The donation from Bishop Rainaldo to Abbot Arderico in 1063 is probably connected with the building already in progress and it can be assumed that the church was ready about 1080 since the team of sculptors from Sant' Abondio (and Santa Margherita) was, by the 1080s, working on the decoration of the convent church of St Servatius at Quedlinburg in Saxony, where the Ottonian church had been destroyed by fire in 1070. The new church was consecrated in only 1129 but the rebuilding was put in hand soon after the fire and the Italian sculptors were already present when the crypt was being built.[19] Consequently, the date proposed for Sant' Abondio by M. Magni, namely between 1050/70 and 1085,[20] seems to me very probable and should also apply to the doorway of Santa Margherita, though of the two, Santa Margherita must be a little later, since it includes some features not yet present at Sant' Abondio.

Of the three arches of the Santa Margherita doorway it was the outer one which received the most lavish sculpture. In contrast to the orderly and repetitive motifs on the first two arches, the decoration here looks at first sight chaotic and confusing. It involves real and imaginary animals engaged in ferocious combat, what I am tempted to call, a 'march of death', in which almost every creature is being attacked by its neighbour and scrolls of foliage entwine their bodies like snakes.

There are numerous precedents for arches decorated with carved animals, for instance, the beautiful Roman example in the Musée archéologique at Saintes (Plate 10b) on which dove-like birds are facing vases

---

[17]   For a description and good illustrations of the sculpture of Sant' Abondio, see Zastrow, op. cit., pp. 61–77.

[18]   M. Magni, *Architettura romanica comasca*, Milano, 1960, pp. 77–88. See also Porter, op. cit., 2, 1917, pp. 301–12.

[19]   A. Goldschmidt, 'Die Bauornamentik in Sachsen im XII. Jahrhundert', *Monatshefte fuer Kunstwissenschaft*, 3, 1910, pp. 302ff. Goldschmidt's cautious dating of Quedlinburg to the end of the eleventh century was based on the belief that the Italian models for its decoration date from the end of the eleventh and the beginning of the twelfth centuries (p. 307). For a summary of the history of St Servatius, see F. Oswald, L. Shaefer, H.R. Sennhauser (edit.), *Vorromanische Kirchenbauten: Katalog der Denkmaeler bis zum Ausgang der Ottonen*, Muenchen, 1968, 2, pp. 263ff.

[20]   Magni, op. cit., p. 87. Porter (op. cit., p. 312) dated Sant' Abondio to the years 'immediately preceding' 1095; Zastrow (op. cit., 62) to the first half of the eleventh century.

11a The Book of Durrow, Dublin,
Trinity College, MS 57, fo. 192v.

11b Pavia, San Michele, detail of north doorway in west facade.

12a Pavia, San Michele, detail of central
doorway.

12b St Augustine, *Quaestiones in Heptateuchon*,
Paris, Bibl. Nat., MS Lat 12168,
frontispiece.

12c Cahors Cathedral, detail of north doorway.

or foliage.[21] In another example, the fifth-century ivory diptych in the Metropolitan Museum in New York, the lambs are shown marching towards a cross at the apex of the arch.[22] In both cases, the animals are docile and arranged in regular, symmetrical compositions. The animals on the Como arch, in contrast, are vicious and in spirit more akin to the barbaric art of the early Middle Ages in the north, than to the classical or classical-derived art of the Mediterranean world. Writing about the carpet page of the Book of Durrow (Dublin, Trinity College, MS 57, 192v) (Plate 11a), Otto Paecht could almost have been describing the Como arch: ' ... an endless entwining of form, ... with its nightmare of writhing organic life, linked by clenched teeth each to the other, inter-penetrating one another in a mortal struggle for existence'.[23]

If the lions supporting the columns at Como caught the imagination of many sculptors of succeeding generations, so did the 'march of death'. It is found repeatedly in Romanesque doorways in Lombardy but nowhere is the connection with Como more evident than on the north doorway of San Michele at Pavia (Plate 11b). On the inner arch of the central doorway in the same church, in addition to the usual animals, there are mermaids and nude human figures which are being attacked by animals in an almost perverse way (Plate 12a). On the outer arch of the north doorway of Cahors Cathedral in Quercy, there is an echo of this type of subject which, in this case, may have acquired a moral, didactic meaning (Plate 12c).

The affinity of the Como animals to the insular art of the seventh century need not cause much surprise if it is remembered that the Irish monastery in Bobbio, founded in 612, was a centre for the dissemination of insular influences in northern Italy.[24] But there were other means by which insular animal ornament could have reached Lombardy, namely the Merovingian manuscripts from north-eastern France, which contain many elements derived from insular art. In her recent article on what she calls the porch portals of northern Italy, Christine Verzar Bornstein illustrated a page from a mid-eighth century manuscript, probably from Laon (Paris, Bibliothèque Nationale, MS Lat. 12168, frontispiece), be-cause it shows an arcade supported by a pair of lions.[25] These lions present a particularly significant parallel for the Como lions, since they are shown in profile (Plate 12b). In addition, this manuscript includes

[21] R. Crozet, *L'art roman en Saintonge*, Paris, 1971, p. 18, pl. 3a.

[22] Hubert, Porcher, Volbach, op. cit., p. 209, pl. 216–17.

[23] O. Paecht, *Book Illumination in the Middle Ages: An Introduction*, Oxford, 1986, p. 60. For a review of literature on the Book of Durrow, see J.J.G. Alexander, *Insular Manuscripts: 6th to the 9th century*, London, 1978, pp. 30–32 (no. 6).

[24] For a summary of the role of Bobbio in artistic matters, see Hubert, Porcher, Volbach, op. cit., p. 157.

[25] C. Verzar Bornstein, 'Matilda of Canossa, Papal Rome and the Earliest Italian Porch Portals', *Romanico padano, Romanico europeo*, A.C. Quintavale (ed.), pp. 143–58.

numerous representations of animals in violent movement and entwining with each other or being entangled in rope-like interlaces. The manuscript was in the possession of the abbey of Corbie near Amiens, as is proved by the corrections to its text by the hand of Maurdramnus, who was abbot there between 772 and 781.[26] According to Jean Porcher, the manuscript 'combines motifs stemming from the eastern Mediterranean with an insular ground. It is from the East (perhaps from Coptic embroidery) that these standing quadrupeds, confronted on each side of a small tree, originate, though their wispy legs and clawlike feet are treated in the British manner'. He then suggests that the influence of the Coptic textiles and other objects from the eastern Mediterranean, reached Corbie through Lombard intermediaries. 'Corbie had been gathering together (from Greece, from Roman and Lombard Italy and the British Isles as well) all that was needed for the shaping of Carolingian painting ... '.[27] It was also at Corbie that a new type of writing, the 'Caroline', was evolved and this was inspired by the script current in northern Italy.

Thus, it can be taken for granted that there was ample opportunity for the exchange of ideas and artistic motifs between northern France and Lombardy. However, even if it is accepted that there is some connection between the lions supporting columns and the fierce animals on the pages of the Laon manuscript from Corbie on the one hand, and the Santa Margherita doorway on the other, it is most unlikely that the Como sculptor knew that particular manuscript. But there were, of course, other books produced in northern France with similar motifs. One of them is the *Sacramentarium Gelasianum* of *c.* 750 (in the Vatican Library, MS Reg Lat 316) which contains arcades supported by single winged animals in profile (172v) or by pairs of quadrupeds (3v), thus reinforcing the probability that one such illumination was known to the Como sculptor and gave him the idea of a doorway with lions supporting columns and the 'march of death'.

This possibility becomes particularly compelling when it is borne in mind that after his conquest of Lombardy in 774, Charlemagne exiled its last king, Desiderius, to the Abbey of Corbie where he spent the last years of his life in prayer, fasting and good works. His wife, who had always been a zealous builder of churches and monasteries, doubtless shared his pious last years.[28] Is it not likely that they kept their interest in the churches of their former kingdom by sending them gifts, including insular and Merovingian books?

---

[26] *Bibliothèque Nationale: Les manuscrits a peintures en France du VIIe au XIIe siècle*, Paris, 1954, no. 12.

[27] Hubert, Porcher, Volbach, op. cit., pp. 178–206.

[28] T. Hodgkin, *Italy and her Invaders*, 7, Oxford, 1899, p. 381, n. 2.

5

'Porta Patens Esto': Notes on Early Cistercian Gatehouses in the North of England

Peter Fergusson

One of the most difficult problems confronting the student of monastic architecture lies at the very entrance of the complex. Today's chain link fence and ticket office prelude access to what is often little more than the monastic nucleus of church and cloister. And once inside the site, lawn and landscape encourage a permeable passage across foundations or through fractured walls. The reality of the precinct in the Middle Ages and the scale, relationship, and circulation among its parts was different. A masonry perimeter wall about 3.6 m (12 feet) high normally circumscribed the entire monastic complex with entry severely limited through one or more gatehouses. Within the wall the precinct presented a series of enclosures corresponding to the different areas of the monastery, each discreetly set apart from the other. Some were courtyards like the outer and inner courts, or the cellarer's yard; others were cloistered like the infirmary, the abbot's residence, or the great cloister; others again were simply walled like the orchards or gardens. The intention of such enclosures was seclusion; they kept the world out and the community in, walling off secular contamination on the one hand, and ensuring the ordered discipline of the monastic routine, on the other.

Until recently study of these areas was overlooked by both historian and archaeologist. Compared to the more obviously important monastic buildings like the church or cloister, the relevance of the inner or outer court, of the agricultural areas, and of individual structures like the guest houses, mills, almonry, or gatehouse, looked peripheral; at best they were treated as vernacular architecture, at worst as crude farm yard structures.[1] Recovery of their form and planning is important, however,

---

[1] Recent archaeological investigation has provided a wealth of new evidence, see G. Coppack, 'Thornholme Priory: The Development of a Monastic Outer Court', in R. Gilchrist and H. Mytum (eds.), *The Archaeology of Rural Monasteries*, British Archaeological Reports, British Series, 203, 1989, pp. 185–222; G. Coppack, 'The Excavation of an Outer Court Building perhaps the Woolhouse, at Fountains Abbey', *Medieval Archaeology*, 30, 1986, pp. 46–87; P. Huggins, 'Monastic Grange and Outer Close Excavations, Waltham Abbey, Essex, 1971–2', *Transactions of the Essex Archaeological Society*, 4, 1972, pp. 127–184; P. Huggins, 'Excavation of the Monastic Forge and Anglo Saxon Enclosure, Waltham Abbey, Essex, 1972–73', *Essex Archaeological and History Society*, 5, 1973, pp. 127–184.

if a broader characterisation of the architecture of monastic communities is to emerge.

Reconstruction of precinct architecture is complicated nonetheless. No medieval monastery in England retains the full sequence of original enclosures and buildings, and few the complete circuit of walls and gatehouses. The extent of the loss and the problem of reconstruction can be illustrated by Kirkstall in Yorkshire, a Cistercian abbey founded in 1152. The claustral nucleus is well preserved and covers about six acres, but the precinct overall, which originally covered seven times the present area in care, has disappeared.[2](Plate 13a) Lost to the modern visitor in consequence is any sense of where or how the monastery was entered, of patterns of circulation, of the location, nature, or purpose of service areas.

This essay looks at one of the many buildings associated with the precinct, the gatehouse. Depending on the institution's size, there could be more than one. At least two gatehouses may be regarded as normal, although in a major monastery like Christ Church, Canterbury, six were built, and are shown on Prior Wibert's famous plan of *c.* 1160.[3] The gatehouse closed the walls of the monastery and secured and monitored passage in and out. Traffic regulation and security determined the disposition of the ground floor only, however. The upper chambers, in either one or two storeys, served other functions. Prominent among them were secular business and legal administration, both conducted by the abbot; the first to negotiate the monastery's business operations with the outside world, the second to adjudicate matters involving the abbey's tenants.[4] The latter, legal function, for instance, gave the name Court Gate to the principal gatehouse at Christ Church, Canterbury (Plate 13b). Further uses include the gatehouse as chapel, residence for guests, and even as 'paradise chamber'.[5]

These general observations conflate gatehouse functions, however, and they sidestep a number of questions. Were gatehouse plans and forms standard? To what extent did the gatehouse develop as an architectural type? Can differences be explained by the nature of the monastic

---

[2] See S. Moorhouse and S. Wrathmell, *Kirkstall Abbey: The 1950–64 Excavations; a Reassessment*, West Yorkshire Archaeological Service, Leeds, 1987, pp. 1–4. At Fountains, by comparison, the precinct encompassed 70 acres with the monastic nucleus about 12.

[3] For the literature see C.M. Kauffmann, *Romanesque Manuscripts, 1066–1190*, London 1975, pp. 96–97.

[4] The precise nature of secular business conducted in the gatehouse is unclear.

[5] For these and for further functions for the gatehouse in earlier centuries including royal audience hall, triumphal arch, Archangel Michael's chapel, see G. Binding, 'Die Karolingische Koenigshalle', in D. Knopp (ed.), *Die Reichsabtei Lorsch*, 2 vols, Darmstadt, 1972, 1977, 2, pp. 273–97; W. Meyer-Barkhausen, 'Die fruehmittelalterlichen Vorbauten am Atrium von Alt St Peter in Rom, zweiturmige Atrien, Westwerke und Karolingisch-Ottonische Koenigskapellen', *Wallraf-Richartz Jahrbuch*, 20, 1958, pp. 7–40.

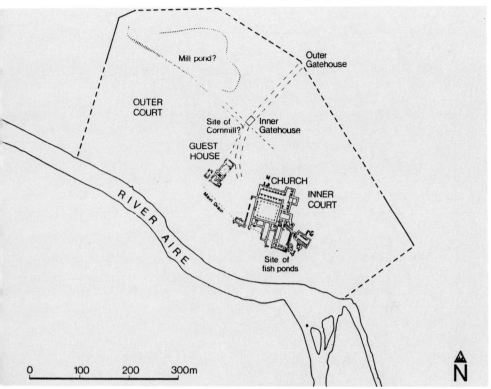

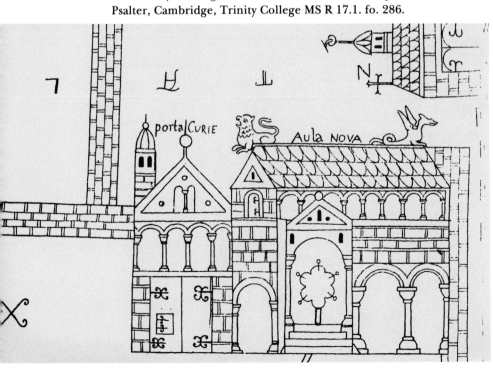

3a Kirkstall Precinct, from Moorhouse and Wrathmell, *Kirkstall Abbey*, Fig. 3.

13b Canterbury, court gate, detail from Prior Wilbert's plan in the Eadwine Psalter, Cambridge, Trinity College MS R 17.1. fo. 286.

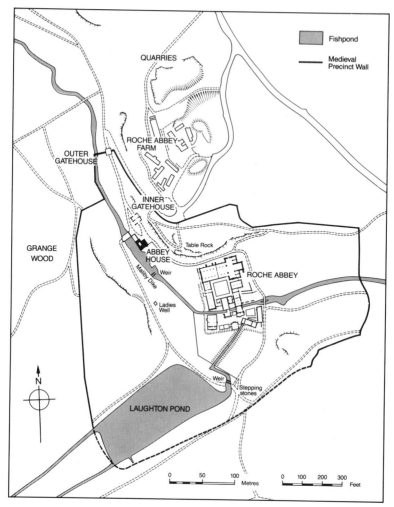

14a Roche Abbey, precinct plan.

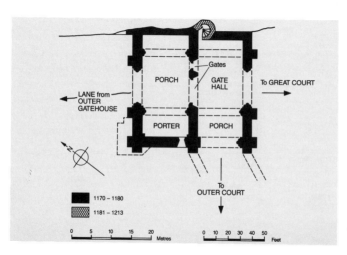

14b Roche Abbey,
gatehouse plan.

institution? Did gatehouse functions change over time? And is it stretching credibility to claim iconographic meanings for the gatehouse?

Restricting discussion to the twelve abbeys established by the Cistercians in the north of England in the twelfth century reveals the challenge of answering these questions. Compared to survivals elsewhere, gatehouses at Cistercian houses are surprisingly few. None survives intact. Yet twelfth-century gatehouses can be reconstructed at half of them, and these the major foundations (Fountains, Kirkstall, Furness, Rievaulx, Byland and Roche) and they permit discussion of the gatehouse type in the Cistercian's early history.

For the first forty years of the Cistercian order in the north of England no above-ground gatehouse remains have been identified. This puzzling fact suggests either that the gatehouse was among the last buildings to be constructed in a campaign probably replacing an initial wooden structure, or that the gatehouse was relocated as the monastery developed and thus can no longer be sought where present buildings survive.[6]

Aspects of the early history of the gatehouse are found in Cistercian documents. In the *Summa cartae caritatis*, written *c.* 1119, for instance, the founders specified the buildings that had to be in place prior to the establishment of a new community. Enumerated are: '...an oratory, a refectory, a dormitory, a guest house, and a gatekeeper's cell'.[7] From the beginning, therefore, the gatehouse was indispensable for a new monastery. In the north of England, immediately after the order's first settlement at Rievaulx in 1132, the gatehouse is mentioned in several contexts. In Walter Daniel's *Vita Ailredi*, for instance, it figures in Ailred's admission to Rievaulx around 1134. The day before he joined, Ailred went with the abbey's founder, Walter Espec, to visit the new community then in its second year of operation. Despite his high social standing and the presence of his host, the party was not allowed inside the monastery. Instead they were met by 'the prior, the guestmaster, and the keeper of the gate (*portarius*)' and prayers and a homily followed.[8] The next day when Ailred returned to request admission to the house, the same officials spoke with him. He then divided his worldly goods, and divested himself of all but one servant, transactions that occurred in the guesthouse. It can be inferred that this building lay inside the precinct but outside the inner court. In accordance with the Rule of St Benedict, Ailred waited there four days, a period of exclusion that seemed 'like a

[6] At Thornholme, for instance, it is clear that the gatehouse was only raised in phase 2 or 3 suggesting a removal from an earlier location, see Coppack op. cit., (as in n. 1), pp. 185 ff.

[7] J. de la Croix Bouton and J.B. Van Damme, *Les Plus Anciens Textes de Cîteaux*, Achel, 1974, p. 121.

[8] F. M. Powicke (ed. and trans.) *The Life of Ailred of Rievaulx*, London, 1950, p. 14. Dr Norton kindly drew my attention to this passage in the *Vita*.

thousand years'.[9] Only after further interrogation was he allowed to proceed inside the monastery to the novice house (*probatorium*).

A further gatehouse reference comes seven years later after Ailred had become novice master. One of the future saint's proudest claims was that no postulant to Rievaulx reneged on his initial commitment. But one stretched Ailred's powers to the limit, a man unnamed, but characterised by Walter Daniel as '*instabilis*'. This man's vocational vacillations involved several departures and returns to Rievaulx. On one such occasion Walter Daniel narrates: 'Meanwhile the fugitive comes to the gate, hastening to get away, but at the open doors he felt the empty air, as though it were a wall of iron. Again and again he tries with all his might to break through and get out, but every effort was in vain ... at last in intense rage he takes hold of the hinges of the gate with both hands and, stretching out his leg, tries to put one foot forward, but in no way did he contrive to reach even the boundary'.[10] Commenting on this episode, Walter Daniel writes that 'though the gates were open, <Ailred> had shut the air against him ...' through the power of prayer.

Apart from the existence of the gatehouse and the office of its keeper, can one assume from Walter Daniel's account that the gates were habitually open? Unfortunately the narrative omits all reference to the time of day when the episode above occurred. But to take the account literally is probably unmerited in any event. Walter Daniel's intention was to impress his reader with a miracle rather than to describe a building, and the references to the gatehouse could be seen as metaphorical as much as factual. Furthermore, on the occasion of the 'unstable' monk's third appearance in the *Vita*, after Ailred had become abbot, it is clear that the gatehouse was barred, at least at night, as it probably was at most other times.[11] Yet the image of openness as a paradigm of the community's ideals remained fundamental, even if in reality the gates were shut. At Cleeve in Somerset, a Cistercian foundation of the late twelfth century, Abbot Dovell rebuilt the upper storey of the original gatehouse just before the Dissolution, and had carved over the main entrance arch *Porta patens esto/ nulli claudaris honesto* (Gate be open, shut to no honest person).[12]

Turning to the physical remains, the most complete early Cistercian gatehouse survives at Roche in Yorkshire. At the outset a distinction needs to be drawn about types of gatehouse. The northern abbeys had at least two: an outer or precinct gatehouse that closed the precinct walls,

---

[9] See chapter 58, J. McCann, *The Rule of St Benedict*, London, 1952, pp. 129–133. For Ailred's reaction to the wait, see Powicke op. cit., (as in n. 8), p. 14.

[10] Ibid., pp. 24, 30–32.

[11] Ibid., pp. 35–36. Other narratives confirm this. For the community sent out by Furness to found Calder and their return to the mother house to find the gates barred, see Victoria History of the Counties of England, *Yorkshire*, iii, London, 1913, pp. 131–134.

[12] R. Gilyard-Beer, *Cleeve Abbey, Somerset*, London, 1959, p. 12.

15a Roche Abbey, great gatehouse from the south.

15b Roche Abbey, gatehouse vaults from anonymous photo, 1922.

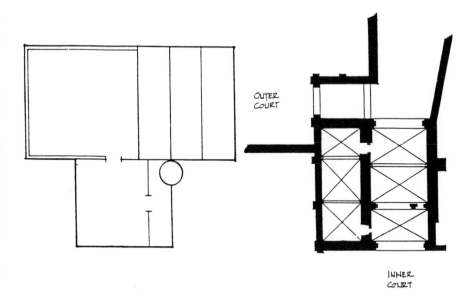

16a Roche Abbey, gatehouse, schematic
     plan of upper floor.

16b Fountains Abbey, gatehouse plan.

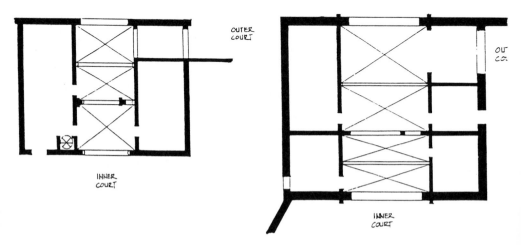

16c Kirkstall Abbey, gatehouse plan.

16d Furness Abbey, gatehouse plan.

and an inner or great gatehouse that controlled access to the various enclosures within the monastery (Plate 14a). Of the first type no remains survive at any house and archaeology has as yet recovered no information about them. At Roche the precinct gatehouse was located about 61 m (200 feet) west of the great gatehouse and was connected to it by a walled lane of which fragments survive. By contrast, the great gatehouse involved more complicated planning and a more ambitious architecture (Plate 15a). Tucked against the rocky hillside that gave the abbey its name on the north, and abutted by the enclosing wall of the outer court on the south, the gatehouse faced three ways, to the east, west, and south, through broad arches and vaulted vestibules. Originally with an upper storey crowned by a high pitched roof, the building would have dominated the entrance to the monastery. What is now visible therefore is a truncated remnant of a once much more impressive structure, essentially the ground storey, along with much of the original paved roadway underneath.

At ground storey the gatehouse consisted of two distinct parts (Plate 14b). Dividing them were the gates which were hung from two archways and opened inwards, a wider one with double doors for vehicles, a narrower one for pedestrians. The outer or west part, constituted the gateway proper, and comprised the single wide west archway and a rib-vaulted vestibule with a broad centre vault and two narrow flanking vaults.[13] A porter's lodge, required by the Rule of St Benedict, occupied the south bay, and was originally framed by wooden screening; it was entered from a small doorway towards the stream.[14]

The second part of the gatehouse consisted of the gatehall, the space within the building extending from the gates *inward* towards the inner court in which visitors would find themselves after passing through the gates. It was likewise rib-vaulted with a flanking narrow barrel vault on the north from which a doorway gave access to a circular stair leading to the upper storey. Exits from the gatehall consisted of two large arched openings, one towards the inner court and the monastic nucleus, the other at right angles that opened south, towards the outer court of the monastery which lay across the stream.[15] Regulation of these important areas where the agricultural and industrial buildings essential to the monastic economy lay, and control of traffic to them, would have

[13] The terminology of gatehouses is confusing. I have adhered to the terms employed by Willis. These are: *gatehouse* for the overall building, *gateway* for the parts lying within the building but outside the actual wooden doors that opened to allow entry, *gatehall* for the parts within the building that lay on the inner side of the doors.

[14] McCann op. cit., (as in n. 9), chapter 66, pp. 152–53 and 201.

[15] The gatehouse plan published in the Department of the Environment guide, A. Hamilton Thompson, *Roche Abbey, Yorkshire*, London, 1971, omits the south opening altogether and dates the building (see fold out plan) to the 14th century.

occurred through the south facing arch which otherwise today incongruously confronts river bank and empty meadow.[16]

If the three arched openings of the lower storey indicate the character of a traffic hub, the second storey had an entirely different purpose. For outsiders it was reached by a newel stair in the north corner of the gatehall, and for the abbey's officials from either an external stairway of wood or stone or from an adjoining building.[17] The two entrances need to be seen in relation to the function of the upper storey as business office and abbot's court; the newel stair provided for the tenants, the upper one for the abbot.

A photograph taken in 1922, when the site came into possession of the government, shows the gatehouse in the process of consolidation (Plate 15b) and permits with the present remains a schematic plan of the first floor (Plate 16a). A large rectangular room occupied the south side and was clearly the principal chamber. Wall benches along three sides served the tenants of the monastery summoned to appear before the abbot. Three lesser rooms lay to the north, the two outer ones ledged into the rock outcrop, although with carefully cut ashlar in the external walls.

Recent examination of the gatehouse has occasioned a redating. Instead of a unitary fourteenth-century structure, two distinct campaigns of work can now be recognised. The earlier, comprised the nucleus of the structure and dates to *c.* 1200 (Plate 14b). About a century later, however, parts of the central vault over the gateway were rebuilt. Vault construction differs. From above (Plate 15b), the east and west compartments of the central vault were composed of thin wedge-shaped stones like the transept chapels vaults of *c.* 1180, while the north–south compartments were filled with larger more accurately cut ashlar typical of *c.* 1300 construction. At the same time capitals and bases were replaced. Structural weakness most likely led to the renewal; the subsequent construction of a buttress counteracted the still discernible outward tilt of the wall.

Associated with the Roche gatehouse is the one at Fountains. Largely ruined, and with the lower walls now about 1.21 m (4 feet) below ground, sufficient proportions nonetheless survive of the north and south passage walls to permit reconstruction (Plate 16b).[18] As at Roche, the builders took advantage of topographical conditions and placed the gatehouse close to the rising hillside on the north, thereby making closure of the inner court easier on this side. In keeping with the larger size of the monastery, the Fountains gatehouse measured 18.3 m (60 feet) in length and about half that in width. Likewise two storey with the

---

[16] Evidence of the outer court disappeared under Capability Brown's terracing in 1774.

[17] The surviving steps placed over the barrel vault indicate an adjoining building. It abuts a former window opening and must therefore date from phase 2 (see text below).

[18] See J.A. Reeve, *A Monograph on the Abbey of St Mary at Fountains*, London, 1892, pp. 50–51; and pl. 44 where the plan and sections show a number of details missing in R. Gilyard-Beer, *Fountains Abbey, North Yorkshire*, London, 1987, p. 77.

lower divided into gateway and gatehall by a pierced cross wall, which anchored the wooden doors for wheeled and pedestrian traffic, it also opened through three vaulted vestibules. Yet the design differed in two ways. First, much larger quarters were assigned the porter; his office occupied the entire south half of the building. This official's responsibilities demanded more extensive space commensurate with the abbey's status and scale and provided him access to both gateway and gatehall, in front and behind the gates in other words. Second, on account of the increased room for the porter, the vaulted vestibule to the outer court was moved to the west of the gateway. This simplified the design and avoided the tighter turning radius for carts under the building proper, and perhaps, more importantly, it moved the roadway to the service areas of the monastery outside the enclosed ground storey.

Architectural details, notably vault responds and capitals, are similar to those in the parlour and refectory, both dating to the 1170s, and thereby establish the gatehouse as another of the buildings raised under the prolific Abbot Robert of Pipewell (1170–79). It preceded Roche by about ten to twenty years, a chronology consistent with the general building history of each house. Roche was a related house of Fountains, a foundation of Newminster which was in turn a direct foundation of Fountains. The west parts of the complex at Roche, including the gatehouse, were completed by Abbot Osmund (1184–1213), who had formerly been cellarer at Fountains. This office ensured his detailed knowledge about the architecture. The gatehouse sequence therefore indicates a shift in planning ideas at Roche. The entrance to the outer court was now moved within the gates, a change that reflected a tightening control of agricultural and industrial activity that can be paralleled elsewhere in the Cistercians' stiffening legislation aimed to regulate all aspects of daily life.[19]

Three other gatehouses in the north can be associated with the Roche and Fountains type. The earliest, and the earliest Cistercian example in England, is at Kirkstall (Plate 16c). The building's survival is due to its conversion into a domestic residence for the abbot at the Dissolution, and in the present century from residence into museum.[20] On the exterior the north and south walls stand nearly to full gable height. Interior arrangements on the ground floor can be discerned since the 1960s thanks to the stripping of nineteenth-century plaster and the removal of wall divisions. These show triple arched entrances like Roche and Fountains, with that to the outer court in the first gateway bay. The

[19] Compare for instance, the process that led to the re-ordering of refectories in the 1170s and 80s see P. Fergusson, 'The Twelfth Century Refectories at Rievaulx and Byland', in C. Norton and D. Park, ed., *Cistercian Art and Architecture in the British Isles*, Cambridge, 1986, pp. 160–80.

[20] See W.H.St John Hope, 'Kirkstall Abbey', *The Publications of the Thoresby Society*, 16, 1907, pp. 1–72, particular p. 10.

original vaults over the passage with responds and capitals remain and are contemporary with the last work on the church of *c.* 1170.

The gatehouse at Furness in Lancashire is a few years later than Kirkstall. Far less survives, although the lower masonry courses up to plinth level are exposed. The building was nearly square, measuring about 24.4 m (80 feet) to a side, larger than Fountains and nearly twice the size of Roche (Plate 16d).[21] Set in the neck of a tight valley which expanded in a north south direction, the gatehouse likewise took this orientation. A third archway opened to the east in the first of the two bay gateway.[22] Spacious apartments flanked the west sides of the traffic passage. Architectural detailing of the plinths of the main entry arches resembles that in the transepts of the abbey church from *c.* 1170.

Two more examples may be added although the remains are much more fragmentary. At Rievaulx the Dissolution Inventory and Rutland Surveys recently published by Glyn Coppack mention a substantial building of at least two storeys.[23] Today, however, only the jamb plinths of the two outer archways and of the gate arch can be traced, all embedded in the hedge of the roadway that still runs on top of the passage. Since the northern plinths are twice the distance from the gate of the southern, a two-bay gateway can be assumed on the north, a single bay gatehall on the south, the same arrangement as Furness and Kirkstall. At right angles to the entrance gate on the east, a single chamfered arch still stands amid the hawthorn, its span indicating a doorway. At Byland, the remains of the great gatehouse consist only of the archway that supported the wooden doors and the jamb of a smaller arch to the north dating to *c.* 1180.[24]

The gatehouses discussed in this essay span the period *c.* 1170–1200. Two distinctive features set them apart from earlier gatehouse types. One is the absence of towers, either flanking as at a large cathedral monastery like Canterbury (Plate 13b), or central as at a Benedictine community like Bury St Edmunds.[25] Both arrangements continue earlier traditions such as Anglo-Saxon at Winchester and Glastonbury (the latter

---

[21] W.H.St John Hope, *The Abbey of St Mary in Furness, Lancashire*, Kendal, 1902, pp. 16–17. The gatehouse is omitted altogether in the official guide; see J.C. Dickinson, *Furness Abbey*, London, 1965. Dr. Jason Wood kindly showed me the remains.

[22] The east wall of the passageway is more complicated than Hope shows on his plan.

[23] G. Coppack, 'Some Descriptions of Rievaulx Abbey in 1538–39: The Disposition of a Major Cistercian Precinct in the Early Sixteenth Century', *Journal of the British Archaeological Association*, 139, 1986, pp. 100–33. Dr. Coppack kindly drew my attention to the gatehouse remains at Rievaulx.

[24] See discussion in S. Harrison, *The Architecture of Byland Abbey*, unpublished M. A. thesis, University of York, 1988, p. 19.

[25] For Bury see G. Webb, *Architecture in Britain: The Middle Ages*, Harmondsworth, 1956, pl. 56.

in association with a chapel)[26], and may be linked in turn to Carolingian and Early Christian forms.[27] Avoidance of towers parallels the Cistercians' legislation prohibiting towers on churches. A second distinctive feature is the creation of the triple portal gatehouse fronted by walled lanes. The building provided access to both inner and outer courts. The creation of this type derives from the order's control of service activities within the precinct, particularly the outer court.

No survey of gatehouses in England has been undertaken and the history of the building type remains unclarified, but the Cistercian material indicates a break from older traditions. Although today gatehouses in the order's northern abbeys survive as barely noticed fragments in one's path to the claustral nucleus, in the Middle Ages the building's importance was not only central but its relation to the precinct and to the monastery's enclosures, and its form and plan, conveyed to visitor and community alike a clear Cistercian identity at the entry of the monastery.

Acknowledgements: In the preparation of the paper I happily acknowledge the help of a number of people. At Roche on snow-swept days in the spring of 1985 Glyn Coppack, Principal Inspector, English Heritage, provided patient help in unravelling the history of the Roche gatehouse and first stimulated my interest in the building type. In different ways I am indebted to others, in particular Stuart Harrison, Christopher Norton, Richard Gem, Tim Tatton-Brown and Jason Wood. Lilian Armstrong read an early draft of the paper and helped clarify the murkier passages of writing.

[26] Both are known through documentary reference. For Glastonbury see W. Stubbs (ed.), *Memorials of Saint Dunstan: Auctore B. Life of St Dunstan*, Rolls Series, 63, 1874, pp. 8, 189. For Winchester see *Sanctae Swithuni Wintoniensis Episcopi Translatio et Miracula*, *Analecta Bollandiana*, 4, 1885, pp. 386–87 and A. Campbell (ed.), *Frithegodi Monachi Breuiloquinum Vitae Beati Wilfredi et Wulfstani Cantoris Narratio Metrica de Sancto Swithuno*, Zurich, 1950, p. 100. Dr. Richard Gem kindly provided me with these sources.

[27] See E. Baldwin Smith, *Architectural Symbolism of Imperial Rome and the Middle Ages*, Princeton, 1956, pp. 8–9, 75.

6

Southwell, Worksop, and Stylistic Tendencies in English Twelfth-Century Facade Design

J. Philip McAleer

'The inordinate love of decoration which is so characteristic of later Anglo-Norman buildings, and which contrasts so strongly with the austerity of the first generation works, may very well have been a symptom of the resurgence of Anglo-Saxon taste.'[1]

During the Romanesque a familiar stylistic progression from simple to complex forms can be observed, a pattern of development characteristic of many other periods. In England, the stylistic evolution started with forms of blunt austerity, exemplified by those earliest remaining structures belonging to buildings begun during the two decades following the Norman Conquest. All display thickly jointed masonry, a sparing use of jamb shafts and mouldings, and simple capital types. As a result, emphasis is placed on the angular nature of the forms which stresses the planes and, consequently, on the apparent structuralism of individual elements: the supports, arches, and layered planes of the walls.

The severe, even 'abstract' nature of these early Romanesque structures was quickly left behind. The departure took the form of enrichment rather than fundamental redefinition. Most obviously, this development is demonstrated by the increasing numbers of shafts to jambs and mouldings to arches, at all levels in the buildings.[2] The earlier simplicity was abandoned and so also, in a sense, was clarity of form or at least the clarity of the individual parts. The enrichment of the forms resulted in the creation of a greater homogeneity. Individual elements are no longer so easily discernible: it is more difficult to determine how many layers

---

[1] The quotation at the head of the paper is from P. Kidson in P. Kidson and P. Murray, *A History of English Architecture*, London, 1962, p. 37. With respect to the buildings mentioned in the text, see the bibliography cited in the relevant catalogue entry of my Ph. D thesis, 'The Romanesque Church Facade in Britain', University of London, 1963 (Garland Publishing, Inc.), New York and London, 1984, and/or the appropriate volume of N. Pevsner, *The Buildings of England*, as, in the interests of economy, only bibliographical items more recent than my thesis are given in the following notes. Some of the ideas in this paper were first presented to the Canadian Conference of Medieval Art Historians held at the University of Victoria, Victoria (British Columbia), in 1983.

[2] The nave of Durham Cathedral is a familiar example of what could and did take place as early as *c.* 1110.

there are to the wall or orders to an arch or shafts to an opening. These changes in style, along with the appearance of a wide variety of ornamental motifs and richer forms of capitals, all combined to produce buildings that were increasingly three dimensional in emphasis, plastic in form, and sculptural in effect.

During the twelfth century there was a progressive enrichment or complication in other ways as well. Wall surfaces which survived the encroachment of jamb shafts or arch mouldings were no longer left bare but were covered by blind arcading, a phenomenon which was particularly evident on the exterior, at aisle and clerestory levels, and especially obvious on west facades.[3] Indeed, by the middle of the century and thereafter, the west fronts of English churches appear to have had as their purpose the provision of a field for an orgy of arcading: the (stylistic) tide of the times drenched the facades: arcading of varied and various forms washes over nearly all available surfaces.

Obviously such stylistic changes did not everywhere take place at the same pace in the identical manner to an equal degree. Even so, there are notable exceptions to these general trends particularly evident in west facades dating to the middle or third quarter of the twelfth century. Two tendencies emerge which conflict with the broad stylistic evolution favouring complexity, richness, multiplicity, and plasticity, or at least go against the urge to arcade. One is the unexpected reassertion of a certain simplicity, even bareness, involving an apparent rejection of most ornamentation; the other is a surprising retreat to an unrelieved flatness of the larger form, the west wall as simply a plane. Both tendencies are vividly demonstrated by the facades of Southwell Minster, *c.* 1140/75, and, even more so, Worksop Priory, *c.* 1170–80 (Plates 17, 18).

These two facade designs are basically bare and blunt enough to sustain comparison with late eleventh-century ones like that of Lincoln Cathedral, or even with a non-Insular post-Conquest construction such as the facade-block of St-Etienne at Caen.[4] The absence of arcading is reinforced by the severe restriction in the size and number of windows or portals, and, in the case of Worksop, is further exaggerated by the sparing use of stringcourses which at Southwell almost become the decorative leitmotif *faute de mieux*. In their assertion of smooth unblemished surfaces these two major facades boldly confront the primary preference of the period for incrusted surfaces as demonstrated, for example, by the destroyed facade of Hereford Cathedral (Plate 19), or

---

[3] A beginning seen in a modest way, both inside and outside, already in the choir aisles of Durham shortly after 1093 (where it has been interpreted as an 'English' or Anglo-Saxon phenomena: see below n. 28).

[4] The facade of Lincoln was most likely complete by the consecration of 1092. Its details compare favourably with those of St-Etienne, Caen, where the main block of the facade is usually considered to have been complete by 1081/86.

17 Southwell Minster, west facade.

18 Worksop Priory, west facade.

the ruined facades of Castle Acre Priory, Malmesbury Abbey,[5] Croyland Abbey, and St Botolph's, Colchester, and the altered facade of Rochester Cathedral.[6] Seen against the accepted fashion, the austerity of the twin-tower facades of Southwell and Worksop at this advanced date in the twelfth century is, in a way, shocking, certainly unexpected and, frankly, rather boring: surely they are two of the dullest surviving Romanesque facades.[7]

How could facades like those of Southwell and Worksop have been built contemporary with or, especially, *after* Hereford and Castle Acre? They form a startling contrast of attitudes. What is the explanation? Worksop was an Augustinian priory, while Southwell was secular. Both, however, are close together in Nottinghamshire. Other examples, farther afield, of a similar extreme simplicity or severity may be mentioned, even if on a smaller scale: the facades of the aisled parish churches of Bishop's Cleeve (Gloucestershire), Ledbury (Herefordshire), and Crondall (Hampshire), all apparently of the 1170s,[8] as well as Blackmore Priory (Essex), also Augustinian, of the 1170s-80s.[9] They spread the geographical net a bit wider, to the west and south, suggesting it was not just a matter of a regional school, as is made yet more evident by the inclusion of the two-tower facade of St Germans (Cornwall), a collegiate church, then an Augustinian priory after 1161/89.

It may be more appropriate to ask if these austere facades reflect Cistercian influence. Unhelpfully, actual remains of the earliest Cistercian buildings and their facades are meagre, and, in any case, Nottinghamshire in particular does not seem to have been a centre of great Cistercian activity.[10] The closest of the great Yorkshire houses was Roche,

[5] G. Zarnecki, 'English Twelfth-Century Sculpture and its Resistance to St-Denis', *Tribute to an Antiquary: Essays Presented to Marc Fitch*, London,1976; reprinted in *Studies in Romanesque Sculpture*, London, 1979, iii, p. 88 (*c.* 1160).

[6] See J.P. McAleer, 'The Significance of the West Front of Rochester Cathedral', *Archaeologia Cantiana*, 99, 1983, pp. 139-58. The facade of Norwich, before drastic 19th-century restorations, was more restrained in its use of arcading and a little more plastic than this group of *c.* 1150–70 flat facades. See J.P. McAleer, 'The Romanesque Facade of Norwich Cathedral', *Journal of the Society of Architectural Historians*, 25, 1966, pp. 136–40.

[7] The facade of Worksop is even barer than it need be due to the absence of a south portal, and the placement of the lower two tower windows on the south rather than west face; the first two stages, therefore, are notable for the absence of both arcading and openings.

[8] These parish churches contrast with examples better known because of their arcaded decoration such as Castle Rising (Norfolk), *c.* 1160, or Iffley (Oxfordshire), *c.* 1180 (both heavily restored and rebuilt).

[9] Blackmore was founded 1155/65.

[10] There was only one Cistercian house, Rufford (founded. 1146); there were none in Derbyshire, only one in Leicestershire (Garendon, founded. 1133); but there were five in Lincolnshire, to the east (Swineshead, founded. 1135; Louth Park, founded 1139; Kirkstead I, founded 1139; Revesby, founded 1142; and Vaudey, founded 1147). At none of these sites do the facades (or the churches) survive. See P. Fergusson, *Architecture of Solitude: Cistercian Abbeys in Twelfth-Century England*, Princeton, 1984, Catalogue, pp. 142–3, 127, 150, 131–33, 130–31, 139–40, 152, respectively.

where, unfortunately, the facade does not survive.[11] The earliest surviving facade is that of Fountains in Yorkshire, probably complete by 1160.[12] The second is Kirkstall, also Yorkshire, finished by *c.* 1175.[13] The facade of Fountains is indeed bare, but that of Kirkstall, even though the west wall lacks arcading, is more sculptural due to its projecting portal, buttresses, and large twin windows: there is actually little blank wall space. The slightly later facade of Byland, perhaps begun *c.* 1177, is yet more decorative and plastic due to the appearance of blind arcading.[14] It is, therefore, far from clear that Southwell and Worksop can be explained as the product of Cistercian influence. Indeed these two facades, as well as the others cited, are really more severe and restrained than their surviving Cistercian 'contemporaries'.[15]

Aside from their bareness, the facades of Southwell and Worksop share an additional obvious stylistic feature, one actually held in common with other, decorated, facades of the period. Both facades are conspicuously planar in design, and therefore again appear in conflict with the general tendencies, evident in the evolution of the Romanesque, exploring three-dimensionality and modelling of form.

The basic forms of even the earliest facade structures are characterised by considerable depth of relief: for instance, the west block of Lincoln Cathedral,[16] or the west front of Tewkesbury Abbey, with its single, dominating, recess.[17] The north or 'Ethelbert' tower of the facade of St Augustine's Abbey, Canterbury, also revealed a considerable sculptural effect in the disposition of the forms, especially due to the appearance of a gallery at low level, above a deep portal recess.[18]

These facades impress mainly through the boldness of their fundamental geometric forms, rather than through the richness of small scale 'ornamental' motifs; bare wall surfaces and unmoulded arches are often present. In these respects, they are a contrast to a number of later Romanesque facades, several already mentioned: Hereford, Castle Acre,

---

[11] See Fergusson, op. cit., pp. 62–66.

[12] Fergusson op. cit., pp. 43–44.

[13] Fergusson, op. cit., pp. 49, 50, 51, and pl. 30.

[14] Fergusson, op. cit., pp. 73, pp. 82–83, and pl. 85.

[15] The sectional facades of Cistercian churches, of course, make less of an impact than twin-tower facades which, even if devoid of arcading, offer a much greater expanse of wall.

[16] *Courtauld Institute Illustration Archives*, gen. ed. P. Lasko: *Archive I. Cathedrals and Monastic Buildings in the British Isles*, Pt 1. *Lincoln: Romanesque West Front*, eds G. Zarnecki and P. Kidson, London, 1976, esp. I/1/5-I/1/25. Presumably the facade of Bury St Edmunds was another example.

[17] The facade of Tewkesbury may have been closely imitated by that of Gloucester Abbey (almost certainly), and Bath Abbey (probably).

[18] St Augustine's is usually dated *c.* 1120–30, but I believe it could be as early as *c.* 1100: see J.P. McAleer, 'The Ethelbert Tower of St Augustine's Abbey, Canterbury', *Journal of the British Archaeological Association*, 140, 1987, pp. 88–111.

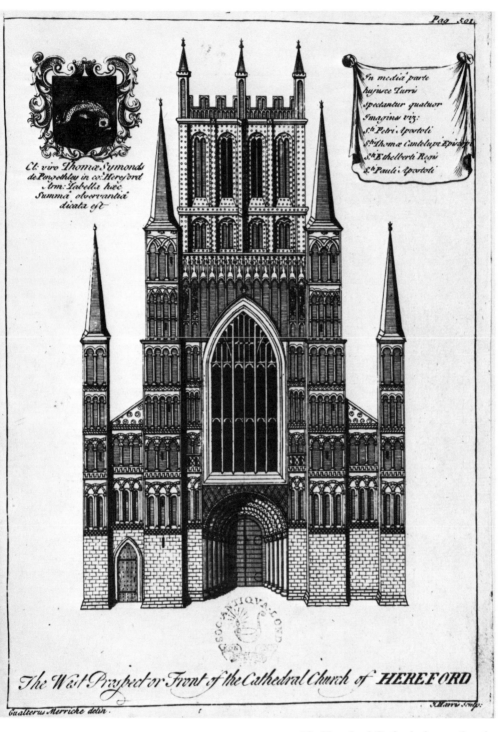

Cl: viro Thomæ Symonds de Pengethley in co: Hereford Arm: Tabella hæc Summâ observantiâ dicata est

In media parte hujusce Turri spectantur quatuor Imagines viz: S.ti Petri Apostoli S.ti Thomæ Cantelupi Episcopi S.ti Ethelberti Regis & S.ti Pauli Apostoli

The West Prospect or Front of the Cathedral Church of **HEREFORD**

Gualterus Merricke delin.   N. Hurr. Sculp.

19 Hereford Cathedral, west facade.

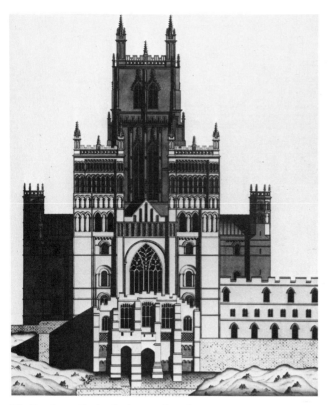

20a Durham Cathedral, west facade.

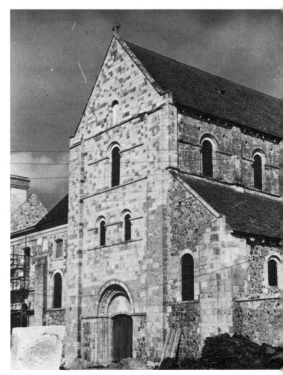

20b Lessay Abbey, west facade.

Malmesbury in particular.[19] A curious aspect of these arcaded facades is their extraordinary flatness. Although they represent facades of several different types, sectional (Hereford), twin-tower (Castle Acre), screen (Colchester, Malmesbury, Croyland), they each exist almost in a single thin plane. This is due not so much to the effect of numerous tiers of blind arcading, as it is to the shallow projection of broad flat buttresses, and to the lack of depth given to windows or doors. Even if the latter are multi-jambed, they are so small that they make little indentation, and hence little impact. There is a rather curious contradiction between the development of the ornamental repertoire and its mode of application, and the articulation of the basic forms. The more three-dimensional facade designs seem to be the earlier facade structures.[20]

This assertion of planarity in the mid twelfth century strikes one as contrary to the general stylistic development of Romanesque to Gothic, especially as seen in northern France where a continuous increase in 'structural relief' is demonstrated by a sequence of facades, beginning with St-Etienne Caen, jumping to St-Denis, with its strongly projecting buttresses, and continuing with Sens and Senlis to Laon, where the buttresses are 'justified' by porches, and so to Amiens and Reims. In England, the Gothic facades of the cathedrals of Wells and Salisbury, for instance, however different in other major aspects from their (Gothic) contemporaries in the Ile-de-France, seem to share a similar sculptural quality, due primarily to the very deep, strongly projecting buttresses.[21]

It may be possible to trace 'anti-sculptural tendencies' to an earlier stage in Insular Romanesque facade compositions. The two-tower facade of Durham Cathedral (Plate 20a) forms an interesting contrast with that of St-Denis. The differences between the two are illuminating and highlight the non-French qualities of Durham. The major gulf between them is created by the form of the buttresses. At St-Denis, as already observed, they project strongly, creating a forceful vertical element, powerfully suggesting support, anticipating the towers which sit on the westwork. At Durham (where the free-standing stages of the towers date from a century later), the buttresses are broad and flat, in one shallow order: the plane of the wall is stressed. The facade of Durham also must have formed a strong contrast with that of St Augustine's, although the facade

[19] The facade of Rochester Cathedral, roughly contemporary with these buildings, adheres to the sculptural tradition.

[20] The late 12th-century west transept at Ely Cathedral, before the addition of the strongly projecting Gothic porch, formed one immense flat plane covered by profuse and rich forms of arcading.

[21] In contrast to these very plastic facades, there are others of the 13th century emphasising planarity: Dunstable Priory, the Gothic additions to Lincoln, and Lichfield Cathedral. The false screen facade of the Augustinian priory of Newstead (Nottinghamshire) also continues the flat theme into the late 13th century.

of the cathedral of Canterbury might have been more similar to it.[22]

Another example of a similar attitude, although on a less monumental scale than Durham, was the Romanesque facade of sectional type at Shrewsbury Abbey.[23] What little is left suggests a design of near perfect flatness: four narrow pilaster-like buttresses have only a minimal projection.

In England, there was not a gradual movement towards increased depth of relief in facade compositions during the second half of the twelfth century, or even a gradual return to three-dimensionality in the early thirteenth century; rather, there seems to have been an abrupt shift. For instance, Malmesbury may have been the direct prototype for Salisbury, but there is still a considerable gap in conception between the former's flatness and the latter's depth.[24] The flat facades of the mid to late twelfth century certainly do not form an intermediate stage (as a parallel to St-Denis, Sens, and Senlis) marked by an increasing depth to the west wall, even if only due to features such as layered buttresses.

As an exception to the general trend, this particular feature of flatness raises the question of whether it was due more to traditional attitudes coming to the fore, than to temporary shifts in contemporary fashion. Can a similar parallel explanation account for the sporadic and somewhat locally limited manifestations of the contradictory preference for severity and austerity in facade design?

It is tempting to associate the flat facades and their parallel use of bands of small scale arcading with the tendency in sculpture to look backwards for inspiration to the pre-Conquest period, a period which has been identified with the rise in national feeling that came to the fore during the reign of King Stephen.[25] In architecture, a similar kind of archaism was first identified by J. Bony as, 'an effort to return to the good old days of Edward the Confessor'.[26] More recently, M.F. Hearn, writing of Romsey Abbey, elaborated the concept of a specifically English, as opposed to a Norman, tradition.[27] Continuing along these lines, it could be proposed that such pre-Conquest, early eleventh-century build-

---

[22] The facade of Christ Church was probably complete *c.* 1077/8. It survived into the 19th century as only a north tower.

[23] The nave of Shrewsbury was probably complete *c.* 1100; the west portal has been dated just after.

[24] The flatness of some of these 12th- (and some 13th-) century facade designs becomes all the more curious considering the boldness of some other English Gothic facades later than those of Wells and Salisbury, e.g. York Cathedral.

[25] See G. Zarnecki, 'The Sources of English Romanesque Sculpture', *XVII Congrès International d'Histoire de l'Art*, The Hague, 1955, pp. 171–78.

[26] J. Bony, 'French Influences on the Origin of English Architecture', *Journal of the Warburg and Courtauld Institutes*, 12, 1949, p. 4, n. 1. He, however, identifies the single factor of this 'backwardness' as the lack of interest in vaulting evident after 1140.

[27] 'Romsey Abbey: A Progenitor of the English National Tradition in Architecture', *Gesta*, 14/1, 1975, pp. 27–40, esp. pp. 27, 39–40.

ings as Earls Barton [28] might have suggested to the mid twelfth-century designers that the use of flat, decorated surfaces constituted a pre-Conquest national tradition.[29]

If the tendency so obvious in the twelfth century, towards an increasingly ornamental character, along with an apparent fondness for flat and arcaded surfaces, can be taken as evidence of a resurgence of Anglo-Saxon tastes, the 'reversion' to severely undecorated facades at Southwell, Worksop, and elsewhere would have to be accepted as an 'Early Norman Revival', recalling the austere grimness of the early post-Conquest structures.[30]

Interestingly enough, neither facade follows a bleakly bare nave. The nave of Southwell has multiscallop capitals, billet and other decorative motifs, and little bare wall space except between the clerestory openings. The elevation of Worksop is even more decorated because of a generous use of dog-tooth (nave arcade abaci and hood moulds) a large nutmeg (gallery hood moulds and clerestory string); and the idiosyncratic employment of continuous and alternating sized arches in the gallery level. After the exuberance of the nave design, its facade seems all the more disappointing.[31]

The exterior elevations of both buildings are notable for the lack of arcading at either aisle or clerestory levels, although its absence there did not necessarily preclude its appearance on the west front. The fact that both facades were of the twin-tower, rather than the screen, type does not provide an explanation, because the twin-tower facade of Castle Acre is one of the outstanding instances of the mid twelfth-century passion for arcading.

Only two major Norman facades remain from the twelfth century. They are those of the abbeys of La-Trinité at Lessay (Plate 20b) and St-Georges at St-Martin-de-Boscherville. Both are likely to date variously

[28] And others such as Barton-on-Humber (tower nave), Barnack (west tower), Deerhurst (apse), Wing (apse), Stanton Lacy (nave wall), and Woolbeding (nave wall); see J. Bony, 'Durham et la tradition Saxonne', in eds. S.M. Crosby, A. Chastel, A. Prache, A. Chatelet, *Etudes d'art médiévale offertes à Louis Grodecki*, Paris 1981, pp. 80, 82.

[29] Whether or not there were enough architectural monuments like Earls Barton for them to have been recognised in the 12th century as constituting a pre-Conquest *national* style is possibly a problem.

[30] A love of the linear and the flat has often been attributed to the English: e.g., G. Zarnecki, '1066 and Architectural Sculpture', *Proceedings of the British Academy*, 52, 1966; reprinted in *Studies in Romanesque Sculpture*, I., esp. p. 104. See also N. Pevsner, *The Englishness of English Art*, London, 1956, pp. 88–91, 120.

[31] N. Pevsner, *The Buildings of England, Nottinghamshire*, Harmondsworth, 1951, p. 213, had even wondered: 'Could not the facade have been begun earlier than the nave and then carried on essentially without a change of style?' This suggestion was eliminated from the second edition, 1979.

from the period 1120–40.[32] Compared to their English cousins, they are remarkably restrained. Their austerity is often described in positive terms (noble and sober simplicity) and regarded as a characteristic Norman virtue, one associated with and continued from the eleventh century and buildings such as St-Etienne, Caen.[33]

In addition to the restraint in decoration, almost total at Lessay, both Norman facades are also notable for their quality of planarity or flatness. The buttresses in particular are still broad and shallow. These qualities may certainly be paralleled by many English twelfth-century designs.[34] Can Norman preferences account for both tendencies under discussion: one, forming a continuous undercurrent, the other an occasional re-assertion of a traditional value, the virtue of restraint?

[32] These tendencies are a remarkable contrast to Norman facades, if those of Lessay and Boscherville can be taken as typical of the mid-century. For Lessay (after 1130/40?), see L. Musset, *Normandie romane*, i. *La Basse-Normandie*, La Pierre-qui-Vire, 2nd edition 1975, p. 205, pl. 76. For Boscherville see Musset, op. cit., 2, *La Haute-Normandie*, p. 149, pl. 64.

[33] J. Daoust, *L'abbaye de St-Georges-de-Boscherville*, Fécamp, 2nd edn, 1958, p. 17; and Musset, op. cit., 2, p. 149.

[34] Interestingly, Pevsner, op. cit., *Nottinghamshire*, p. 213, commented: 'The buttresses (of the facade) are as shallow as Normandy made them in the 11th century, and have no set-offs on the way up'.

7

Medieval 'Service' Architecture: Undercrofts

Virginia Jansen

Because undercrofts or cellars (I use the terms interchangeably) constitute a subordinate class of building, they have rarely been studied, and, despite the significant number of surviving examples, not at all as a group so far as I know.[1] Yet they point up two significant issues which historians of medieval architecture overlook at times, but which would expand the way they do their work: first, there may be another concept of architecture, perhaps a counter-version to ecclesiastical style; second, the very simplicity of cellars limits any discussion of forms to interpretations based on their functional, economic and social character.

Most ecclesiastical architecture of the central Middle Ages, whether Romanesque or Gothic, shows a highly articulated, analytical structure, in which the repetition of vertical responds divides the walls into bays. Even in the most open of these, the relatively narrow span tends to emphasise the longitudinal direction, desirable for processions and for separated circulation. In the late Middle Ages, however, divisions became less marked, the arcades wider and higher, and spatial openness paramount. These qualities are found particularly in churches outside the regions of the so-called 'classic' French Gothic and in ecclesiastical types other than cathedrals, such as German hall churches, English parish churches, and friars' churches all over Europe. Whether vaulted or not, whether one storey or two (though seldom three), these late Gothic structures have wide arcades, thin piers (often simply round, directionless columns), and thin walls. Articulation by bay division is seldom seen, or if apparent, is treated as unobtrusively as possible. New features are invented to increase the unification of the architecture, such as dying mouldings, which dissolve the clear distinction between arch and pier established by the capital in the architecture of the earlier Middle Ages.[2]

---

[1] This essay (which forms part of a larger study including other building types, such as hospitals, dormitories, granaries and arcades) is drawn from early work-in-progress, and is perhaps especially appropriate to honour Peter Kidson, because his conversations encourage one to cast the net more widely, to think more broadly and to examine the unexpected. Thus, I dedicate this work to him with gratitude, pleasure and affection.

[2] Virginia Jansen, 'Dying Mouldings, Unarticulated Springer Blocks, and Hollow Chamfers in Thirteenth-Century Architecture', *Journal of the British Archaeological Association*, 135, 1982, pp. 35–54.

As is well-known, these characteristics of thin walls, reduced supports, wide open spaciousness and lateral movement are associated with the beginnings of Gothic, as seen in the ambulatory of St-Denis. But what is less generally recognised is that another line of medieval building, both Gothic and pre-Gothic, also contains these spatial qualities and may have played a role in the developments of late Gothic openness. These are the utilitarian structures which I have termed 'medieval service architecture' (Plate 21a). They include a variety of buildings, domestic, industrial, and utilitarian of all sorts: cellars, storerooms, workrooms, hospitals, refectories, dormitories, chapter houses. These types survive not only in monastic complexes, but also in domestic and municipal environments (Plate 22a). Here I shall restrict discussion to masonry examples, even though some of the types, such as hospitals and halls, developed from or run parallel to timber structures.

Cellars, or undercrofts, are the bottom floor of a multi-storey (often two-storey) building. Sometimes they are at ground level, sometimes partly subterranean like a crypt in a church. For this essay I shall emphasise aisled masonry undercrofts, which means cellars of at least a certain size, and hence an indication of the patron's status.

These rooms served primarily for storage, whether for casks in storerooms (Plate 22b) or for monks in workrooms. Their location on the ground served well for heavy, bulk storage, whether of grain, beer and wine, or animals. Their spaces had to be as commodious as possible. This primary function of openness dictated a well-defined syntax, a body of forms and spatial treatment directed toward reducing the mass of supports and freeing the interior.

Examination of undercrofts, however, suggests several lines of inquiry beyond formal ones. Who in the Middle Ages could afford a multi-level building and why was it desirable? Who wanted and could afford to build in stone? What do the answers to these questions connote?

Different from single-story halls, undercrofts were almost always vaulted, and unless the span was small, one or two (or more) rows of supports provided a strong platform for the structure above. Thus the subdorter increased the warmth, dryness, and cleanliness of the dormitory raised above the ground.[3] The undercroft podium also rendered the size and pattern of the upper story more visible and commanding, particularly true of the piano nobile in substantial domiciles. Because vertical planning saved space, it indicated a large settlement; it grouped structures more compactly, possibly implying centralised control, and dramatised the imposing power of the outline. It created a display of status worthy of a significant institution or patron, particularly of one operating in a hier-

---

[3] On the plan of St Gall, the cellar supported the larder; Walter Horn and Ernest Born, *The Plan of St Gall: A Study of the Architecture and Economy of, and Life in a Paradigmatic Carolingian Monastery*, 3 vols., Berkeley, 1979, i, p. 292.

archically structured society. On a large scale, especially in monastic examples of the agriculturally successful Cistercian Order, undercrofts reached an impressive size and openness, immediately conveying economic wealth and probably also socio-political strength. The use of masonry reinforced this sense of well-being, as it reflected and represented the continuity and durability of the community. What I wish to emphasise here is the relationship of cellars to economic prosperity and social status.[4]

The undercroft of the lay-brothers' wing at Fountains Abbey, immediately visible to all who pass through the monastic gateway, may be the most noteworthy example, its length a product of two stages of building at the end of the twelfth and beginning of the thirteenth century (Plate 21b). Still impressive, if much more modest, examples are found at Fontenay, and at Eberbach, where the cellar of the lay-brothers' wing was particularly renowned.[5] These earlier structures, whether ribbed or groin vaulted, with low vaults and short columns, still achieve a remarkable openness; they imply that the type itself as much as chronology determined the spaciousness. By the mid thirteenth century, however, undercrofts became even more open. Technical advances in building enabled the walls to become thin, the supports more attenuated, and the vaults steeper, as seen at Fontaine-Guérard, a Cistercian nunnery in Normandy. The so-called 'workroom' underneath the dormitory at Fontaine-Guérard shows a wide-open double-aisled room, with the thinnest of columns carrying pencil-thin moulded ribs 'cleanly' arching, uninterrupted by bosses or complicated with rich mouldings, over an amply proportioned space (Plate 21a).[6] These sparely formed ribs are caught by corbels which are unsupported by shafts so that any pretence of an intellectual system of supports is gone, deemed an unnecessary burden in a utilitarian structure such as this. The walls are pierced by generous windows and the door is segmental-headed to give requisite breadth rather than unneeded height. Such qualities of breadth and openness can be seen in most undercrofts, even in low ones such as the

---

[4] See further Ibid., vol. 1, pp. 286, 292–305; 3, 109–11, 118–20, with discussion of the order and centrality of the stores and cellarer intrinsic to monastic life.

[5] J.L. Lekai, *The Cistericans: Ideals and Reality*, Kent, Ohio, 1977, pp. 316–18. Fontenay and Eberbach are illustrated in Marc-Anselme Dimier, *L'Art Cistercien*, i: *France*, 2nd edn, La Pierre-qui-Vire, 1974, pl. 13, and ii: *Hors de France*, La Pierre-qui-Vire, 1971, pl. 31, respectively.

[6] Marcel Aubert, *L'Architecture Cistercienne en France*, 2 vols., 2nd edn, Paris, 1947, ii, pp. 74–85, discusses several examples of the dormitory undercroft, usually termed the monks' workroom or dayroom, noting that at first the space was often used as the dormitory for novices until a separate building was constructed. At Fountains, R. Gilyard-Beer, *Fountains Abbey*, London, 1970, pp. 48–49, posits that the earlier subdorter was 'probably a workroom', but the use of the remodelled undercroft is unknown. Recognising the architectural significance of this structure, Roger Stalley in *The Cistercian Monasteries of Ireland*, New Haven, 1987, pp. 166, 217, reviews further speculative functions.

21a Fontaine-Guérard Abbey, undercroft.

21b Fountains Abbey, undercroft of west range (cellarium and lay-brothers' refectory).

22a Provins, Grange-aux-dîmes, cellar (probably originally a covered market; later a tithe storehouse for St-Quirace).

22b Santes Creus Monastery, cellar.

twelfth-century undercroft of Burton Agnes Hall in Yorkshire, where the ribs describe an almost flat arch in order not to take up any more height than necessary.[7] The supports remained minimal. In fact, in walking through well-preserved cloisters at the ground level, one moves through a sequence of airy rooms, much more expansive than the constricted space of the monastic church, as can be well experienced today in the Catalan monasteries of Santes Creus and Poblet.

At this point we can isolate the features which create the open spaces of these structures and produce their specific architectural typology.[8] Foremost are the pared down supports, both the thin columns of the arcades and the absence of shafts on the wall. The absence is an obvious economic saving, which corresponds to the spare treatment of the capitals and even of the supports, but the willingness to carve capitals and corbels suggests that the primary reason their wall responds are missing is functional rather than economic.[9] Moreover, the form of the supports in these undercrofts, which are generally columns rather than simple, rectangular piers, suggests not only a desire to increase functional roomi-ness, but also a visual goal, in other words, a conscious preference that governs the building and qualifies it as architecture.[10] Both economic and functional factors merge in producing these qualities, the essence of spareness, simplicity, and plainness.

Allied with narrow supports are three techniques which increase the openness by reducing the thickness of the vaults as they meet the columns. First, in both groin or ribbed vaults, the arches (and ribs in the case of the latter) are fused together into one block at the springing;[11] the darker stone of the springer block at Fontaine-Guérard illustrates this monolith (Plate 21a). The vaults then intrude less upon the width of the span and the resulting effect increases the breadth of the space.

A second technique exists also in both groin-vaulted and ribbed-vaulted versions. Here the diagonal section of the vault is 'squeezed out' as it comes down to the springing (Plate 22a). In ribbed vaulted specimens the result is particularly startling: the tapering diagonal rib combined with pencil-thin columns creates a nearly visionary spaciousness in the chapter houses at Santes Creus in Catalonia or L'Escale Dieu in south-western France.[12]

[7] Illustrated in Margaret Wood, *The English Medieval House*, London, 1965, pl. 14a.

[8] In a paper on medieval houses in Kent delivered to the Medieval Academy of America in 1989, Sarah Pearson emphasised that the very presence or absence of architectural details can inform discussion of the use of medieval structures.

[9] Something of this sort has to be the explanation for the piers in the chapter house and refectory at Bebenhausen, where the shafts suddenly stop below the capital; illustrated in Courtauld Institute Illustration Archives, London, 1977, 3/3/72-73.

[10] For example, the Purbeck marble columns in the lay-brothers' undercroft at Waverley Abbey are noteworthy.

[11] Jansen, ibid., pp. 41–43.

[12] Illustrated in Dimier, ibid., ii, pls 110–11; and i, pl. 23, respectively.

Third, occasionally the wall corbels and capitals are entirely omitted so that the vaulting ribs simply die or continue into the walls or central supports, as seen in the undercrofts at Fountains (Plate 21b), Forde, and Silvanès. These dying mouldings increase the spans of the arches and the spaciousness even more.

All over the medieval world, then, numerous structures provided spatial experiences different from that of most ecclesiastical building but embodying the Sugerian words: 'the beauty of length and width'. Modern viewers will find, as did medieval inhabitants, that this other version of architecture, of utilitarian, service-oriented building, has the appeal of austerity, dynamic spaciousness, and a more direct reception of the craft of skilled masonry work, the last a way to express economic power other than through the elaboration typical of church architecture. The uncluttered lines, the airy openness, the spareness present another version of building, a 'dearticulated' rival to decorative ecclesiastical art. In the twelfth century this alternative view is suggested by the words of Alexander Neckham: 'The extent of human affectation is shown in part by the expenditures dedicated to pleasure which an empty boastful pride consumes and squanders in the superfluous magnificence of buildings'.[13] This other line could have provided a response to critics of elaborate church architecture such as Bernard of Clairvaux and Peter the Chanter as well as Alexander Neckham, and it corresponded to the ecclesiastical component seen in the church architecture of the Cistercians, the friars, and middle-class townspeople. In what degree there may have been a connection between these storage facilities and late Gothic church building remains to be considered, but parallels may be suggested by a similar austerity found in the late Antique and early Christian reaction to the highly articulated buildings of classical antiquity as well as in the much better documented influence of industrial building on modern architecture. The spaciousness of undercrofts, free from cumbersome, heavily articulated supports, and their reductive architecture express a plainer, more functional and perhaps reformist vision of medieval architecture. Like the cellarer himself, it is 'prudent. . . temperate. . . not wasteful'.[14]

[13] *De Naturis Rerum*, ed. Thomas Wight, London, 1863, as translated and quoted in Teresa G. Frisch, *Gothic Art 1140-c. 1450*, Englewood Cliffs, New Jersey, 1971, p. 31.

[14] *The Rule of Saint Benedict*, chapter 31, ed. and trans. Justin McCann, London, 1952, pp. 80–83.

8

Auckland Castle: Some Recent Discoveries

Jane Cunningham

Restoration work carried out between 1978 and 1983 by the Church Commissioners in the chapel of Auckland Castle at Bishop Auckland in County Durham has revealed valuable evidence for the form of the building when it was the hall of one of the most important residences of the bishops of Durham.[1] The discoveries include portions of the internal jambs of doorways and windows, the possible foundations of a south porch, additional fragments of internal blind arcading across the west wall, the arcade plates on both north and south sides and a relieving arch in the west wall which differs slightly from one already known to exist in the east wall. The implications of the discoveries are important: fragments found reused in later work suggest that there may already have been stone buildings at the site when the building of the hall was begun, and the hall itself, possibly the first aisled stone hall in the diocese of Durham, seems to have had a fully developed screens passage across its lower end.[2]

Auckland Castle stands on a peninsula high above the rivers Wear and Gaunless, about twelve miles south-west of Durham.[3] The site has belonged to the see of Durham since the tenth century or earlier;[4] by the late twelfth century it was one of the principal manors of the bishops of Durham, probably on account of the hunting to be had there. It was known as the Manor or Hall of Auckland until about 1500, after which it

---

[1] I am very grateful to Peter Roach and Peter Bartle of the Official Architects Office of the Church Commissioners, who carried out the restoration, both for making their findings available to me, and for much additional assistance. I am also most grateful to John Heward for discussion of much of the material in this paper.

[2] A 12th-century aisled stone hall is now thought to have existed at the manor of the bishops of Durham at Howden in Yorkshire; see M.W. Barley, *Houses and History*, 1986, p. 87.

[3] For illustrations of the castle, including photographs and early representations, see John Cornforth, *Auckland Castle, Co. Durham*, in *Country Life*, 151; Part I, Jan. 27, 1972, pp. 198–202; Part II, Feb. 3, 1972, pp. 260–270; Part III, Feb. 10th, 1972, pp. 334–37.

[4] Auckland seems to have been part of the lands temporarily alienated by Bishop Aldhune, *c.* 1000, and returned to St Cuthbert by Cnut; *Historia de Sancto Cuthberto* in *Simeon of Durham*, i, *Surtees Society*, 51, 1867, p. 151.

was generally called either the Castle or the Palace of Auckland. It is now the Bishop of Durham's only official residence in the diocese.

Until 1665 the present chapel was the hall of the medieval manor:[5] it is on the north side of the manor site and may have been close to a gate.[6] A hall is first mentioned at or near the manor in an entry in Boldon Book, the survey made for Bishop Hugh du Puiset in 1183 which records the services and rents due to the bishop on his lands. It states that:

> All the villeins of Aucletshire...find for every bovate one rope for the great hunts, and they build the bishop's hall in the forest, 60 feet in length and 16 feet in breadth (18.3 by 4.87 m), between the posts (arcades?) with a buttery and a larder and a chamber and a privy. Also they build a chapel 40 feet in length and 15 feet in width (12.2 by 4.57 m), and they have 2s as a favour and they make their part of the hedge among the lodges. And on the bishop's departure they have a full tun of beer or the half if he stayed away.
>
> In Stanhope each villein carries game to Durham and Auclet. Also all the villeins construct a kitchen, a larder, a dog kennel for the great hunts, and they find litter for the hall, chapel and chamber.[7]

Although this hall was evidently also aisled, it cannot be the existing one as the dimensions are very different. The buildings mentioned were presumably of timber construction and had to be rebuilt or at least repaired annually, possibly to provide additional accommodation for the bishop's retinue or for guests; they may also have been close to the scene of the hunt.

No documentary evidence remains for the late twelfth century and early thirteenth-century building of the existing early Gothic hall, but on stylistic grounds it appears to have been built for Bishop Hugh du Puiset (1153–95), late in his episcopate. It is unlikely that building had proceeded very far before Hugh died; as his successor, Philip of Poitou (1197–1208), seems to have spent more of his time with the king than in his diocese, and the see was vacant until 1217. The building was probably not completed until the manor was brought back into regular use during the episcopates of Richard Marsh (1217–26), Richard Poore (1228–37)

---

[5] Although Raine published most of the documentary material on Auckland Castle, he was under the impression that the present chapel was the original medieval one built by Bec in 1307–8, James Raine, *A Brief Historical Account of the Episcopal Castle, or Palace, of Auckland*, Durham, 1852. The inconsistency of this argument was demonstrated by J.F. Hodgson, 'The Chapel of Auckland Castle', in *Archaeologia Aeliana*, New Series, 8, 1896, pp. 113–240.

[6] A stone gateway was built by Bishop Skirlaw (1388–1405), but its site is unknown, *Historia Dunelmensis Scriptores Tres*, ed. James Raine, *Surtees Society*, 9, 1839, p. 144. The present entrance, from the south-west, is in the same position as that depicted in a painting of *c.* 1680 (Cornforth, op. cit., I, fig. 5). Cornforth suggests that an old gatehouse further north may formerly have been the main entrance, Ibid, I, p. 200.

[7] *Boldon Book*, ed. W. Greenwell, in *Surtees Society*, 25 (1832), pp. 26, 29; the translations are from the Victoria History of the Counties of England, *Durham*, i, pp. 333, 334.

and possibly Nicholas of Farnham (1241-49). This accords well with the stylistic differences between the west piers and the three arches to the domestic offices, which were almost certainly built for Hugh, and the second and third piers from the west, which have moulding profiles of the first half of the thirteenth century in all but their bases. The pointed trefoil-headed blind arcading across the west wall and the details of the north door which have recently been discovered also suggest a completion date well after Hugh's death (Plate 24c).

Godwin de Praesulibus misleadingly stated that Bishop Antony Bek (1284–1311) 'built the Great Hall, wherein were divers pillars of black marble speckled with white'.[8] Bek may indeed have been responsible for large-scale alterations, but there is little doubt that he did not build the hall; his work may have included raising the aisle walls and the provision of large windows to replace smaller gabled ones similar th those formerly in the Great Hall in Winchester Castle: the shapes of the gables can be made out in the ashlar against the rubble of the north aisle wall and between tall buttresses of a form appropriate to a building of Bek's episcopate (Plate 23a). Mention should also be made of the account roll of Peter de Midrigg, the bishop's steward at Auckland, which shows that in 1337–38 the guttering of the hall and of the seneschal's chamber were repaired with lead, that of the hall also being covered with shingles or boards (*cindulis*). In the same year John of Allirton, carpenter, was paid 21s 6d for cutting 1500 *cindulis* for a covering over the hall; 4000 brodds (short nails or 'prods') were needed for this, and cost 6s 8d.[9] The *lover* or louvre of the hall was still in existence in 1543–44: in the 1660s it was called a lanthorne.[10]

The Castle suffered greatly during the Commonwealth, especially after it was bought by Sir Arthur Haslerigg;[11] he had many of the older parts demolished, including the two chapels set one above the other which had been built for Bishop Bek in 1307–8.[12] Immediately after the Restoration Bishop John Cosin (1660–72) set about restoring the Castle: amongst other works he made a new chapel by restoring and refitting the old aisled hall, which was consecrated in 1665. It is thought that he rebuilt the south hall, refaced most of the end walls and probably replaced the tracery of the clerestory windows.[13] The building was already orientated;

---

[8] See n. 5.

[9] Raine, op. cit., p. 21. According to Robert of Graystanes, Bek 'manerium de Auckland cum capella et camera sumptuosissime construxit', *Scriptores Tres*, p. 90, quoted in n. 6.

[10] Raine, op. cit., pp. 27–31.

[11] Ibid., p. 66.

[12] For the details of Cosin's work, see *Bishop Cosin's Correspondence*, ii, in Surtees Society, 50, 1872; for a discussion of the ideas behind it, see Cornforth, op. cit., who also describes the later building history of the castle.

[13] Thomas Cocke has suggested, in a verbal communication, that the clerestory itself may have been built in the first half of the 16th century.

23a Auckland Castle, chapel, exterior: three east bays of north wall.

23b Auckland Castle, chapel, lower portion of east wall drawn by C. Hodgson Fowler in 1882.

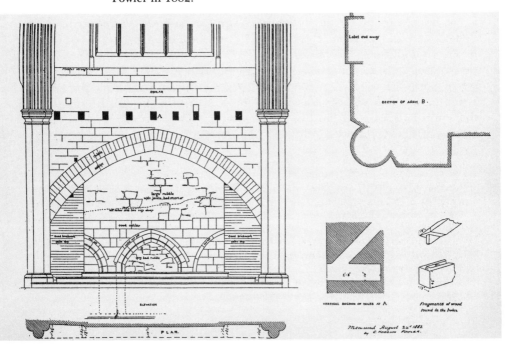

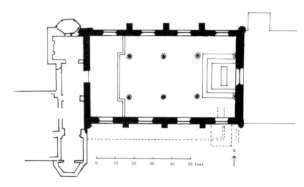

24b Auckland Castle, chapel, plan.

24a Auckland Castle, chapel, recently discovered head stop.

24c Auckland Castle, chapel, transverse section looking west. (Thin dotted lines = recent discoveries; thick dotted line = suggested hipped roof line)

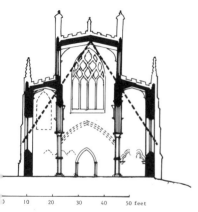

24d Auckland Castle, chapel, longitudinal section looking north. (Thin dotted lines = recent discoveries; thick dotted line = suggested hipped roof line)

24e Auckland Castle, chapel; interior, north aisle, eastern bay. Shared jamb of cross-passage door and tall door to the east of it.

he placed the altar at the east end, where the screens had been, and made the high table end the entrance, at the west end. He also had the floor paved with black marble and white stone slabs, and may have had the floor level raised by 45 cm (18 inches) in all but the west bays and the aisles; the latter were raised to a similar level in the 1820s. Repairs to the east wall in the early 1880s disclosed a pointed relieving arch and, below it, three blocked arches to the service block; all these were below a row of holes in the ashlar at the level of the arcade capitals. The findings were drawn by C. Hodgson Fowler in 1882 (Plate 23b).

The existing building has been described fully by Hodgson.[14] It is an aisled hall of four bays and measures about 26 by 14.6 m (85 feet by 48 feet) externally. The east and west bays of the arcade are 6 m (20 feet) long and the two inner ones 5.2 m (17 feet) long. The richly moulded arches are pointed and rise from quatrefoil piers consisting of two shafts of local grey Frosterley marble, polished and set *en délit*, and two of light-coloured coursed sandstone which are linked in the middle; most of the capitals, shaft rings, bases and plinths are also of polished marble, or of dark stone, which increases the richness of the design. The western bay is particularly elaborate, as is perhaps appropriate for the high table end of the hall. The marble capitals of the western pier are carved with varied waterleaf forms. The simple ones resemble multiple capitals, of Purbeck marble, which have been found at Wolvesey Palace in Winchester, built by Hugh du Puiset's uncle, Henry of Blois.[15] This connection is reinforced by the fact that the more elaborate versions of waterleaf capitals, those on the south-west pier, find parallels only in the eastern parts of the church of St Cross Hospital, which Henry of Blois built in Winchester; the bases of this pier have spurs which are very like those on a marble base again found at Wolvesey.[16] The corbels which support the arcade at the west end are also elaborate. The style of the carving suggests a date after about 1225, with paired heads of kings and bishops forming brackets and with some stiff-leaf foliage comparable to that in the Chapel of the Nine Altars in Durham Cathedral. The remains of blind trefoil-headed arcading across the west wall appear to be of similar date. The arcade mouldings are very rich, but are composed of numerous simple forms, the arcade side having what appear to be the earlier profiles.[17]

[14] Hodgson, op. cit., pp. 152–79.

[15] Winchester Research Unit fragments 532 and 535; photographs are in the Conway Library, Courtauld Institute of Art. For Henry of Blois see G. Zarnecki, *Henry of Blois as a Patron of Sculpture*, S. Macready and F.H. Thompson, eds., *Art and Patronage in the English Romanesque* Occasional Papers, New Series, VIII, The Society of Antiquaries of London, 1986, pp. 159–72.

[16] Winchester Research Unit fragment 1028.

[17] See Hodgson, op. cit., plates XXV and XXVI.

The discoveries made during the restoration of 1978–83 include fragments from at least one earlier stone building in the vicinity; they are a fragment of chevron moulding and part of a waterleaf capital with a deep, square abacus and little trefoils between the main leaves. The style and squat proportions of the latter are similar to those of capitals in the Galilee Chapel in Durham Cathedral which was built for Hugh du Puiset and was probably begun in about 1175,[18] and also to capitals in the chapel in the keep at Newcastle Castle, which was being built between 1168 and 1178.[19] Neither fragment fits stylistically with the earliest work in the hall. These and other fragments were discovered in the rubble infill of the walls supporting Cosin's stalls in the east bay of the south aisle and in the rubble used as infill during the construction or restoration of the clerestory, in the two middle bays on the south side. A simple moulded angle capital was also found, as well as portions of shafting; they may have come from windows or doors in the hall or elsewhere. Three carved heads were found, of which two appear to have been label stops. Although one is very damaged, the other is of high quality and was probably carved in the early thirteenth century (Plate 24a); it is of a clean-shaven man, possibly a monk, with a line of curls across his forehead. The face is lean, with compressed lips, and the planes of the brows, eyes and nose are sharply defined. The third head is less striking, but it is too mutilated for its use to be clear.

Other important remains were found *in situ*. The remains of three further arches of the blind arcading at the west or high table end of the hall were discovered to the south of the seventeenth-century entrance door, which cut through the arch of one of them. From these and the two already visible it can be calculated that there were probably nine arches across the wall, and that their disposition took no account of the division of the wall into main vessel and aisles (Plate 24c).

At the east or low end of the hall the removal of the plaster from the east bay of the north aisle wall revealed the jambs of a blocked main doorway in the middle of the bay and the left jamb of the tall, narrow doorway immediately to the east of it; the existence of both was already apparent from outside (Plate 23a, 24d). The right jamb of the main door has a shaft set *en délit* and the remains of a capital with a round impost and wind-blown stiffleaf foliage similar to the capitals of the arcading at the west end of the hall, and the upper capitals of the north-west arcade corbel above them; the impost continues as a shaft ring on the left shaft of the taller door (Plate 24e). The arches of both doors were partially revealed; they were slightly pointed and had large single soffit rolls, one other order and a hoodmould. The taller door may have been reached

[18] Richard Halsey, *The Galilee Chapel*, in *Medieval Art and Architecture at Durham*, British Archaeological Association Conference Transactions, 1980, p. 62.

[19] R. Allen Brown, H.M. Colvin, A.J. Taylor, eds., *The History of the KIng's Works*, H.M.S.O., 1963, ii, p. 746.

on the outside by a flight of steps, as the first eight courses of masonry are disturbed, and are unlike the straight joints of the jambs visible above (Plate 23a, furthest bay); furthermore, there may have been a passage within the wall which returns in the east wall, to the south, possibly indicating the presence of an intramural staircase leading to an upper chamber in the service block, which could thus be reached from inside as well as outside.

The south wall of the hall was entirely rebuilt by Cosin, but it is likely that there was a door in the east bay equivalent to that on the north side, forming a screens passage. This interpretation is supported by the discovery, during repairs to the pews, of paving stones at the original floor level, 45 cm (18 inches) below the present one; these are situated precisely where one would step through such a door. Traces of foundations were apparently found outside the probable position of the south door, but it seems that there was not enough to prove that there was a porch. There was also an unexplained line of footings running along south of the south wall; they returned to the north a metre or so short of the east end (Plate 24b).

Fragments of internal window shafts and bases were found in the second bay from the east in the north aisle wall. They correspond to the levels of the sills which can be seen on the exterior of the wall; the jambs of a blocked fireplace were also found in the next bay to the west in the same wall: it was probably inserted in about 1500 (Plate 24d).

Among the most important finds were the rotted arcade plates on both north and south sides, which have had to be replaced with load-bearing bricks, and a pointed relieving arch in the west wall; the latter has one order of ashlar and one of rubble, and is similar to that at the east end, though set about 2.1 m (7 feet) higher (Plates 24c and 23b).

The implications of these discoveries require consideration. In the first place, the discovery of stone fragments earlier than any part of the existing hall suggests that the manor already had other stone buildings; their location and purpose are quite unknown. At least some of the fragments were used as rubble infill in work done for Cosin, and may have come either from buildings destroyed during the Commonwealth, or from those parts of the hall which he rebuilt, such as the south wall, with its probable door and possible porch, although these would be more likely to be of thirteenth-century date. Alternatively they may have come from buildings cleared away by him, probably including the service block adjoining the hall to the east.

The reconstruction of the blind arcading as equal arches across the west wall suggests that there was no entrance at this end. By contrast, the existence of the north door in the east bay, and possibly an equivalent south door, suggests a fully developed screens passage, especially when considered with the three blocked service doors to the buttery, kitchen passage and servery, which seem to have had continuous rolls along the angles of their jambs. East of the hall there is a turfed platform of earth which seems to have existed from at least the late eighteenth century;[20] beneath it, against the bottom of the east gable wall, there is a vaulted passage which may be a precaution against damp (Plate 23b). None of this reflects the service block which still existed on this site in 1628, when an inventory listed first the hall, followed immediately by the 'Olde Pantry', the 'Olde Kitchen' and the 'Olde Scullerie'.[21]

The inventory of 1628 indicates that there was almost certainly at least one chamber (a word which can indicate more than one room) over the buttery, servery and kitchen passage, and that there was a way down to a hall porch; the entrance to the latter may well have been the tall door east of the main north door. The drawing made in 1882 shows a row of nine holes across the east wall at the level of the arcade capitals and fragments of wood found in the holes; each of these made a joint between a rafter coming down from the *outside*, that is from the roof of a building set transversely across the east side of the gable wall, and the sole-plate (Plate 23b). The latter would have been set on top of the wall at arcade capital height, to receive the rafter, and the wall would then be continued above it, to secure it. The repair of gutters to the hall in 1337–38 could refer to guttering at this point, especially as the senschal's chamber (which could have been the chamber in this position) needed guttering at the same time.[22] The fact that the relieving arch in the east wall is below the row of holes, whereas that at the west end is about 2.1 m (7 feet) higher, suggests that provision had to be made for a building against the east wall, but not for one against the west wall.

The discovery of the arcade plates permits a reconstruction of the angle of the hall roof, and allows an independent assessment of the line taken by the rafters, using as fixed points the arcade plates and a point just below the outer angle of the window gables (visible in the north aisle wall) (Plate 23a, 24c) This produces a ridge at approximately the same height as the existing one, suggesting that whether the roof covered low or high aisles, or a clerestory, its height remained constant (Plate 24c). Such a suggestion is supported by the fact that the height of the hall, from its original floor level, is almost exactly the same as its external width.

The reconstruction of the roof may be tentatively taken a stage further, using the unusual irregularity of the bay lengths as a starting point, the two end bays being some 90 cm (3 feet) longer than the two middle ones. While this would merely provide more room at the high table end, where extra space might be desirable, it would be less practical at the screens end. The length of the two end bays, each about 6 m (20 feet) long, is very nearly half the total internal width of the hall. Thus a roof at

[20] Hodgson, op. cit., p. 143 and note.
[21] Raine, op. cit., pp. 75, 76.
[22] Ibid., pp. 27, 29.

the same angle as that reconstructed for the side walls can be suggested for the east end, forming a hipped roof. It would just clear the arches of the east bay and meet the end wall at the wall at the same level as the holes which held the rafters from the transverse service and chamber block (Plate 24d). Such a roof construction would not have worked at the west end, however, because of the greater height of the relieving arch, but it should in any case be stressed that the reconstruction is very tentative: the irregular spacing of the piers which such a roof would have necessitated might have been carried over from an earlier building on the same site, probably of timber construction.

The new discoveries have not changed the position of the hall at Auckland Castle in relation to other aisled halls of the period. This is not the place to discuss in detail the stylistic and historical connotations of the design: it will suffice to say that the hall was intended to rival and emulate buildings at the highest level, such as Archbishop Roger of Pont l'Eveque's hall in York,[23] and the hall of the king's palace at Clarendon,[24] and that if it was begun for Bishop du Puiset, it expressed his aspirations both in its form and in the use of finely worked, valuable materials.[25] The discoveries do, however, shed further light on the relatively little-known disposition of a hall intended to be both impressive and functional. As it was still in use in 1628, when it was 'newe wainscotted and seated' and contained 'four long tables and a short table and eight joyned formes', it was still performing an important function, although the bishop's regular appearances probably declined sharply once the Great Chamber with its own service quarters was built by Bishop Bek.[26] If this hall was indeed built on the foundations of an earlier one, as is suggested by the spacing of the piers, it demonstrates a continuity of use tempered only slightly by the development of such conveniences as a screens passage, the innovation of *c.* 1200, and a fireplace, the innovation of *c.* 1500.

---

[23] Giraldus Cambrensis described Roger's hall in 1174, when the archbishop was showing it to Geoffrey Plantagenet: '... archiepiscopus ei aulam suam ostendit, nuper extructam, regiam scilicet, in signem miro lapideo tabulata, et columnis sublimibus', *De Vita Galfridi Archiepiscopi Eboracensis*, Rolls Series, 21, 1873, iv, p. 367.

[24] Colvin (in R. Allen Brown, H.M. Colvin and A.J. Taylor, eds., op. cit., ii, p. 911) suggests that the aisled hall at Clarendon was being built in 1181–83; marble columns were recorded as being brought to Clarendon in 1175–77, and associates these with building of the chapel.

[25] For the connotations of the use of marble see G. Zarnecki, op. cit. According to William of Newburgh, Hugh wished to be among the greatest in the world, and the more he was anxious to build on earth, the more remiss he was in building in heaven, William of Newburgh, *Historia Rerum Anglicarum* in *Chronicles of the Reigns of Stephen, Henry II and Richard I*, Rolls Series 82, 4 vols, 1884–89, ii, pp. 225ff.

[26] See n. 9.

9

The Sculpture of Burmington Manor, Warwickshire

Allan M. Brodie

The remains of the thirteenth-century house at Burmington Manor in south Warwickshire were discovered by the Royal Commission on the Historical Monuments of England in 1984. In the Annual Review of the Royal Commission Nicholas Cooper described these remains as 'a significant addition to the corpus of domestic aisled halls'.[1] His reasons for this assertion were that the house was 'in an area where such structures are rare, its early owners can probably be identified and thus its status can be established, it can be dated reasonably closely, and it possesses certain affinities with the hall of the Bishop's Palace at Hereford which may throw light on some of the problems presented by that building'.[2]

Within the confines of the Annual Review of the Royal Commission, there was little opportunity to discuss the corbel sculpture and since the publication of that article the capital of one of the posts of the aisled hall has been uncovered. In this note the sculpture will be described and its significance considered. To the reasons cited above for Burmington Manor's importance, others may be added. It is an early and rare example of high quality sculpture in a domestic building. The sculpture has affinities with a number of contemporary West Country workshops, and the use of capitals without astragals was one of the motifs Harold Brakspear identified as peculiar to his West Country School of Masons.[3] Burmington Manor also contains a rare example of the survival of a carved wooden capital, one without close parallels in wood but with clear links to contemporary stone carving.

The Manor House and its Discovery

Prior to 1984 Burmington Manor was believed to be a house of late sixteenth- or early seventeenth-century origin.[4] Externally apparently of this date, only the presence of a medieval buttress and window might

---

[1] N. Cooper, 'Burmington Manor, Warwickshire: The Thirteenth-Century Building' *Annual Review of the Royal Commission*, 1984–85, p. 27.

[2] Cooper, op. cit., p. 27.

[3] H. Brakspear, 'A West Country School of Masons', *Archaeologia*, 81, 1931, pp. 1–18.

[4] Burmington Manor was described as this when first listed in 1966.

have suggested that the house had older origins (Plate 25a). A programme of internal renovation in the 1980s revealed elements of an early thirteenth-century hall. Three stone corbels with varying degrees of damage were uncovered, along with a fragment of leaf carving on one post. Dendrochronology provided a tentative felling date of 1208–1215 for the timber of the hall.[5] In 1987 a small section of wall was removed in the area where the top of the post of the south arcade of the hall was expected to be located. As some leaf carving had survived on the post of the north arcade, it was hoped that some further carving might be revealed. This expectation was exceeded, and a large section of a wooden capital was found to have survived.[6]

The Manor House lies a short distance to the south of the parish church. The hall and solar are both aligned approximately west to east. However, the solar is on a slightly different alignment from the hall, prompting Nicholas Cooper to speculate on whether or not it was coeval with the hall.[7] Examination of the junction between the north walls of the hall and the solar suggests that there might be substance to this speculation. The north wall of the hall is rubble in its lower parts with timber framing above, reflecting the sixteenth-century heightening of the thirteenth-century aisle wall. The solar is quoined against the timber-framed walling, but the quoins also continue a short distance down into the rubble of the aisle wall. Beneath these quoins there is a ragged joint. At one point this is rectangular in shape, as if caused by the removal of a quoin. The only feature of the solar which could provide any indication of its date is the blocked window in the north wall. A two-light composition with a hood moulding, internally it has a segmental rear arch and retains clear evidence of shutters.[8] Its form suggests a date in the late twelfth or early thirteenth century. The date range is sufficiently wide to allow the solar and hall either to be contemporary, or to be of different dates. If contemporary the hiatus between the two ranges would therefore be the result of misalignment during construction or later rebuilding.

The aisled hall of Burmington Manor survives to a greater extent than the solar, though it has been substantially altered since the sixteenth century. It was almost square in plan, 9.75 by 9.45 m (32 by 31 feet) with stone outer walls and two-bay wooden arcades. The only bay of the arcade which has survived is the west bay of the north arcade. Its arch is formed from a pair of chamfered, curved braces which describe a true semicircle. The spandrels of the arches were filled with a plastered

---

[5] Cooper, op. cit., p. 27. Dendrochronology report by Nottingham University in NBR file number 60167.

[6] My involvement with Burmington Manor began when Nicholas Cooper invited me to accompany him to the removal of this section of walling.

[7] Cooper, op. cit., p. 27.

[8] A similar window appears at Boothby Pagnell Manor House (Lincolnshire), *c.* 1200 according to Wood, plate LIII.

25a Burmington Manor, Warwickshire, north wall of solar and hall.

25b Burmington Manor, Warwickshire, south-west corbel.

25c Glastonbury Abbey, Somerset, capital of easternmost nook shaft on exterior of south choir aisle.

diaphragm, the dowel holes and grooves for this infilling surviving in the soffit of the arcade plate and in the posts. Grooves in the north and south faces of the north arcade post led Nicholas Cooper to suggest that similar wooden arches spanned the aisles and the nave on the line of the open hall truss.[9] The form of the hall seems to suggest a deliberate attempt to produce the effect of a masonry building in timber. John Blair noted that the hall of Hereford's Bishop's Palace was 'a careful, deliberate timber version of contemporary stone halls'.[10] Nicholas Cooper has already described the features which Burmington shared with Hereford, and in addition to sharing certain specific details, both appear to be consciously imitating stone forms.

The imitation of stone in wood could have been heightened by paint. There are early references to the use of paint to simulate masonry by whitewashing and picking out a jointing pattern in red paint.[11] References also exist in the thirteenth century to paint simulating marble, presumably Purbeck or a similar coloured, polishable limestone. In 1245 the posts of Henry III's chamber at Ludgershall (Wiltshire) were ordered to be painted a marble colour.[12] Ten years later Henry III ordered that the piers and arches of Guildford Castle (Surrey) were to be marbled.[13] If even a simple paint scheme was adopted at Burmington, this could have improved the impression that the wooden arcades were stone. It could also have disguised the very different visual effect of the stone corbels in the gables and the wooden capitals of the arcade posts.

The evidence for the original roof and fenestration is fragmentary. The roof appears to have been a collar rafter roof with passing braces. No thirteenth-century rafters remain *in situ* but ten were reused in the sixteenth-century roof. The only evidence for the form of the fenestration is the presence of a mortice in the centre of the aisle side of the arcade plate of the north-west bay. Nicholas Cooper suggested that this might indicate that the aisles had gablets.[14]

The sculpture

The timber arcade of the hall sprang from wall posts, supported by corbels in each gable, and from a pair of wooden, arcade posts. Due to the insertion of a floor in the sixteenth century, the capitals of the

[9] Cooper, op. cit., pp. 28–29.

[10] John Blair, 'The 12th-Century Bishop's Palace at Hereford', *Medieval Archaeology*, 31, 1987, p. 63.

[11] M. Wood, *The English Medieval House*, London, 1983, p. 395; L.F. Salzman, *Building in England down to 1540*, Oxford, 1952, p. 158. Fragments of this type of paint scheme survived at Clarendon Palace (Wiltshire). T.B. James and A.M. Robinson, *Clarendon Palace*, Reports of the Research Committee of the Society of Antiquaries of London, no. 45, 1988, p. 251.

[12] Salzman, op. cit., p. 159.

[13] Salzman, op. cit., p. 159.

[14] Cooper, op. cit., p. 29.

arcade posts and the corbels are now at floor level on the first floor.[15] Three of the four stone corbels survive, the south-eastern having disappeared with the creation of a stair into the attic.[16] The shafts of the corbels are ogee keeled in plan, a common form in the West Country after Worcester and Wells, and their abaci can also be associated with western workshops (Plates 25c and 26b). The only substantially complete abacus is that of the south-west corbel (Plate 25b). Though its part octagonal plan and its profile might seem simple enough to be commonplace, their combined occurrence is not particularly common around 1200. The choir of Glastonbury Abbey, the nave of Slymbridge church and Wells Cathedral are perhaps the most significant examples of the combined use of these motifs, though in the case of Wells the top member of the abacus is considerably taller than at Burmington. While distant Somerset or Gloucestershire parallels may seem fanciful, another feature of the general design might have had a similar source. The corbels lack astragals, a feature restricted in date to the late twelfth or early thirteenth century, and in geographical distribution to a number of sites scattered across the West Country (Plates 25b, 25c, and 26b). This is another form which can be found at Glastonbury, Wells and Slymbridge, but it is too widely, and too arbitrarily distributed to point to any particular source for the motif's appearance at Burmington. However, in examining the detailed handling of the sculpture, more persuasive evidence for links with large ecclesiastical workshops in the West Country can be uncovered.

The south-west corbel is the least damaged of the three corbels (Plate 25b). Two of its five trumpets are intact, but none of the motifs separating the mouths of the trumpets have survived. The underside of the trumpets appear to have a membrane drawn across their contours, as if the trumpets spring from a larger outer shell. This effect is difficult to parallel precisely, though comparable designs appear at Old Sodbury (Gloucestershire), Alderminster (Warwickshire) and at Bromyard (Hereford and Worcester). None of these have more specific similarities to Burmington, and they are all works of less skilled sculptors than the Burmington master.

Dangling in the mouth of each trumpet of the south-west corbel is a trefoiled leaf with a C-shaped channel in its central lobe. The pronounced lip of the trumpets curve round above the trefoiled leaf and form its stem. The use of a trefoiled leaf in the mouth of a scallop is a common method of elaborating the basic design. However, most examples appear in parish churches and rather than being strongly plastic, their design is executed using simple, stylised leaves cut into the flat, vertical mouth of rigid scallops. One of the nook shafts on the exterior of the

---

[15] The sculpture, being at floor level on the first floor, presented problems for photography. I would like to thank Pat Payne for crawling on the floor to take Figs 3, 5 and 7–11.

26a Burmington Manor, Warwickshire, north-west corbel.

26b Burmington Manor, Warwickshire, north-east corbel.

26c Burmington Manor, Warwickshire, west face of wooden capital of south arcade.

26d Burmington Manor, Warwickshire, south-west corner of wooden capital of south arcade (photograph taken looking into a mirror).

27b St Mary's, Shrewsbury, north-west face of south-west crossing pier.

27a Glastonbury Abbey, Somerset, capital of internal nook shaft on east side of sixth bay.

27c St Mary's, Shrewsbury, south-west face of south-east crossing pier.

south choir aisle of Glastonbury Abbey includes a trumpet design similar to Burmington (Plate 25c). Each delicately executed trumpet has a trefoiled leaf in its mouth. The stems appear to be continuous with the rims of the trumpets and there is a channel in the central lobe and stem of each leaf. Though these are simple forms, their combined occurrence at both Burmington and Glastonbury seems to be more than just coincidence. As noted earlier, both sites shared general design features such as neckless capitals and their abaci designs.

The other corbel in the west gable has suffered considerable damage, but enough has survived to demonstrate that it reproduced, at least in general form, the design of its companion (Plate 26a). It was composed of five trumpets and retains traces of the distinctive membrane motif linking their undersides. None of the ends of the trumpets remain intact. If the corbel was symmetrical, and there is no reason to doubt it, its dimensions would have been the same as those of the south-west corbel. Only the northern of the two corbels in the east gable survives (Plate 26b). Unlike those in the west gable this corbel consists of nine trumpets, alternately keeled and round in section. All the trumpets of the west gable corbels were keeled in section. None of the mouths of these trumpets has survived.

In addition to three stone corbels, a large section of one wooden capital and a fragment of another has survived (Plate 26c). Early thirteenth-century in date, the survival of such carving is a great rarity. Twelfth-century wooden capitals survive in the hall of the palace of the bishops of Winchester at Farnham (Surrey) and in the Bishop's Palace at Hereford.[17] Both are larger and higher status buildings than Burmington, but unlike Burmington their capitals are straightforward scalloped designs, an indication of their date rather than a reflection on the skill of their carvers. The capitals of *c.* 1200 in Old Court Cottage at Limpsfield (Surrey), though of a different type, exhibit a level of skill in their execution comparable to Burmington.[18]

[16] Describing these as corbels implies that the shafts beneath them terminated before reaching ground level, but definite evidence to support this belief is lacking. Beneath the north-eastern corbel 15 cm (6 inches) of shaft remains *in situ*, along with an uncertain length of shaft beneath the south-west corbel. No traces of shafting survives below first floor level.

[17] On Farnham Castle see M.W. Thompson, *Farnham Castle, Surrey*, HMSO, London, 1961; A. Oswald, 'Farnham Castle, Surrey', *Country Life*, December 23, 1939, pp. 653–56; December 30, 1939, pp. 682-86. On Hereford the principal recent articles are Blair, op. cit.; C.A. Ralegh Radford, E.M. Jope and J.W. Tonkin, 'The Great Hall of the Bishop's Palace at Hereford', *Medieval Archaeology*, 17, 1973, pp. 78–86; S.R. Jones and J.T. Smith, 'The Great Hall of the Bishop's Palace at Hereford', *Medieval Archaeology*, 4, 1960, pp. 69–80.

[18] I. Nairn and N. Pevsner, *Surrey*, The Buildings of England, Harmondsworth, 2nd edn, 1971, p. 344. I would like to thank Kathryn A. Morrison for bringing this house to my attention.

The wooden capital at Burmington is very different in shape from the stone corbels. This is partly to be explained by the different material used, but also by its different position and function within the hall. Forming part of a post at the centre of an arcade, the capital had to remain essentially cubic in form. In consequence, there are marked differences between the wooden capital and the stone corbels not only in their architectonic form but also in their detailed execution. The capital is irregularly octagonal in plan, long main faces alternating with shorter corner faces. Most of the west face and a five centimetre (two inch) wide slice of the north face of the capital have survived (Plate 26c). The south-west corner face and a small piece of the south face are also intact, but a large section of the north-west corner was destroyed by later building work (Plate 26d). The west face of the capital is now extremely friable, but the slice of the north face and the fragment of the north-west corner face are in almost pristine condition.

Each long face of the capital was ornamented with three trumpet scallops (Plate 26c). Only the lower half of the mouth of the trumpet is seen and a small, recessed, blank area separates it from the abacus.[19] Flanking each trumpet are a pair of leaves which spring from the astragal. The face of each leaf is slightly concave and curves upwards and outwards following the contours of the trumpet, but the leaves also curve laterally towards the adjacent leaf of the next trumpet. At the astragal the pair of leaves between each trumpet are clearly separated by a V-shaped groove, but part of the way up the capital they fuse to share a single tip, the constituent leaves now only being separated by a sharp ridge.

The south-west face is the only complete corner face which has survived (Plate 26d). Beneath the mouth of the single trumpet on this face is a motif resembling a fir cone clasped perilously between two multi-lobed leaves, leaves which are arranged like six-fingered hands. The lowest lobe turns beneath the leaf, while the uppermost curls upwards and slightly backwards. The whole of this motif survives on the south-west corner face, along with one of the hand-shaped leaves of the north-west face.

The paired leaf form with cone, set halfway up the capital, is the most distinctive motif used in the wooden capital. A trilobed leaf following the general design of one of these hand-like leaves occurs in the nave of Whichford (Warwickshire), a small parish church five miles south-east of Burmington. Similar leaves with pronounced 'thumbs' also appear in the south wall of the choir of Glastonbury Abbey, but only singly, and without an accompanying cone. The same wall of Glastonbury Abbey also provides an example of a pair of opposed leaves, set halfway up the

---

[19] C. Wilson discusses this and other types of trumpet scallops in 'The Sources of the Late Twelfth-Century Work at Worcester Cathedral', *Medieval Art and Architecture at Worcester Cathedral*, British Archaeological Association Conference Transactions, 1975, pp. 82–84.

capital (Plate 27a). A similar arrangement exists on the western capital of the south door of Stoke Prior (Hereford), though it too lacks the cone between the leaves.

The double-handed, cone-holding motif has no local parallel nor any precise one at Glastonbury. However, one capital on the south-west crossing pier of St Mary's Shrewsbury is decorated with a motif similar in form to the Burmington 'hands'. It is comprised of two five-lobed leaves, the second and fourth lobes being ornamented with a line of beading (Plate 27b). The leaves are arranged like clasped fists, and like Burmington the bottom lobe curls beneath the leaf. On the capital adjacent to this one is a motif which includes another hand-like leaf, overlapping a smooth leaf. Both these leaf forms are in the position of volutes, rather than half way up the capital. Hand-like leaf forms also appear part of the way up capitals on the south-west and south-east crossing pier (Plate 27c). In both cases the leaves face each other, but neither example has the cone motif between the leaves.

Conclusion

Burmington Manor is a house of modest size in south Warwickshire. Although small, and apparently a property of a person of local rather than national or regional importance, it has sculpture of a quality fitted to an ecclesiastical project of some scale. The most complete stone corbel shares motifs with capitals at Glastonbury Abbey, and although none of the common forms are exclusive to these two sites, the combination appears to be without parallel in any other contemporary workshops. The wooden capital also has one leaf form similar in spirit to Glastonbury, but this capital appears to be more closely related to St Mary's at Shrewsbury. No clear parallels in wood have survived for the detailing of this capital. Though it can be related to contemporary stone carving, it is very different in its architectonic form from stone capitals in general, and the corbels in the gables in particular. This can be explained by a combination of the structural role the capital played in the building and the characteristics of thee material being used.

The only local buildings of comparable size and date to Burmington are parish churches. The much-restored chancel arch at nearby Alderminster (Warwickshire) has a capital with some forms in common with Burmington. In both buildings astragals are omitted and a membrane is drawn across the underside of the trumpet scallops. This combination of forms is sufficiently unusual in the area to suggest some type of link between the two buildings. However, in explaining any connection, it is necessary to acknowledge the striking difference in the quality of the carving. Alderminster is coarse and stiff compared to Burmington, and they are unlikely to be the work of one sculptor. It is more plausible either to propose that the carver of the Alderminster capital had seen the hall at Burmington, and within his capabilities had sought to reproduce the design, or that both were drawing on a lost common model.

Parish churches do not supply many useful parallels for either the wood or stone carving at Burmington. The quality of the sculpture found in them is coarser, probably reflecting the combination of a lack of funds and an absence of skilled craftsmen. Domestic buildings do not prove more helpful in supplying parallels for the Burmington sculpture, this being due to the poor survival rate of early domestic architecture. Those which have survived are relatively large structures, the result of the patronage of major secular or ecclesiastical patrons. Even the relatively modest sized hall of Old Court Cottage at Limpsfield was the manorial court of the Abbot of Battle. Limpsfield like Burmington, provides an indication that relatively small buildings might contain high quality sculpture. Although both could be the result of a statistical distortion in the rate of survival, they are more likely to be representatives of a once larger class of buildings, few of which have survived.

Acknowledgements: I would like to thank my colleagues in the Royal Commission on the Historical Monuments of England for their assistance, particularly Nicholas Cooper, Joanna Smith, Pat Payne and Terry Buchanan. I would also like to thank the owner of Burmington Manor, Michael Macdonald, for his cooperation and hospitality.

10

The West Portal of Ivry-la-Bataille

Kathryn Morrison

All that survives of the abbey church of Ivry-la Bataille (Eure) is a section of the west facade corresponding to the central and southern portions of the former nave (Plate 28a).[1] It contains the rapidly disintegrating remains of a twelfth-century portal which now forms the gateway of a private property.[2] The Abbey of Ivry was already described as 'ruinous' in fifteenth and sixteenth-century texts, and in 1563 the Huguenots reportedly destroyed the nave and pillaged the monastery.[3] The facade was largely remodelled in the 1570s when the (demolished) funeral chapel of Jacques de Poitiers was erected against its south bay, but the general lines of its original design can still be deciphered.[4]

The three facade bays were separated by column-buttresses: the one to the left of the portal survives to a level corresponding to the top of the archivolt springers, but the one to the right has been cut back. Similar column-buttresses defined the angles of the facade. This system of facade articulation suggests an influence from western France, which recurs in aspects of the sculptural decoration.

The south facade bay contains a round-headed blind arch with a continuous roll archivolt carved with shallow zig-zag. This arch would have formed the centrepiece of the interior east wall of the sixteenth-century funeral chapel. Above the blind arch is a blocked round-headed window, probably original, and higher still an arch traced in brick marks where the chapel vault abutted the facade. From this trace of vaulting one can determine that the north wall of the sixteenth-century chapel would have masked not just the buttress separating the south and central

---

[1] Despite the tripartite division of the facade there is no evidence that the twelfth-century church had aisles.

[2] The most important literature concerning the west portal of Ivry-la-Bataille is as follows: Fleury, G., *Etudes sur les portails imagés du XIIe siècle, leur iconographie et leur symbolisme*, Mamers, 1904, pp. 137–47; Lapeyre, A., *Des façades occidentales de St-Denis et de Chartres aux portails de Laon*, 1960, pp. 193–99; Sauerlaender, W., *Gothic Sculpture in France, 1140–1270*, 1972, p. 393, and Suau, J., 'Les débuts de la sculpture gothique dans l'Eure. 1. Le portail de l'abbaye Notre-Dame d'Ivry', *Nouvelles de l'Eure*, no. 39, 1973, pp. 49–59.

[3] Maudit, *Histoire d'Ivry-la-Bataille et de l'abbaye Notre-Dame d'Ivry*, 1899, pp. 433–34.

[4] The stone and brick chapel can be seen in the view of the abbey made from the east, published in *Monasticon Gallicanum*, 1687.

bays of the facade, but also the recess on the extreme south of the central bay which contains an engaged column and capital. We will see that this recess, together with the equivalent member on the north side of the bay, probably formed part of the original portal.

The portal, as it exists today, consists of three recessed orders: the first two orders each incorporate a single archivolt while the outer order includes both an archivolt and a label. The additional outer recesses mentioned above form a lateral continuation of the embrasures and determine the frontal plane of the upper facade wall. This plane is sustained for only a couple of courses above the impost blocks before the wall recedes back to meet the plane determined by the label. In addition, the nature of the masonry changes: that on the level of the label is coarse and irregular, presumably dating from the 1570s, while the blocks carried by the outer recesses, when examined closely, prove to be voussoirs. There are three voussoirs on the left and four on the right. Those on the left have deteriorated considerably, but those on the right retain the shape of voussoirs, including bevelled angles, and on three traces of carving survive: two were carved with figural scenes, now too weathered to be identified, and one with a bird or animal of some sort.[5] The remodelling of the archivolts must have been accomplished *c.* 1570 to enable Jacques de Poitiers' chapel to overlap the central bay of the facade. An additional spur could have been Huguenot damage, and it is reasonable to assume that the best preserved voussoirs from the original four orders were selected for the reconstruction.[6] The iconographic confusion of the existing figural orders lends credence to this notion, but determining the original existence of a fourth archivolt, although it increases our knowledge of the portal design, does not provide the key to their present disorder.

The present outer archivolt, carved with thin *rinceaux,* survives worn but intact while the weathered label survives only in its lower portions. This label preserves some traces of carving which would be difficult to interpret without the help of a drawing make in 1853 by Raymond Bordeaux which shows quite clearly that it was decorated with a series of

---

[5] In a drawing of the portal by Raymond Bordeaux dated 15 August 1853 (*Papiers et notes archéologiques sur Evreux et le département de l'Eure,* Paris, Bibl. Nat. Nouv. Acq. Fr. Ms. 21595, carnet II, fo. 7), the first and third voussoirs appear to be carved with half-length figures and the fourth with a bird or siren.

[6] Fleury, in a letter of 20 February 1905 to Louis Régnier (A.D. Eure, III, fo. 204, *Notes Louis Régnier.* Ivry, no, 352), suggested that the arrangement of the archivolts dates from the late 16th century, but he did not postulate the original existence of a fourth archivolt. Lapeyre, op. cit., 1960, p. 199, offered an alternative explanation for the present disorder. He suggested that funds ran out in the 12th century, before the portal sculpture had been completed.

radially disposed heads or masks with pointed ears, perhaps a further influence from western France.[7]

The majority of the voussoirs composing the two inner archivolts carry scenes relating to either the Last Judgement or the Passion of Christ, but one or two scenes cannot be convincingly associated with either theme. Heaven on the lower left (1:1) and Hell on the lower right (1:11) of the inner archivolt probably occupy their original positions.[8] This archivolt would have presented the Last Judgement in a similar manner to the inner archivolt of the central portal of the west facade of St-Denis.[9] Other scenes which would have originally belonged to this archivolt are Abraham with souls in his bosom (1:2), an angel carrying souls (1:4), a demon carrying a soul over his shoulder (1:10), and perhaps St Michael fighting the dragon (1:9). The majority of those scenes also occur at St-Denis.[10] As only two Elders of the Apocalypse (1:5 and 2:13) survive it is unlikely that an entire arch was devoted to them, as, for example, at St-Denis and Chartres.[11] Similarly only one full-length censer-swinging angel (1:7) survives, suggesting that a full archivolt of such figures, as found at Le Mans and Bourges, did not figure at Ivry.[12] Another figure which one would not expect to encounter singly is the Virtue, *Sobrietas* (2:14), depicted in armour trampling the corresponding Vice, *Gasrimas* (Gluttony), underfoot. No other Virtue survives. All of those figures are associated with the theme of the Last Judgement, particularly on the archivolts of churches in western France, e.g.: Aulnay, west portal (*c.* 1135), and were probably gathered together on the second archivolt. The Passion scenes (2:12, the Arrest of Christ; 2:7, the Crucifixion; 2:6, the Deposition; 2:5, the Holy Women at the Tomb; 2:4 and 2:5, the Descent into Limbo) would have belonged to a separate archivolt.[13] According to Guilhermy, writing on 15 August 1839, the programme

[7] Bordeaux, op. cit., *Papiers*, fo. 5v. This drawing shows that the label did not consist of 'une bordure de palmettes entremelées de tetes d'anges', as stated by Fleury, op. cit., p. 137. The same drawing also shows that the *rinceau* on the outer archivolt emerged from an inverted head on the left-hand side.

[8] The voussoirs are numbered by archivolt (inner to outer) and, within each archivolt from left to right, eg: (2:5) refers to the fifth voussoir from the left on the second archivolt.

[9] On the inner archivolt of Provins, which is often compared to Ivry and St-Denis, by some curious inversion Heaven is on the right and Hell on the left.

[10] The right side of the St-Denis archivolt, containing Hell scenes, was totally recarved by the sculptor Brun in the mid nineteenth century. See S.M. Crosby and P. Blum, 'Le portail central de la facade occidentale de St-Denis', *Bulletin Monumental*, 131, 1973, p. 236.

[11] Lapeyre, A., op. cit., 1960, p. 199, suggested that an entire archivolt of the Ivry portal would have been reserved for the Elders of the Apocalypse.

[12] Voussoir 1:8 is also carved with an angel, but apparently of a different type. The angels on voussoirs 2:8 and 2:10 are discussed below.

[13] Suau, op. cit., p. 51 alludes to the presence of the Flagellation, presumably on voussoir 2:7, but he does not justify this identification.

28a Ivry-la-Bataille, Abbey Church of Notre-Dame, remains of west facade.

28c Le Mans Cathedral, South Portal, voussoir 1:7: censing angel.

28b Ivry-la-Bataille, Abbey Church of Notre-Dame, voussoir 1:7: censing angel.

29a Ivry-la-Bataille, Abbey Church of
Notre-Dame, column statue of an Old
Testament queen drawn by Bordeaux.

29b St-Denis, Abbey, column statue of a
king from the cloister drawn by Benoit
(d. 1717).

included an angel holding the nails of the Passion (2:8).[14] The figure is now too damaged for this to be verified, and Guilhermy's iconographic observations are not always reliable, yet the inclusion of such a figure would have expressed very clearly the relationship between the themes of the Passion and the Last Judgement. The significance of several voussoirs remains enigmatic. An enthroned female accompanied by a standing angel (1:3) is usually identified as an Annunciation but considerable doubt remains: there are no other Infancy scenes on the portal and this voussoir does not display standard twelfth-century Annunciation iconography.[15] It is more likely that this voussoir represents the Virgin enthroned in Heaven on the Day of Judgement, as she had appeared in earlier Last Judgements, for example on the tympanum of Autun (*c.* 1125–28). At Autun the figure enthroned beside the Virgin is generally identified as St John, who may also appear at Ivry (2:15). The paired heads carved on the lower voussoirs of the second archivolt (2:1 and 2:16) are puzzling: it seems too easy to dismiss them as decorative conceits. Clearly the iconography of the archivolts remains problematic in a number of respects.

The vicissitudes of the portal did not end with the reassemblage of the voussoirs in the sixteenth century. It was probably during the Revolution that the tympanum, lintel and all but one column-statue were lost, although this is not documented. Fortunately, those elements were described by Jacques Le Gris in a letter dated 6 November 1726 to Dom Bernard de Montfaucon.[16] The five column-statues described by Le Gris seem to have represented a prophet between two kings on the north embrasure and a prophet and queen on the south embrasure; Le Gris claimed that the sixth column-statue had disappeared in the sixteenth century when the funeral chapel was built. The queen alone survives: in the eighteenth century she occupied the second recess on the right, but she was probably moved to her present position in the third recess when a road was constructed through the portal in the nineteenth century with its kerb abutting the second recess. This contributed to the decay of the portal by concealing its plinth courses and altering its proportions.

From Le Gris' description it is clear that the tympanum contained Christ in Majesty surrounded by the four Evangelist Symbols, with the twelve apostles seated below on the lintel, as on the south portals of Le Mans and Bourges.[17] Blocks carved with colonnettes above each doorpost are the only remains of the lintel.

---

[14] Baron F. de Guilhermy, *Notes*, Paris Bibl. Nat. Nouv. Acq. Ms 6094, fo. 325. Voussoir 2:10 seems to have been carved with a comparable figure which would have formed a pendant for 2:8.

[15] Suau, op. cit., p. 52 attempts to justify the presence of an Annunciation within a Last Judgement programme.

[16] Dom B. de Montfaucon, *Dessins et gravures pour les monumens de la monarchie françoise*, Paris Bibl. Nat. Ms. Fr. 15634, folios 90r, 90v and 91.

[17] Le Gris, 1726.

The Ivry portal is usually classified as 'Chartrain', but in its architectural design and iconographic programme it is more closely related to other mid twelfth-century portals. The presence of a full college of seated apostles, possibly within a framework of individual architectural canopies, on the lintel relates the portal to Le Mans and Bourges rather than to the central portal of Chartres, and the iconography of the archivolts, although unique, displays striking similarities with St-Denis. The design and technique of several figures reveal that the workshop included sculptors who had previously been employed at Le Mans and in the *chantier* of St-Denis: the resemblances to those monuments are not fortuitous.

The most striking stylistic comparison one can draw between Le Mans and Ivry concerns the censer-swinging angel (1:7) which, if it was not executed by the same hand as the Le Mans south portal angel (1:7) was certainly produced by a member of the same workshop (Plates 28b, c). The head of the Ivry angel is missing and the left hand, which is broken off at Le Mans, carries an incense boat. Both angels are slender and graceful. They stand on wavy clouds and, advancing to the left, flex their right legs at the knee while their left legs curve gently backwards. The drapery arrangement over their lower bodies is closely comparable. The design of the censers, the conventional fly-away drapery of the mantles and the depiction of the wings, with one lying flat against the ground and the other lying at an oblique angle across the planes of the relief, with deep undercutting behind the left arm, all reveal a relationship which must be direct.

At Chartres, although the voussoir angels are all three-quarter length, a similar design was used for the right-hand angel on the south portal tympanum.[18] In contrast to Ivry and Le Mans the Chartres angel raises its right wing to conform to the shape of the tympanum, it does not stand on a cloud bank and the escaping drapery of the mantle is not blown upwards. Those design differences indicate that the Ivry and Le Mans angels cannot have derived independently from Chartres. Moreover, between Ivry and Le Mans one finds a high degree of technical affinity not shared with Chartres, especially in the finely chiselled surface of the drapery, avoiding thick or deeply channelled folds, and in the gentle gradation of the carving. Interestingly, none of the other angels on the inner archivolt of Le Mans share those characteristics.

The relationship between Le Mans and Ivry does not end with the two censer-bearing angels. The design and technique of the sole surviving column-statue at Ivry (Plate 29a) finds a counterpart in the Old Testament queen on the right embrasure of Le Mans. The positioning of the (broken) hands, which once held a scroll, is reversed at Le Mans but

---

[18] Another variation on this design is found on the tympanum of the portail Ste-Anne in Paris.

otherwise the poses and costumes of the two figures are very close. The robes which they wear, the *bliaut*, have bodices with rectangular panels in the centre of the neck. The skirts fall from the hips in numerous fine folds, fanning out just above the feet into similar patterns of pleats. Over their robes they wear mantles which fall over their arms and nearly reach their feet. Their shoes were decorated with drilling. It is in the treatment of the headgear, however, that a direct relationship between the two queens is suggested most forcefully. A swathe of cloth falls over the chest in concentric folds, leaving the neck bare. The area below the ears is deeply drilled, and long plaits emerge from beneath the headdress and lie flat against the shoulder and upper arm until they taper out at the hip. Certainly there are differences between those two figures: in particular the Ivry queen has more attenuated proportions and an extra tail of cloth falls from the headdress onto the left shoulder, but there is little doubt that they follow the some model and there is a strong possibility that they were carved by the same workshop, especially bearing in mind the relationship between the voussoir angels discussed above.

Just as the design of the angels recurs at Chartres, so does the design of this queen.[19] At Chartres it was employed for the queen on the buttress between the central and north portals, but incorporating a number of features which distinguish it from Ivry and Le Mans. Here the bodice is almost completely concealed by the mantle, which falls in two loops over the chest. The forehead is not bound, as at Le Mans, and the hair,parted in the middle, is visible underneath the crown. The girdle, tied in a reef knot as at Ivry, masks the seam between the bodice and the skirt while at Ivry it was tied about the waist. From those differences it is clear that the Ivry and Le Mans queens cannot have independently copied this figure. On the other hand, the splayed hemline above drilled shoes, the long sleeves of the mantle, the positioning of the hands, the plaits appearing beneath the head-scarf and the deep drilling on either side of the neck show that the same technical procedures and designs were circulating in the Chartres workshop as in the Le Mans and Ivry workshops. More significantly, the scarf falling over the left shoulder of the Ivry queen, absent from the Le Mans queen, reappears here suggesting that the sculptor of the Ivry figure had a knowledge of the Chartres as well as the Le Mans version of this design.

The design and technique of the Ivry queen is also related to a slightly recut column-statue of a king from the cloister of St-Denis, now in the Metropolitan Museum in New York (Plate 29b).[20] At 1.15 m (3 feet 9

---

[19] Suau, op cit., p. 55.

[20] This statue is indubitably authentic. It corresponds very closely to a drawing of a king from the cloister of St-Denis made by Benoist (d. 1717) for Montfaucon, and Leon Pressouyre ('Did Suger Build the Cloister at St-Denis?', *Abbot Suger and St-Denis*, ed. P. Gerson, new York, 1986, p.236) succeeded in tracing its history from the 18th century until it entered the Metropolitan Museum from the collection of Alphonse Kahn in 1920.

inches) high this column-statue is considerably smaller than column-statues which stood in the embrasures of mid twelfth-century portals, but it is of the same type. The most striking parallel between the Ivry queen and the St-Denis king is the treatment of the lower part of the skirt and the feet, a part of the Ivry queen which is now very damaged. A drawing made by Raymond Bordeaux in 1853 (Plate 29a), and old photographs show that the queen wore drilled shoes and that the skirt flared out slightly above the hemline into three major pleats, each composed of several fine folds.[21] The lower part of the St-Denis king displays almost exactly the same features, as does the Le Mans queen. The same parts of the Chartres queen are not dissimilar while, perhaps significantly, most of the other Chartres column-statues have straight hems. Other striking resemblances between the Ivry queen and the St-Denis king include their long thin arms and rounded stomachs covered by tight folds which run cross-wise and then fan upwards to suggest the form of the belly. The resemblance between the drapery of the Ivry queen and the St-Denis king is so close that one must consider the possibility that they were carved by the same workshop.

The Ivry voussoir representing Abraham with souls in his bosom (1:2) also finds a stylistic parallel in a work from St-Denis: this time a statue of Dagobert, now lost, which was in the narthex of St-Denis until the eighteenth century although it is thought to have been carved for the cloister. This sculpture is only known through drawings, which renders any technical comparison with Ivry inconclusive.[22] As they are depicted, the drapery conventions seem to have been very similar to those in the Ivry Abraham. It has been claimed by several art historians that the notion of placing a Last Judgement cycle on the inner archivolt of Ivry must have been inspired by the central portal of St-Denis, and now it is possible to explain this in terms of a workshop or individual sculptor who can be associated with the cloister workshop of St-Denis. At St-Denis they would have seen the west portals of the abbey church, which provided the inspiration for the iconographic scheme on the inner archivolt of Ivry.

We can now consider the date of the Ivry portal. Fleury thought that it was produced during two medieval campaigns. An initial late eleventh- or early twelfth-century portal, comprising round arches decorated with geometric or foliage patterns, would have been reconstructed in the late twelfth century with pointed arches carrying figural carving, and at the same time the original plain columns would have been replaced with column-statues.[23] Lapeyre dated the portal to a single unfinished campaign in the last quarter of the twelfth century, but more recently

[21] Bordeaux, op. cit., fo. 6r.

[22] The statue was published in Dom B. de Montfaucon's *Monumens de la monarchie françoise*, 1, Paris, 1729, pl. 12. The drawing is reproduced by Sauerlaender, op. cit., p. 382.

[23] Fleury, op. cit., p. 141, and in the letter of 1905 cited above, n. 6.

Sauerlaender and Suau have dated it *c.* 1150-55.[24] Neither of the monuments with which the sculpture has been compared here are precisely dated. The south portal of Le Mans is generally dated *c.* 1150–55, after Chartres and before the consecration of Le Mans Cathedral nave in 1158. The sculpture from the cloister of St-Denis is stylistically related to sculpture from the choir of St-Germain-des-Prés which was consecrated in 1163, and in fact the inner capital on the right of the Ivry portal finds a close parallel in that building, corroborating the relationships outlined above. It is reasonable to conclude that the Ivry portal was produced in a single campaign *c.* 1160 by a workshop including sculptors who had previously been employed in Paris, in the orbit of St-Denis and St-Germain-des-Prés, and at Le Mans.

[24] Lapeyre, op. cit., p. 279; Sauerlaender, op. cit., p. 393 and Suau, op. cit., p. 56.

11

The Choir of St-Etienne at Caen

Lindy Grant

The Benedictine abbey of St-Etienne at Caen was founded by William the Conqueror in 1060 in expiation for his consanguineous marriage. It was intended from the first as his mausoleum, and was a key element in his attempt to establish Caen instead of Rouen as the capital of Normandy. In the twelfth century political interest shifted back to Rouen and the Seine valley, and neither Caen nor St-Etienne ever quite recaptured their initial prestige and importance. Nevertheless, the ducal family continued to accept their special relationship to the abbey, and the abbots, though not of the stature of Anselm or Lanfranc (but then who, in twelfth-century Normandy, was?) worked closely with William's successors.[1]

William's church was large and splendid. In the early twelfth century, the nave was vaulted, but otherwise the building stood unaltered for more than a century.[2] Eventually, however, the church was provided with a new choir (Plate 30a). There is no documentary evidence to date this choir conclusively, and one has to have recourse to stylistic dating. Most

---

[1] St-Etienne always obtained substantial confirmation charters from the duke-kings, and those of both Henry II and, in particular, Richard I add many new and valuable privileges, see *Gallia Christiana*, 11, p. 425 and J. Lechaudé d'Anisy, *Extraits des chartes dans les archives du Calvados*, Caen, 1834 1, p. 279, no. 55. Henry II held his important Christmas court at Caen in 1183, see Roger of Howden, *Chronica*, ed. W. Stubbs (Rolls Series), 1869, 2, p. 273. See also Archbishop Rotrou of Rouen's letter of 1171, warning off a predatory baron: 'carissimos filios nostros a domino rege plurimum dilectos abbatem et monachos Sancti Stephani de Cadomo', in *Receuil des Actes de Henri II*, ed. L. Delisle and E. Berger, Paris, 1916, 1, p. 453, no. ccciv. In return, late 12th-century abbots were often closely concerned in royal business. For Abbot Robert's expedition to check on Hubert Walter at Richard's behest see A. Du Monstier, *Neustria Pia*, Rouen, 1663, p. 653: for his successor Abbot Samson's key role as baron of the Norman exchequer see *Rotuli Normanniae*, ed. T. D. Hardy (Record Commission), London, 1835, passim, eg. pp. 22–23, 36.

[2] For William's church see E.G. Carlson, *The Abbey of St-Etienne at Caen in the Eleventh and Twelfth Centuries* (University Microfilms), Ann Arbor, 1968. 19th- and 20th-century restorations are well documented in the archives of the Monuments Historiques in Paris, carton 212, and the choir has not changed since it was recorded in A. Pugin, *Specimens of the Architectural Antiquities of Normandy*, London, 1825, pls. 7, 12–17. The problematic restoration is that carried out by Jean de Baillehache in the mid 17th-century see L. Grant, *Gothic Architecture in Normandy, 1150–1250* (unpublished Ph.D. thesis, University of London, 1987), p. 120, n. 2.

previous commentators have assumed it to be a building of the early thirteenth century [3] and it is generally supposed to be the result of two completely different designs and campaigns, with a 'French' architect responsible for the ambulatory, and a later 'Norman' architect for the elevation.[4] Both assumptions are open to question.

It was the striking similarity in design between the ambulatories, but not the elevations, of Caen and Vézelay that first led Lambert to suggest that Caen was the result of two quite different campaigns. The necessary break in construction was duly identified between the double columns of the apse (Plate 30b). The rear column is distinctly fatter than the inner one; the front abacus is circular, while the abacus above the rear pier is a broad rectangle with lopped corners; and there is an ugly scar in the masonry between the front and rear capital of each pair of columns. From these observations, it has been argued that the rear columns were built as part of the first campaign, intended to remain single, and to support a thin upper wall in the French manner; and that the inner columns were added only in the second campaign when the second architect, a Norman, redesigned the buildings with a thick upper wall.[5]

But if one looks closely, there is no question of the inner and outer apse columns at St-Etienne belonging to different campaigns. All the columns course perfectly with their pair, and sometimes a single masonry block serves both columns. The discrepancy in their design is easily explained. The rear column is fatter, and the rear abacus a different, broader shape from its inner counterpart because the outer column and abacus have to support the thicker section of apse wall – the thicker end of the wedge – and the broad spread of three ambulatory ribs, as against the single rib shaft on the main elevation. The scarring between the capitals of the double columns (it appears also in the same position on the composite piers of the straight bays) is best explained as the legacy of the previous wooden choir screen dismantled in 1925.[6] So the usually accepted campaign break at St-Etienne simply does not exist, and there are no other masonry breaks which might suggest that the choir should

---

[3] E.g. J. Vallery-Radot, *La cathédrale de Bayeux* (Petits Monographies), Paris, 1922, p. 68; L. Serbat, 'Caen. Eglise Saint-Etienne et abbaye aux hommes', *Congrès Archéologique*, 75, 1908, p. 21; J. Bony, *French Gothic Architecture of the 12th and 13th Centuries*, Berkeley/Los Angeles, 1983, p. 318.

[4] First suggested by E. Lambert, 'Caen roman et gothique', *Bulletin de la Société des Antiquaires de Normandie*, 43, 1935, p. 46, followed by P. Héliot, 'La diversité de l'architecture gothique à ses débuts en France', *Gazette des Beaux Arts*, 69, 1967, p. 299.

[5] Carlson, op. cit., pp. 232–33, and Bony, op. cit., pp. 318 and 514, n. 23.

[6] Report to the Commission des Monuments Historiques by Nodet, 21st Jan, 1925, Archives des Monuments Historiques, carton 212.

30b Caen, St-Etienne, choir: apse piers.

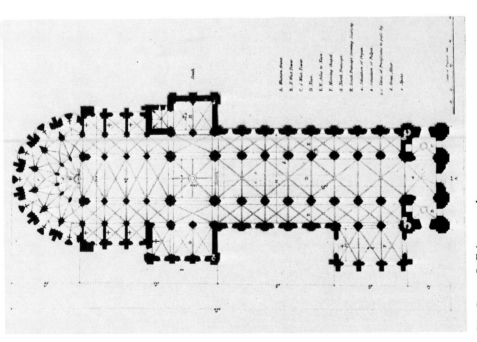

30a Caen, St-Etienne, plan.

31b Caen, St-Etienne, choir.

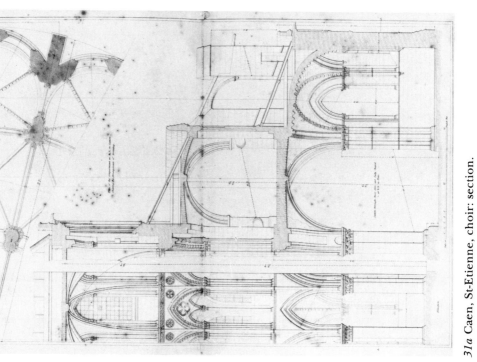

31a Caen, St-Etienne, choir: section.

32b Caen, St-Etienne, ambulatory and radiating chapel.

32a Caen, St-Etienne, choir: exterior.

be considered the result of more than one campaign.[7] Besides, Pugin's section of the choir reveals the neat integrity of its design: the lower levels at St-Etienne are the perfect support for the upper levels (Plate 31a).[8] There is stylistic integrity too, in that all features, with the single exception of the ring mouldings, which appear in the ambulatory are repeated throughout the rest of the choir. The tombstone of the architect William, built into the wall of the axial chapel, claims all the new work unequivocally as his own: 'Guillelmus jacet hic petrorum summus in arte iste novum opus det praemia christus, amen'.[9]

So we must take William's word for it, and regard the choir of St-Etienne as a single integral build and design. It would be nice but unprofitable to ask who William was; it is worth asking what were William's design sources and what the workshop tradition in which he had been trained, and whether this throws any light on when he built St-Etienne.

The choir of St-Etienne at Caen is the building which first successfully wedded French Gothic precepts to Norman traditions. William was clearly conversant with an indigenous, Norman building tradition, first adumbrated at Fécamp in Upper Normandy in the rebuilding begun in 1168.[10] These underlying Norman elements are important. There is no trace of alternation at Caen (Plate 31b), and the vaults spanning the bays are quadripartite and rectangular. The piers in the straight bays are composite and coursed. The elevation is of three levels with a substantial vaulted tribune comprising the middle storey. Caen, like Fécamp, Eu and the nave of Coutances, adopts the thick wall system with clerestory passage, and, like Fécamp and Eu, has stair turrets at the junction of the straight bays and the apse (Plate 32a). At the same time, certain elements suggest an awareness of what might conveniently be labelled the Franco-Norman as opposed to Fécampois strain in twelfth-century Norman Gothic architecture, notably the choir of Mortemer, with which Caen shared the rather unusual feature of undulating chapels caught at cornice level into a single sweeping semi-circle of roof (Plate 32a), which probably, at Mortemer, reflected Parisian sources such as St-Martin-des-Champs.[11]

Along with Mortemer in Normandy, and Vézelay and Pontigny in

[7] The sole break visible in the Early Gothic work at St-Etienne is between the south transept chapel and tribune above, and the main body of the choir. It is clear on the exterior that at both chapel and tribune level the choir is built up against the south transept. The south transept chapel is very elaborate, but is stylistically all of a piece with the rest of the building, and it makes no sense to regard this break as anything more than rather odd building procedure, possibly dictated by having to build around the previous choir.

[8] Pugin, op. cit., pls. 15 and 16.

[9] Illustrated in L. Musset, *La Normandie Romane*, i, La-Pierre-qui-Vire, 1967, pl. 9.

[10] For Fécamp and this early Norman Gothic building tradition see Grant, op. cit., pp. 51–73.

[11] Ibid., pp. 85–87.

Burgundy, St-Etienne is one of a group of grand abbeys with connections at the very highest levels, which seem rather belatedly to have found that Suger's choir at St-Denis provided the perfect blueprint for an intimate abbatial as opposed to a vast cathedral choir. Mortemer is a securely dated building, begun in 1174 and finished before 1200,[12] and Vézelay and Pontigny too surely belong to the late twelfth rather than the thirteenth century. Vézelay and Caen (Plate 32b) are particularly close to St-Denis, in that in both churches the radiating chapels are divided only by low walls, an interpretation in stone of the low wooden or metalwork screens which must have divided the cells of the outer ambulatory at St-Denis into separate chapels. Caen too has something of the breadth and scale of St-Denis, boasting seven as opposed to the more normal five radiating chapels.

St-Etienne at Caen, like most Norman Gothic architecture, consistently responds to Parisian architectural stimuli.[13] Many features derive from the more recent and fashionable cathedral of Notre-Dame in Paris. The ambulatory piers, with their round coursed cores surrounded by *en délit* fasciculated shafts (Plate 32b), find their closest analogy in the nave aisles of Notre-Dame in Paris. The double span flyers, with an intermediate buttress, in the straight bays of the choir relate to the original nave flyers at Notre-Dame.[14] The tribune windows at Caen are mainly oculi, and the comparison to the Parisian Mantes,[15] and its source, the tribune windows at Notre-Dame in their original form, is obvious. In other words, St-Etienne incorporates into a design which owes much to St-Denis a large number of fashionable features from Parisian building of the 1170s and early 1180s.

There is another, more surprising external influence at work at St-Etienne. It is the only major Norman building where English influence from a consistent and plausible source can be felt. That source is Canterbury, and its influence is revealed by a series of telling details, particularly of articulation.

Many of the shafts involved in the articulation of St-Etienne are very slender (especially those in the apse), and in the straight bays single shafts and capitals support triple ribs. This articulation is quite different from the wide splayed and emphatic triple shafts rising uninterrupted from base to vault of Fécamp or Eu, or the naves of Rouen or Coutances.

[12] Mortemer is securely dated by the abbey chronicle, published in J. Bouvet, ed., 'Le recit de la foundation de Mortemer', *Collectanea ordinis Cisterciana reformatorum*, 22, 1960, pp. 149-68, and see the discussion in Grant, op. cit., pp. 196–98.

[13] Grant, op. cit., pp. 341–50.

[14] See the reconstruction of the original flyers in M. Aubert, *Notre-Dame de Paris; sa place dans l'architecture du XIIe au XIVe siècles*, 2nd. ed., Paris, 1929, pp. 43–44, 103–6. Aubert's reconstruction was based on drawings by Viollet-le-Duc.

[15] See Aubert, op. cit., p. 109, for the original design of the tribune windows at Notre-Dame. For Mantes, see J. Bony, 'La collégiale de Mantes', *Congrès Archéologique*, 54, 1946, pp. 163-220.

33b Caen, St-Etienne, choir: south side, upper levels.

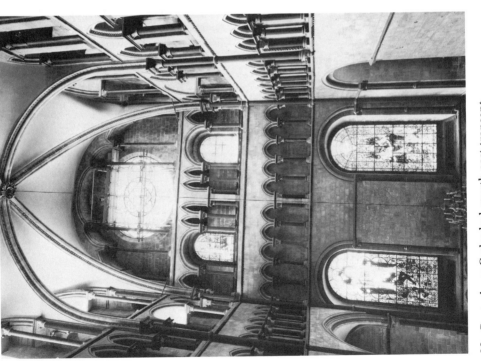

33a Canterbury Cathedral, north-east transept.

34b Eu, St. Laurent, choir: apse piers.

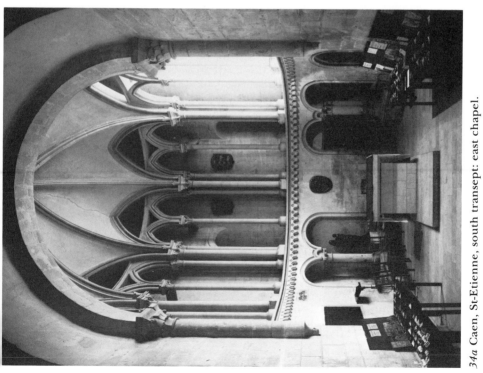

34a Caen, St-Etienne, south transept: east chapel.

The shafts in the straight bays at Caen are broken at the arcade abaci and at the tribune cornice by capitals. At arcade level they are *en délit*, above this, coursed. Moreover, the diameter of the shaft expands considerably at the point of transition from *en délit* to coursing (Plate 31a). Such expansion is very unusual, but it can be found, though unassociated with a change in masonry cutting, on the east walls of the eastern transepts at Canterbury (Plate 33a).

En délit shafting is used not only to articulate the main lines of the elevation, but also in smaller passages of screen work. The twin clerestory windows are set behind a triple-arched screen (Plate 33b), resulting in a contrapuntal effect which has long since been compared to window screen design on the interior west wall of St-Remi at Reims, or over the eastern transept roses at Canterbury (Plate 33a).[16] The relationship between the Caen and Canterbury window screens is tightened by a detail common to both, but unknown elsewhere in the twelfth century: at Caen the heads of the outer arches, and at Canterbury the heads of the median arches, sit directly on the inner capital. This form is rare at any time. The only other examples I have found (at Chartres, Dreux, Salisbury, and, in association with windows, on the west wall at Eu) are all in buildings to be dated well into the 1220s, which is patently far too late for either Canterbury or Caen.

Delicate *en délit* shafting screens the remois passage in the small south transept chapel (Plate 34a). Here the fragile screen is stabilised by a small buttressing strut between the capital and the back wall of the remois passage. This seems to be the only appearance of this small buttressing element in France, but its use in a series of English clerestories (the east wall of Chichester retrochoir, the west transept at Rochester, St Hugh's choir at Lincoln) suggests that the source might once again be Canterbury, where indeed it appears, albeit rather discreetly, in the clerestory of the west wall of the eastern transepts.

The double column form of the apse piers (Plate 30b) was widespread in later twelfth-century France, though this is its first occurrence in Normandy. I suspect that originally the Caen piers had small additional columns at their interstices, a very specific design feature, which would here again reveal the direct influence of Canterbury. The evidence for these additional shafts is circumstantial, but cumulatively convincing. All the direct evidence for their existence was destroyed by the wooden choir screen dismantled in 1925, which left the deep gouges in the masonry at the junction of every set of capitals. The dismantling of this screen is documented with minute bureaucratic efficiency in the archives of the Monuments Historiques.[17] When it was removed, it was discovered that the section of base between the two columns had been destroyed

16 Serbat, op. cit., p. 40.
17 See above, n. 6

when the screen was erected, so that on all the piers these sections of base, which might have revealed the existence of the additional shafts, are twentieth-century replacements. The indirect evidence is that additional shafts do exist in the apses of the cathedrals of Lisieux and Bayeux, which are almost slavishly dependent on Caen. At Lisieux, the earlier of the two, the additional shafts are very thin and serve no useful purpose whatsoever. It is hard to see the architect of Lisieux – not otherwise an original artist – inventing this feature. But shafts in this position at Caen would have provided a neat solution to the minor design problem, which has certainly disturbed most recent commentators, created by the practical but undeniably awkward junction of fatter rear and thinner inner column, topped by rectangular rear and rounded inner abaci. Additional *en délit* shafts, inspired by the example in the presbytery at Canterbury, and the related folly in the Trinity Chapel, where there are miniature intersticial capitals but no shafts to support them, would have been the perfect solution.

Caen is the building which introduces rounded abaci and bases to Normandy. Canterbury, where they appear in the eastern crypt and the east transepts, provides the most likely source. The remois passage in the south transept chapel at Caen is the earliest in France apart from the prototype at St-Remi at Reims itself; and its appearance in Normandy, in an area and a building otherwise impervious to Champenois influence, is at first sight surprising. Canterbury again provides the connecting link. Both architects at Canterbury were in close touch with eastern French and Champenois architectural traditions.[18] There is no remois passage as such at Canterbury, but there are two closely related types, in the elegantly screened pseudo-passage running in front of the Trinity Chapel ambulatory windows, and in the wall passage at the level of the upper set of choir windows.

Canterbury was easily assimilated at Caen because Canterbury too was drawing on French sources. The elegant articulation, the screen work, the play on columnar forms with additional shafts at Canterbury are all essentially French imports, and they are all imported from the north and east of France. The importance of Canterbury for Caen is that it allows St-Etienne access to aspects of the architectural traditions of north east France and Champagne, an area with which the Paris-oriented Normandy seems otherwise to have had little connection.

The links with Canterbury are very specific. William of Caen must have visited the Canterbury chantier; details such as the small buttressing strut could only have been learnt on site. He seems to have been particularly conversant with work on the eastern transepts, the eastern crypt, and the early work in the Trinity Chapel, in other words with the work of William

[18] J. Bony, 'French Influences on the Origins of English Gothic Architecture', *Journal of the Warburg and Courtauld Institutes*, 12, 1949, p. 8.

the Englishman as he took over from William of Sens. The specificity of William's borrowings from Canterbury suggest to me that he used them in his own work at Caen very soon after he first absorbed them. They are surely evidence that the choir of St-Etienne at Caen is a building of the mid 1180s, not of the early 1200s. This, after all, is exactly what the links with early work in the nave at Notre-Dame in Paris would suggest, and it is fully borne out by all the parallels that can be made with dated building within Normandy itself. Capital design at Caen for instance is remarkably close to that at Eu, begun in 1186,[19] particularly for the crossed crockets in the apse arcades of both buildings (Plate 34b), and to the nave and south porch at Bayeux, built in the 1180s and 1190s for the foliate types on the composite piers.[20] The broad waterleaf types which appear between several of the radiating chapels can, indeed, be compared to capitals from the first nave campaign at Fécamp, which must have been completed by around 1180.[21]

[19] For the dating of Eu see *Gallia Christiana*, 11, cols, 294-95, and see Grant, op. cit., pp. 63, 72, n. 45.

[20] For the late 12th-century work at Bayeux see Grant, op. cit., pp. 64–65. The refashioning and vaulting of the nave aisles and the building of the new chapter house can be dated to the episcopate of Henry of Salisbury (1165–1205) on documentary evidence. Henry arranged for the revenues from the canons's prebends to be diverted to the cathedral building fund in the year following the death of the incumbent. Henry's charter is undated, but must predate 1181, since it was confirmed by Pope Alexander III (1159–81). Building continued into the 1180s, since it was reconfirmed by Urban III in 1186 or 87. Henry also established a local confraternity to fund rebuilding; see *Antiquus Cartularius Ecclesiae Baiocensis*, ed. V. Bourrienne, 2 vols (Société de l'Histoire de Normandie), Paris/Rouen, 1902–3, 1, p. 105, no. 82. p. 217, no. 174; p. 252, no. 205; p. 58, no. 47. The south nave porch at Bayeux is particularly close to the choir of St-Etienne. It, too, has rounded socles below bases, spandrel oculi, and a pier (admittedly much restored) composed of a columnar masonry core surrounded by *en délit* shafts. This porch was built as an integral part of the Bayeux nave campaign. The inner plinth of the porch is continuous with the inner plinth of the south nave aisle. The most sensible explanation of these new elements in the south porch is that they are in response to the new work at St-Etienne. They are once again corroborative evidence for a date in the 1180s for St-Etienne.

[21] The choir and five eastern bays of Fécamp nave, up to a glaringly obvious break, were built by Henri de Sully, abbot from 1140–88: the western bays were completed by his successor, Raoul d'Argences. The evidence for this is in P. Labbé, ed., *Novae Bibliothecae Manuscript. Librorum*, Paris, 1657, 1, p. 328. Immediately after his transcription of the Fécamp chronicle, Labbé gives a catalogue of the abbots of Fécamp, 'ex veteris schedis exscriptus et deductus'. This includes the sentence: 'Radulfus ortus apud Argentias ... mediatatem navis ecclesie et duas turres acervorum construxit'. This vital sentence was given an incorrect reference by J. Vallery Radot, *L'église de la Trinité de Fécamp*, (Petits Monographies), Paris, 1928, 15, who claimed it was part of the Fécamp chronicle itself, and referred to the recension in the *Receuil des Historiens des Gaules et de la France*, ed. M. Bouquet and others, 24 vols, Paris 1867–1904, 23, pp. 430–32. This error has been repeated frequently. The evidence is thus less absolutely convincing than it is usually considered; it is not clear whether it was 'ex veteris schedis exsciptus' or whether 'deductus' by Labbé himself. One suspects the former, since Labbé would only have been tempted to deduce that Raoul was responsible for the western bays, in the absence of documentary evidence, had he noticed the break, which seems unlikely.

St-Etienne at Caen thus emerges as a particularly potent amalgam of Norman Gothic tradition with a fresh and lively response to Parisian design, together with some very specific, and slightly undigested good ideas from Canterbury. In spite of this St-Etienne is a remarkably coherent design. It presented a whole new approach to Gothic building in Normandy. The intercommunicating chapels, the remois passage, and the mannered syncopation of clerestory window and screening shafts open up the possibility of complex and shadowed subsidiary spaces. Its slender shafting is often *en délit* and often carried on corbels. The dosserets on both aisle and tribune responds and main piers are softened into convex or concave curves, and shaft groups united by single rounded bases or abaci. The result of all these devices (and their importance cannot be underrated in the formation of the mature Norman Gothic style) was to undermine the integrity of the bay, and introduce a measure at least of spatial fluidity to an architecture of stiffness and mass, in spite of the determination of Norman architects to retain the outdated composite pier. St-Etienne at Caen must stand as the seminal Norman Gothic building: certainly all future architectural speculation in Lower, and much in Upper Normandy, depended on it.

Acknowledgements: the research for this paper was partly financed by a grant from the University of London Central Research Fund. I would like to thank the editors, my colleagues in the Conway Library for their help with photographs, and Monsieur Yves Lescroart of the *Monuments Historiques* for access to the upper levels of St-Etienne. Above all, of course, I would like to thank PK for his continual encouragement, help, conversation, and the inspiration to study Gothic architecture in the first place.

12

Villard de Honnecourt's Perception of Gothic Architecture

M.F. Hearn

The architectural drawings of Villard de Honnecourt permit us, by observing what he illustrated (or did not) and how he illustrated it, to deduce his qualitative perception of Gothic architecture.[1] Many points remain controversial: How professional was his architectural involvement? What was the purpose of the portfolio of drawings? Why do the drawings deviate from the buildings they purport to represent? Yet despite this, deductions concerning his perceptions are valid, regardless of his personal situation. Whether he was a practitioner or merely a connoisseur, whether he drew for the benefit of others or only for himself, whether he made mistakes or 'improved' upon the examples he copied, he clearly was knowledgeable about Gothic architecture. By analysing the available data we can begin to divine what formal quality in Gothic architecture seemed crucial to its effectiveness for a discerning witness in the early thirteenth century.

Considering the range of building types that anyone would be likely to illustrate when evincing a serious engagement with architecture, it is significant of a particularised interest that Villard included only great churches and even then only examples exhibiting limited aspects of some recent developments in the Gothic mode. There are, for instance, no castles, urban fortifications, bridges, or any other types that an architectural expert would include in order to demonstrate a comprehensive grasp of the subject (with or without an awareness of the scope of Vitruvius). The buildings he did illustrate, or rather the portions of the buildings he illustrated, appear to represent not a collection of favourite solutions to some specific design problems (either practical or aesthetic) but a predilection for high-art architecture and even for certain formal concerns within that category. One can go further: Villard's drawings indicate an interest in cutting to the stylistic core of Gothic

---

[1] The most comprehensive bibliography of scholarship on Villard, up to 1982, was compiled by Carl F. Barnes, Jr., in *Villard de Honnecourt, the Artist and his Drawings: A Critical Bibliography*, Boston, 1982. Scholarship after that date has been noted and summarised in the *Forum* published by the Association Villard de Honnecourt for the Interdisciplinary Study of Medieval Technology, Science and Art, since 1986.

architecture. The task at hand is to determine the aspect of Gothic architecture that Villard regarded as conveying style and to define what it does.

It is important to emphasise that I do not regard the drawings as being limited to the issue of style. Indeed, some of the drawings (for instance, the flying buttresses of Reims Cathedral and the miniature representations of the plans of a Cistercian church and the chevet of Cambrai Cathedral) were probably intended to address matters other than style. My purpose is simply to suggest that style is very much an issue with Villard and that most of his architectural drawings are more concerned with style than has yet been established.

In his sketch of the bar-tracery frame of a nave aisle window in Reims Cathedral (Plate 35a), he depicted the way in which the geometry of its paired lancets was integrated with the sexfoil rose above them and he showed how the jamb shafts ought to be related to the adjacent clusters of vault-responds on the aisle wall. He also included an inset profile on the central mullion so that one could see exactly how its shafts were to be moulded and how the flanges to hold the glass were to be arranged. He captioned this sketch with an enigmatic remark about a journey to Hungary, concluding: '...I drew it because I liked it better'. Obviously this portion of the cathedral design had struck him as being particularly important. The fact that Villard drew it indicates that he recognised the value of certain details for the overall formal effect of the building.

Reflective of this recognition is the page devoted to profiles (Plate 35b).[2] Four different designs for piers, appropriate to different locations in the cathedral, are shown, with indications of how the stone composing their complex forms should fit together. The most elaborate is one of the crossing piers, on the faces of which the unequal numbers of shafts, representing the different groupings for the crossing itself and for the aisles, are accurately depicted. Sketched adjacent to it is the cluster of respond shafts that divides the bays of the aisle walls, showing the logical correspondence of the shafts to the three types of arches in the aisle vaults: the transverse, diagonal, and wall arches. The third type is a main-arcade pier of the nave, its four shafts corresponding to the vault and elevation elements, shown with tongue and groove joints.[3] The fourth pier purportedly depicts the version situated in the ambulatory between the radiating chapels. Contrary to the actual building, though, it adds subsidiary shafts responding to the vault ribs in order to improve the consistency of the linear articulation. Together the plans of these piers

---

[2] Identification of the forms on the page is based on François Bucher, in *Architector: The Lodge Books and Sketchbooks of Medieval Architects*, New York, 1979, p. 170.

[3] This particular formulation apparently was of great interest to Villard because he had illustrated it earlier in a less detailed version on another page, along with the rose window design from Chartres Cathedral and floor tiles from Hungary.

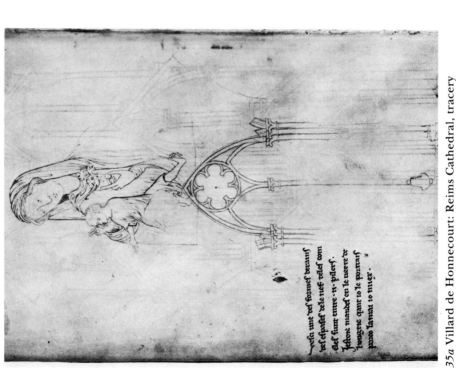

35a Villard de Honnecourt: Reims Cathedral, tracery of a nave window.

35b Villard de Honnecourt: Reims Cathedral, pier plans and window mullion profiles.

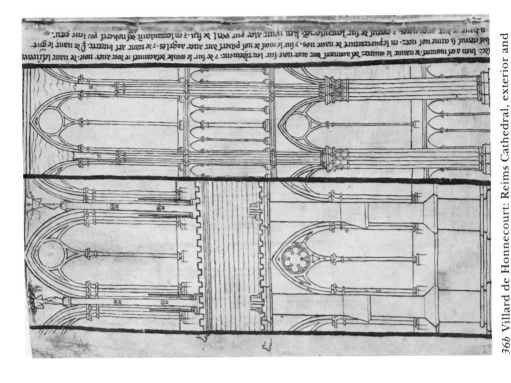

36b Villard de Honnecourt: Reims Cathedral, exterior and interior of main elevation.

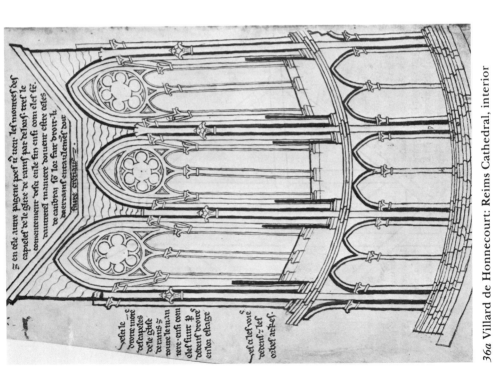

36a Villard de Honnecourt: Reims Cathedral, interior of radiating chapel.

indicate the basic articulating elements of the main elevation and the vault-responds for the crossing and adjacent bays and for the ambulatory and aisles.

Even more explicit are the profiles shown in two rows below the piers, which Villard's caption assigns to the radiating chapel he had illustrated (Plate 36a). The first three details of the upper row most nearly represent the jambs and mullion of a traceried aisle window, like that shown in Plate 35a, followed respectively by profiles of the sexfoil rose, its framing oculus, the lancet arches beneath the rose, and a repeat of the central mullion. The last profile belonging to the window series appears to be the framing arch above the rose, which indicates the depth of the double-shell wall. The last two items in the upper row have been tentatively identified as a triforium base of the south transept and a blind arcade, possibly referring to a drawing now lost. The lower row begins with what may be the sill and stringcourse at the base of a window, followed by profiles of a transverse arch and a rib. The last two items show bases with shafts. In general, these details represent the elements for which an architect made templates and they depict the contours of bases, shafts, and arch mouldings, including all rolls, hollows, quirks, and fillets. Each roll and virtually every shaft that is supposed to be truly round in profile is so indicated by a dot in the centre which implies a compass point in the drawing of a template. Finally, in regard to technical details, it is particularly interesting that on the aisle window of the nave exterior Villard indicated exactly where the joints between the individual segments of the tracery were to occur (Plate 36b).[4] While all these various data have a certain value for the process of construction their primary purpose is to determine the exact configuration of the surface articulation, especially of the shafts and arch mouldings, which, for reasons of scale, could not be included on the elevation. The formulation of the contours is of crucial importance in determining the highlights of rolls and the shadows of concavities, those visual properties that endow the system of articulation with the character of sculptural lines, against the foil of the flat ashlar wall. That Villard chose to select these mouldings for his set of Reims Cathedral drawings indicates that for him the linear effect was the real point of Gothic architecture.

The elevation drawings, particularly of the interior, emphasise nothing so much as the pattern of plastic, linear articulation. In both the chapel and the main elevation (Plate 36a, b), the bar tracery of the windows has the same value as the system of moulded arches and respond shafts on the wall. Indeed this system is represented much more in terms of a consistent, overall pattern than of a skeletal structure. In this regard, one feature of the chapel interior is truly extraordinary: flanking the

---

[4] He showed the tracery joint-pattern also on one of the windows of the chapel exterior, not illustrated here.

shafts that are superimposed upon the wall and the arch mouldings that are separated from the wall by concave channels, a dark shadow is represented by a a black band, wider than any line. Here Villard portrayed the sense of distinctness of these articulating members. In the same vein, he also blacked in the holes of the wall passages above the chapel dado and beneath the clerestory on the exterior elevation (Plate 36b), underlining the fact that the wall is formulated in two planes and that the articulating system thereby appears to stand free of the wall. This very distinctness from the courses of mural ashlar, together with the co-ordination of shafts and pointed arches, endows these linear forms with the character of an interior order of architecture superimposed upon the outer. Describing a trajectory from the bases of the shafts to the keystones of the arches, this linear system is imbued with the illusion of inner vitality, as if it were a dynamic force leaping upward, be it in the main elevation and high vaults or in a blind arcade running beneath the windows. In this context Villard's fixation on bar tracery assumes its full meaning, for this framework in the windows permits the extension of the illusory effect across the voids as well as on the structural surfaces.

Villard expressed the same concern in a different way in his drawings of a tower on the west facade of Laon Cathedral (Plate 37a, b), an example, he averred, that was singular in his experience. In both the plan and elevation he drew only the upper portion that stands above the facade, the portion formulated as an open-work cage of arches and tabernacles. As he states in the caption, he considered drawings of the tower to be conveying its *manière*, a term virtually equivalent to style. Indeed he represented the tower as being more conspicuously composed of slender shafts than it really is. On the canted turrets of the middle stage of the actual tower, for instance, his triplet of monolithic shafts is a reasonably thick octagonal pier with one attached shaft on its outer face, both of which are constructed of coursed masonry. Similarly on both stages of windows the shafts are misleadingly presented as mono-lithic rather than coursed and as more conspicuous and closer together than they really are. There can be no mistake about his intentions, though, for the shafts on the plan, representing only the middle stage of the tower, are shown as fully round, hence as detached, monolithic colonnettes. Although such shafts were already old-fashioned when Villard drew them, *c.* 1220, they are the sort that contrast most sharply with ashlar masonry and so emphasise the illusion of inner vitality in the linear articulation. This emphasis underlines the reason Villard was so taken by the tower: it makes the first instance in which Gothic linear articulation had been extensively applied to an exterior, extending the stylistic effect of the interior to the outside. As he represented the tower, it gives the impression of being reduced to an ethereal composition of sculptured lines.

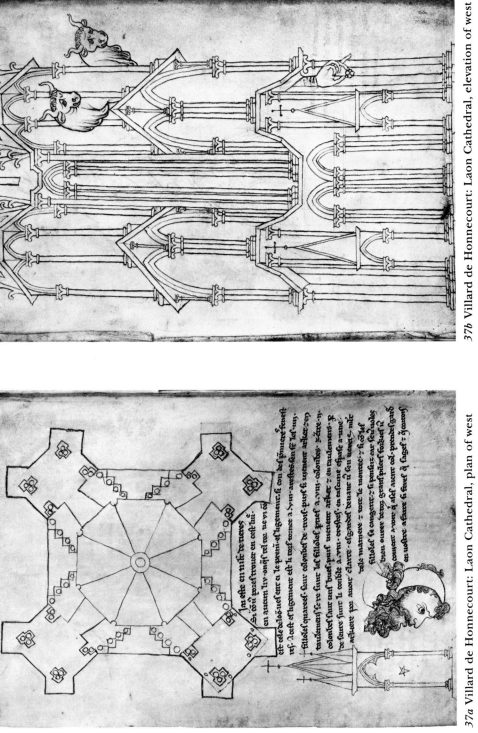

37a Villard de Honnecourt: Laon Cathedral, plan of west facade tower.

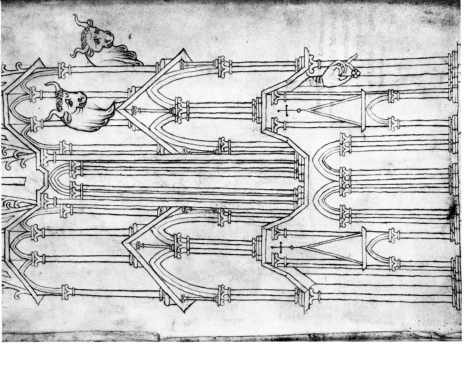

37b Villard de Honnecourt: Laon Cathedral, elevation of west facade tower.

38a Villard de Honnecourt: Chevet plans, an 'ideal' church and Meaux Cathedral

38b Villard de Honnecourt: Miscellaneous details, including a square chapel with star vault

Unexpectedly Villard seems to have focused on a similar aspect of Gothic style when setting out three different plans for Gothic chevets, each drawn in the same manner. Two of them are labeled as actual churches, namely the abbey church of Ste-Marie at Vaucelles and the cathedral of St-Etienne at Meaux. The unlabeled example, often called an 'ideal plan' appears on the page above the chevet of Meaux (Plate 38a). For the purposes of this discussion these latter two suffice to represent the group. Because the plans differ from each other primarily in regard to the number, shape, and disposition of their radiating chapels, it might be assumed that his chief concern in them was spatial distribution; that they represent only the eastern arm of the church could be regarded as adequate for his purpose because the chevet is the most complex portion of a church plan. Upon closer study we can observe that the most conspicuous feature seems to be not so much the arrangement of spaces as the geometry of the vault arches, namely how the vaults are divided into cells and how those cells relate to each other. In each case the geometry has been ideally regularised in order to circumvent the problems of awkward ambulatory bay disposition experienced in actual buildings when the hemicycle severies of the main apse vault radiate more than 180 degrees from the keystone. On all these plans the keystone of the main apse is located on the chord of the apse and is the centre from which the entire vaulting scheme radiates with strict regularity. The vault arches are carefully connected to indications of columnar piers and shafts. Indeed the plan is mainly an ichnographical projection of a pattern of linear articulation, much more concerned with what is above rather than what is at ground level.

That a diagram of the articulation system is the intended emphasis of the chevet plans seems to be confirmed by the plan of a square chapel (Plate 38b), where, because its shape is so simple and ordinary there can be no question of concern for spatial composition. Villard announces its purpose as a demonstration of how to make ribs from eight capitals converge on a single capital without crowding, illustrated in the context of other drawings related to techniques of stoneworking. The ultimate aim of this particular technical solution is to create a star vault (earlier than any constructed example) that, integrated with corresponding wall shafts, determines the entire architectural interest of the structure; in other words, the linear articulation. Since this star vault probably antedates by some years that in the crossing of Amiens Cathedral (which Villard appears not to have visited anyway), it represents an important early instance of the urge to elaborate the linear pattern beyond the configuration of structure.

It is perhaps more than an interesting coincidence that the buildings Villard chose to represent in greatest detail, the cathedrals of Reims and Laon, are those in which linear articulation underwent an historically auspicious new development.[5] The first important application of Gothic linear articulation to any portion of an exterior occurred in the north transept tower of Laon Cathedral where the portion above the facade block was richly articulated with shafts and arch mouldings on diagonally-canted tabernacles as well as enormous openings in the straight faces of the tower. The dual replication of this example in the pair of towers on the west front, on a facade block enriched with a triple porch and flanking pinnacles at ground level and an arcaded passage at the top, produced the first elaborately decorated facade in Gothic architecture. The Laon facade launched a model that would become the paradigm for great churches in the thirteenth century and beyond. But before the next such project was actually undertaken, another development in exterior decoration occurred, at Reims Cathedral.

The introduction of bar tracery in the chevet windows at Reims meant not only the extension of the interior articulation system (hitherto confined to elevation and vaults) across the voids, but also made it visible on both interior and exterior. Appropriately the Reims chevet was the first one to be richly decorated in the Gothic manner. In the spandrels between the radiating chapel windows are carved angels. Above the windows is a cornice-like balustrade articulated as a tracery arcade. Higher up, the flying buttress piers are adorned with shafts and arch mouldings, culminating in the openwork pinnacles which contain large figures of angels, and atop the flyer arches are atlas figures. Between the buttresses are the traceried clerestory windows, decorated with naturalistic masks, and above them, another crowning balustrade of tracery.

From these two examples, Laon and Reims, the application of the linear articulation system to church exteriors became a general pheno-menon. Only at that point can it be said that a building was Gothic both inside and out. Villard's set of drawings depicting the High Gothic choir of Cambrai Cathedral, mentioned in one of his captions but now lost, recorded a design that was the most advanced in his ken, one in which the composition had been arranged so as to permit the articulation system alone to represent the structure.[6] Thus not only the most consistent and conspicuous features of Villard's architectural drawings, but also the examples he chose, reveal to us what he regarded as most important about Gothic architecture, namely that the linear articulating members which animate its surfaces are the key to the aesthetic expressiveness of the Gothic style.

[5] For the sake of concision I have omitted discussion of a decorative tower, the west rose window of Chartres Cathedral, the tracery pattern of a round window of Lausanne Cathedral, and the tabernacle from a choir buttress at Reims Cathedral, all of which are clearly devoted to an interest in the decorative articulation of Gothic architecture.

[6] This loss has now been verified in terms of the codicology of the portfolio by Carl F. Barnes, Jr., and Lon Shelby in 'The Codicology of the Portfolio of Villard de Honnecourt (Paris, Bibliothèque Nationale, Ms. Fr. 19093)', *Scriptorium*, 42, 1988/1, pp. 20–48.

13

'Seeing that it was Done in all the Noble Churches in England'

Peter Draper

Of the many factors which determined the regional variations of English medieval architecture there is one which may not have been accorded sufficient importance: the alleged misogyny of St Cuthbert. In his history of the bishops of Durham, Geoffrey of Coldingham records that Hugh of Le Puiset:

> began to contruct an aisle (*plagam*) at the east end of the church and had marble columns and bases brought from across the sea. However, although employing the most skilful masons at great expense, there were as many beginnings as masters as whenever the walls were built to any great height cracks appeared in them to the peril of the workmen; which was enough to indicate to him that God and his servant Cuthbert disapproved. The work was stopped and transferred to the west where women would be allowed to enter; so those who had not had access to the secret and holy places might gain solace from the contemplation of them.[1]

This account may be construed as implying that the intended new work was in connection with the setting of the shrine but the later construction put upon it by the compiler of the *Rites*, that the intention was to provide a Lady chapel 'whereunto it should be lawful for women to have access', should not be dismissed without further consideration.[2]

Whatever the original function or functions of the 'Galilee' that was finally erected at the west end of the church, an altar to the Virgin there is attested by a charter datable to the 1180s, certainly before 1189. While it has been reasonably argued that in the 1170s and 1180s it is easier to find more examples of the relocation and refurbishment of shrines than it is to find eastern Lady chapels, there is no reason why the intended campaign should not have included provision for a Lady chapel as well as improving access to the shrine.[3] This is just the period when altars dedicated to the Virgin began to be accorded greater importance, sometimes involving the construction of a new chapel. It would not be surprising to find Hugh of Le Puiset at the forefront of this development. The likelihood that the intended building

[1] *Historia Dunelmensis Scriptores Tres*, ed J. Raine, Surtees Society, 9, 1839, p. 11

[2] *Rites of Durham*, ed. J.T. Fowler, Surtees Society, 108, 1902, p. 43.

[3] R. Halsey, 'The Galilee Chapel', in *Medieval Art and Architecture at Durham Cathedral*, British Archaeological Association Conference Transactions, Leeds, 1980, p. 61.

was to include a Lady chapel may be gauged by considering the reasons for the provision of such chapels in the later twelfth century.

It is something of a commonplace in books on the period to refer to the growing importance of devotion to Virgin and to see the increasing number of Lady chapels as one manifestation of this. The implication is that this is an example of a change in devotional practice having a direct effect on architecture. In a general sense all religious buildings have to take account of liturgical practice, but establishing a direct correlation between developments in devotional practice and changes in architectural design is seldom easy, not least because buildings are adaptable and many changes of use can be accommodated within an existing structure. The setting-up of a new chapel might require only minor internal modifications. In the late twelfth and the early thirteenth century, however, a sufficient number of chapels were being built specifically as Lady chapels to warrant the search for an explanation that goes beyond a generalised reference to a rise in the cult of the Virgin during the twelfth century and tries to define more precisely those changes which led to the construction of these chapels.

The architectural historian attempting to pursue this is confronted by several problems. The first and most immediate difficulty is to define what is meant by a Lady chapel. For, in addition to those chapels explicitly dedicated to the Virgin, there are chapels bearing other dedications where masses in honour of the Virgin are known to have been celebrated, as for example at Salisbury, where the grand eastern axial chapel was dedicated to the Trinity but from the beginning the altar was used for Lady masses.[4] On the other hand the known variations in the siting of chapels dedicated to the Virgin means that it cannot be assumed,[5] as it too often is, that a prominent eastern chapel was necessarily a Lady chapel.[6]

Within the Anglo-Norman tradition an additional altar in the central apse-echelon plan was more likely to be in connection with the relics of a saint (as at Durham and Ely) than dedicated to the Virgin, but it may be observed here that if the exceptional late eleventh-century eastern chapel

[4] 'In parte orientali in honorem Sanctae et Individuae Trinitatis et Omnium Sanctorum, super quo de cetero cantabitur missa de beata Virgine singulis diebus', *Registrum S. Osmundi Episcopi*, 2 vols, ed. W.H. Rich Jones, Rolls Series, London, 1884, ii, p. 38. For the dedications of altars in Old Sarum see W.St John Hope 'The Sarum Consuetudinary and its Relation to the Cathedral Church of Old Sarum', *Archaeologia*, 68, 1917, pp. 111-26 where he notes that the only altar dedicated to the Virgin was the high altar. This practice was continued in the new cathedral. The altar of Holy Trinity is referred to as being 'in capella beate Virginis' in a 15th-century processional.

[5] Lady chapels are found at the west end (Glastonbury, Durham), in nave aisles (Canterbury, York), in transepts (Rochester, St Albans, Tewkesbury), and in choir aisles (Ely, Croyland) as well as at the east end.

[6] St John Hope, op. cit., argues that the eastern chapel at Old Sarum was dedicated to St Martin. At Romsey M.F. Hearn, 'The Rectangular Ambulatory in English Medieval Architecture', *Journal of the Society of Architectural Historians*, 30, 1971, pp. 187-209, prefers a dedication for the double eastern chapel there to the two titular saints.

at Winchester did serve as a Lady chapel, it would provide a convenient precedent for the frustrated project at Durham as Le Puiset had been archdeacon at Winchester.[7] In the alternative plan with an ambulatory and radiating chapels the central chapel as often carried other dedications; at Norwich to the Saviour and in the two abbeys at Canterbury to the Trinity. It was common for crypts to be dedicated to the Virgin, again in both abbeys at Canterbury, and at Worcester and Bury St Edmunds. The tradition continues into the thirteenth century with the undercroft of St Stephen's chapel. This association may be significant for this enquiry with the introduction in the twelfth century of the plan with rectangular ambulatory, a form which seems to have been derived from Lotharingian outer crypts.[8] Most, if not all, such crypts were dedicated to the Virgin and this dedication could be retained even when the function of the outer crypt had been incorporated into the main building and the altars placed on the main level.[9] The primary purpose of such crypts was to improve the display of relics and, while this function does seem to have been carried with the form to England, it is less easy to establish that the close association with the Virgin also followed. In those cases where this connection was maintained (the retrochoir at Winchester is a possible example of this) the chapel of the Virgin was part of a larger rebuilding and it would be difficult to claim that the building of the Lady chapel was the prime motivation.[10] There is, however, from the late twelfth century a sufficient number of examples of the addition of prominent Lady chapels to existing churches to suggest that they were being built in response to a newly-felt need.

In the present state of knowledge about architecture in the middle years of the twelfth century it would be unwise to try to claim a first example of such an addition, but the practice would seem to date mainly from the last quarter of the twelfth century and to have gathered momentum through the first half of the thirteenth century. Only a few examples can be quoted here: in the late twelfth century chapels were added at Chichester (almost certainly predating the fire of 1187), at Great Malvern, at Hereford, at Lichfield and at Holy Trinity, Aldgate. In 1220 a substantial Lady chapel was added to Westminster Abbey, though this may have been part of an intended rebuilding of the east end, as was the new Lady chapel which replaced the axial chapel dedicated to the Saviour at Norwich in the

[7] Martin Biddle, *Excavations near Winchester Cathedral, 1961-68*, 1969, p. 70, argues for a dedication to the Virgin following the comparable chapel in the Old Minster whereas Arnold Klukas, 'The Continuity of Anglo-Saxon Liturgical Tradition in Post-Conquest England in the Architecture of Winchester, Ely and Canterbury Cathedrals', *Actes du Colloque Anselmienne*, Bec, 1982, Paris 1984, p. 115 suggests that 'the axial chapel to the east of the high altar now provided a second choir for the additional offices dedicated to All Saints and the Dead' in accordance with the requirements of the *Regularis Concordia*.

[8] M.F. Hearn, op. cit., pp. 187–209.

[9] R. Wallrath, 'Zur Bedeutung der mittelalterlichen Krypta', *Beitraege zur Kunst des Mittelalters*, Berlin, 1948, pp. 54–69.

[10] Draper, 'The Retrochoir of Winchester Cathedral', *Architectural History*, 21, 1978, pp.1–17.

mid thirteenth century. At Lincoln, where the axial chapel in which St Hugh was buried was dedicated to St John the Baptist, the chapel enlarged in the early thirteenth century as the Lady chapel was the northern chapel of the north-east transept. A Lady chapel in a similar position dating from about 1220 is found at St Augustine's, Bristol but this position adjacent to the north transept was to become a particular feature in East Anglia: at Thetford in the first half of the thirteenth century, at Bury *c.* 1275, at Peterborough in the 1270s, and most spectacularly at Ely in the 1320s.

Were these chapels built in response to a need arising from some change in the devotional life of the community served by these churches, and if so, what was that change? Or was the response to a wider, more popular demand? The compiler of the *Rites* mentions the access that women were to have to the Lady chapel. This is a theme which deserves more attention than it has been given. At Ely, for example, Bishop Walpole refers to the commotion caused by the laity, especially women, attending the Lady chapel in the south choir aisle.[11] In general we know little about the access that the public had to the east ends of these churches, especially the monastic churches. Some access was certainly allowed, as is attested by miracles at various shrines. We can easily imagine the sort of problems that could, and obviously did, arise from this to judge from the strictures of the same bishop at Ely, who had to enjoin the monks not to hold illicit conversations with women among the shrines at the east end of the church.[12] St Cuthbert, it seems, wisely foresaw these problems.

Some element of popular demand there may have been for the provision of these chapels, but there is evidence of more direct pressure arising from the greater importance being accorded to the Virgin in the liturgical life of religious communities. Early in the century came the introduction of the Feast of the Conception of the Virgin.[13] This was accepted in the 1120s in a number of major Benedictine houses (Reading, St Albans, Gloucester, Winchcombe, Worcester and Westminster Abbey) led it seems by Bury St Edmunds under Abbot Anselm. Despite opposition to it, notably from St Bernard, it was adopted at the Council of London in 1129. It was also under Abbot Anselm at Bury that it became customary to recite the Office of the Virgin daily. He may also have been responsible for introducing the celebration of a daily mass in honour of the Virgin where it had been traditional to celebrate this weekly on Saturdays.[14] Knowles suggested that this may have begun as a private rather than a communal mass, but the practice seems to have spread widely by the end of the century.[15]

---

[11] S.J.A. Evans, 'Ely Chapter Ordinances and Visitation Records 1241–1515', *Camden Miscellany*, 17, 1940, p. 23.

[12] Ibid., p. 13.

[13] E. Bishop, *Liturgica Historica*, Oxford, 1914, pp. 238–59.

[14] This practice seems to have begun in the Carolingian period and is found in the Sacramentary of Alcuin and later in the *Regularis Concordia*.

[15] D. Knowles, *The Monastic Order in England*, 2nd ed. 1963, pp. 540–41.

In 1194 the Chapter General of the Cistercians ordered a daily mass *De Beata* to be said at a special altar.[16] This was necessary because the solemn mass of the day was celebrated at the high altar, which in Cistercian churches was customarily dedicated to the Virgin. Before 1205 Bishop Savaric instituted a daily mass at Wells and this was confirmed by his successor, Jocelin.[17] In this connection it is interesting that in 1196 the chapter at Wells had taken the decision to preserve the eastern Lady chapel of the earlier church even though it was separate from, and out of alignment with, the rising new church [18] and would mean that Wells would have two Lady chapels.[19] At Salisbury the feasts of the Virgin are given a specially honoured place in the Use of Sarum and Richard Poore instituted a daily mass at the altar of the Trinity in his new church. The wide acceptance of this practice by the turn of the thirteenth century is attested by an entry in the *Gesta Abbatum* at St Albans where it is recorded that hitherto the Lady mass had been held weekly on Saturdays but that Abbot William had ordained, with the full consent of the convent, that a solemn, sung mass of the Virgin should be celebrated daily 'seeing that it was done in all the noble churches in England'.[20] Not only was there to be a daily, rather than a weekly, mass but this was now to be celebrated as a full sung mass and to become the mass next in importance to the celebration at the high altar. This is a clear change in liturgical practice which was almost bound to have consequences for the architectural design of churches. In some churches the need for a new chapel seems to have been felt acutely but at others the effect seems to have been delayed. At St Alban's the altar of the Virgin was greatly embellished with paintings and sculpture during the abbacy of William of Trumpington but the new Lady chapel was not begun for some fifty years and at Ely the Lady chapel remained in the south choir aisle until the new chapel was completed in the 1340s.

In the light of this change in devotional practice, there is no reason why Le Puiset's frustrated building project at the east end of the cathedral

---

[16] Cap. Gen. 1194, LXIII.

[17] A grant of land by Bishop Giso (1061–88) to the 'Chapel of St Mary' was confirmed in 1136. Savaric's institution was 'ut in ecclesia ipsa continua eiusdem dei genetricis virginis habeatur memoria et in eius veneratione missa diebus singulis solemniter celebretur'.

[18] W. Rodwell, 'The Anglo-Saxon and Norman Churches at Wells', in L.S. Colchester, ed., *Wells Cathedral: A History*, pp. 1–23.

[19] In the documents the earlier Lady chapel is referred to as 'iuxta claustrum' to differentiate it from the Lady chapel at the east of the new church.

[20] 'Hic etiam felicis memoriae Abbas Willelmus <Abbot William of Trumpington, 1214–35>, videns quod in omnibus nobilibus ecclesiis Angliae missa de Beata Virgine ad notam solemniter cotidiana decantatur...' *Gesta Abbatum Monasterii Sancti Albani*, Rolls Series, i, p. 284. A daily celebration at the Lady altar is recorded in the time of William's predecessor, Abbot John de Cella (1195–1214): 'Ricardus quoque de Clohale ... contulit unum calicem aureum altari Sanctae Mariae ubi canitur cotidie de ea et pro ecclesia', ibid., I, p. 234. Practice in different orders varied. According to A.A. King, *Liturgies of the Religious Orders*, London 1955, pp. 360–66, the Dominicans only introduced a daily mass *De Beata* during the Octave of the Assumption in 1314.

should not have included a Lady chapel, even though it is not clear what form this eastern extension was intended to take. The chronicler's description of it as *plagam*, usually translated as 'aisle', might imply a returned ambulatory around the former apse.[21] A projecting chapel is a possibility, but given the prevailing tradition in the north, stemming mainly from Roger of Pont l'Eveque's York, it is much more likely to have been in the form of a chapel beneath a high eastern gable or in a low aisle outside the gable.[22] Yet neither form is well suited to the provision of an impressive Lady chapel. This problem was certainly felt later at York, where in 1361 it was stated that there was no suitable place where the mass of the Virgin could be celebrated appropriately in the church.[23] In the Nine Altars Chapel at Fountains the central altar seems to have been dedicated to the Virgin but in the later medieval period the two altars flanking the central one had to be removed to make more space for the Lady chapel. At Durham the central altar of the Nine Altars was dedicated to St Cuthbert and St Bede as the Lady chapel had been firmly established at the west end. At Ripon the Lady chapel was placed over the sacristy adjacent to the south choir aisle.

The rather modest provision for Lady chapels in these northern buildings is in marked contrast to the prominence so often given to these chapels in the south. The regional variation is striking, with the high gable prevailing north and east of a line drawn approximately between Chester and Lincoln and the low ambulatory with projecting chapel to the south and west of that line. The geographical distribution cuts across the opposing diagonal of the oolite limestone belt and the architectural affiliations include both secular and monastic churches. Of course other factors, such as the display of relics, influenced the design of east ends but it is noticeable that the most prominent Lady chapels are to be found in the province of Canterbury.[24] York retained its own Use throughout the Middle Ages, independent of Sarum, and it may be that the rivalry between the two provinces was itself a factor in determining the arrangements made for Lady chapels. It is diverting to speculate how differently provision might have been made in the north if Hugh of Le Puiset's ambitions had not been frustrated by St Cuthbert.

---

[21] R.E. Latham, *Revised Medieval Latin Word List*, Oxford, 1965.

[22] The full-height east gable seems the more likely reconstruction though Willis's suggestion of an eastern aisle with chapels like Byland is still favoured by Eric Gee, 'Architectural History until 1290', in G.E. Aylmer and R. Cant, eds, *A History of York Minster*, Oxford, 1977, p. 122.

[23] 'Non fuerat aliquis locus congruus ubi missa gloriosae dei genetricis et Virginis Mariae cotidie in ipsa ecclesia celebranda decenter poterat celebrari', Chapter Act, Register Gc, fo. 52.

[24] In the 'southern' outliers of the 'northern' high gable type, the Lady chapel at Lincoln led off the north-east transept, at Ely it was in the south choir aisle, but at Old St Paul's it is worth noting that two full bays were allotted to the spacious Lady chapel at the east end.

14

Cui Bono? The Saint, the Clergy and the New Work at St Albans

Nicola Coldstream

The Trinity chapel of Canterbury Cathedral is a shrine built to immortalise the memory of a British saint who was unequivocally martyred. In shape and function it follows the tradition of the *martyrium*; the Trinity altar, important though it was, had at best only an equal claim to its place in the chapel. The example of Canterbury, if not its plan, was presumably partly responsible for the cavernous eastern extensions that from the late twelfth century sheltered other British saints resting in elevated grandeur behind the high altar. Many of the great thirteenth-century extensions to or replacements of Anglo-Norman choirs are associated with shrines, and it has become commonplace to see their primary purpose as the setting for the main shrine. Attention is drawn to the shrine-like decoration of Ely, Lincoln and Winchester, which seems to confirm the hypothesis.[1] At Durham the fund raisers placed considerable emphasis on the need to provide a suitable setting for the shrine of St Cuthbert, and at Ely, Westminster, Lincoln and London a grand renewal of the shrine itself was undertaken at the same time as the rebuilding.[2]

The history of St Albans suggests that if this interpretation is valid for some churches, for others it takes insufficient account of all the interests involved in a major rebuilding where the needs of the dead saint and his pilgrims had to be balanced by those of the living clergy. For all the post-Reformation destruction, misuse and restoration, St Albans has retained a palimpsest of the medieval arrangement of the eastern arm, back to the Anglo-Norman abbey church. Its late medieval liturgical layout has survived, and there is also some record of the changes made by successive abbots to altars, images and shrines. From these we can derive a clear picture of the clergy's intentions as they strove to create ordered logic out of disordered confusion.

---

[1] P. Draper, 'Bishop Northwold and the Cult of St Etheldreda', British Archaeological Association Conference Transactions, *Medieval Art and Architecture at Ely Cathedral*, 1979, p. 10; P. Draper, 'The Retrochoir of Winchester Cathedral', *Architectural History*, 21, 1979, pp. 1–17; V. Glenn, 'The Sculpture of the Angel Choir at Lincoln', *Medieval Art and Architecture at Lincoln Cathedral*, British Archaeological Association Conference Transactions, 1986, p. 102.

[2] *Rites of Durham*, ed. J.T. Fowler, Surtees Society, 107, 1902, p. 150.

Like Becket, St Alban was martyred, but he was unlike him in other ways. He could never have been the focus of political protest, and he deserved sympathy, or he would have if his story were not historically doubtful. Alban was the protomartyr of Britain, and his was the only cult that was continuous from Roman times. [3] The pre-Conquest site of his shrine has not yet been found, [4] but in 1129 the saint's remains were translated to the new Anglo-Norman church, probably to a position behind the high altar, for which precedents had been established at Durham, Winchester and elsewhere. In any case, the shrine was certainly there when, according to Matthew Paris, it was completed by Abbot Simon (1166–83) and set up on high so that it could be seen by the celebrant at the high altar.[5] In 1177 the relics of St Alban's mythical companion Amphibalus were discovered at Redbourne in Hertfordshire, and the cult was further boosted in 1257 when the grave of St Alban himself came to light while they were preparing to rebuild the east end of the church.[6]

The Anglo-Norman presbytery of the abbey church ended in three parallel apses (Plate 39a), and the aisles were divided from the main vessel by solid walls. The monks' choir occupied the crossing and the first three bays of the nave. When in 1257 cracks were discovered in the eastern arm, the apses were demolished and the presbytery renovated and extended eastwards. The presbytery itself was divided into five bays; the solid walls of the first three were retained, but cut back, with upper entrances newly opened from the aisles into the bay next to the crossing. The two eastern bays of the presbytery, which became the feretory or shrine chapel, were properly arcaded, and the arcade extended across the east wall under the high gable. East of the high gable was built the new work, a single-storey structure consisting of an aisled vestibule or ante-chapel leading to an aisleless Lady chapel, in a slightly echelonné plan that allowed for short lengths of east-facing walls very suitable for altars (Plate 39b). The vestibule was decorated with foliage sculpture whose high quality can still just be seen *in situ* where the restorers could not reach it, but it is also apparent in the fragments excavated by Biddle.[7]

As a setting for a shrine the new work, while by no means as spectacular as Canterbury, Ely or Lincoln, nevertheless seems admirably planned.

[3] D.H. Farmer, *Oxford Dictionary of Saints*, Oxford, 1978, p. 8 (hereafter cited as Farmer).

[4] M. Biddle, 'Archaeology, Architecture and the Cult of Saints in Anglo-Saxon England', in L.A.S. Butler and R.K. Morris, ed., *The Anglo-Saxon Church. Papers on History, Architecture and Archaeology in Honour of Dr H.M. Taylor*, CBA Research Report 60, London 1986, pp. 13–16.

[5] *Gesta Abbatum*, Rolls Series, i, p. 189.

[6] *Chronica Maiora*, Rolls Series, v, p. 608. Farmer, p. 8. The site of the Anglo-Saxon church was almost certainly not beneath the Anglo-Norman building, and this auspicious discovery is decidedly reminiscent of the discovery of the tomb of Arthur at Glastonbury.

[7] For references see Biddle, op. cit., p. 13.

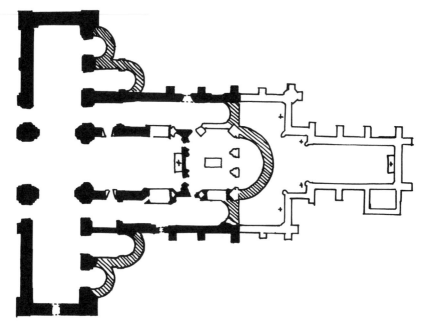

39a Schematic plan of St Albans Abbey Church showing Anglo-Norman
   presbytery (solid), apses (hatched: destroyed), and thirteenth-century
   extension (outline). The positions of the main altars are marked with
   crosses, and the shrine is shown between the apse and the high altar.

39b St Albans Abbey Church, looking north-east from the shrine chapel to the
   ante-chapel (left) and the Lady Chapel (right).

There is ample space for pilgrims to gather in the vestibule, whence the feretory is clearly visible through the arcades. Pilgrims could not, however, have entered the church directly opposite the shrine as they could at the non-monastic Lincoln: the monk's cemetery to the south and their vineyard to the north precluded any such doors.

The present liturgical arrangement at St Albans is, courtesy of the nineteenth and twentieth centuries, that of the fifteenth: the site of the high altar in the late fifteenth century can be deduced from the altar screen, which was erected by 1484 and completely blocks the view into the feretory from the west. The watching loft on the north side of the feretory was made between 1400 and 1420, and the tomb of Humphrey, Duke of Gloucester, on the south side dates from *c.* 1450.[8] The base of the shrine of St Alban was reconstructed from fragments in the nineteenth century and placed in what was presumed to be its position after 1308, the middle of the feretory.[9] In the late Middle Ages, two altars, of the Relics and the Salutation, stood against the east arcade.[10] This layout is not the fruits of an ecclesiologist's dream: the late medieval additions of tomb, watching loft and screen were embellishments to an arrangement that existed from the early fourteenth century. There is good reason to suppose that this itself reflected the Anglo-Norman layout except in one particular detail. Essential to the argument is the Anglo-Norman site of the high altar, and as understanding of what the clergy were trying to do with their new thirteenth-century building stems from that, the point is worth pursuing.

At Durham, which also had three parallel apses but choir arcades, the high altar was on the chord of the central apse and the shrine of St Cuthbert in the apse itself. Matthew Paris gives evidence that at St Albans the shrine was in the apse, but not that the high altar was on the chord, and Peers collected other evidence, some negative, that the altar stood some way west of it.[11] In all the records of embellishments to altars and chapels there is no evidence that the high altar was ever moved; and its position relative to the thirteenth-century architecture is itself suggestive. It is set, not opposite two piers, but stranded in the middle of a bay, with the shrine chapel oddly occupying a bay and a half to its east. The solid walls of the presbytery stop half a bay short of the altar. The impression is most strongly given that the measurements for the vaulting took priority over the high altar; the bay divisions of 1257 have every appear-

---

[8] Victoria History of the Counties of England, *Hertfordshire*, 2, p. 494 (hereafter cited as VCH).

[9] VCH, 2, p. 493; J.T. Micklethwaite, 'The Shrine of St Alban', *Archaeological Journal*, 29, 1872, pp. 201–11.

[10] VCH, 2, p. 493

[11] *Chronica Maiora*, 5, p. 608; Peers, in VCH, 2, p. 493, accepts in the main text that the altar was on the chord, but in a footnote he expresses doubts. What follows here is the result of testing Peers' doubts.

ance of being established in spite, rather than because, of the altar, as if it were an immovable fixture. The pragmatists seem to have won the argument.

More seriously, what is known of the disposition of other altars in the Anglo-Norman church also suggests that the high altar is in its original place. There were two other altars at the east end of the main vessel, dedicated to Saints Oswin and Wulfstan. That of St Oswin was almost certainly set up after Tynemouth became a cell of St Albans in 1085;[12] the monks had further reason to emphasise it when Durham was trying unsuccessfully to recover Tynemouth during the twelfth century. St Oswin's was the matutinal altar. St Wulfstan's altar was not dedicated to him until after 1218, when Abbot William of Trumpington (1214–35) returned from the translation ceremony at Worcester bearing one of the saint's ribs.[13] There was not room in the apse for a big shrine base and two altars, and it is more likely that they were placed to the right and left of the apse entrance, where their successors, those of the Relics and Salutation, are known to have stood from the early fourteenth century.[14] As the solid presbytery walls prevented movement to or from the aisles, all moves had to be made within the main vessel. The high altar would have to be sited well clear of the two altars, one of which was used for the morrow mass, to allow sufficient space. Between 1302 and 1308 Abbot John de Maryns 'moved and adorned' the shrine of St Alban;[15] the direction can only have been westward into the newly designed feretory. Had the high altar stood east of its present position, the shrine would have displaced it. *Gesta Abbatum* does not mention the altar.[16]

The present layout, then, reflects that of Anglo-Norman times (with the possible addition of the Wulfstan altar), with the exception of the shrine. After 1257 the major altars of the central vessel remained in place. Those at the ends of the aisles presumably moved two bays to the east, and two new ones were established either side of the entrance to the Lady chapel. The only piece of liturgical furniture in the main vessel that did not stay in its original place was the shrine, which was moved a few feet westward, clear of the new work.

The shrine was not the only object in the eastern arm to have been shifted about. In 1257 the whole east end was cluttered and obstructed. Abbot Trumpington was an energetic rearranger of the church furniture, his main effort being the creation of a Lady chapel in the south choir aisle, an operation requiring some architectural reworking. He moved Amphibalus' relics from the north aisle, where they had lain since 1186,

[12] Farmer, p. 307.
[13] VCH, 2, p. 493; Farmer, p. 414.
[14] VCH, 2, p. 493.
[15] *Gesta Abbatum*, 2, p. 107.
[16] The freedom of movement now given by the aisles and arcades presumably obviated the inconvenient bulk of the shrine base.

to a place over the new Rood in the nave, and the old Rood and a statue of the Virgin were put in the north aisle.[17] With the new building, the shrine of Amphibalus was set up in the vestibule, more or less on the previous site of St Alban's shrine, and the Lady altar was established at the extreme east of the church.

It is significant that the plan chosen for the new work at St Albans was quite different from its immediate forerunner at Ely and its contemporaries at Lincoln and Old St Paul's. The new work shows none of the makeshift adaptation characterising the presbytery. The design was evidently chosen with care, and it belongs to a type by then well-established and exemplified by the cathedrals of Winchester and Salisbury. These buildings are quite unlike Ely, Lincoln and London, where the eastern arm, running full height from the crossing to the east wall, surrounded and enclosed the shrine in an architecturally unified space that matched, in its expensive and glossy materials, the shrine itself. Winchester and Salisbury have low extensions beyond the east gable, like St Albans. It has been argued that both were intended as shrine chapels.[18] Although Osmund of Salisbury was not canonised until 1457 they had tried for canonisation soon after his remains were translated to the eastern chapel in 1226; at Winchester, however, the retrochoir and the shrine area were completely reorganised and a new shrine base made in 1476, which, with the efflorescence of superb funerary monuments there in the fifteenth century, suggests that it was then that the shrine was moved, and that whatever Bishop de Lucy's building may have been, it was not intended as a shrine chapel.[19]

Evidence at Durham, Ely, Lincoln and London is more equivocal. At Durham the shrine is separated from its 'setting' by the change of level and the transverse plan of the chapel of the Nine Altars, an effect that may have been dictated by geology but probably suited the clergy who used the altars. At both Lincoln and London the extreme east was set aside for a Lady chapel, giving the same arrangement as St Albans, but marking it by screens rather than the architectural design. At Ely alone does the emphasis seem to have been wholly on the shrines, with St Etheldreda's two companions given space at the east, and the Lady chapel remaining in the south choir aisle (where it stayed until the

[17] VCH, 2, pp. 493–94.

[18] P. Draper, 'The Retrochoir of Winchester Cathedral', *Architectural History*, 21, 1978, pp. 1–17.

[19] I am grateful to Mr John Crook for discussing with me his findings at Winchester, which are to be published in J. Crook, 'The Architectural Background for the Cult of St Swithun in Winchester Cathedral', in M. Biddle and B. Kjolbe-Biddle, *The Anglo-Saxon Minsters of Winchester* (Winchester Studies, 4, ii, in preparation); see also, P. Tudor-Craig and L. Keen, 'A Recently Discovered Purbeck Marble Screen of the Thirteenth Century and the Shrine of St Swithun', *Medieval Art and Architecture at Winchester Cathedral*, British Archaeological Association Conference Transactions, 1983, pp. 63–72; E.C. Norton, 'The Medieval Tile Pavements of Winchester Cathedral', ibid., pp. 78–93 (p. 80).

burial requirements of the bishops and possibly the threatened collapse of the central tower forced the monks to build a new Lady chapel out to the north). Even at Ely the main saint stayed where she had rested since the Anglo-Norman translation, and the new building was put up round and well to the east of the shrine. At Lincoln and London the shrine did move eastwards, at Lincoln to move it out of the north-east transept, in London because the whole liturgical choir was moved eastwards. These were nevertheless special cases; it was not usual to move a shrine far from its traditional, holy site, and what happened to St Erkenwald in London contrasts strongly with the fate of, for example, St Wenceslas in Prague, whose shrine chapel remained the one fixed point in a cathedral that extended to its north, east and west in successive rebuildings.[20] In England, Saints Cuthbert and Swithun stayed, like Etheldreda, in their traditional places, and as if to emphasise the sense that a shrine may be part of a new work but not 'of' it, the Durham and Winchester shrines were on elevated platforms, as at St Albans, marked out as distinct spaces by arcading.

At St Albans we know what was moved and the exact journey of each piece; we also know what was not moved. From this we can draw a few conclusions about the purpose of the moves. The new design opened up the aisles for circulation and allowed the altars, shrine and people to be arranged in an ordered sequence. It clarified and enlarged the liturgical spaces. The new work was a setting for the cult of the Virgin and some extra chantry altars; its relation to the shrines of Saints Alban and Amphibalus was secondary. There was a tripartite emphasis in the eastern arm on high altar, shrine and Lady chapel, and the high altar, not the shrine, dictated the layout. This is true of all the big eastern extensions, but in the buildings of boxlike design, where the divisions were marked by screens, the clarity of purpose has been lost in post-Reformation reorderings that continue to this day. At St Albans, however, the architectural design has ensured the survival of the medieval arrangement, and it shows how a thirteenth-century monastic community tried to balance its own requirements against those of the lay world. The monks and priests were screened by the solid walls of their choir and presbytery, which they chose not to demolish; the area beyond the presbytery was now accessible through the aisles, and until the late fifteenth century the feretory was so arranged that the clergy could see the shrine from the west and pilgrims could have access to it from the aisles and vestibule; the vestibule was both assembly hall and chantry chapel; and the Virgin was now properly celebrated in her own chapel. St Albans offers a rare glimpse of the medieval clergy setting out a building appropriate both to the patron saint and the *Opus Dei*.

---

[20] P. Crossley, *Gothic Architecture in the Reign of Kasimir the Great*, Cracow, 1985, p. 48.

15

The Iconography of the Angel Choir at Lincoln Cathedral

T.A. Heslop

Medieval architecture and the sculpture attached to it are currently regarded as two separate areas of study. There are some benefits in this division. As far as sculpture is concerned, it focuses attention on the development of certain forms; for instance the portal or the roof boss. As a result typologies emerge which facilitate the approximate dating of individual examples and the assessment of their relative conformity with earlier monuments. If they are seen to break new and subsequently influential ground, they may be deemed historically important. The Angel Choir at Lincoln (*c.* 1255–80) has been a prime example of this separatist approach since many of the papers devoted to its sculpture deal with one aspect alone. Thus we have C.J.P. Cave's short monograph on the bosses, Arthur Gardner's pamphlet on the angels, and Marion Roberts' discussion of the Judgement Portal and its possible relationship to Westminster Abbey.

Helpful as such works are in clarifying chronological sequences and exposing 'seminal monuments' within a notional evolution, there is a clear danger that important issues will be lost to view. Principal among them is the reason for making the sculpture in the first place. We may be fairly sure that no portal or roof boss was created either to allow historians an extra means of dating a building nor, as Clement Greenburg was to put it, 'to keep culture moving'. So what was the sculpture for? At one level the answer is obvious enough; a building with certain pretensions can signal its status by sculptural embellishment. Of course, the nature, location and iconography of sculpture is subject to fashion. The Angel Choir is a case in point; it has a Judgement Portal (which was a popular species) and its roof bosses do fit comfortably in a line of descent from those at Worcester and Ely cathedrals and Westminster Abbey. However, there is arguably more to the siting of these features at Lincoln than the desire to be identified with other recent and prestigious churches. There is a relative consistency in the placing and association of the sculpture which suggests that the viewer was being informed about the meaning of the building. For, as well as articulating it architectonically, the sculpture specifies a significant reading of the whole eastern extension.

This is a large claim, but the means which the designers employed to carry it through were actually very simple and based on a series of primary oppositions. Essentially east was better than west and higher was better than lower. If we begin by looking at the Judgement Portal with these hierarchies in mind various 'problems' are resolved at once. For example, it has always been regarded as an oddity (typical of Lincoln) that the figure of Synagogue is placed on Christ's right, traditionally the side of the Blessed. However, what matters here is that it is to the west and that the corresponding figure of Ecclesia is to the east, which is liturgically the more important direction. As a consequence of the partial subversion of the normal meanings of left and right within the iconography of Judgement, various accommodations have been necessary. The mouth of Hell has been placed in the centre below Christ's feet, rather than in the more usual position in the lower right hand, 'sinister' corner of the composition. Had it been placed there at Lincoln, it would have been adjacent to Ecclesia, an association which would have conveyed precisely the wrong message. A similar difficulty arose over the Wise and Foolish Virgins, represented on the outer voussoirs. Only the Wise Virgins would normally be on Christ's right hand side, but at Lincoln this was the side of Synagogue so the Foolish Virgins had to appear there. Rather than move the Wise Virgins to the sinister side, it was decided to signal their greater virtue by placing them above their Foolish sisters in the same archivolt. Although it is not carried out with absolute consistency (there are devils on the tympanum to Christ's left), the logic of the system is clear. The principal drawback as far as art historians are concerned is that these rules are not those we are accustomed to on 'canonical' French doorways.

The priorities manifest on the Judgement Portal extend to the roof-bosses in the interior (Table 1). One walks though the door into the central bay of the south aisle. Looking up at the ridge rib of its vault one sees at the junction of the western tiercerons a 'man and monster' combat scene. On the eastern boss of the same bay is a scholarly disputation. These subjects set the tone for the series beyond them. Further west are dragons, while to the east are the Coronation of the Virgin, David enthroned in the Tree of Jesse, then a prophet speaking to a king followed by an enigmatic scene in which a young man approaches a crowned woman seated with two dogs. Whatever uncertainties exist about the precise identification of some of these scenes, the east/west divide is clear enough. The monsters, combat and dragons to the west are generally different from the graceful histories and holy mysteries to the east. If anything the distinction between the two directions in the aisle is even clearer than it was on the portal. The general implications of the scheme are obvious. The holiest part of the church, with its altars and shrines, is the eastern end. By contrast the associations of the westerly direction were with temporal existence, its snares and tribulations.

To elucidate any further involves unravelling the subject matter of

Table 1

Lincoln, Cathedral, Angel Choir: layout of the basic subject
matter in the south aisle and main vessel.

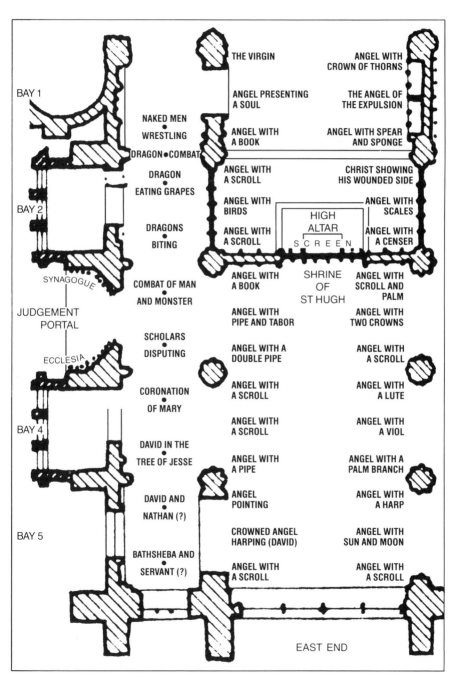

BAY 1

BAY 2

BAY 4

BAY 5

SYNAGOGUE

JUDGEMENT
PORTAL

ECCLESIA

THE VIRGIN

ANGEL WITH
CROWN OF THORNS

ANGEL PRESENTING
A SOUL

THE ANGEL OF
THE EXPULSION

NAKED MEN
•
WRESTLING

ANGEL WITH
A BOOK

ANGEL WITH SPEAR
AND SPONGE

DRAGON • COMBAT

DRAGON
•
EATING GRAPES

ANGEL WITH
A SCROLL

CHRIST SHOWING
HIS WOUNDED SIDE

ANGEL WITH
BIRDS

HIGH
ALTAR
SCREEN

ANGEL WITH
SCALES

DRAGONS
•
BITING

ANGEL WITH
A SCROLL

ANGEL WITH
A CENSER

COMBAT OF MAN
•
AND MONSTER

ANGEL WITH
A BOOK

SHRINE
OF
ST HUGH

ANGEL WITH
SCROLL AND
PALM

ANGEL WITH
PIPE AND TABOR

ANGEL WITH
TWO CROWNS

SCHOLARS
•
DISPUTING

ANGEL WITH A
DOUBLE PIPE

ANGEL WITH
A SCROLL

CORONATION
•
OF MARY

ANGEL WITH
A SCROLL

ANGEL WITH
A LUTE

ANGEL WITH
A SCROLL

ANGEL WITH
A VIOL

DAVID IN THE
•
TREE OF JESSE

ANGEL WITH
A PIPE

ANGEL WITH A
PALM BRANCH

DAVID AND
•
NATHAN (?)

ANGEL
POINTING

ANGEL WITH
A HARP

CROWNED ANGEL
HARPING (DAVID)

ANGEL WITH
SUN AND MOON

BATHSHEBA AND
•
SERVANT (?)

ANGEL WITH
A SCROLL

ANGEL WITH
A SCROLL

EAST END

individual bosses. David harping in the Tree of Jesse and the Coronation of the Virgin are unmistakable, but the other three compositions present problems of interpretation. The suggestion that the next boss in the series depicts David and Nathan was made by C.J.P. Cave, apparently on no other grounds that it is the obvious interpretation of a scene in which a prophet talks to a king. It is quite likely to be an Old Testament subject since both figures hold scrolls, and bearing in mind that the adjacent image to the west shows the Tree of Jesse, the onus of proof surely lies with those who think it represents anything other than David and Nathan. If, as I am supposing, the sequence of bosses contains a coherent story, then the next scene must surely represent Bathsheba visited by David's servant (2 Samuel 11:3), shown as a quasi-Annunciation. It may be thought that this is far too disgraceful an episode for representation at the east end of a church interior. Yet exegetes in the Middle Ages, while acknowledging the literal impropriety of David courting another man's wife, were at pains to point out the wholesome spiritual meaning of the story, which was that in freeing Bathsheba from an undesirable union with Uriah the Hittite, David presented a typological analogy to Christ's rescuing humanity from subservience to inferior religion for a more fulfilling congress with him though his church. In that sense Bathsheba, like Mary, signified Ecclesia.

This identification of the boss might be questioned on the grounds that the lady already wears a crown, which Bathsheba ought not to do as early as her reception of David's servant. However, we are in no position to know how the 'commission' was worded. If the sculptor were instructed 'to depict a beautiful woman, the beloved of the king, receiving his messenger' he might arrive independently at such an image, but it could equally be that the crown was stipulated so as to make more obvious the association between Bathsheba and Ecclesia/Mary. This is necessarily pure speculation. The point of principle at issue is that the general context of the boss, relative to the adjacent sculpture and to the devotional arrangements in the church itself, may be more help in understanding the subject matter than the minutiae of the individual composition, and ought therefore to be given at least as much weight in any argument.

The final uncertain subject in this sort of sequence of five figurative scenes in the south aisle is the pair of men disputing, on the most westerly boss, just inside the Judgement Portal. One of the men holds a scroll and the other has the long beard and receding hairline which usually characterise St Paul. We may suppose that they are representative, respectively, of the Old and the New Law, and that their purpose is to alert the spectator to the continuity which links the veiled reference to Christ and the Church in the story of David and Bathsheba and the revealed truth of it in the Coronation of Ecclesia/Mary.

So far we have considered only one set of sculptural signposts in the

church. The visitor entering the building though the Judgement Porch
can take the road of strife and temptation to the west or the road to
union with Christ and his church to the east. But most people using the
door would have been drawn neither left nor right, but straight on
towards the principal glory of the minster, the shrine of Great St Hugh.
This probably lay at the western end of the central bay of the five bay
extension. The desire for a prominent site for St Hugh's body was
arguably the main reason for the whole Angel Choir project, so it is not
surprising that his relics were in this focal position. But what was the
nature of this place where Hugh lay?

The Angel Choir gets its name from the heavenly host which occupies
the spandrels of the gallery. Strictly it is a misnomer since this part of the
building was not used by the canons of Lincoln as their liturgical choir.
Nor does the term describe the angels themselves who are an orchestra
rather than singers; or at least half of them are. The musicians, in fact,
inhabit only the zone east of the screen behind the high altar, which is
represented as celestial paradise. The associations of the figures in the
two western bays are altogether different. Christ displays his wounds,
angels carry Instruments of the Passion (crown of thorns, sponge and
spear) or scales. Another presents a soul to the Virgin Mary. None of this
is about being in paradise, rather it is about getting there. As a starting
point we are given, apparently, the Expulsion of Adam and Eve. Then
follow the means of redemption though the Passion, through the blood
of Our Saviour, through judgement, and by means of the love and pity of
Mary.

The dividing line between this region and 'paradise' is marked by an
angel with a scroll in his left hand and a palm branch in his right. The
palm is of course a symbol of those who have entered paradise and
another attribute of that blessed state, crowns, are held aloft by his
immediate neighbour. Those entering this part of the church are being
given intimations of the eternal bliss which St Hugh, whose shrine was
directly below, had already attained. It is clear enough that the paradise
within Lincoln Minster was where one would expect, at this eastern
extremity (Genesis 2:8).

As all those who have played the game have discovered, considerable
ingenuity is required to explain in detail the iconography of some of the
spandrel figures. In the western bays, the angel seated upon two 'hawks'
and feeding a third is particularly enigmatic. Given the setting of this
composition within the same zone as the Angel of Judgement but also
adjacent to the high altar table, a suitable text would be Revelation
19:17: 'an angel saying unto the fowls that fly in the midst of heaven.
Come and gather yourselves unto the supper of the great God'. Within
the eastern bays the most surprising subject is the bearded and crowned
'angel' with a harp in the central spandrel of the south-eastern bay.
Arthur Gardner, in his pamphlet on the Lincoln Angels, identified this

figure unequivocally as 'King David', notwithstanding the large, spreading wings which emerge from his shoulders. Gardner was surely right. Angels may have harps and head fillets, though hardly crowns, but they do not have beards so this is not really an angel. Then again, the wings can hardly be a mistake since, had they been carved in error, they could have been pared away when the anomaly was recognised. The intention must always have been, for some reason, to show David assimilated to an angelic orchestra, and the wings were an obvious way to do it. It may or may not be significant that the position chosen for him is above the two bosses in the south aisle identified earlier as Davidic subjects.

The fact that there are elements of the iconography of the Lincoln Angel Choir which seem inscrutable should not prevent us from trying to make broad sense of the whole. There is indeed a general methodological issue at stake here; do we try to identify all the parts and then see what kind of whole they constitute, or do we allow our perception of a total scheme (albeit across the centuries, darkly) to guide us in our attempts to explain the parts? I prefer the latter course not, as a cynic might suppose, because it suits my purpose but because it has two mutually supporting factors in its favour. The first is that if we believe in the concept of an iconographic programme at all, then the parts which constitute it are likely to be subservient either to a narrative sequence or to a theme (or occasionally both). The second is that the notion that the sculpture in mid thirteenth-century English buildings works in tandem with the buildings themselves can be tested in other cases. In fact it already has been. The explication outlined above for the eastern extensions of Lincoln is based on one that was developed to account for the disposition of various sculptural subjects in Westminster Abbey.

The Westminster story may be recapitulated very briefly. In the nave aisles there are secular subjects: heraldry in the spandrels of the blind arcading and combat bosses in the aisle vaults above. Only in the eastern and therefore in the most important bay is this modified. There one finds foliate bosses above the shields of the Edward the Confessor, the Holy Roman Emperor and the kings of France and England. In the western aisles of the transept arms there are sacred subjects in the bosses and to a large extent also in the spandrels. Further east the bosses are foliate (perhaps signifying the verdancy of paradise) and the spandrels show angels attending crowned figures (the Blessed), or an angel holding crowns, or more foliage. The significant exception to this general scheme is the richly sculptured area to the west side of the south transept now known as the Muniment Room. Here are found the famous and beautiful combat scenes and the corbel of a crowned man and a woman. There is a current of a opinion, to which I subscribe, that this vantage point, with its separate access staircase, was the king's pew. The change of content in the sculpture certainly implies a relatively secular function.

At Westminster the idea that the sculpture indicates the status and the function of parts of the building is not fully exploited. Nonetheless, the thought processes are visible enough. In the Lincoln Angel Choir there seems to be a more concerted effort to integrate the portal, roof bosses and spandrel angels into the overall scheme. The idea which the scheme serves is the commonplace that part at least of the church is an image of the Heavenly Jerusalem or of paradise on earth. To enter it one passes from this world through Judgement either as represented on the portal or in the equivalent redemption sequence in the westernmost spandrels of the gallery. If one makes the 'mistake' of turning to the west on entering the portal, there are warnings within the bosses overhead that one is heading in the direction of strife and deceit. To the east is the solace of Christ's union with his Church. Straight ahead lies paradise, where one can commune with St Hugh.

It may be objected that if these sculptures are signposts, then they fail in their first duties which are to be easily visible and readily intelligible. Yet we are hardly in a position to say quite what the intended 'audience' was, how it looked at the buildings or how good it was at reading sculpture. As the examples accumulate of changes in pier design which indicate main altar spaces, or of the disposition of rich marble to emphasise the position of a shrine, it becomes clear that there were at least two categories of people who knew that buildings contained signs: those who designed them and those who were persuaded to part with the money that was required to fund expensive variation. It is nigh on impossible to believe that these two parties, each with its vested interest, did not use such ingenuity to increase the mystique of their profession or the allure of their church. Similar 'designatory' sculpture may be found in many other buildings, English and continental, and in other centuries, and yet as a mode of medieval artistic behaviour it has gone largely undiscussed. Thanks largely to the advocacy of Emile Mâle, French portal sculpture has gained the modern academic award for logic and programmatic consistency. One may argue that the prize should really have gone to Mâle. However that may be, a more broadly significant use of sculpture, elucidating as it does the meaning of the architecture itself, was current at the same time and is writ large in one of PK's favourite buildings, Lincoln Minster.

Bibliographical Note:

In deference to the recipient's well-known aversion to footnotes, this offering is provided with no more than a short bibliography.

C.J.P. Cave, *Lincoln Roof Bosses*, Lincoln Minster Pamphlets, no. 3, 1951.
A. Gardner, *A Handbook of Medieval Sculpture*, 1935.
A. Gardner, *The Lincoln Angels*, Lincoln Minster Pamphlet, no. 6, 1960.

V. Glenn, 'The Sculpture of the Angel Choir at Lincoln', *Medieval Art and Architecture at Lincoln Cathedral*, British Archaeological Association Conference Transactions, 1986, pp. 102–8.

T.A. Heslop, 'The Sculpture of Westminster Abbey, 1245–72', *The Cambridge Guide to the Arts of Britain, ii, The Middle Ages*, ed. Boris Ford, 1988, pp. 178–84.

W.R. Lethaby, 'Notes on the Sculpture Lincoln Minster: The Judgement Porch and the Angel Choir', *Archaeologia*, 60, 1907, pp. 379–90.

A.J. Minnis, *The Medieval Theory of Authorship: Scholastic Literary Attitudes in the Later Middle Ages*, 1984, pp. 103–8.

M.E. Roberts, 'The Relic of the Holy Blood and the Iconography of the Thirteenth-Century North Transept Facade of Westminster Abbey', *England in the Thirteenth Century: Proceedings of the 1984 Harlaxton Symposium*, ed. W.M. Ormrod, 1985, pp. 129–42.

David Stocker, 'The Mystery of the Shrines of St Hugh', *St Hugh of Lincoln: Lectures Delivered at Oxford and Lincoln to Celebrate the Eighth Centenary of St Hugh's Consecration as Bishop of Lincoln*, ed. Henry Mayr-Harting, 1987, pp. 89–124.

L. Stone, *Sculpture in Britain: The Middle Ages*, 2nd edn, 1972.

Acknowledgements: I would like to thank Veronica Sekules, Mary Dean and the editors for helpful comments on and corrections to an earlier draft of this essay, and Patricia Banham for writing a stimulating essay, many years ago, on the cloister bosses at Lincoln.

16

The Architecture of the Cloister of Burgos Cathedral

Christopher Welander

Whereas the sculpture of the cloister of Burgos Cathedral has been studied at length, its architecture has received little attention.[1] Hopefully, the following remarks will help to redress the balance.

Situated to the south of the chevet, it is an unusually grand cloister, possessing two stories and with walks some 40 m long and 5 m wide (130 by 16 feet 6 inches). Rib vaulted throughout, the arcades are full of tracery.[2] Entry was originally effected by the portal in the south transept. This leads into the upper storey which is lavishly embellished with sculpture. An addition to the original project for the cathedral, the cloister was erected in isolation, the earliest of its adjacent buildings being La Capilla de Sta Catalina begun on 13th September 1316.[3] Deknatel dated it c. 1270–80.[4]

Some of its unusual features have practical explanations. The position of the cloister to the south of the church (cathedral cloisters normally occur to the north) and its possession of two stories is the result of the fact that the cathedral is situated on the southern face of a steep hill.[5] Its position by the chevet rather than the nave is the consequence of the fact that the normal site was already occupied by the Romanesque

---

[1] The most important works on the sculpture are: E. Bertaux, 'La Sculpture Chrétienne en Espagne des origines au XIV siècle'; A. Michel, *Histoire de l'Art*, Tome ii, Vol. i, Paris, 1907, p. 276–79; F.B. Deknatel, 'The 13th-century Gothic Sculpture of the Cathedrals of Burgos and Leon', *Art Bulletin*, 17, 1935, pp. 243–389, especially pp. 298–322. On the architecture there is G.E. Street, *Some Account of Gothic Architecture in Spain*, ed. G.G. King, 1, London-Toronto, 1941, p. 32–36.; L.Torres Balbas, *Arquitectura Gótica*, Ars Hispaniae, 7, Madrid, 1952, p. 237.

[2] Only the tracery of the upper storey is original.

[3] Two points show that the cloister was not planned with the rest of the cathedral in c. 1220: the fact that its portal lies off-centre in the west wall of the outer bay of the south transept and the way the right jamb of this portal crudely cuts short the plinth which originally ran along the bottom of all three sides of the south transept's outer bay.

[4] M. Martinez y Sanz, *Historia del Templo Catedral de Burgos*, Burgos, 1866, pp. 141, 296–98. The chapel's portal is obviously a later insertion. Deknatel, op. cit., pp. 298–303.

[5] E.E. Viollet-le-Duc, *Dictionnaire raisonné de l'architecture française du XIe au XVIe siècle*, Paris, 1858–68, iii, p. 409, n. 3.

cloister or episcopal palace.[6] Two of its unusual features are more revealing.

The first is the cloister's figural sculpture. French cloisters of the thirteenth century, like those of the cathedrals of Noyon and Rouen are devoid of this. Instead, they have foliate capitals and tall, window-like, arcades. At Burgos, in addition to that decoration there is, in the upper storey, the portal, complete with jamb statues, tympanum and archivolts; groups of figures attached to the piers at the angles of the arcade (Plate 40a); twenty-one statues arranged on brackets along the walks; and busts of angels decorating the corbels which support the vaults against the walls.

Smart twelfth-century cloisters like that of Moissac (1100) have historiated capitals and large-scale figural sculpture, so the basic explanation of this feature is that our structure was an attempt to combine that old formula for a cloister with the thirteenth-century one.[7] However, the architect seems to have had a more specific aim in mind. The clue is the way the figures are arranged on the arcade at Burgos. For, broadly-speaking, there are two ways in which large-scale, figural sculpture is distributed on cloister arcades. In one, it is found on the piers in the angles. This occurs in southern France and northern Spain and is Romanesque because the sculpture takes the form of reliefs or statues embedded in the respond. Moissac belongs to this series.[8] In the other, it is attached to the colonnettes of the arcades along the sides of the walks. This is centred on northern France and is Early Gothic as the sculpture consists of column-figures. An example is the cloister of Notre-Dame-en-Vaux, Châlons-sur-Marne.[9] Our cloister, then, with its figures grouped in the angles of the arcade belongs to a particular, locally-distributed, twelfth-century series which suggests that the real aim of the architect was to revive his own, Castilian, formula for an expensive cloister and to combine it with the new one from the north. Perhaps his model was the cloister of Santo Domingo de Silos (early twelfth century). After all the two communities were very much in contact with each other at the time our structure was being planned. On 4 November 1260, for example, the Bishop of Burgos, Martín González (1259–67), sorted out the division of the revenues of the abbey between the abbot and the monks.[10] The idea of placing large-scale, figural sculpture in the angles

[6] Ibid., p. 409. On the Romanesque cloister cf. V. Lampérez y Romea, 'La Catedral de Burgos (obras ultimamente ejecutadas)', *Arquitectura y Construccion*, 1918, pp. 5–20.

[7] M. Schapiro, *The Sculpture of Moissac*, London, 1985, p. 4 and fig. 24.

[8] Others of it are: St-Trophîme, Arles (late 12th century), St-Guilhem-le-Desert (1150s/early 1160s); Ganagobie (late 12th century); Montmajour (early 13th century); S Domingo de Silos (early 12th century); Tudela Cathedral (c. 1180–1200); and probably St-Martin, Savigny (second half of the 12th century), and St-Bénigne, Dijon.

[9] W. Sauerlaender, *Gothic Sculpture in France, 1140–1270*, London, 1972, pp. 411–12, where it is dated c. 1180.

[10] M. Férotin, *Recueil des chartes de l'abbaye de Silos*, Paris, 1897, no. 197.

of cloister arcades was kept alive there during the twelfth century. In the late twelfth century the south-west pier was embellished with two reliefs just as the other angle piers had been.[11] The fact that the subject of one of them, the Annunciation to the Virgin, occurs in our cloister makes this suggestion all the more likely (Plate 40a).[12]

The second feature is the design of the cloister's wall (Plate 40b). To the north, thirteenth-century cloisters normally have flat, plain walls although there are examples with arcading (Langres Cathedral) and tracery (Westminster Abbey). At Burgos, the wall consists of a continuous run of huge, decorated, niches.

Lambert suggested that this feature derived from the cloister of Bayonne Cathedral (begun shortly after 1258).[13] Certainly the walls of three of the walks are treated in a similar fashion with recesses, covered by pointed barrel vaults, filling the whole of the space between each respond. There is another candidate to consider. This is the cloister of the Old Cathedral of Salamanca (begun 1178) for its walls have a continuous series of low recesses covered by round barrel vaults.[14] Could not the niches at Burgos be expanded versions of these? This is unlikely: the ones at Salamanca are not separated by responds although one would not expect anything else in a wooden-roofed cloister.

To establish that the way the wall was treated at Burgos came from Bayonne, not Salamanca, is only half the answer.[15] To explain fully the feature we must also examine the design of the niches, for those at Burgos are very different from the ones in the French cloister.

One difference is that at Bayonne the recesses are simply gaps between the responds, being framed by the formeret and formeret colonnettes of the cloister vaults. At Burgos they have their own identity as each is picked out by a roll-moulding supported on recessed colonnettes fitted in beneath the vaults.[16] Exactly the same design as that found at Burgos occurs at Salamanca and there its character is easily recognisable for tomb niches as in the cloister of San Pedro, Soria, are framed in the same way.[17] What this means is that the recesses at Burgos and Salamanca have a funerary function and are intended to house sarcophagi, whereas those at Bayonne are purely architectural. This should come as no

[11] Fray Justo Pérez de Urbel, *El Claustro de Silos*, Vitoria, 1975, pp. 151–69, discusses the views on its date.

[12] At S Domingo de Silos, however, it is combined with the Adoration of the Magi.

[13] E. Lambert, *L'art gothique en Espagne aux XIIe et XIIIe siècles*, Paris, 1931, p. 254, n. 1. On the cathedral and cloister of Bayonne see E. Lambert, '(Bayonne) cathédrale et Cloître', *Congrès Archéologique de France*, 102, 1939, pp. 522–60.

[14] M. Gómez-Moreno, *Cátalogo Monumental de Espana: Provincia de Salamanca*, text, Madrid, 1967, p. 108.

[15] E. Lambert, op. cit., 1931, p. 254, n. 1 suggested that at Bayonne it originated with the remois passageway used in the radiating chapels there.

[16] This is also the case with the side chapels of the chevet of Soissons Cathedral.

[17] I. Robertson, *Blue Guide: Spain, The Mainland*, London, 1980, p. 336.

40a Burgos, Cathedral, cloister: upper storey, north-east pier, the Annunciation to the Virgin.

40b Burgos, Cathedral, cloister: upper storey, wall.

41b Burgos, Cathedral, cloister: upper storey, arcade.

1a Salamanca, Old Cathedral, Tomb of Precentor Aparicio Guillén (d. 1287).

41c Burgos, Cathedral, western towers from the north east.

surprise as cloisters in Spain as in France had long been used for burials;[18] Salamanca seems to be the first one to have been expressly designed as a cemetery.[19] The design of our cloister's wall should be seen as an attempt to combine the unusual treatment of the walls of Bayonne with the Castilian idea, from Salamanca, of a cloister as a luxurious necropolis.

Another difference is that at Burgos unlike at Bayonne there is an arch covered in foliage at the back of each niche. This detail is not found in tomb niches but is a characteristic of thirteenth- and fourteenth-century altar tombs in Castile.[20] Examples include the tombs of Dean Martín Fernández (d. 1250) and Archdeacon Juan Martínez de Díaz (c. 1300–50) in Leon Cathedral [21] and the tombs of Precentor Aparicio Guillén (d. 1287) (Plate 41a) and Canon Alfonso Vidal (d. late thirteenth century) in the Old Cathedral of Salamanca.[22] Perhaps the niches at Burgos are giant, ready-made altar tombs awaiting the sarcophagi, and tympana, of clients.

Several observations indicate that this is indeed the case. First, there are examples of altar tombs framed like the tomb niches of Salamanca.[23] Second, the iconography of the niches occurs on contemporary Castilian altar tombs. The busts of angels which decorate the corbels supporting the vaults between each recess are then the equivalents of those strung out along the arch framing such tombs as that of Bishop Martín II Rodríguez (d. 1250) in Leon Cathedral.[24] In both they represent a heavenly Mass for the Dead with, for example, one angel holding open a missal and another swinging a censer or displaying the crown of the righteous. Similarly the foliage which adorns the arches inside the niches is an expanded version of that decorating altar tombs like the one of Bishop Rodrigo II Alvarez (d. 1232) in Leon Cathedral.[25] In this case there might seem to be nothing specifically funerary about the feature. Surely the foliage is simply decorative? The persistent way in which twelfth- and thirteenth-century altar tombs from both France and Castile are laced with foliage indicates that here it probably symbolises the Garden of Paradise. Third, as Deknatel recognised from its iconography,

---

[18] On burial places see P. Ariès, *The Hour of Our Death*, translated H. Weaver, London, 1983, chapter 2.

[19] It was followed by the cloisters of two Cistercian monasteries, La Espina (Valladolid) and Santes Creus.

[20] In altar tombs it frames the tympanum which indicates that it derives from those contemporary portals whose tympana are bounded by foliate arches.

[21] M. Gómez-Moreno, *Cátalogo Monumental de Espana: Provincia de Leon*, text, Madrid, 1925, pp. 243 and 251; plates, Madrid, 1926, Nos. 299 and 325.

[22] M. Gómez-Moreno, op. cit., text, Madrid, 1967, p. 118; plates, Madrid, 1967, Nos. 54 and 55.

[23] Such as, in the Old Cathedral of Salamanca, the tomb of Canon Fernando Alonso (d. 1279), and in Leon Cathedral, the tomb of Maestrescuela Munio Velasquez (d. 1260).

[24] M. Gómez-Moreno, op. cit., text, Madrid, 1925, p. 244; plates, Madrid, 1926, Nos. 305.

[25] M. Gómez-Moreno, op. cit., text, Madrid, 1925, p. 238; plates, Madrid, 1926, Nos. 290.

one of the niches (at the south end of the west walk) contains the tympanum of an altar tomb.[26] Clearly at least one client furnished a niche as he was intended to. The reason why this did not happen more often was presumably because it was decided to place statues on brackets in all the recesses instead. The cloister continued to be used as a cemetery during the Middle Ages but epitaphs and then sarcophagi were all that were installed.[27]

Altar tombs were introduced shortly before 1250 from France to Leon Cathedral (the earliest example appears to be that of Bishop Rodrigo II Alvarez) and immediately proved popular with the cathedral clergy of Leon, Avila and Salamanca.[28] In turning the niches into altar tombs, our designer would appear to have been intent on equipping the cloister with the most up-to-date and fashionable type of tomb.[29] In the final analysis the design of the cloister's wall represents the transformation of that of Bayonne in the light of Castilian ideas about the proper function of a cloister and what constituted a suitably impressive tomb.

To turn from examining the general conception of the cloister to looking at its detail is a considerable wrench because their sources lie in Rayonnant Paris. For example, the tracery pattern of the arcade of the upper storey is the same as, and was probably copied from, that of the windows of the straight bays of the upper chapel of the Ste-Chapelle, Paris (1241–46) (Plate 41b).[30] The way in which it was made is characteristic of contemporary Parisian Rayonnant. Originally, as befits a cloister, only the oculi would have been glazed because the lower part constitutes a free-standing arcade. It is the treatment of the latter which is interesting. For the trefoils of the lancets as well as the lancets themselves have colonnettes, complete with capitals and bases, exactly the sort of delicate work based upon a reduction in the scale of forms which was practised from the 1240s in the French capital.[31] The model was probably the triforium of the north transept of Notre-Dame, Paris, built by Jean de Chelles between about 1246/47 and 1257.[32] Other smaller details like the profile of the bases confirm this picture which should come as no

---

[26] Op. cit., p. 307.

[27] The epitaphs are cited by P. Orcajo, *Historia de la Catedral de Burgos*, 2nd ed., Burgos, 1846, p. 166–72. Martinez y Sanz, op. cit., pp. 135, 184; Deknatel, op. cit., p. 300. For the sarcophagi see Orcajo, op. cit., pp. 162ff.; A. Dotor y Municio, *La Catedral de Burgos: Guia Historica-Descriptura*, Burgos, 1928, pp. 228ff.

[28] On the spread of this type of tomb see J. Gardner, 'The Tomb of Cardinal Annibaldi by Arnolfo di Cambio' *Burlington Magazine*, 114, 1972, pp.136–41.

[29] This explanation of the niches helps to explain an otherwise curious feature of Burgos Cathedral in comparison with its neighbours, namely the absence of individual 13th-century altar tombs. There was no need of any once the cloister had been built.

[30] R. Branner, *St Louis and the Court Style in Gothic Architecture*, London, 1965, pp. 64–65.

[31] Ibid., p. 67ff.; J. Bony, *French Gothic Architecture of the Twelfth and Thirteenth Centuries*, Los Angeles, 1983, pp. 396ff. and 423ff.

[32] Branner, op. cit., p. 76–77.

surprise given the fact that as Deknatel pointed out the sculptor of David and Isaiah in the right jamb of the cloister portal also hailed from Paris, his style being that of the Apostles of the Ste-Chapelle.[33]

Rayonnant details did not first appear at Burgos in the cloister for they also occur on the west towers, which were built either by 1257 or between then and 1260 because a document of 11 November 1257 mentions the west portal [34] and the cathedral was dedicated on July 20th 1260.[35] In fact, not surprisingly, these two structures are closely related: two of their details occur nowhere else in Leon-Castile at this time. One is the motif of a pointed arch on tall colonnettes containing a pointed trefoil and capped by a crocketed gable with finial. In the cloister, it forms the jambs of the cloister portal (with the addition of pinnacles flanking the gables) and the canopies of the figures at the angles of the arcade (without the colonnettes). On the towers, it decorates the buttresses in the gallery zone where it resembles most closely the blind arcading of the culées of the nave of St-Denis, Paris (*c.* 1260–81)(Fig. 41c).[36] Another detail is the small console which sometimes supports the overlapping lower torus of a base. In the cloister it occurs on some of the bases of the responds along the walls of the upper storey. This is not a particularly Rayonnant feature but its appearance here does indicate that it was introduced as such. Burgos's consoles look like those of the three eastern chapels on the north side of Notre-Dame, Paris (*c.* 1245–50), attributed to Jean de Chelles.[37] The same relationship between the cloister and the towers is indicated by the style of their figural sculpture: Deknatel's argument that, in the cloister, the four princes attached to the north west pier and the king and prince against the walls nearby were carved by the chief sculptor of the towers' figures and his assistants is wholly convincing.[38] The two structures have an underlying affinity, both being concerned with the lavish display of figures. The cloister and the towers probably belong to a single project, one which began in all likelihood with the west portals, work proceding from the towers to our structure.[39] This suggests that the cloister may have been started earlier than normally thought, namely shortly after the completion of the towers in the early to mid 1260s.

[33] Op. cit., pp. 315–17.

[34] F.J. Pereda Llarena, *Documentacion de la Catedral de Burgos, (1254–93)*, Burgos, 1984, No.37.

[35] L. Serrano, *Don Mauricio, Obispo de Burgos y Fundador de su Catedral*, Madrid, 1922, p. 66; this is broadly in agreement with Deknatel, op. cit., pp. 297–98.

[36] C.A. Bruzelius, *The Thirteenth-Century Church at St-Denis*, Yale, 1985, p. 153.

[37] Branner, op. cit., pp. 69–70; J. Bony, op. cit., p. 427.

[38] Op. cit., p. 303 and pp. 311–13.

[39] This is because, first, the design of the lintel of the cloister portal was found in the lateral portals of the west facade (see A. Ponz, *Viaje de Espana*, Madrid, 1788, xii, p. 24, and Lambert, op. cit., p. 233), and secondly because some of the sculptors working on the cloister may have begun work on the west portals (see Deknatel, op. cit., pp. 317–22).

Branner pointed out that Parisian Rayonnant designs occur in Leon Cathedral (begun *c.* 1255).[40] Their discovery at Burgos indicates that in fact they spread more widely. But what is the relationship between the two cathedrals? Did the Rayonnant vocabulary of the cloister/towers arrive via Leon? This is improbable because the two projects, the west portals at Burgos and Leon Cathedral, were begun at roughly the same time and there is no significant overlap in Rayonnant designs between the two buildings.[41] This does not mean that Rayonnant architecture arrived at the two cathedrals independently. It simply suggests that, once it had arrived, the lodge of each cathedral maintained its own repertoire of designs. For the Parisian character of it at each place and the fact that the same man, Henri (d. 1277), was architect of both monuments indicates that it must have been introduced at one go for use on both cathedrals.[42] Master Henri was presumably responsible for this as Branner suggested.[43] If Master Henri had either of the two projects uppermost in his mind when he was sent to France in 1253 or 1254 it is more likely to have been that at Burgos than Leon Cathedral, for he had long been the architect of Burgos and so would naturally have wished to finish it before embarking on a new cathedral.

Finally it should be noted that the cloister became the model for such buildings across Northern Spain into the fourteenth century. The cloisters of Leon (*c.* 1284/95-early fourteenth century) and Oviedo (*c.* 1296/1301 to early fourteenth century) are veritable copies of it.[44] At both there is much figural sculpture (on religious and royal themes just as at Burgos) although it is largely small-scale and decorates the corbels which supports the vaults against the walls. Leon even has a version of our cloister portal. At both the walls consist of a continuous series of enormous, empty, altar tombs. Their style, to begin with, is also derived from the cloister: its arch profile, for example, is found in both.

The architecture of the cloister at Burgos Cathedral is then of considerable interest. In a broad context, the way Castilian ideas about cloisters and tombs were combined with Rayonnant architecture to form a popular design becomes highly significant. Elsewhere in Christendom native ingenuity was stimulated, a new departure provoked, by the arrival of

---

[40] R. Branner, op. cit., pp. 118–20.

[41] The profile of the bases is the same at Leon but it is such a minor feature and so widespread that it is not significant. Small consoles beneath the overlapping lower torus of bases and depressed spurs also occur there, but they are very rare and look different from those of the cloister. The balustrade, punctuated by pinnacles, in front of and above the portals at Burgos is not connected with that at Leon because it is an 18th-century addition (see Lambert, op. cit., p. 237, n. 1).

[42] Martinez y Sanz, op. cit., pp. 182–83; Lambert, op. cit., pp. 229–31, 241–42.

[43] Branner, op. cit., p. 120.

[44] Gómez-Moreno, op. cit., text, Madrid, 1925, pp. 232ff; Torres Balbas, op.cit., p. 237.

Rayonnant architecture in the mid thirteenth century.[45] Clearly a similar, creative, development took place in Spain as well. Leon Cathedral is only part of the story.[46]

Acknowledgements: I would like to take this opportunity to thank those who attended the 1987 Conference of Historians of Medieval Spain held at Liverpool University for the welcome they gave an earlier version of this paper.

[45] Branner, op. cit., pp. 118ff. J. Bony, *The English Decorated Style: Gothic Architecture Transformed, 1250–1350*, Oxford, 1979, is a study of one such new departure.

[46] I discuss this, and other matters, more fully in my doctoral thesis, 'The 13th-century Cathedrals of Toledo'.

17

Lincoln and the Baltic: The Fortunes of a Theory

Paul Crossley

In 1937, and then more fully in 1958, Karl Heinz Clasen, sometime Professor of the History of Art at the University of Koenigsberg in East Prussia, put forward a seemingly outlandish theory about the contribution of England to the history of late Gothic architecture in Germany. Peter Kidson, with his genius for inspiring a love of the unexpected, introduced me to Clasen's theory over twenty years ago, and it has fascinated me ever since.

Clasen argued that late Gothic vaults (vaults with ribs forming purely decorative patterns) were an overlooked but essential component of the German late Gothic style, and they made their first concentrated appearance on the continent in the late thirteenth and early fourteenth centuries in a most unexpected quarter: on the lower Vistula, at the time the territory of the Teutonic Knights. Their debut, in the choir aisles of the Cistercian abbey church of Pelplin (c.1276–1300) took the form of tierceron star vaults directly inspired by the nave vaults of Lincoln Cathedral (Plate 42a, b). Pelplin triggered a sudden fascination for patterned vaulting in the neighbouring workshops of the Teutonic Knights, where however the English tierceron ribs were immediately discarded in favour of the un-English 'triradial', or three-pronged rib figure, which the Knights had first used c. 1300 in their castle chapels at Lochstedt and Marienburg (Malbork) (Plate 42c, d). Using the triradial as the essential building block of the vault, the Knights proceeded, in the first half of the fourteenth century, to create an astonishing variety of decorative patterns without parallel at the time in continental Europe (Plate 42e-h). According to Clasen, Prussian patterns soon spread southwards to Silesia, and from there found their way to Prague, just in time to inspire Peter Parler to use decorative vaults in the cathedral, and thus to alter the whole course of German late Gothic architecture.[1]

Clasen's derivation of the Silesian vaults from Prussia was soon exploded by Józef Frazik, who convincingly traced their origin to the

---

[1] K.H. Clasen, 'Deutschlands Anteil am Gewoelbebau der Spaetgotik', *Zeitschrift des Deutschen Vereins fuer Kunstwissenschaft*, 4, 1937, pp. 163–85; idem, *Deutsche Gewoelbe der Spaetgotik*, Berlin, 1958, esp. pp. 27–71.

triradial vaults over the eastern bay of the choir of Kraków Cathedral.[2] As far as I know, no one has ever taken seriously Clasen's belief that Peter Parler was directly or indirectly influenced by East Prussia,[3] but three issues in Clasen's thesis still seem to call for special attention: the origins and dating of the choir vaults at Pelplin, the sources for the Knights' early use of triradials, and the inspiration for the great 'umbrella' vaults in the double-aisled chapter house and Grand Master's remter at Marienburg.

In recent years Janusz Ciemnołoński has argued that the choir of Pelplin was not begun in 1276 and finished by 1323 (as Clasen and others had assumed)[4], but was started in the last quarter of the fourteenth century, and not completed until before 1447.[5] If he is right, then Pelplin ceases to have any importance in the development of decorative vaults in Europe. But Ciemnołoński's case begs too many questions to carry conviction. Why did the monks of such a large foundation have to wait one hundred years for their main church and (he argues) about fifty years for a stone oratory? Why does the Pelplin Chronicle, in recording the collapse of a tower in 1323, refer to a 'church' (*ecclesiam*) and the damage throughout it, when, according to Ciemnołoński, there only existed at that time a small oratory? And if Pelplin belongs to the late fourteenth century how do we explain certain idiosyncratic forms, obviously borrowed from Pelplin, in buildings which date to before *c.* 1350? The 'giant order' used in the basilican nave of St John at Wormditt (Orneta) (begun *c.* 1340, consecrated 1374) is exactly prefigured in the octagonal pillars at Pelplin whose front three faces rise through the elevation wall to the high vaults.[6] The similarities between Pelplin and the choir of its daughter house at Krone (Koronowo) are obvious: its flat east end across all three aisles, with two prominent staircase turrets, its four-pointed star vaults, its distinctive and strongly projecting aisle responds (Plate 42i). But Krone was begun in 1289 and consecrated in

[2] J.T. Frazik, 'Zagadnienie sklepień o przęsłach trójpodporowych w architekturze średniowiecznej', *Folia Historiae Artium*, 4, 1967, pp. 89–91; and Idem, 'Sklepienia tak zwane Piastowkie w Katedrze Wawelskiej', *Studia do Dziejów Wawelu*, 3, 1963, pp. 127–47.

[3] In fact it was strenuously denied by Henning Bock, 'Der Beginn spaetgotischer Architektur in Prag (Peter Parler) und die Beziehungen zu England', *Wallraf-Richartz-Jahrbuch*, 23, 1961, pp. 191–220. See also my article, 'Wells, the West Country, and Central European Late Gothic', in *Medieval Art and Architecture at Wells and Glastonbury*, British Archaeological Association Conference Transactions, Leeds, 1981, pp. 85–98; and K.J. Philipp, 'Zur Herleitung der Gewoelbe des Prager Veitsdoms. Ikonographie spaetgotischer Gewoelbefigurationen', *Kritische Berichte*, 13, 1985, heft 1, pp. 45ff.

[4] Clasen, op. cit., 1958, p. 32, and P. Skubiszewski, *Architektura Opactwa Cysterskiej w Peplinie* (Studia Pomorskie, 1) Wrocław, 1957, p. 34.

[5] J. Ciemnołoński, 'Ze Studiów nad Bazyliką w Peplinie', *Kwartalnik Architektury i Urbanistyki*, 19, 1974, pp. 27–66.

[6] M. Kutzner, 'Społeczne warunki kształtowania się cech indywidualnych sakralnej architektury gotyckiej na Warmii', in *Sztuka Pobrzeża Bałtyku* (Materiały Sesji Stowarzyszenia Historyków Sztuki, Gdańsk 1976), Warszawa, 1978, pp. 61–62.

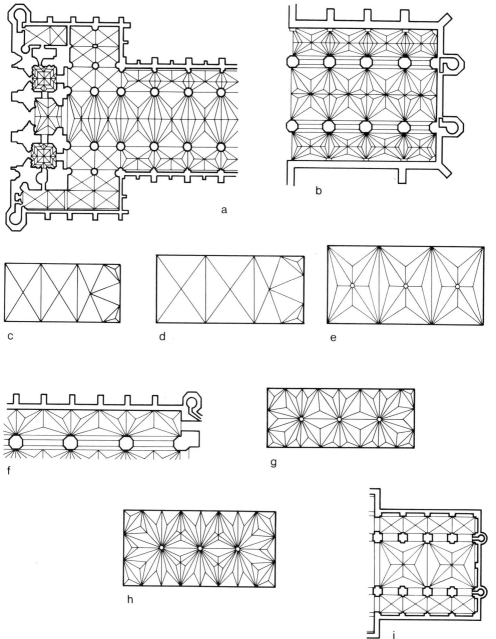

42 a) Lincoln Cathedral, western bays of nave.
    b) Pelplin, Cistercian church, choir.
    c) Lochstedt, Castle chapel.
    d) Marienburg (Malbork), Castle chapel, *c.* 1309.
    e) Golub (Golub-Dobrzyń), Castle chapel.
    f) Marienwerder (Kwidzyń) Cathedral, nave vaults.
    g) Marienburg Castle, chapter house.
    h) Marienburg, Grand Master's Palace, Great Remter.
    i) Krone (Koronowo), Cistercian church, choir.

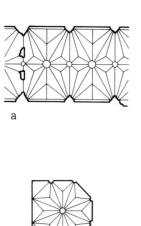

a

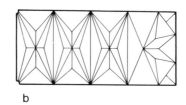

b

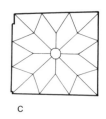

c

d

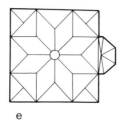

e

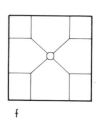

f

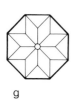

g

h

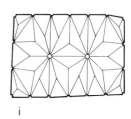

i

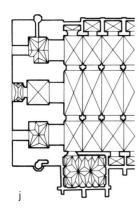

j

43 a) London, St Stephen's Chapel, undercroft vaults.
   b) Thorn (Toruń), St James, choir.
   c) Worms Cathedral, Silberkammer.
   d) Alt-Breisach, St Stephen, crypt vault.
   e) Regensburg, Auerkapelle.
   f) Vyšší Brod, Cistercian church, chapter house.
   g) Kouřím, St Stephen, crypt.
   h) Neuenburg (Nowe), Franciscan church, crypt.
   i) Luebeck, St Mary, Briefkapelle.
   j) Luebeck, St Mary, western bays of nave.

1315.[7] Ciemnołoński's arguments, based on inadequate stylistic analysis and on our fragmentary knowledge of the monastery's economic fortunes, are simply not enough to dislodge the established chronology of Pelplin: until new evidence is found, the choir must remain an essentially late thirteenth-century conception. Its vaults are remarkably close to English patterns. The high vault, although very similar to the lierne vault planned in 1292 for the undercroft of St Stephen's chapel in London (Plate 43a),[8] could have a local origin, since it is made up entirely of conventional 'Prussian' triradials. There can be no doubt however about the origins of the aisle vaults in the tierceron vaults of the nave at Lincoln, even (as Peter Kidson spotted) down to the use of a continuous ridge rib in the north aisle and an interrupted one in the south. Clasen got Pelplin absolutely right.

The origins of the Prussian triradial do not point to England, since the form rarely appears there. Nor was it, as Clasen implied, a largely Prussian phenomenon, having little connection with its use elsewhere in the Empire.[9] Triradials make their debut in East Prussia as corner in-fills in the Knights' castle chapel at Lochstedt (dated not much before 1305) [10] and in the original, now much rebuilt, chapel at Marienburg (*c.* 1309) (Plate 42c, d).[11] They appear in the same position in three contemporary choirs in Germany: at Our Lady at Herford, of the first quarter of the fourteenth century,[12] at St James at Rostock (begun after 1280 and completed by 1334)[13] and in the choir of the Cistercian church at Salem in Swabia (begun in 1299).[14] Dispersed though these buildings are, they represent a wide interest in late thirteenth-century Germany in enlivening conventional flat east ends with triangular or polygonal terminations,[15]

[7] S. Skibiński, *Gotycka Architektura Pocysterskiego Kościoła w Koronowie* (Prace Komisji Sztuki Bydgoskiego Towarszystwa Naukowego, 2), 1967, especially pp. 20–36.

[8] N. Pevsner, Review of Clasen's *Deutsche Gewoelbe der Spaetgotik*, in the *Art Bulletin*, 49, 1959, pp. 333–36.

[9] Op. cit., 1958, p. 35.

[10] C. Steinbrecht, *Preussen zur Zeit der Landmeister: Beitraege zur Baukunst des Deutschen Ritterordens.* Berlin, 1888, p. 112; idem, *Schloss Lochstedt und seine Malereien*, Berlin, 1910; T. Mroczko, *Architektura Gotycka na Ziemi Chełmińskiej*, Warsaw, 1980, p. 190, dates the chapel to 'after 1299 to *c.* 1305'.

[11] For the original, late 13th-century chapel see M. Kilarski, 'Pierwotna forma kaplici zamkowej w Malborku', *Biuletyn Historii Sztuki*, 45,1983, pp. 127–62. About 1309, perhaps in connection with the arrival of the Grand Master, this chapel was given a pseudo-polygonal apse with triradial vaults modelled on Lochstedt's. See S. Skibiński, *Kaplica na Zamku Wysokim w Malborku*, (Universitet im AM w Poznaniu, Seria Historia Sztuki, 14), Poznań, 1982, pp. 12ff., 45ff.

[12] H. Thuemmler, H. Kreft, *Weser Baukunst im Mittelalter*, Hameln, 1970, p. 265.

[13] Mroczko, op. cit., p. 178, fig. 78.

[14] J. Michler, 'Die urspruengliche Chorform der Zisterzienserkirche in Salem', *Zeitschrift fuer Kunstgeschichte*, 47, 1984, pp. 3–46.

[15] See P. Crossley, 'The Vaults of Kraków Cathedral and the Cistercian Tradition', in *Podług Nieba i Zwyczaju Polskiego. Studia z historii Architektury: Sztuki i Kultury Ofiarowane Adamowi Miłobedzkiemu*, Warszawa, 1988, pp. 63–72.

and given the Knights' extensive network of bailiwicks and commanderies in the Empire,[16] it is not unlikely that they were aware of these experiments. Certainly St James at Rostock was an important inspiration to the Knights' architect when he came to design, in around 1330, very similar corner solutions in the vaults of the choir of St James at Thorn (Toruń) (Plate 43b).[17] It should also be remembered that the general 'courtly' character of the Marienburg and Lochstedt chapels derived from a type of *capella speciosa* common in Germany throughout the later thirteenth century, and particularly well represented in Austria and Bohemia.[18] None of these *capellae*, as far as we know, possessed corner triradials,[19] but it was in Bohemia that the greatest concentration of triradials vaults, in cloisters, crypts and chapter houses, could be found in Germany before 1300.[20] The strong influence of Bohemia in the military architecture of the Knights up to the 1270s,[21] as well as the close administrative and political ties between the two territories,[22] makes a Bohemian source for these early triradials the most likely hypothesis.

The final problem raised by Clasen's analysis centres on the stylistic pedigree of the Knight's greatest architectural achievements: the chapter house (Plates 42g, 44) and the Grand Master's remter at Marienburg (Plate 42h). The dating of the earlier room, the chapter house, is crucial, for it stands as the first of the Knight's secular interiors with lavish umbrella vaults supported on free-standing columns. Clasen's pre-war publications dated the chapter house to '*c.* 1325–30', but in 1958 he strenuously argued for a beginning '*c.* 1300'.[23] It is now clear that this latter date is far too early, and recent Polish research has convincingly dated the room either to the early 1320s, or even later, to the reign of

---

[16] K. Górski, *Zakon Krzyżacki a powstanie Państwa Pruskiego*, Wrocław-Warszawa-Gdańsk, 1977, pp. 52–53.

[17] Mroczko, op.cit., pp. 183–84.

[18] Skibiński, op. cit., 1980, pp. 46–63.

[19] But the chapel of Horšovský Týn, *c.* 1270, in southern Bohemia, uses a pseudo-polygonal vault with triangular corners divided by a single ridge rib. See D. Menclová, *České Hrady*, Prague, 1972, pp. 261ff. This solution, and other Austrian-Bohemian chapels and their eastern vaults are discussed in Crossley, op. cit., 1988.

[20] Zvikov castle, Kouřím crypt, the chapter house and transept chapels of Vyšší Brod Cistercian monastery, Sedlec.

[21] J. Frycz, 'Die Burgbauten des Ritterordens in Preussen', *Wissenschaftliche Zeitschrift der Ernst-Moritz-Arndt-Universitaet Greifswald* (Gesellschafts- und Sprachwissenschaftliche Reihe), 29, 1980, pp. 45–56, especially p. 51; idem. 'Architektura zamków krzyżackich', in op. cit. *Sztuka pobrzeża Bałtyku...*, 1978, pp. 44ff.

[22] See Górski, op. cit., pp. 52–53. For the Bohemian initiatives of the early 14th-century Landmeister Konrad Sack, see 'Konrad Sack', in *Altpreussische Biographie*, ed. K. Forstreuter and F. Gause, 2, lief. 4, p. 580; and Frycz, op. cit., 1980, p. 51; I. Sławinski, *Zamek w Golubiu*, Warszawa-Poznań-Toruń, 1976.

[23] *Die mittelalterliche Kunst im Gebiete des Deutschordenstaates Preussens*, i, *Die Burgbauten*, Koenigsberg, 1927, p. 78; idem, op. cit., 1937, p. 173; idem, op. cit. 1958, pp. 38–41.

44 Marienburg Castle, chapter house.

45a Luebeck, St Mary, Briefkapelle.

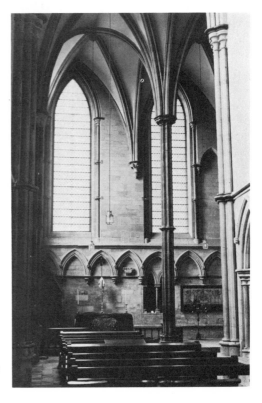

45b Lincoln Cathedral, nave:
north-east chapel.

Grand Master Luther von Braunschweig (1331–1335).[24] A pattern of possible sources now becomes clearer.[25]

What distinguishes the chapter house at Marienburg from all other previous secular halls is its bold use of triradial umbrella vaults over the whole space. It was this palm-like vaulting which led Pevsner, and later Frazik, to see the chapter house and retrochoir of Wells Cathedral as sources for the Marienburg rooms.[26] The similarities are striking but superficial (there are no tiercerons or ridge ribs at Marienburg), and the real sources can be found in Germany itself.

It may be significant that the practice of vaulting a subsidiary space, a crypt, or chapter house or house chapel, with an umbrella of triradial ribs supported on a centrally-placed column took deepest root on the continent in the late thirteenth and early fourteenth centuries in Middle Germany and Bohemia. This type of construction, given canonical form in Villard de Honnecourt's design for a square chapel (Plate 38b), appeared in the Silberkammer at Worms Cathedral of *c.* 1270, in the crypt of Alt-Breisach in Swabia (*c.* 1300), in the Auerkapelle in Regensburg (*c.* 1300), and in Bohemia, in the chapter house of Vyšší Brod and the crypt of the church at Kouřím, both of *c.* 1280 (Plate 43c-g).[27] Given the Knights' close administrative contacts with Franconia and Bohemia, it is not unlikely that their architects knew of these small but ingenious buildings; and it seems that at least one example of the type had reached the lower Vistula in the first decade of the fourteenth century, probably under Bohemian influence. From 1300–6 East Pomerania was under the sovereignty of Waclaw II and III, both kings of Poland and Bohemia.[28] Here, on the left bank of the Vistula, the Franciscans made a settlement at Neuenburg (Nowe), and sometime between *c.* 1300 and 1311 began a new church with a large crypt, octagonal in plan, with a central column and a fan of triradials, far closer in form to the crypt at Kouřím than, as Mroczko argues, the chapter house of Salisbury (Plate 43h).[29] The Knights must have known the crypt, for they bought the whole town of Neuenburg

[24] Skibiński, op. cit. 1982, pp. 86–87, dates it to circa 1320. Frycz, op. cit. 1980, p. 53, thinks that the chapter house belongs to the period of Grand Master Luther von Braunschweig (1331–35).

[25] The destruction of many of the Knights' castles has, however, left serious gaps in our knowledge of their early vaults. Nothing survives of their headquarters at Elbling (Elbląg). Did the chapter house in the east wing of the destroyed castle at Thorn, dated '*c.* 1310–40', and perhaps double-aisled, have an umbrella vault? And the ruined remter at Rheden (*c.* 1320?) seems to have had a star vault very like the Pelplin chapter house (*c.* 1300), which Clasen (op. cit., 1958, pp. 39–40) saw unjustifiably as the principle source of the chapter house at Marienburg. See Frycz, op. cit. 1980, pp. 50, 53.

[26] Pevsner, op. cit. 1958, p. 335; Frazik, op. cit. 1967, p. 83.

[27] For a discussion of all these buildings see Clasen, op. cit. 1958, pp. 25–27, 56–58.

[28] Górski, op. cit. p. 59.

[29] Mroczko, op. cit. pp. 278–80

in 1313.[30] Admittedly this crude, squat little space hardly prepares us for the splendours of Marienburg; but the functions of crypt and chapter house were often close in Germany in the Middle Ages,[31] and it is tempting to see Neuenburg as a modest reminder to the Knights, when they began their chapter house a few years later, of a distinguished Bohemian and German tradition of triradial umbrella vaults.

The second, and long-recognised, source for the Marienburg chapter house is the famous Briefkapelle at St Mary's in Luebeck, begun, according to its contemporary inscription, in 1310 (Plate 43i, 45a).[32] Despite Clasen's contorted attempts to date this chapel to '*c.* 1320 and after', in order to give Marienburg the priority (and prove that the form originated in East Prussia), recent conservation work on the chapel has confirmed the 1310 date.[33] The Briefkapelle had no local progeny, but there can be little doubt of its influence in the later chapter house at Marienburg: the same double-aisled plan, the same elegant octagonal columns, the same all-over canopy of triradial umbrella vaults. The most likely channel for the transmission of ideas from Luebeck to Marienburg was the Baltic Hansa, of which Luebeck was the head. Two of the Knights' towns, Thorn and Elbling, were members of the League, the latter (the headquarters of the Landmeister until 1309) founded on the *Luebisches Recht*.[35] The Knights of the Inflant (eastern Baltic), had representatives in Bremen and Luebeck.[36] The Grand Master of the Knights enjoyed the title of *Caput Hansa*. The close-knit Baltic world of Thomas Mann's *Buddenbrooks* was rooted in the trading networks and maritime exchanges of the Hansa of the high Middle Ages.

[30] J. Heise, *Die Bau- und Kunstdenkmaeler der Provinz Westpreussen: Kreis Schwetz*, 4, Danzig, 1887, pp. 330, 334; Dehio-Gall, *Deutschordensland Preussen*, Muenchen-Berlin, 1952, pp. 101–2; E. Gall, *Danzig und das Land an der Weichsel*, Muenchen, 1953, p. 141. Gall doubts if the vaults are original, and indeed they have been rebuilt, together with much else in the crypt; but the original springers survive, and allow a reconstruction with eight triradials divided by transverse ribs, see Frazik, op. cit., 1967, fig. 83, p. 79.

[31] R. Wagner-Rieger, 'Gotische Kapellen in Niederoesterreich', in *Festschift fuer K.M. Swoboda*, ed. Otto Demus et. al., Vienna, 1959, pp. 295–96; and W. Götz, *Zentralbau und Zentralbautendenz in der gotischen Architektur*, Berlin, 1968, pp. 250ff.

[32] For a survey of the German literature on the Briefkapelle see W.A. Steinke, 'Die Briefkapelle zu Luebeck, ihre Herkunft und ihre Beziehung zum Kapitelsaal der Marienburg', *Jahrbuch des St Mariens-Bauvereins (Luebeck)*, 8, 1974, pp. 55–71. See also M. Hasse, *Die Marienkirche zu Luebeck*, Muenchen-Berlin, 1983, pp. 40–43.

[33] Clasen, op. cit., 1958, pp. 42–48; E. Gąsiorowski, 'Die Briefkapelle der St Marienkirche zu Luebeck', *Deutsche Kunst und Denkmalpflege*, 35, 1977, pp. 148–63; and in the same volume, S. Kummer, 'Archaeologische Aufschluesse zur Baugeschichte der Briefkapelle an St Marien in Luebeck', pp. 139–47.

[34] Apart from the contemporary umbrella vaults in the Strobukkapelle in St Catherine at Luebeck, possibly by the same architect, see Dehio, *Handbuch der Deutschen Kunstdenkmaler: Hamburg Schleswig-Holstein*, Muenchen-Berlin, 1971, p. 357; Clasen, op. cit., 1958, p. 48.

[35] E. Christiansen, *The Northern Crusades: The Baltic and the Catholic Frontier, 1110–1525*, London, 1980, p. 86.

[36] Górski, op. cit., p. 52.

The Briefkapelle may be the clue to the origins of the Marienburg remters, but its own origins lie, as many authorities have long recognised, in England.[37] The north west tower of St Mary's, begun in 1304, has a tierceron vault with longitudinal and transverse ridge ribs that look remarkably English (Plate 42a, 43j). The position of the Briefkapelle, flanking the western bays of the nave of the parent church, is exactly prefigured in the two rectangular chapels (*c.* 1240) opening off the western bays of the nave at Lincoln (Plate 42a and 43j). In addition, the northern chapel at Lincoln anticipates Luebeck by supporting its cone of ribs on an elongated central pillar (Plate 45b). Here, as in Pelplin, the impact of Lincoln seems incontrovertible.

Clasen was wrong about Luebeck, and he overstated the autonomy of East Prussian architecture and its contribution to the genesis of decorative vaulting in Germany, but he was correct in seeing the encounter of Lincoln and Pelplin as the mere catalyst for a movement that soon left English ideas far behind. English architecture did not provide the powerful and constant model for German *Backsteingotik* that many scholars have recently supposed. Most of the so-called English forms in northern Germany can be better explained by local inspiration.[38] They are symptoms of what Panofsky once called 'pseudo-morphosis', the emergence of a form A morphologically analogous to, or even identical with, a form B, yet unrelated to it from a genetic point of view. We know that Hanseatic Luebeck and Cistercian Pelplin (both, significantly, sites with international connections) had some (probably indirect) knowledge of Lincoln, not simply because their forms are remarkably close to their model, but because those forms resist any local explanation. The anglicisms of both buildings were however quickly absorbed into very different currents of thought, in much the same way as English ideas in Prague and central France had a distinct but short-lived impact a half century later. This receptive pattern of momentary impact and rapid transformation may be partly explained by the presence of two new forces in Gothic architecture. First, the growth and circulation of architectural drawings in the late thirteenth century gave architects access to a heterogeneous collection of forms detached from the full force and authority

---

[37] The mid 13th-century church of St John at Krummesse, ten miles south of Luebeck, does anticipate the chapel in being a double-aisled hall, but that is as far as the analogy goes; see R. Hootz, *Deutsche Kunstdenkmaeler: Ein Bildhandbuch, Hamburg, Schleswig Holstein*, Darmstadt, 1961, plate 163 and p. 374.

[38] There is no space here to criticise all these 'English' attributions. I deal with some in Crossley, op. cit., 1981, pp. 82 and 104, n. 3; see particularly J. Bony, *The English Decorated Style, Gothic Architecture Transformed, 1250–1350*, Oxford, 1979, pp. pp. 64–67. For extreme anglophilia see W. Steinke, 'The Influence of English Decorated Style on the Continent: St James in Toruń and Lincoln Cathedral', *Art Bulletin*, 56, 1974,, pp. 505–16, comprehensively demolished by T. Mroczko, op. cit., pp. 158–208, and ignored by M. Kutzner, 'Lubelski Styl Architektury Gotyckiego Kościoła Sw Jakuba w Torunia', *Sztuka Torunia i Ziemi Chełmińskiej, 1233–1815*, ed. J. Poklewski, Warsawa-Poznań-Toruń, 1986, pp. 55–75.

of their original context. Like nineteenth-century pattern books, these details invited eclecticism and easy transformation. Secondly, the hegemony enjoyed by France over European architecture in the early thirteenth century was something exceptional in the history of Gothic and was not, as some have argued, transferred to England, or to any other single country, when France lost its supremacy around the year 1300.[39] From then on European architecture had no single orthodoxy to obey. Unhampered by any dominant international language, but stimulated by a chance(?) encounter with English patterned vaults, architecture in the southern Baltic in the early years of the fourteenth century could begin an eclectic and creative experiment. The outlandish had become possible.

Acknowledgements: Peter Kidson allowed me as a research student to pursue the problem of England and the Baltic, and then generously supported me when I changed my allegiance from Prussia to Poland. For his tolerance, and for countless other kindnesses, I shall always be in his debt. In the preparation of this paper I happily acknowledge the generous help of Jack Lohman, who has drawn my attention to a number of works cited here, and has kindly sent me xeroxes and lent me published material. All the drawings for this essay and for that by Jean Bony were specially drawn by Alan Adams to whom the authors wish to express their thanks.

[39] Notably N. Pevsner, *An Outline of European Architecture*, 7th ed., Harmondsworth, 1964, p. 128; and J. Bony, op. cit., pp. 1 and 62ff.

18

The Tomb of Henry IV
and the Holy Oil of St Thomas of Canterbury

Christopher Wilson

Henry IV was the first king of England who chose to break with the tradition of burial in Westminster Abbey inaugurated by Henry III. A sufficient explanation for his decision to seek burial elsewhere may be the fact that room was no longer available for tombs in the Chapel of St Edward the Confessor, but there is also the possibility that the abbey was shunned because it contained the monument intended for the king whom Henry had usurped and whose murder was widely regarded as his responsibility. The considerations of space and of posthumous *bella figura* which seem to have ruled out Westminster worked in favour of Canterbury Cathedral, a church housing a shrine even more prestigious than the Confessor's and one which was still hardly encumbered by tombs. Henry's first will of January 1409 reveals his decision to be buried within the cathedral 'aftyr the discrecion' of Archbishop Arundel,[1] the chief supporter of his seizure of the throne, but it is very doubtful whether this deference was anything more than a way of avoiding being seen to demand the most honorific position in the church, that immediately north of St Thomas's shrine. A clear indication that the present site had indeed been earmarked for the king by the time his first will was drawn up is the burial in 1410 of his half-brother John Beaufort, earl of Somerset, in the next bay to the east,[2] an event hardly explicable except as an instance of the fairly widespread late medieval usage of entombment at the feet of a close associate of superior rank.

Records of various kinds indicate that the funeral on Trinity Sunday 1413 was as solemn and elaborate as tradition required,[3] but no documentation at all has survived for the making of the monument. In 1424 Henry's executors had still not received enough money to pay off the

---

[1] J. Nichols, ed. *A Collection of Wills of the Kings and Queens of England ...* London, 1780, p. 203. A will which superseded that of 1409 has not survived; J.L. Kirby, *Henry IV of England*, London, 1970, p. 222.

[2] J. W. Legg, W.H.St J. Hope, *Inventories of Christchurch, Canterbury*, London, 1902, p. 151.

[3] F. Devon, *Issues of the Exchequer*, London, 1837, p. 325; J.H. Wylie, *History of England under Henry IV*, 4 vols, London, 1884–98, iv, pp. 111–13; idem, *The Reign of Henry V*, 3 vols, Cambridge, 1914–29, i, pp. 47–48; C.E. Woodruff, 'The Sacrist Rolls of Christ Church, Canterbury', *Archaeologia Cantiana*, 48, 1936, pp. 43, 50.

debts which were the first charge on his estate,[4] and it is very likely that his widow Joan of Navarre stepped in some time during the 1420s and ordered the existing joint monument to Henry and herself. The style of the effigies is very close to that of the many others produced during the 1420s in the workshops of the alabasterers Thomas Prentys and Robert Sutton at Chellaston in Derbyshire, and the absolute equality of Joan's and Henry's heraldic commemoration suggests strongly that she was the patron (Plate 46a).

Burial in Canterbury Cathedral had a significance for Henry IV which would not have been lost on contemporaries, although it appears to have escaped the notice of historians and antiquarians of later generations. One of the elements of the propaganda put out around the start of Henry IV's reign, in the hope of reinforcing his shaky title to the throne, was the claim that the anointing at his coronation fulfilled a well-known prophecy revealed by the Virgin Mary to St Thomas during his French exile. The Virgin had predicted that future, unspecified kings of England would be anointed with the oil in a small stone phial which she enclosed within a golden eagle and presented to the archbishop. The first of these kings would recover peacefully the lands lost by his predecessors, including Normandy and Aquitaine; he would be 'greatest among kings'; he would build churches in the Holy Land and would expel the pagans from Babylon. As often as he carried the oil-containing eagle in his breast he would have victory over his enemies and his kingdom would prosper. A number of late fifteenth- and sixteenth-century writers claimed that Henry hoped sincerely to accomplish the feats enumerated in the prophecy,[5] and it is not unlikely that awareness of his failure in this respect was one of the causes of the stress which has been identified as a possible contributory factor in the sudden and alarming attacks of illness to which he was subject from 1405.[6] To most kings the fulfilment of the terms of the prophecy would have seemed too high a price to pay for the benefits of unction with St Thomas's oil, but in 1399 Henry was in his prime and very probably believed himself equal to the task. After all, he had acquired a kingdom without bloodshed, and his Prussian expeditions of 1390–91 and 1392 had given him first-hand experience of crusading warfare. His visit to Jerusalem in early 1393 may well have fired him with the desire to recover the Holy City for Christendom.

A simpler and slightly different version of the prophecy existed by 1318, when Edward II petitioned pope John XXII to sanction a second anointing with the oil, which he believed had come into his possession in 1308. The suggestion had evidently been made to Edward that his

---

[4] Wylie, op. cit. at n. 3 above, 1884–98, iii, p. 235, iv, p. 144; Wylie, op. cit. at n. 3 above, 1914–29, i, pp. 26–27; A.C. Reeves, *Lancastrian Englishmen*, Washington, 1981, p. 16.

[5] Wylie, op. cit. at n. 3 above, iv, 1884–98 p. 105, n. 4. See also T. Rymer, *Foedera*, viii, p. 738.

[6] P. McNiven, 'The Problem of Henry IV's Health, 1405–1415', *English Historical Review*, 100, 1985, pp. 768–70.

political difficulties were due to the omission of the unction with this oil, but it would have been obvious to the pope that an undeclared motive was to achieve parity with the French kings, who were anointed with the most famous and potent of all coronation oils, that in the *sainte ampoule* which the Holy Spirit itself had brought straight from heaven for the baptism of King Clovis in 496.[7] The fourteenth-century English kings were anointed with two oils, those of St Mary of Sardinia and St Nicholas, of which the former at least was miraculous in origin, although by comparison with the French coronation oil they suffered from being abundant and hence widely available. Edward II's possession of the heaven-sent oil of St Thomas and his unsuccessful bid to make use of it seem to have remained secret, and by *c.* 1340 the prophecy had evolved into what proved to be the definitive version, which as well as acquiring a certain number of accretions, most notably the golden eagle, had shed its allusion to Edward II.[8]

An official Lancastrian account of the recovery of the oil and its history down to 1399 was probably circulated around the time of Henry IV's coronation, and though the original text has not survived, its main elements were incorporated into four contemporary or near-contemporary chronicles.[9] The fullest account, that in the *Annales Ricardi Secundi et Henrici Quarti* by the strongly pro-Lancastrian monk of St Albans, Thomas Walsingham, tells how the eagle and oil came into the possession of Henry, first duke of Lancaster,[10] who handed them over to the Black Prince on the assumption that he would be the next king. Before Richard II's coronation a fruitless search was made for the oil;

[7] The only evidence for the form of the prophecy in 1318 is a letter written in that year by John XXII in response to an inquiry from Edward II; L.G.W. Legg, ed., *English Coronation Records*, London, 1901, pp. 69–72, 170–71; M. Bloch, *Les Rois Thaumaturges*, Strasbourg, 1924, pp. 238–40.

[8] That is, the prediction that the first king anointed with St Thomas's oil would be the fifth after the one reigning at the time of the prophecy; Legg, op. cit. at n. 7 above, pp. 170–71. The manuscripts of the definitive version of the prophecy are listed in T.A. Sandquist, 'The Holy Oil of St Thomas of Canterbury', in T.A. Sandquist, M.R.Powicke, *Essays in Medieval History Presented to Bertie Wilkinson*, Toronto, 1969, pp. 331 n. 4, 334 n. 11.

[9] Thomas Walsingham, *Historia Anglicana, 1272–1422*, 2 vols. ed. T.H. Riley, Rolls Series, 1863–64, ii, pp. 239–40; idem, *Ypodigma Neustriae*, ed. T.H. Riley, Rolls Series, 1876, p.388; idem, *Annales Ricardi Secundi et Henrici Quarti*, in *Johannis de Trokelowe et Henrici de Blaneforde ... Chronica et Annales*, ed. T.H. Riley, Rolls Series, 1866, pp. 297–300. Anon., *Eulogium Historiarum*, 3 vols, ed. F.S. Haydon, Rolls Series, 1858–63, iii, pp. 379–80, 384. T.A. Sandquist, op. cit. at n. 8 above, has doubted whether Henry IV's successors were actually anointed with the oil of St Thomas and has denied that the unction was part of the official Lancastrian propaganda, but the evidence adduced consists mainly of the absence of references to the oil from some 15th-century accounts of the coronations of Henry V and the manifestly untrustworthy testimony of Adam of Usk, who incurred Henry IV's anger and suffered hardship as a consequence; cf. A. Gransden, *Historical Writing in England*, ii, London, 1982, pp. 141, n. 166, 175–76.

[10] Henry of Grosmont, Henry IV's maternal grandfather, obviously introduced into the story to establish Lancastrian fair-dealing.

46a Canterbury Cathedral, tomb of Henry IV, painting on tester (from R. Gough, *Sepulchral Monuments in Great Britain*, ii, part 2, London, 1796, facing p. 32).

46b Canterbury Cathedral, Tomb of Henry IV, crowned eagle on tester.

46c Canterbury Cathedral, Tomb of Henry IV, detail of collar with flying eagle on tester.

The Ampulla or Eaglet.

I

47a Coronation eagle of 1660 (from
F. Sandford, *The History of the
Coronation of ... James II ...*,
London, 1687, part of plate
between pp. 36 and 37).

47b Canterbury Cathedral, north-west transept,
tracery light of north window, detail of
figure of St Thomas of Canterbury.

and when later Richard stumbled across it in a chest in the Tower of London, Archbishop Arundel refused to anoint him on the grounds that he had already been anointed at his coronation. Despite failing to obtain a second unction, Richard attempted to exploit one of the powers attributed to the oil in the prophecy by taking it with him on his abortive Irish expedition of May-July 1399. At the first confrontation between Richard and Henry at Chester around 19 August, Arundel confiscated the eagle and oil, which remained in his custody until he used them at Henry's crowning on 13 October. How much credence was given to all this in 1399 it is impossible to say, but the claim to have received unction with the oil of St Thomas put the Lancastrian succession under the patronage of Canterbury's and England's premier saint in the most public and unambiguous manner. It seems prima facie highly likely that the idea of expressing this allegiance through the physical closeness of Henry's tomb to the shrine had been discussed with Arundel some time in the months preceding the coronation.[11]

At the east and west ends of the tomb stand large painted panels showing respectively the Virgin crowned by the Trinity and the Martyrdom of St Thomas. It is possible that these paintings commemorate the main protagonists in the prophecy of the coronation oil, though this is not demonstrable since neither illustrates the story, and the association of the Virgin and St Thomas in art and legend was in any case established long before the emergence of the prophecy. The two panels join onto the tester whose soffit is decorated entirely with heraldry, badges and mottoes (Plate 46a). Three large shields of England, England impaling Navarre and Navarre are set against a background of diagonal bands formed alternately of Henry's well-known motto *soverayne* [12] punctuated with crowned golden eagles (Plate 46b) and what must be Joan's motto *a temperance* on account of its punctuation by the ermine device of her first husband, Jean IV, duke of Brittany.

Around the large shields are Lancastrian livery collars of SS of a unique pattern with golden eagles incorporated into their tirets (Plate 46c). The basic collar of SS was, as is well known, a device inherited by Henry from his father John of Gaunt, and many such collars were made for Henry's personal use and as presents both before and after his accession.[13] The collar was a badge in its own right, and seems to have been worn in Henry's time with only non-figural pendants hanging from the tiret,

[11] The intention to create a Lancastrian mausoleum at Canterbury can be inferred from the burial east of the site of Henry IV's tomb of the earl of Somerset in 1410 and the duke of Clarence in 1421, both bodies later reburied later in St Michael's chapel; Legg, Hope, op. cit. at n. 2 above, pp. 150–52.

[12] On this motto see most recently C. Blair, I. Delamer, 'The Dublin Civic Swords', *Proceedings of the Royal Irish Academy*, 88, section C, 1988, pp. 87–142. I am very grateful to Claude Blair for lending me a typescript of this article in advance of publication.

[13] For bibliography on collars of SS see ibid., p. 121 no. 106.

most commonly the simple ring shown on Queen Joan's effigy at Canterbury. It was apparently no earlier than Henry V's reign that the fashion
emerged for wearing collars of SS with beasts and other badges as
pendants, a borrowing perhaps from the collars of chivalric orders. The
many differences between the collar on Joan's effigy and those on the
tester exemplify the diversity possible in the decorative treatment of the
collar proper, and in the collars made to Henry's order diversity extended
to the treatment of the tiret, which could enclose a variety of beasts. The
swan, the griffon and oliphant and the lamb are all documented within
the period 1401–3.[14] It seems reasonable to assume that collars with
tirets so decorated were marks of the king's special favour and in some
cases a personal allusion will have been intended. No documentary
evidence for collars with tirets bearing eagles has come to light so far,[15]
but because three such collars are shown on the tester, and two of these
enclose arms other than the king's, it seems clear that gold collars of this
pattern did actually exist and that the queen at least was entitled to wear
them. Perhaps collars with eagles in their tirets were a form of Henry's
livery reserved to members of his immediate family, and if so there is a
possibility that he was consciously following his grandfather Edward III,
the great pioneer of late medieval badge culture in England, who is on
record in 1352 as ordering for himself, the Black Prince and John of
Gaunt three hoods of blue Brussels cloth sewn with eagles in cast or
stamped sheet gold.[16] Hoods were regularly given to retainers throughout the fourteenth century, and the luxurious royal headgear made in
1352 would probably have registered with contemporaries as an exclusive
version of a very common form of livery.[17] After the death of his father,
if not before, Gaunt ordered many eagle-decorated items of plate, jewel-
lery, clothing and furnishing,[18] though in his case eagles had the extra
significance of alluding to his Evangelist name saint. That eagle badges
were regarded as proper to Gaunt by his son is suggested by the lack

[14] Public Record Office, E 101/404/18 (account of the receiver of the chamber of the
household). For the swan badge and its association with collars of SS see J. Cherry, 'The
Dunstable Swan Jewel', *Journal of the British Archaeological Association*, 3rd ser., 32, 1969, pp.
38–53. The reference to the swan as the livery of Henry Prince of Wales in a statute of 1401
(*Rotuli Parliamentorum*, iii, 1377–1411, pp. 477–78), and the absence of swans from the
Canterbury tomb, suggest their lesser importance after Henry's accession although, if Joan
of Navarre did indeed pay for the tomb, swans may have been excluded on account of
association with the family of Henry's first wife, Mary de Bohun.

[15] Unfortunately there was not time to read more than a few of the accounts for Henry
IV's jewels and plate in the Exchequer and household records before sending this article
for printing. However, see n. 14 above.

[16] Stanilands, 'Medieval Courtly Splendour', *Costume*, 14, 1980, p. 18.

[17] C. Given-Wilson, *The Royal Household and the King's Affinity*, New Haven and London,
1986, pp. 234–45.

[18] H.S. London, *Royal Beasts*, London, 1956, p. 61.

of evidence of their use by Henry before Gaunt's death. Gaunt was almost certainly the original owner of the only *objet de luxe* known to have combined his two devices of the eagle and collar of SS, a silver-gilt salt in the shape of an eagle with letters of 'S' around its neck. This came into Henry's possession late in 1399 along with many other of Richard II's treasures.[19] As Gaunt's heir, but also in tribute to his military prowess and his kingly aspirations, Henry was saluted as the eagle in several poems written around the time of his landing at Ravenspur,[20] and his liberal use of Gaunt's former badge is clear from some accounts of the receiver of the chamber of the household for 1401–3 which show the eagle to have been much the commonest of several personal devices embellishing the jewels and plate given away as presents.[21]

The 'official' status of the crowned gold eagle badge which punctuates the motto *soverayne* on the tester of the Canterbury tomb is confirmed by its use for the subtlety of the third and final course of the feast after his wedding to Joan of Navarre in February 1403.[22] But whereas the crowned eagles on the tester are close relations of the fierce, tousled-feathered species of heraldic eagle which became general in the fifteenth century (Plate 46b), the uncrowned eagles on the collars are all slight, rather innocuous-looking birds with wings extended as if about to fly (Plate 46c). The variation must have had a significance of some kind, and for Henry IV the most obvious meaning specific to the very rare device of fluttering golden eagles would have been as a commemoration of the sacred oil-containing eagle first used at his coronation. The incorporation of the eagle into the central element of the collar of SS conforms not only to the prophecy that the first king anointed with the oil would prosper so long as he wore the gold eagle on his breast, but also to a detail of the later history of the oil preserved in the near-contemporary continuation of the *Eulogium Historiarum*, namely that Richard II wore the eagle hung around his neck continuously from the time of his discovery of it in the Tower of London.[23]

No visual record of the appearance of the coronation eagle was made before its destruction under the Commonwealth, and the only written references to it are too laconic to permit comparison with the representations in the collars on the tester. Nevertheless the mistake made by

[19] F. Palgrave, *The Antient Kalendars and Inventories of the Treasury of his Majesty's Exchequer*, 3 vols, London, 1836, iii, p. 364 (no. 61). The entry describes the salt as a falcon, but there is a considerable amount of evidence from the late 14th century onwards that heraldic and quasi-heraldic representations of falcons and eagles were indistinguishable visually; cf. J. Parker, *A Glossary of Terms Used in Heraldry*, new edition, Oxford, 1894, pp. 246–47.

[20] *Political Poems and Songs*, 2 vols, ed. T. Wright, Rolls Series, 1859–61, i, pp. 364–65, 368.

[21] See n. 14 above.

[22] T. Austin, 'Two Fifteenth-Century Cookery Books', *Early English Text Society*, 1st ser., 91, 1888, p. 58.

[23] Anon., op. cit. at n. 9 above, p. 380.

the official responsible for drawing up the 1649 inventory of regalia kept at Westminster Abbey when he entered the eagle as a 'dove of gould'[24] is suggestive of a rather slight bird resembling not only those on the tester collars, but also the eagle made for Charles II's coronation (Plate 47a). The latter can be presumed to follow its medieval predecessor in its basic shape at least, for considerable care is known to have been taken to reproduce the remembered features of the originals of other items of regalia.[25] The different wing positions adopted by the eagle of 1660 and the birds on the tester collars are not a serious obstacle to the theory of their both being reflections of the late medieval coronation eagle. The downturned points of the former might be due to incorrect transmission of the details of the original, and the eagles within the collars could well owe their upturned wings to aesthetic considerations, namely the need to fit into the inverted trefoil shape of the tirets and the wish to continue the line of the collars.

The oil of St Thomas continued to be used in the coronation of English kings at least until 1483 and probably until 1509. If it never attained the kind of prestige which attached to the *sainte ampoule*, this can perhaps be attributed in part to its all too evident failure to prosper the fifteenth-century kings. An indication of a certain loss of importance in the late fifteenth century is the order made by Richard III directly after his coronation that in future it should stay among the regalia kept in the abbey rather than in any of the royal jewel repositories. The implication behind this change must be the discontinuance of the solemn ceremony on the eve of the previous coronations in which the eagle and oil had been conveyed from Westminster Palace to the high altar of the abbey, a procession obviously modelled on that which escorted the *sainte ampoule* from St-Remi in Reims to the cathedral.[26]

Within the context of the cult of St Thomas the story of the oil remained popular,[27] and there is a good chance that it was commemorated at Canterbury far more prominently and explicitly than on Henry IV's tomb. Most of the glass of *c.* 1480 in the great north window of the north-west transept was destroyed in 1642, but the heraldry surviving in the heads of the uppermost tier of lights indicates a scheme of six saints associated with the English royal house.[28] St Thomas took pride of place

[24] Legg, op. cit. at n. 7 above, p. 274.

[25] The 1660 eagle, known as the 'ampulla', differed from its predecessor in being a container for oil rather than for the oil-containing stone phial, the ampulla proper. It was also larger. My thanks to Ronald Lightbown for discussion of the eagles.

[26] W. Ullmann, 'Thomas Becket's Miraculous Oil', *Journal of Theological Studies*, new ser., 8, 1957, p. 131; J.W. McKenna, 'The Coronation Oil of the Yorkist Kings', *English Historical Review*, 82, 1967, pp. 102–4.

[27] Sandquist, op. cit. at n. 8 above, pp. 332–33, 343.

[28] M.H. Caviness, *The Windows of Christ Church Cathedral, Canterbury*: (Corpus Vitrearum Medii Aevi Great Britain, ii), London, 1981, p. 268, calls the object in St Thomas's hand a scroll curled into a cone.

on the dexter side of a central image of the Trinity and stood immediately above a crowned and kneeling figure of Edward IV in the tier below. That the iconography reinforced Thomas's role as patron of the king by showing him as purveyor of the coronation oil is very likely, for in the surviving glazing of the tracery lights, where he occupies the central dexter position, he holds in his left hand a small conical vessel which must surely be the stone phial containing the oil inside the golden eagle (Plate 47b).[29] The fact that this image and the much larger one below survived the proclamation of Thomas Becket as a traitor in November 1538 suggests that the myth of the coronation oil had declined to the point where no attack was needed to consign it to oblivion.

[29] The conical form is admittedly not very ampulla-like but may have been intended to recall the horn used at the prototypical kingly unction, that of David by Samuel. No doubt the glass painter was as ignorant as we are of the form of the phial concealed within the eagle.

19

Gaelic Friars and Gothic Design

Roger Stalley

The fifteenth-century Franciscan Friary at Muckross (Co. Kerry) is one of Ireland's most frequently visited medieval monuments. This popular status is to be ascribed, not to any general perception of the friary's historic or architectural worth, but to the fact that it lies in a beautiful setting, beside Lough Leane in the Killarney National Park (Plate 48a). What most visitors may fail to realise is that Muckross is a remarkable monument, of a type quite unlike anything surviving in England. Apart from the roofs, the buildings are virtually intact and these include a delightful set of late Gothic cloister arcades, surrounding an intimate cloister garth (Plate 48b). The friary was founded between 1440 and 1448 by Donal MacCarthy, the local chieftain, and it is one of about a dozen Franciscan houses in Ireland that have survived almost complete.[1] The Franciscans were particularly well adapted to the needs of Irish society in the later Middle Ages and at least twenty new houses were founded in the fifteenth century alone, a time when the movement was reinvigorated by the Observant reform. In addition to the main order, there were also many foundations belonging to the third order, the lay branch of the movement.[2] The success of the Franciscans, and to a lesser extent the Dominicans, seems to have occurred at the expense of the parochial clergy and in many areas of the Gaelic west friaries virtually replaced parish churches as the focus of religious life.

---

[1] The best description of Muckross is to be found in the official guidebook, written by Harold Leask (?) and published by the Office of Public Works, *The Friary of Muckross Commonly Called 'Muckross Abbey'*, Dublin, n.d.. See also H.G. Leask, *Irish Churches and Monastic Buildings*, 3, Dundalk, 1960, pp. 51, 97, 104–6. 140–42 and A. Gwynn and R.N. Hadcock, *Medieval Religious Houses: Ireland*, London, 1970, p. 256. The official guidebook (p. 4) may be wrong in supposing that some time elapsed between the building of the east and west ends of the church, as the same hood moulding is employed over both the east window and the west doorway. Nor is it certain that the tower is an insertion, as the guidebook argues.

[2] The most convenient introduction to the friars in Ireland can be found in J. Watt, *The Church in Medieval Ireland*, Dublin, 1972, especially pp. 60–84, 193–201. Watt shows that between 1400 and 1508 some 67 new Franciscan houses were founded, comprising 14 Conventual, 10 Observant and 43 Third Order foundations.

What makes the Irish friaries particularly interesting for students of English architecture is the dearth of such monuments in Britain. The English friaries suffered badly after the Reformation, and, with their urban locations, most of the buildings were reduced to fragments long before the twentieth century. Consequently it is difficult to form much impression of mendicant design and the influence it may have exerted. What remains are usually isolated buildings or fragmentary walls, the sort of thing architectural historians tend to leave to local archaeologists.[3] For anyone desiring a more complete view of English ecclesiastical architecture in the Middle Ages a trip to Kerry, Limerick, Galway or Mayo is a *sine qua non*.

There has been no modern study of mendicant architecture in Ireland and many issues await clarification.[4] Most of the buildings belong to the later Middle Ages and it is not clear how far they represent traditions established in the thirteenth century when the friars arrived.[5] Nor is it certain whether the well-preserved friaries in the west of the country reflect the situation in the more anglicised areas in the east, particularly in the Pale.[6] In the late thirteenth century the life of the Franciscans was badly disrupted by internal racial disputes and it is possible that the different cultural outlooks within the order may have had an effect on architecture.[7] There appear to be few obvious architectural contrasts

[3] The architecture of the Franciscans in England was examined by A. R. Martin, *Franciscan Architecture in England*, Manchester, 1937, but there is no equivalent survey of Dominican building. The general neglect of mendicant design is reflected in the mere two pages accorded to the subject by Geoffrey Webb in *Architecture in Britain: The Middle Ages*, Harmondsworth, 1956.

[4] There is an excellent series of articles on the Franciscan friaries by Canice Mooney, 'Franciscan Architecture in Pre-Reformation Ireland', *Journal of the Royal Society of Antiquaries of Ireland*, 85, 1955, pp. 133–73; 86, 1956, pp. 125–69; 87, 1957, pp. 1–38 and 103–24. For a recent general account of the Franciscans in Ireland see P. Conlan, *Franciscan Ireland*, Mullingar, 1988, and for the Dominicans see D.D.C. Pochin Mould, *The Irish Dominicans*, Dublin, 1957.

[5] The Dominicans arrived in Ireland in 1224, establishing houses at Dublin and Drogheda. The Franciscans came some years later and their first houses at Youghal and Cork were founded by 1231–32, Gwynn and Hadcock, op. cit., pp. 218, 236.

[6] The rural friaries in the west have survived far better than the urban foundations in the east. No medieval mendicant buildings exist in Dublin and architectural remains at Drogheda, Dundalk, New Ross, Waterford and Wexford are fragmentary. Surviving cloisters all have a western distribution. As many of the friaries in Munster and Connacht are of 15th-century date, it is difficult to decide how far they are following earlier practices, established in the east. Some of the eastern friaries were evidently in a poor state in 1540, when it was reported that the Dominican church at Drogheda and a great part of the dormitory 'had fallen down from age before the dissolution', *Extents of Irish Monastic Possessions, 1540–41*, ed. Newport B. White, Dublin, 1943, pp. 244–45. The state of things at Drogheda contrast with the smart new Franciscan friaries at places like Askeaton, Moyne, Rosserk etc., on the Atlantic seaboard.

[7] The most notorious episode occurred at the General Chapter of the Franciscan order, held at Cork in 1291, when racial quarrels led to a fracas in which sixteen friars were killed, Watt, op. cit., pp. 78–79.

48a Muckross Friary, general view from the south east.

48b Muckross Friary, east range of the cloister.

49a Askeaton Friary, interior of the north range of the cloister walk.

49b Muckross Friary, interior of the east range of the cloister.

between the Dominicans and the Franciscans, apart from the form of their belfries, though this may be an uninformed view.[8] Within the Franciscan movement some distinction might be expected between the Observants and the Conventuals, with the strict ideals of the Observants being expressed in architectural terms. These are broad issues, however, and this essay deals with two rather specific matters, namely how the Irish friars set about planning their buildings and the rationale behind their distinctive organisation of the cloisters. Implicit in both issues is the extent to which the Irish friars really belonged to the architectural world of Western Europe.

The cloisters at Muckross, along with those at Askeaton (Plate 49a), Quin, Moyne and Rosserilly, form one of the most delightful and least known groups of cloisters anywhere in Europe.[9] The dimensions tend to be small, with the garths rarely exceeding 12 to 15 m (40 to 50 feet) in width. At Muckross the sense of enclosure is enhanced by a huge yew tree, which envelopes the whole of the central court. In one fundamental respect, the Irish friary cloisters differ from the customary arrangements in Benedictine or Cistercian abbeys in that the walks are frequently integrated into the adjoining ranges and not covered by lean-to roofs. While this was not unique to Ireland, it was a common feature of the Irish houses. At first the scheme may have been adopted where space was short, most probably in an urban environment (though paradoxically such constraints did not apply in many of the Irish friaries, with their open, rural locations). The integrated system was employed extensively in England, whence it presumably spread to Ireland.[10]

In cloisters of this type the walks served as a support for chambers above and as a result they were usually vaulted in stone. In Ireland either barrel or groin vaulting was employed, (Muckross uses both) in preference to more expensive ribbed vaulting. The cloister arcades were required to lend support both to these vaults and to the upper walls of the various ranges. As a result they were designed in robust fashion and reinforced with buttresses. At Muckross, and at almost every other Irish friary, the arcades rest on twin shafts linked together, forming what is

[8] The typical Dominican belfry, as at Cashel or Kilkenny, extended the full width of the chancel, whereas the Franciscan towers, as at Moyne, Rosserk, Rosserilly, Quin and Kilconnell were narrower and considerably more elegant. Exceptionally the Franciscan belfries at Muckross, Clonmel and Dundalk followed the 'Dominican' pattern, Leask, op. cit., 3, pp. 51–52.

[9] Irish cloister design in the later Middle Ages is described by Leask, op. cit., 3, pp. 133–53; see also R. Stalley, *The Cistercian Monasteries of Ireland*, London and New Haven, 1987, pp. 153–60.

[10] Integrated cloisters were built in the Francisican houses at Ware, Walsingham, Dunwich, London, Bedford and Yarmouth. The system was also employed by the Dominicans at Bristol, Hereford, Newcastle and Norwich and by the Carmelites at Hulne and Aylesford, Martin, op. cit., p. 30. The west range of the Cistercian abbey at Cleeve was also built in this way, R. Gilyard Beer, *Cleeve Abbey, Somerset*, London, HMSO, 1960, pp. 41–43.

known as the 'dumb bell' pier (Plate 49a, b). The pseudo shafts can be either round (as at Askeaton) or octagonal (as at Muckross), and the arrangement is an interesting development of Romanesque design.[11] The twin colonnettes of the typical Romanesque cloister, however, were too fragile to support the heavy forces applied to them in the fifteenth century without some means of reinforcement. While the 'dumb bell' form has 'cousins' elsewhere in Europe, as in the north walk of the thirteenth-century cloisters at Noirlac, the stout proportions and dearth of tracery provide a distinctively Irish flavour.[12] The earliest surviving examples appear to be those in the cloister at Jerpoint, (c. 1390–1400), but it is likely there were precedents long before. Jerpoint was a Cistercian house, where the need for such piers was far less pressing than in the friaries, with their integrated cloisters.[13]

The cloisters at Muckross are flanked on the north and east sides by narrow vaulted chambers, dimly lit. It is difficult to believe that these claustrophobic spaces were rooms of much importance and at Muckross the vaulted ground floor of the east range, with internal dimensions of 16.61 x 3.19/3.30 m (54 feet 6 inches by 10 feet 6 inches/10 feet 10 inches), would have been most unsatisfactory as a chapter house.(Plate 50a)[14] The floors above, containing the dormitory and refectory, are better proportioned, since they extend over the vaults of the cloister below (Plate 50b). Clearly the builders could not have enlarged the ground floor chambers without making the upper rooms impractically wide. The drawback of the integrated cloister, therefore, was that it restricted the size and character of the adjoining ranges. In many cases the latter were reduced to little more than basements, providing a solid foundation for the sequence of upper halls and chambers, where the main living quarters of the friars were situated.[15] At Muckross this meant that space was not used all that effectively and, in contrast to traditional cloister design, the cloister walks provided only part of the necessary circulation system. Much of the traffic of the friars must have been up and down the various staircases and around the upper floors, rather than

[11] In one respect Muckross is unusual in that a raking buttress, forming part of the cloister pier, separates every arch in the arcade. The moulding of the buttress is neatly turned above the arch to form an architrave.

[12] M. Aubert, *L'Architecture Cistercienne*, ii, Paris, 1947, pp. 15–16, 19.

[13] Stalley, op. cit., pp. 154–55, 189–93.

[14] The north range has an equally narrow basement, measuring 3.24 m (10 feet 8 inches) at its maximum width. Leask, in the official guide to Muckross, suggested that the ground floor of the east range served as a 'day room', since it had a fireplace and there are traces of a garderobe in the north wall, op. cit., *Muckross Abbey*, p. 11. If this chamber was not the chapter house, it is hard to know where else in the friary the chapter house was situated.

[15] The descriptions of friaries made at the time of the Dissolution make reference to numerous 'cellars', *Extents*, passim. Nonetheless there are plenty of cases where the refectory was situated on the ground floor of the north range, Mooney, op. cit., 3, 87, 1957, pp. 22–23.

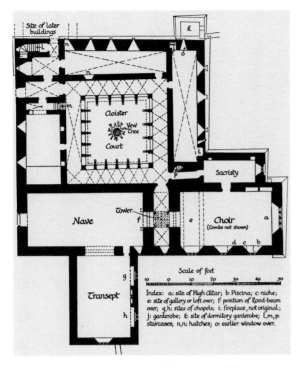

50a Muckross Friary, plan of the ground floor.

Index: a: site of High Altar; b: Piscina; c: niche; e: site of gallery or loft over; f: position of Rood-beam over; g,h: sites of chapels; i: fireplace, not original; j: garderobe; k: site of dormitory garderobe; l,m,p: staircases; n,n: hatches; o: earlier window over.

50b Muckross Friary, plan of upper floors.

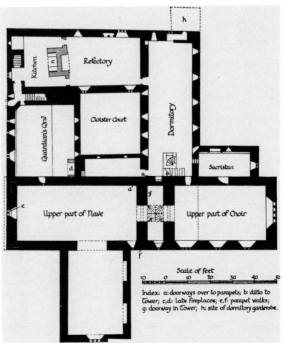

Index: a: doorways over to parapets; b: ditto to Tower; c,d: late fireplaces; e,f: parapet walks; g: doorway in Tower; h: site of dormitory garderobe.

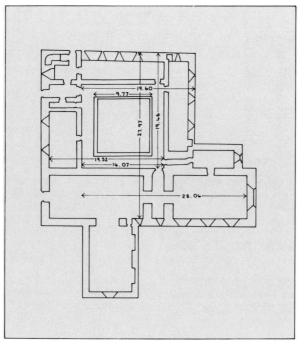

51a Muckross Friary, measurements mentioned in the text.

51b Muckross Friary, diagram showing the geometrical steps used to lay out the plan.

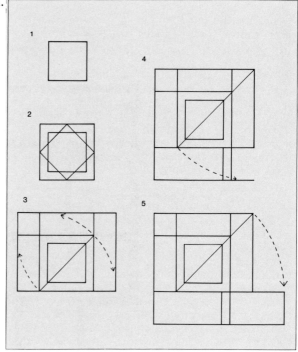

through the cloisters themselves.[16]

The narrowness of the ranges is one of several aspects of mendicant planning that have been criticised in the past. The late Canice Mooney commented on the irregularities, 'the chance measurements' and apparently arbitrary proportions found in the Irish friaries.[17] The habitual addition of one transept arm (and often one nave aisle) meant that the churches were lopsided and a first glance at the plans gives the impression that buildings were thrown together in all directions.[18] Although the belfry towers (and the passage or 'walking space' below) are usually placed at the junction of nave and chancel, close to the east walk of the cloister, there was no consistency in their precise location. To a large degree the irregularities are the consequence of piecemeal building, for towers, transepts and even western ranges of the cloister were often additions to the original fabric.[19]

Muckross is typical of this apparently arbitrary approach to design. The transept was a sixteenth-century addition and a vertical masonry joint on the facade of the church and at the junction with the north range demonstrates that the west range was erected some time after the nave was complete. The cloister, although square in plan, is divided into five bays to the north and east, but six to the south and west. These last two ranges, which are later in date, were given round rather than pointed arches. Three of the cloister walks are covered by groin vaults, whereas the fourth (the western one) has a barrel vault. Other anomalies at Muckross include the poor alignment of the north and east ranges. Despite these inconsistencies it is difficult to believe that everything was left to chance. Muckross was founded as a new house in the fifteenth

---

[16] The principal stairs were sited at the south end of the east range (leading to the dormitory) at the north end of the west range (to the refectory) and near the centre of the west range. It was possible to walk around three sides of the cloister at the upper level.

[17] Mooney, op. cit., 4, 87, 1957, p. 109.

[18] The single transept arm, which produces the lopsided plan, is a characteristic of Irish friaries and rare in England and Wales. It occurs at Chester and Llanfaes (Franciscan) and Warrington and Newport (Austin friars), Martin, op. cit., p. 16.

[19] The piecemeal building of the friars is discussed by Mooney, op. cit., I, 85, 1955, pp. 154, 168–71. In a large measure this was a result of the spasmodic nature of mendicant patronage, with friaries surviving on a multiplicity of relatively small benefactions. The Franciscan house at Adare (Limerick) had separate benefactors for the bell tower, chapels, wings of the cloister, refectory, choir stalls etc., Mooney, ibid., p. 171. The Register of the Dominican friary at Athenry (Galway) records a similar list of benefactors responsible for individual parts of the friary, M.J. Blake, 'The Abbey of Athenry', *Journal of the Galway Archaeological and Historical Society*, 2, 1902, pp. 65–90. The consequence of this type of funding is not hard to detect in the buildings and there are often sharp breaks, both in masonry and style, around different ranges of the cloister. This is particularly obvious at Quin (Clare) and there are similar breaks at Muckross. On the south-east pier of the cloister the springer for the first south arch was cut for a five bay arcade, rather than the six bay system as built. At the north-west angle the pier was not prepared with a springer for the west range, as if a west range was not envisaged at that time.

century and presumably a full complement of buildings was envisaged at the start, both by the friars and their patron, Donal McCarthy. At least some forethought must have been given to the layout of the buildings.

The cloister was in fact laid out quite accurately as a square, with (internal) sides varying from 13.85 to 14.15 m (45 feet 6 inches to 46 feet 5 inches), with an average of 14 m (45 feet 11 inches). Assuming a wall width was included in the dimensions, the intention may have been to make each side 15.24 m or 50 English feet.[20] If the area of the square of the cloister is halved, according to the drawing shown in Villard de Honnecourt's sketchbook, the inner square of the cloister garth is defined.[21] 14 divided by the square root of two gives 9.90 and, along their inner sides (facing the cloister walks), the walls supporting the cloister arcades measure 9.77 to 9.78 m (32 feet 1 inch).[22]

If the square formed by the cloister garth (9.77 x 9.78 m; 32 feet x 32 feet 1 inch) was used as the geometrical starting point, the layout of the rest of the friary begins to fall into place. If one side is multiplied by root two it gives 13.82 m (45 feet 4 inches), approximating to 14 m (46 feet), the average for one side of the whole cloister. It seems that the 'secret' of the medieval masons may also explain the uncomfortably narrow ranges which flank the cloister. When multiplied by the square root of two 13.82 generates 19.54. The combined width of the cloister and north range (measured along the east walk of the cloister) is approximately 19.46 m (63 feet 10 inches) and the equivalent measurement across the east range is 19.6 m (64 feet 4 inches).[23] These dimensions are (inevitably) almost exactly twice the length of one side of the cloister garth 9.77 m (32 feet). The internal width of the west range is slightly wider than the others, but if the outer (west) wall is excluded, the cloister and west range combined measure 19.52 m (64 feet) (Plate 51a).

It is likely that a ratio based on the square root of two was again invoked to establish the lines of the church. If 19.54 is multiplied by the square root of two it gives 27.64. This is within 33 cm (1 foot 1 inch) of the combined width of the church, the cloister and the north range, which amounts to 27.97 m (91 feet 6 inches). In an east-west direction

[20] One cannot of course automatically assume that the English foot of 0.3048 m was in use in the west of Ireland. For the problems associated with medieval metrology see E. Fernie, 'Historical Metrology and Architectural History', *Art History*, 1, 1978, pp. 383–99. If the average width of the cloister (14 m, 46 feet) is added to the adjoining wall of the church (1.27 m, 4 feet 2 inches) the total is 15.27 m (50 feet 1 inch). However, the walls of the east, north and west ranges are only 80 cm (2 feet 7 inches) in thickness, giving a total of 14.8 m (48 feet 7 inches).

[21] H.R. Hahnloser, *Villard de Honnecourt*, Graz, 1972, pl. 39, pp. 107–8.

[22] The lower walls supporting the east and north cloister arcades are a mere 66 cm (2 feet 2 inches) thick.

[23] The north range fluctuates in width from 2.90 m (9 feet 6 inches) along the east wall to 3.35 m (11 feet) along the west. The measurements include the outer walls of the north and east ranges.

the same methods may have been employed to determine the position of the east wall of the chancel. This projects 14.02 m (46 feet) beyond the end of the east cloister walk and the combined length of the chancel and cloister comes to 28.06 m (92 feet) (Plate 51a).[24] The table below lists the critical dimensions mentioned so far and the accompanying diagram (Plate 51b) illustrates in geometrical terms the successive steps evidently taken in laying out the friary.

Table 2

Muckross Friary, Principal Dimensions

	Ideal (9.77 as base unit)	Actual	
Cloister garth	9.77	9.77	(32' 1")
Cloister	13.82	14.00	(45' 11")
Cloister + E. range	19.54	19.60	(64' 4")
Cloister + N. range	19.54	19.46	(63' 10")
Cloister + W. range	19.54	19.52	(64' 0")
Cloister + N. range + church	27.64	27.97	(91' 9")
Cloister + chancel	27.64	28.06	(92' 1")

Admittedly, the relationship between theory and fact is far from absolute and it is necessary on occasions to switch from internal to external measurements. While this might be exactly how the builders operated, with ropes or marks on the ground sometimes indicating inner, sometimes outer, wall faces, it nevertheless introduces an arbitrary element into the argument. If this major qualification is set aside, the discrepancies between actual and 'ideal' measurements are less than one per cent. Given that Muckross is constructed of rubble and that the builders had difficulties defining right angles, the correspondences seem too close to be dismissed as coincidence. Moreover, the use of the traditional method of 'doubling the square' as a device to define the ranges around the cloister may explain one of the anomalies of Irish friary architecture. With a cloister measuring 30.48 m (100 feet) across, the ratio 1: root-2 produces an additional length of 12.8 m (42 feet), a convenient width for an adjoining range, as found in the twelfth-century abbey at Jerpoint.[25] With the small friary cloisters the use of root two ratios generated rather narrow spaces. While there may have been utilitarian advantages in this, it is worth considering whether, in geo-metrical matters, the builders of Muckross were slaves to tradition, being constrained by an ancient device which they almost unwittingly followed.

---

[24] The measurement 28.06 m (92 feet) does not include the width of the east wall of the chancel and its great battered external plinth.

[25] Stalley, op. cit., p. 75.

Muckross may be an isolated example of these methods of planning and it would be unwise to deduce too much about Irish Gothic from this monument alone. In style, however, it is fairly typical of mendicant architecture in the second half of the fifteenth century, a period when the friars were particularly active as builders. The friary was still unfinished in 1486 when, 950 miles away the Regensburg architect, Mathes Roriczer, enshrined the 'secret of the medieval masons' and the successive use of root-two ratios in his *Buechlein von der Fialen Gerechtigkeit.*[26] Remote in the mountains of Kerry, the friars of Muckross lived on the fringes of Europe, but their builders, at least, appear to have known something about the secrets of Gothic design.

[26] L.R. Shelby, ed., *Gothic Design Techniques: The Fifteenth Century Design Booklets of Mathes Roriczer and Hanns Schmuttermayer,* Carbondale, 1977. For a brief discussion of the so-called secret of the medieval masons see P. Frankl, 'The Secret of the Medieval Masons', *Art Bulletin,* 27, 1945, pp. 46-60, especially pp. 49–62, where Frankl emphasises that root-two ratios were used as a substitute for scale drawing and the employment of cumbersome yardsticks.

20

Remarques sur la Bibliothèque du Chapitre
de Notre-Dame de Paris au XVe Siècle

Anne Prache

Les cathédrales médiévales ont souvent conservé en Angleterre de nombreuses constructions annexes, palais de l'évêque, bâtiments des chanoines ou des moines. En France, peu de cathédrales ont conservé l'ensemble immobilier, qui formait la cité épiscopale, une ville ecclésiastique à l'intérieur de la ville. La sécularisation des biens d'Eglise à la Révolution et la suppression des chapitres cathédraux ont eu pour conséquence la mise en vente et la dispersion des immeubles. En outre, la situation de ces immeubles au coeur de tissus urbains très denses dans notre pays a provoqué des spéculations sur les terrains, des destructions, des remodelages des îlots d'habitations et et de la voirie. Il faut alors recourir aux descriptions et aux plans, aux estampes et aux dessins anciens, pour restituer ce que fut autrefois l'environnement de bon nombre de cathédrales.

Le cas de Notre-Dame de Paris est bien connu de tous les historiens de la capitale. Son site sur l'Ile de la Cité, entre deux bras de la Seine, a accentué les difficultés d'extension dès le Moyen Age et a entraîné de nombreuses démolitions alentour au XIXe siècle.[1] L'Ile de la Cité ne couvre que huit hectares. Dès le Haut Moyen Age, la partie occidentale, le palais, a été réservée au pouvoir civil et la partie orientale dévolue à l'Eglise. La cathédrale, reconstruite dans la seconde moitié du XIIe siècle, a occupé la majeure part de l'espace disponible et sa façade a marqué la limite occidentale de la cité épiscopale, avec une extension le long du bras sud de la Seine pour l'hotel-dieu.[2] Le palais de l'évêque s'élevait aussi sur le flanc sud. Au nord s'étendait, un peu plus au large, le quartier canonial, enclos ou cloître. On disait le *cloître Notre-Dame*, mais il n'y avait pas de cour de cloître entourée de galeries. Le quartier, dont subsistent quelques vestiges, formait un tissu serré d'habitations, de sanctuaires secondaires, de jardins et de vignes. Bien que les descriptions anciennes de ce site soient relativement nombreuses et que l'histoire en

---

[1] Voir par exemple P. Lavedan et J. Hugueney, *L'urbanisme au Moyen Age*, Paris-Genève, 1974, p. 25 et p. 152.

[2] Nombreux documents reproduits dans A. Marty, *L'histoire de Notre-Dame de Paris d'après les estampes, dessins, miniatures, tableaux, exécutés aux XVe XVIe, XVIIe, XVIIIe et XIXe siècles*, Paris, 1907.

ait été établie, les spécialistes de l'architecture médiévale ne se sont guère souciés jusqu'à présent d'étudier les bâtiments canoniaux de Notre-Dame. C'est par hasard, à l'occasion d'une participation à un ouvrage sur les bibliothèques médiévales de France, que je me suis intéressée à la bibliothèque du chapitre de Notre-Dame.[3]

Les chanoines des cathédrales possédaient en général une biblio-thèque. André Masson, dans un livre paru en 1972, en a relevé plusieurs. Il écrit: 'Les chanoines des cathédrales, comme les moines des abbayes, avaient leur bibliothèque, le plus souvent construite au-dessus d'une galerie de cloître'.[4] Et il cite en exemple celles de St-Dié, d'Angers, de Tours, du Puy, celle-ci située dans un bâtiment parallèle à la galerie occidentale du cloître. Il mentionne aussi celle de Bayeux, plantée au milieu de la cour du cloître, celle de Rouen, reliée au bras nord du transept, celle de Noyon, située en dehors de la cour du cloître, mais aussi raccordée indirectement au bras nord, celle de Troyes, d'abord en étage à l'est de la cour claustrale, puis reconstruite perpendiculairement à la quatrième travée de la nef en 1473. Ces bibliothèques datent pour la plupart de la fin du Moyen Age. D'une façon générale, elles sont situées en étage, sans doute pour bénéficier de plus de lumière et aussi pour mettre les livres à l'abri de l'humidité. La structure la plus courante, et pas seulement pour les bibliothèques des chapitres cathédraux, paraît avoir été la galerie, ouverte d'une rangée de fenêtres sur un long côté, les livres disposés en face et entre les ouvertures.

Les documents, qui concernent la bibliothèque des chanoines de Notre-Dame de Paris, ont été publiés en 1877 par Alfred Franklin.[5] De 1682 à sa fermeture définitive en novembre 1790, elle a été installée en étage dans une maison, qui servait d'entrée à l'enclos canonial au nord de la cathédrale. Auparavant, elle avait été conservée dans un bâtiment spécialement construit entre 1462 et 1465, à l'est du chevet, près de la petite église St-Denis-du-Pas. Sans doute ce bâtiment était-il trop exigu, car, dès le XVIe siècle, le chapitre désirait déménager la bibliothèque. Avant la construction de 1462–65, il n'y avait pas de bibliothèque digne de ce nom dans le cloître Notre-Dame. A. Franklin a noté la mention d'une école en 1217, *infra ambitum claustri, quidam locus adherens episcopali curie*, dans le cloître, contre le palais épiscopal, mais il n'y est pas question de la bibliothèque.

Vers 1370 elle existe pourtant et le chancelier Grimier Boniface propose alors de la mettre au-dessus de la chapelle St-Aignan. Cette chapelle du XIIe siècle subsiste encore en partie, rue Chanoinesse, au nord de Notre-Dame. Finalement en 1405, le chapitre décide de trouver une place pour la bibliothèque à l'intérieur de la cathédrale. A la date du 5

---

[3] *Histoire des bibliothèques françaises*, i, *Le Moyen Age et l'Humanisme*, ouvrage collectif publié sous la direction d' A. Vernet, à paraître fin 1989.

[4] A. Masson, *Le décor de bibliothèques du Moyen Age à la Révolution*, Genève, 1972, p. 22.

[5] A. Franklin, *Les anciennes bibliothèques de Paris*, i, Paris, 1877, p. 3–34.

52   Paris, Notre-Dame, nave: drawing by Danjoy, Monuments Historiques, plan no. 21.661.

août 1412, dans les registres du chapitre, on lit: 'Conclusum est quod in turri ecclesiae de sinistro latere, per quam fit ascensus ad libreriam, de novo ordinatum supra testudines seu voltas ejusdem ecclesiae, fiat claritas major, tam per apertionem seu dilationem fenestrarum jam factarum, quam per operationes unius fenestrae novae in loco bassiori'.[6] A. Franklin en a conclu que l'accès se faisait par la tour nord de la façade et que la bibliothèque était, avant 1462, dans les combles de la cathédrale.[7]

Ce n'est guère vraisemblable. Quiconque a monté les marches de Notre-Dame jusqu'au grand comble imagine aisément que les ouvrages placés là auraient été pratiquement inaccessibles. De plus l'éclairage y est très insuffisant. Si, d'après le texte de 1412, les chanoines se souciaient d'améliorer la lumière dans l'escalier d'accès de la tour nord par l'agrandissement des fenêtres existantes et par le percement d'une nouvelle ouverture, ils avaient du déjà aménager un local bien éclairé pour la bibliothèque nouvellement organisée. Les voûtes, sur lesquelles elle était située d'après le texte, devaient être celles du bas-côté intérieur de la nef. Autrement dit, la bibliothèque avait été installée dans la tribune septentrionale de la nef. L'escalier de la tour nord communique directement avec l'ancien cloître canonial et donne accès à une salle en étage, d'où on peut gagner, au même niveau, la galerie de la tribune. Celle-ci, dans sa disposition, peut être comparée à l'étage d'une galerie de cour de cloître, à ceci près qu'au lieu d'ouvrir sur la cour, elle donne sur la nef de l'église. L'éclairage y est tout de même satisfaisant, puisqu'il y a des fenêtres dans le mur extérieur, qui donnent un jour direct dans la tribune.

Il ne reste plus trace de fenêtres anciennes, sauf dans la première travée, contre la tour nord de la façade. Viollet-le-Duc a en effet refait toutes les autres fenêtres de la tribune, une par travée, en leur donnant la forme de larges triangles en arc brisé, courts et haut placés. La structure de Notre-Dame au niveau de la tribune est en effet assez complexe. La tribune elle-même surmonte le bas-coté intérieur de la nef. Or, au rez-de-chaussée, il y a deux bas-côtés juxtaposés et, au-delà, des chapelles ajoutées au XIIIe siècle entre les contreforts du XIIe. Les chapelles sont couvertes de toits à deux pans, perpendiculaires au sens longitudinal de la nef. Du côté de la rue, au nord, ces toits posent sur des pignons triangulaires, percés d'ouvertures pour éclairer les combles des chapelles. Ces combles forment autant de petites pièces rectangulaires, qui s'ouvrent au sud au-dessus du bas-côté extérieur de la nef sur une galerie aveugle, qui double la tribune. Cette galerie est scandée d'arcs-diaphragmes, qui portent une couverture dallée en pente douce, presque une terrasse, pour relier le mur extérieur de la tribune aux toits des chapelles. A l'intérieur, on peut donc, sans sortir, passer de

---

[6] Idem, p. 50.
[7] Idem, p. 20.

la tribune dans la galerie aveugle et de là aux combles des chapelles. L'espace est considérable.

Tout paraît avoir été très restauré au XIXe siècle. Les combles et les toits des chapelles ont été refaits. Dans la galerie aveugle, seuls deux arcs-diaphragmes sont partiellement anciens, mais la galerie existait avant les restaurations. Les Archives des Monuments Historiques conservent des dessins exécutés à la fin de 1843 ou au début de 1844 par l'architecte Danjoy, admis à participer au concours pour la restauration de Notre-Dame (Plate 52).[8] Finalement, c'est le projet de Lassus et de Viollet-le-Duc qui a été retenu.[9] Danjoy, en tout cas, a fait deux dessins, une élévation du côté extérieur nord de la nef sur une travée et une coupe transversale au niveau de la tribune, qu'il appelle 'triforium'. Il indique la galerie aveugle, 'galerie couverte en dalles', et les combles des chapelles, ou 'petites salles'. Il montre les arcs-diaphragmes et note que 'la construction de ces arcs parait être du même temps' que les chapelles.

Sur le dessin de l'élévation extérieure, la fenêtre qui éclaire le niveau de la tribune est différente de la réalisation de Viollet-le-Duc. C'est une baie sans ornement, à deux montants verticaux réunis au sommet par un arc brisé. Danjoy a dessiné deux prolongements de cet arc, à ses extrêmités, sur les murs, jusqu'aux contreforts latéraux de la travée. Il note à propos de la fenêtre, qu'il appelle *croisée* dans la tradition du XVIIIe siècle, 'croisée formée par les jambages de l'ancienne baie et l'arc de la voûte du triforium (tribune) au devant duquel il se trouve un deuxième quelquefois ne s'accordant pas avec lui pour la hauteur. Cet arc extérieur après le dérasement du mur a été ajouté pour supporter la corniche'. La corniche est celle qui court au sommet du mur extérieur de la tribune, dont la couverture a été abaissée au XIIIe siècle pour permettre l'agrandissement des fenêtres hautes.

De toute évidence, l'élévation extérieure de la nef de Notre-Dame a été profondondément transformée au XIIIe siècle. Au XIIe, deux toits en appentis devaient, l'un couvrir le bas-coté extérieur et buter assez haut contre le mur de la tribune, l'autre surmonter la tribune jusqu'à la base des fenêtres hautes primitives, beaucoup plus courtes. L'adjonction des chapelles latérales a conduit à modifier la couverture du bas-côté extérieur, en établissant les arcs-diaphragmes et la galerie aveugle, afin de conserver un minimum de pente jusqu'aux toits des chapelles pour l'écoulement des eaux pluviales. En raison de la galerie aveugle, l'appui des fenêtres des tribunes n'a guère pu être abaissé. Par contre, le dallage posé sur les voûtes de la tribune a permis l'agrandissement des fenêtres

---

[8] Paris, Archives des Monuments Historiques, plan no 21.661. Je remercie très vivement Mme Chantal Hardy, professeur à l'université de Montréal, qui m'a communiqué les références et les reproductions des documents.

[9] Voir J.M. Leniaud, *Jean-Baptiste Lassus (1807–1857) ou le temps retrouvé des cathédrales*, Paris-Genève, 1980, p. 43.

hautes par le bas. Les arcs signalés par Danjoy pour porter la corniche ont dû être montés aussi au XIIIe siècle en même temps que la nouvelle couverture.

Après 1844, en plus des restaurations des couvertures, le mur extérieur de la tribune a été reconstruit. Viollet-le-Duc s'est inspiré des arcs qui portaient la corniche pour dessiner des fenêtres, qui en rappellent la forme. La fenêtre indiquée par Danjoy était différente, on l'a vu. Etait-elle pour autant d'origine? On peut se demander si les chanoines ne l'avait pas faite agrandir par le haut, entre 1405 et 1412, ce qui expliquerait que son encadrement supérieur épousait directement la voûte et que les arcs du XIIIe siècle sous la corniche ne coincidaient pas toujours avec les ouvertures.

Nulle trace ne subsiste aujourd'hui dans la tribune nord de la nef pour rappeler l'ordonnance de la bibliothèque, qui y resta une soixantaine d'années. Les ouvrages pouvaient être rangés le long du mur extérieur, sous les fenêtres. Il y avait aussi beaucoup de place disponible dans la galerie aveugle, parallèle, et dans ce cas, la tribune elle-même aurait été réservée à la consultation et à la lecture. L'histoire de cette bibliothèque inspire deux conclusions. D'une part, il sera toujours difficile de démêler la chronologie des éléments de l'architecture de Notre-Dame, malgré l'existence du journal des travaux du XIXe siècle, parce que, depuis le XIIe, il y eut de multiples remaniements. L'installation de la bibliothéque dans la tribune n'est qu'un épisode, mais qui a pu modifier l'élévation septentrionale de la nef. D'autre part, elle pose la question de l'utilisation des tribunes latérales des églises, après l'abandon de leur fonction liturgique. Edgar Lehmann a indiqué que la première bibliothèque de l'université de Heidelberg a été placée dans la tribune d'une église voisine, à peu près à la même époque qu'à Notre-Dame.[10] Il paraît vraisemblable que, dans les villes où les enclos canoniaux ne pouvaient s'étendre faute de terrain disponible, les chanoines aient songé à des solutions comparables à celle de Notre-Dame pour pallier au manque de construction appropriée.[11]

---

[10] E. Lehmann, *Die Bibliotheksraueme der deutschen Kloester in Mittelalter*, Berlin, 1957. La bibliothèque a été mise dans la tribune de la Heilliggeistkirche vers 1421–41.

[11] Philippe Plagnieux m'a communiqué une note digne d'être ajoutée. Le 19 Germinal an 7, le ministre des Finances écrivit au ministre de l'Intérieur: 'Concernant les précautions à prendre pour mettre la Bibliothèque Nationale à l'abri des accidents du feu je dois vous prévenir que le Directoire exécutif a pensé ... qu'il seroit possible de transporter la Bibliothèque dans la cidevant Eglise Notre Dame' (Paris, Archives Nationales, F13 872).

21

King's College, Cambridge:
Observations on its Context and Foundations

Walter Leedy

King's College, Cambridge, is of remarkable historical importance, and its chapel, as Walpole wrote, is 'alone ... sufficient to enoble any age'. Essential to understanding this achievement are the circumstances surrounding its nascent phase, 1440–50; for it was during this decade that its educational mission and architectural program matured. Relative to this critical decision-making period several fundamental questions can be raised, none of which have easy or necessarily absolute answers: What motivated the king to establish a college in Cambridge? How was its precise location in Cambridge chosen? How was the scale of its architectural plan determined? What can the size of the foundations for the present chapel tell us about its original design?

John Langton, Master of Pembroke College and Chancellor of Cambridge University, lobbied King Henry VI to establish a new college at Cambridge.[1] Meeting with success, Langton, along with John Fray, Chief Baron of the Exchequer, and John Somerset, Chancellor of the Exchequer and a former tutor of Henry VI's, were appointed members of a Royal Commission to select a suitable site. On 14 September 1440 they purchased the first of three parcels of land for the new college, a garden belonging to Trinity Hall.[2] This purchase was followed by two others in October and November. Thus the whole site was quickly acquired (the university owned one of the parcels which it sold to the commissioners) and conveyed to the king in one deed dated 22 January, 19 Henry VI (1440–41).[3] To what degree ease of acquisition influenced the decision to locate the college here is unknown, but a clue was inserted in the deed as to why this location was selected: besides the usual abuttals, the site was described as next to the new Schools of Theology and Canon

---

[1] A list of benefactors indicates that Langton *per instancias suas et labores speciales* secured the foundation of the college, perhaps as the outcome of an earlier effort to establish a 'university college' under royal patronage. See John Saltmarsh, 'King's College', Victoria History of the Counties of England, *Cambridgeshire and the Isle of Ely*, iii, 1959, p. 376.

[2] King's College Muniment, A. 68; cited in Robert Willis and John Willis Clark, *The Architectural History of the University of Cambridge and of the Colleges of Cambridge and Eton*, Cambridge, 1886, I, p. 319.

[3] King's College Muniment, A. 76, cited in Willis and Clark, I, p. 318.

Law, which were then under construction. In addition, the site had primary frontage on Milne Street, which in the fifteenth century was an important collegial thoroughfare (Plate 53).

Henry VI granted the site and founded the college by Letters Patent dated on 12 February 1441 by the title of *Rector et Scolares Collegii Regalis Sancti Nicolai de Cantebrigia.*[4] The statutes were to be written by a commission headed by William Alnwick, Bishop of Lincoln. The foundation stone was laid by Henry VI himself on Passion Sunday, 2 April 1441.[5]

The Letters Patent envisioned a college composed of a rector and twelve scholars (this number could fluctuate based on the revenues of the college), and construction began. To speed the project along, as well as to control costs, reused materials from Cambridge Castle were allocated to the project.[6]

Soon after construction commenced, the initial plans for the college were dramatically altered, and the college was refounded by Letters Patent on 10 July 1443, when it assumed a new title: *Collegium Regale Beate Marie et Sancti Nicholai de Cantebrigia.*[7] At this time, the king himself assumed the responsibility for making the statutes. During this period the endowments for the college were significantly increased and, based on increasing numbers, the provost and scholars petitioned the king for the larger site.[8] By 26 August 1443, the purchase of a larger site had begun.[9] The college was evolving, therefore, into a more substantial institution. By 1445, if not earlier, the new college was to have seventy scholars.[10] The endowment gradually increased, through a number of grants, to a substantial amount, as did the numerous rights and extraordinary privileges that were bestowed upon the college.[11] Over time the king's enthusiasm to enlarge his own creation grew, and the pressures to do so appear to have been substantial. The enlargement of the college was therefore the result of a joint decision between the king, the college, and university officials. Unlike Henry VI's college at Eton, the 1441 foundation charter did not single out King's College as a memorial to his assumption of the governance of the realm. By 1448, however, he referred to it as 'the primer notable werk purposed by me after ... I ... took vnto my silf the rule of my saide Roiames [Realms]'.[12] What reasons may have led the King to establish such a large college, and why at Cambridge instead of Oxford?

---

[4] *Calendar of the Patent Rolls, 1436–41*, pp. 521–23.

[5] King's College Muniment, Box M. 9; cited by Willis and Clark, I, p.321.

[6] *Calendar of the Patent Rolls, 1436–41*, 507 (15 February 1441).

[7] *Calendar of the Patent Rolls, 1441–46*, 197.

[8] *Rotuli Parliamentorum*, v, 163b–164a.

[9] Willis and Clark, I, p. 337.

[10] Great Britain, Public Record Office, Calendar of Papal Letters, 1431–47, 479.

[11] For a discussion of these, see Saltmarsh, 'King's College', pp. 377ff.

[12] J.W. Clark and M.R. James, *The Will of King Henry the Sixth*, Cambridge, 1896, p. 4.

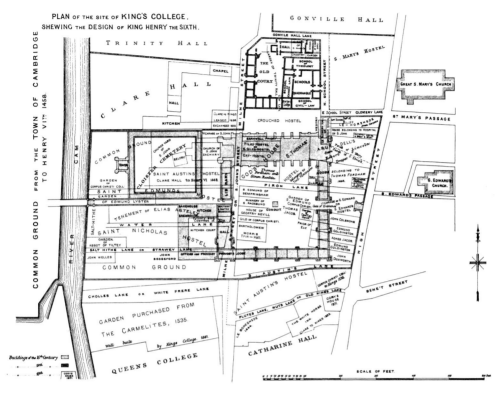

53 Cambridge, King's College, site plan showing plan of Henry VI (from Willis and Clarke, IV, fig. 3).

The statutes for the enlarged foundation, which the King had assumed responsibility for devising, stipulate that out of the seventy projected scholars, only eight might study subjects such as Canon or Civil Law, Medicine, or Astronomy. The rest were to study the Arts, Philosophy or Theology.[13] Broadly speaking, the college's educational goals rejected secular utilitarian values. By doing so they conflicted with the typical medieval student's highly pragmatic view of the purpose of a university education. This was exceptional for most medieval colleges and sets King's College apart from most other colleges at Cambridge.[14] With the goals of the extirpation of the heresy then current in England, the augmentation of the priesthood, and the strengthening of the church, Oxford was probably automatically excluded, as in the fifteenth century it had a reputation as a 'University of Heresies'.[15] In 1458–59 Henry VI revised the statutes to exclude specifically the followers of Pecock (the bishop condemned as a heretic in 1457), as well as Lollards, from the benefits of the foundation.

Fifteenth-century writers deplored the lack of men of spiritual capacity within the church. One of the central themes in thoughtful letters written in fifteenth-century England is the notion that the ills of society might be cured by a spiritual regeneration that would emanate from the universities.[16] The original statutes for King's College deplore the lack of clerics, and notice the acute shortage of teachers. This objective seems to be borne out by the manuscripts in their library and by bequests to the college. The earliest catalogue from around 1452 records 175 manuscripts, out of which there were none on Civil Law, and no Civil Law manuscripts were given by bequest throughout the fifteenth century.[17] This was not the case for other Cambridge colleges. A lavish endowment provided by Henry VI made King's College possible. As medieval universities ran on paltry budgets, non-vocational education required outside funding.

Not all of the Henry VI supporters were impressed with his foundation. In 1451 some members of parliament considered the great expense involved an unwarranted attempt by the king to lay up for himself treasures in heaven.[18] On the one hand King's College can be seen to be an endeavour to stimulate spiritual values in English society by a partial

---

[13] The Queen's Commissioners, *Documents Relating to the University and Colleges of Cambridge*, London, 1852, II, pp. 471–80.

[14] Alan B. Cobban, *The Medieval Universities: Their Development and Organization*, London, 1975, pp. 163, 228. This pattern is detectable at Queens' College (founded 1446) and much later at Jesus College (founded 1497).

[15] *Calendar of the Patent Rolls, 1441–46*, 197 (10 July 1443).   [16] See Henry Anstey, ed., *Epistolae Academicae Oxon.*, Oxford, 1898, esp. letters 81, 106, 177, 181, 189 and 207.

[17] See Saltmarsh, 'King's College', p. 393 and notes for pertinent bibliography.

[18] B. Wolffe, *Henry VI*, London 1981, pp. 7–8.

return to meditative, monastic ideals;[19] on the other hand, it can be seen as an attempt by Henry VI to purchase a place in paradise for himself. For the fifteenth-century mind these were not necessarily inconsistent or paradoxical objectives.

The initial site acquired for the college in 1441 was modest, and it was planned around a quadrangle, which was only partially completed. Construction apparently stopped when the foundation was enlarged, as this quadrangle was to be abandoned. Since no plan or description for the proposed design survives, it is not known whether the college was to have a chapel integral to the quadrangle, a free standing chapel to be placed adjacent to it, or even if a chapel was intended. A clue to answering this question is contained in a gloss that describes where the foundation stone for the college was laid. It states the King laid the first stone in the turret of the gate towards Clare Hall.[20] As it was common practice to lay the foundation stone at the location of the high altar, perhaps a chapel was not originally envisioned, and the college was to use a parish church.

Later, a chapel, which fell down just after vespers in 1536-37, was built just south of the early quadrangle just outside the smaller gate (*portam minorem*) and north of the present chapel.[21] Its first stone was laid on 29 September 1444.[22] This happened after the college was refounded and after additional land for a larger site was purchased in August 1443.[23] Writing about its collapse, John Caius (d. 1573) recalled that it was a mean and inconvenient structure.[24] This may suggest that its fabric was inconsistent with the quality of the architectural work of the quadrangle itself and therefore that this chapel may have been intended as a temporary facility. Yet because of its date of foundation, 1444, a real possibility exists that this chapel might have been part of a projected new architectural plan for the enlarged foundation, which in turn was later abandoned for a still more ambitious undertaking. Support for this developmental process (the aggrandisement of its physical plan in gradual steps rather than in one striking act) finds its parallel in the way the endowments and privileges for the college multiplied during this period.

The enlarged foundation called for a larger site. To amass a large parcel of property in the centre of Cambridge was a mighty task and took several years to accomplish. The site chosen was located contiguous to

[19] Cobban, p. 228, sees this as the direction of the collegiate movement in 15th-century Cambridge.

[20] 'Lapis iste positus est in dextra scilicet meridionali turre porte versus Clare Halle'. Printed in Willis and Clark, I, p. 321.

[21] There is a charge in the Mundum Book, 1536–37, for removing the materials; cited in Willis and Clark, I, p. 497, n. 2.

[22] Saltmarsh, 'King's College', p. 378, n. 32.

[23] Willis and Clark, I, p. 337.

[24] John Caius, *Historiae Cantabrigiensis Academiae ... Liber primus*, posthumously published, 1574, p. 69.

the early site, just south of it, and ran from High Street (now King's Parade) all the way to the river (Plate 53). This was the only way the college could be reasonably expanded without interfering with the other import- ant colleges and schools located on the west, north, and east sides. The area was a built-up section of the city. A church, an inn, private houses and tenements were all demolished, and streets were vacated to make way for the college.

While it is impossible to analyse fully the impact that this clearing had on the town, the evidence seems to indicate that this project increased the already acute housing shortage which resulted in part from the frequency of urban fires (in 1385, for example, over one hundred tenements were gutted by accidental fires) and a general unwillingness of commercial interests in fifteenth-century England to build speculative housing. These factors increased the costs of urban living and resulted in depopulation.[25] In 1446 citizens complained that houses formerly occu- pied by craftsmen were now inhabited by scholars, and were not charge- able for the town relief. They also pointed out that the demolition for King's College had left a large quarter untenanted; and that in conse- quence craftsmen were quitting the town, thereby leaving it impover- ished.[26] Compensation was sought by the Corporation in 1445 for the loss of access to the Salt Hythe, an important quay, by allowing a new way down to the river to be made to the north of Trinity Hall, but this was not granted until 1455.[27] With the foundation in 1446 of Queens' College, Cambridge was effectively divorced from the river trade.[28]

Local geographic conditions did not help matters. The fens reached almost the outskirts of the town, and their stagnant water bred pestilence, which kept King Henry VI from attending the laying of the first stone for the 1444 chapel.[29] Cambridge declined throughout the fifteenth and early sixteenth centuries. While this may have been part of a national phenomenon, there is no question that in Cambridge, the King's College project intensified this decline.

The choice of this specific building site within Cambridge had clear advantages. Besides giving the college frontage on the town's major commercial and religious street, it helped to control building costs. Since an important quay was situated there, stone and other building materials could be brought by boat or barge directly to the site. The river was still tidal and stone delivery could be timed to coincide with

---

[25] *Calendar of the Patent Rolls, 1441–46*, 458 (18 July 1446).

[26] Arthur Gray, *The Town of Cambridge: A History*, Cambridge, 1925, p. 71.

[27] Charles Henry Cooper, *Annals of Cambridge*, 1842–1908, I, pp. 191–193; Willis and Clark, I, pp. 212, 343–44.

[28] See Mary Doreen Lobel, 'Cambridge', in M.D. Lobel, ed., *The Atlas of Historic Towns*, London, 1975, II, p. 15.

[29] British Library, Add. Ms. 7096, fo. 148b. Letter, Henry VI to Abbot Curteys, on 17 September 1444. For the dating of this letter see Saltmarsh, op. cit., p. 378, n. 2.

it.[30] At times transport by river was hazardous: it rose to such heights upon one occasion that men were swept away and drowned.[31] When the river level was too low, stone came by land, at twice the price. This influenced the times at which building materials were purchased to be stockpiled, and, therefore, dates of purchase for materials in the surviving building accounts are not sure indicators of when they were employed.

Henry VI's commissioners thus chose the best site in the city for the college to represent the prestige of the king and his love of ceremony and monumentality. It also gave visibility to the magnitude of its intended function. Henry VI's architectural intentions were laid down in a letter of intent known as the 'Will of King Henry VI'. This document, dated 12 March 1448, describes the architectural plan of the proposed establishment. Dimensions are given in English feet; this fact suggests that the design may have been developed as a scale drawing rather than a proportional one and one that was site-specific.

Following the latest Oxford fashion (there is a preponderance of evidence that Henry VI looked to Oxford colleges to form his ideal vision of King's College) the chapel was planned to form one side of a quadrangle. Henry VI in his 'Will' instructed that the chapel was to 'conteyne in lenghte CCiiijxx viij. fete'; that is, the internal dimension of the chapel was to be 288 feet (87.78 m at 30.48 cm to the foot), much larger than function alone might dictate.[32] In spite of many changes in the design of the chapel, it is to this dimension that the chapel was actually built. Unquestionably, ensuing from the lofty mission of the college, it was intended to be symbolic as well as functional. But how was the chapel's length determined? To what extent was it the result of an arbitrary decision? An investigation into the relationship of Henry VI's plan to the physical conditions and legal limits of the site give some insight into the decision-making and planning process.

The westernmost limit of the chapel is located just off the alluvium laid down by the river.[33] This was probably done to avoid structural problems. (Modern buildings in Cambridge built partially on and partly off the river's alluvium show evidence of uneven settlement, which in some cases has resulted in severe structural problems.) The thinking which influenced this decision is not known, and there is no documentary evidence that soil tests were done in Cambridge while the founder was

---

[30] Dorothy Summers, *The Great Ouse: The History of River Navigation*, Newton Abbot, 1973, pp. 17, 21.

[31] Ibid., and W.M. Palmer, 'Cambridge Castle Building Accounts', *Proceedings of the Cambridge Antiquarian Society,*, 26, 1923–24.

[32] *Will of King Henry the Sixth*, p. 7.

[33] T. McKenny Hughes, 'Superfical Deposits under Cambridge and their Influence upon the Distribution of the Colleges', *Proceedings of the Cambridge Antiquarian Society*, 11 (for 1903–6), 1907, pl. XXVIII, p. 400, shows made ground on the alluvium almost right up to the west end of the chapel.

developing his plan. However, at about that time, he sent for information about the subsoil of the site for Winchester College and had actual soil samples sent to him.[34] In all likelihood the decision to locate the chapel just off the alluvium was premeditated.

The decision as to where the easternmost limit of the chapel should be located is more difficult to establish. It lies on the easternmost boundary of the original site, and a parcel of land just east of the east end of the chapel was not acquired until 1452 from Robert Lincoln. This was several years after the foundation stone was laid on 25 July 1446, by the king himself, west of the intended east wall where the high altar was projected to be.[35] If this parcel had been necessary for the design, it should surely have been obtained earlier; for on 26 August 1446 it was noted that the building of King's College could not proceed without incorporating a tenement called 'Godeshous'.[36] While the legal limit of the site at the time of design can be seen as the determinant, another factor most likely played a role: Henry VI's vision for a college plan based on a rectilinear scheme. The plan was lined up nicely with the north, south and west boundaries of the site, but is set at an angle to High Street (now King's Parade). The basic length (I am not saying the exact length, for it could have been slightly longer or shorter) of the chapel was directly related to the conditions of the site, in conjunction with Henry VI's conceptual model for an ideal college. In turn, the length of the chapel determined the size of the quadrangle. The angled placement of the east wall of the college relative to the street had one additional advantage: it increased viewing distance, and thus gives greater visibility and a sense of presence to the college.

The foundations of the chapel are 3.65 m (12 feet) deep, and are composed of rough stones.[37] First, they descend through a few centimetres of topsoil, then proceed through between 2.75 and 3 m (9 and 10 feet) of mixed chalk, soil and brick rubble (probably this was back fill), and finally sink into 61 cm (2 feet) of gravel. This spread of gravel lies on a solid chalk marl and gault.

The foundation for the north wall, 2.13 m (7 feet) west of the tower, is stepped out 15 cm (6 inches) at a depth of 15 cm (6 inches) below the

[34]   T.F. Kirby, *Annals of Winchester College*, London, 1892, p. 193.

[35]   King's College Muminent, Box M. 9, fo. 16a, printed by Willis and Clark, I, p. 465; Saltmarsh, 'King's College', p. 378.

[36]   *Calendar of the Patent Rolls, 1441–46*, p. 460.

[37]   King's College, Muniment Room, Three Section Drawings by Aston Webb and Son, architects, dated 1 November 1920; the precise location is not noted on them, but internal evidence shows that the water pipe went to the fourth chapel on the north side. In addition John Saltmarsh was able to verify the location as being in the north-east corner, since the college gardner recalled the excavation in 1963. The drawings have been misplaced, but they are carefully described in Saltmarsh's papers, Cambridge University Library, MS. 3559, fo. 8a.

surface, while the north extremity of the first north buttress from the east is stepped out 33 cm (13 inches), 15 cm (6 inches) below the surface.

The foundation of the west side of the north-east tower is stepped out 61 cm (2 feet) at a depth of about 15 cm (6 inches), and is further stepped out at a depth of 1.22 m (4 feet) by another 91 cm (3 feet). As the tower is 4.57 m (15 feet) across at ground level, and if the foundations are the same on all sides, this tower sits on a substructure that is 7.62 m (25 feet) across. This mighty foundation suggests that tall corner turrets were part of the original design and not, as has been recently suggested, the result of a decision not to build a separate bell tower.[38]

An examination of the context of the King's College, from the Henry VI's intentions to specific conditions in Cambridge, constitutes the basis for an understanding of the beginning stages of the design of King's College Chapel, a structure which emerged as a symbol par excellence for collegial education and, as such, served as a prototype of educational buildings located around the world.

Acknowledgements: The late John Saltmarsh of King's College willingly shared his great knowledge on the subject and graciously provided me access to the primary documentary material preserved in the Muniment Room at King's College. I am also grateful to Master and Fellows of Peterhouse, Cambridge, who provided refreshing intellectual fellowship as well as splendid accommodations in Cambridge for extended periods of time. This present article is part of a projected larger study.

[38] Francis Woodman, *The Architectural History of King's College Chapel*, London, 1986, p. 192.

22

Warkworth Keep, Northumberland:
A Reassessment of its Plan and Date

Lesley Milner

The keep of Warkworth Castle, Northumberland (Plates 54a, b), which is situated on the north-east coast of England, overlooking the mouth of the River Coquet, about twenty-five miles to the north of Newcastle-upon-Tyne, has long attracted the attention and admiration of scholars, who have praised the quality of its design in terms which are normally used, during the medieval period, for the architecture of the great cathedrals.[1]

That the keep is a stunningly original building there is little doubt: positioned at the highest and at the least vulnerable point of the castle, on a steep mound which was probably the motte of the twelfth-century fortification, its distinctive outline provides a focal point both from the coastal countryside which surrounds it on three sides and from the sea. It dominates the buildings of the castle and the town of Warkworth which stretch immediately below it to south and north respectively.

For architectural historians the keep's fascination lies in the fact that it is at the same time a very simple and a highly complex building. The essence of its plan is the combination to the square and the greek cross, (see plan, Plate 55a, b). Its main bulk takes the form of a perfect square (80 feet x 80 feet, 24.38 x 24.38 m, at base), from the sides of which four bays project, to north, south, east and west. From a distance it is these cross arms which dominate the design and, together with the high thin tower which rises above the building, give it the aspect of a giant directional compass; from much closer, from the town or the castle, the great bulk of the square comes into predominance. The same duality occurs inside the building. A comparison of the plans of the ground floor with those of the two floors above will show that on the ground floor it is the four long corridors of the cross shape which set the seal on the design; on the first and second floors, the residence of the lords of

---

[1] Cadwallader John Bates, 'Warkworth Castle', in *The Border Holds of Northumberland*, 1891; and idem, 'Warkworth' in *A History of Northumberland*, 15, 1899. W. Douglas Simpson. 'Warkworth: A Castle of Livery and Maintenance', *Archaeologia Aeliana*, Fourth Series, 15, 1938; and idem, 'The Warkworth Donjon and its Architect', *Archaeologia Aeliana*, Fourth Series, 19, 1941. H.L. Honeyman, *Warkworth Castle* (English Heritage Official Handbook), 1954; Nikolaus Pevsner, 'Warkworth', in *The Buildings of England: Northumberland*, Harmondsworth, 1957.

Warkworth, space is opened up and, apart from the chapel in the eastern arm, the corridors of the cross arms are merged into squares and rectangles of domestic chambers.

The most striking feature at Warkworth keep, however, is what has been christened, for want of a better word, the lantern. This narrow space (8 feet 4 inches x 10 feet, 2.54 x 3.048 m) is open to the sky and is situated at the heart of the building. It has two functions, to provide light and air to living rooms and to larders below and to collect rain water, which is then channelled off by a stone conduit in the north arm of the ground floor and was taken to the keep's washrooms and lavatories by a series of ducts.

It is the lantern's relationship to the plan of the keep as a whole, however, which excites interest. Just as, from the outside, the high thin tower seems to mark the centre of the building, inside the lantern seems to lie in the exact centre. In fact neither tower nor lantern are disposed exactly round the centre point of the building. In addition the cross arms' relationship with the square from which they break can be seen to be irregular, the northern one being placed too far east, the eastern too far north and southern too far west (the western is correct). This essay will propose that these anomalies are not, as they have been considered in the past, the result of mistakes made by the keep's architect or his masons, nor the result of placing a later medieval design on pre-existing walls, but that they are an essential and deliberate element in the design of the keep; at the same time a date for the keep will be suggested that differs from those that have previously been made and accepted.

Few documents exist to testify to the construction of the keep at Warkworth.[2] The castle itself came into the ownership of the Percy family in 1332. Their emblem, the lion, sculptured in relief on a stone panel, is set into the north facade of the keep. In 1523 a local wood was felled to provide timber for centring for the keep's chapel windows and in 1538 Warkworth was visited by Henry VIII's commissioners who described the keep as being 'in good reparacion'. One other record has to be taken into consideration; in 1472 general cleaning was carried out to welcome the new wife of the fourth Earl of Northumberland and William Thompson and John Walker were paid 8*d.* for cleaning the Great Hall and 'the donjon'.

Hitherto the keep of Warkworth has been dated to the closing years of the fourteenth century, or the early fifteenth, thus associating it with its best-known lord, Henry, third Lord Percy and first Earl of Northumberland, soldier, king-maker and ultimately traitor, who died in battle against the English Crown in 1408. Yet the irregularities of plan just

---

[2] The Warkworth documents belong to the archive of the Duke of Northumberland, Alnwick Castle, Northumberland. They are published in *A History of Northumberland*, 15, 1899.

54a Warkworth Castle keep from the north-west.

54b Warkworth Castle, aerial view from the south-west.

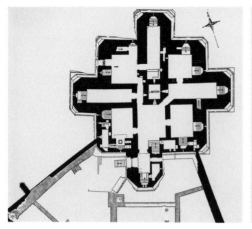

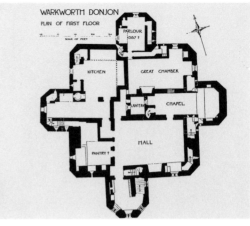

WARKWORTH DONJON

PLAN OF FIRST FLOOR

SCALE OF FEET

PARLOVR
1587?

KITCHEN

GREAT CHAMBER

LANTERN

CHAPEL

PANTRY?

HALL

WARKWORTH DONJON

PLAN OF SECOND FLOOR

SCALE OF FEET

ROOF

UPPERMOST CHAMBER

"MYDDEST" CHAMBER

LOWEST CHAMBER

UPPER VAULT
UNDER WATCH TOWER

PRIVY
CHAMBER

UPPER PART
OF
KITCHEN

DRAWING CHAMBER

"AWMRI FOVND HERE 1340"?

VAVLT
VNDER
WATCH
TOWER

LANTERN

CHAPEL CHAMBER

"CLERKES
CHAMBER"

UPPER PART OF HALL

STVDY
HOVSE

55a Warkworth Castle keep: plans of
ground, first and second floors.

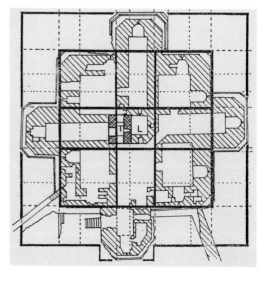

55b Warkworth Castle keep: plan of ground
floor set against a golden-section grid.

T = position of Tower
L = position of Lantern

described, together with the fact that the stone vaulting on the ground floor does not always seem to fit the walls which support it and that rebuilding of crushed walling on the north-western side of the keep has been carried out, have prompted the opinion that the keep is built on the substantial remains, even to the extent of the entire ground floor, of an earlier medieval building which previously occupied the motte.[3] Such a view is unsatisfactory on two counts. First, it is unlikely that either the designer or the patron of what was clearly such a prestigious and expensive building would allow it to be impaired by old walling that could be levelled: secondly, a closer study of the keep's plan raises strong doubts about whether it can in fact be termed 'irregular'.

Plate 55b shows the ground plan of Warkworth set against a grid. It will be apparent that to approach the plan with accepted ideas of proportional harmony will result in disappointment: dividing the building into halves, quarters or thirds and looking for internal divisions to conform to these, results in failure. Nevertheless, the keep is the result of one pervasive and over-all system. Within its 80-foot (24.38 m) main square, it consists of four 30-foot (9.14 m) squares, so disposed as to leave a cross-shape 20 feet (6.09 m) wide between them. The proportional relationship between squares and cross is therefore 3:2:3 (30 feet + 20 feet + 30 feet = 80 feet). Set against the smaller divisions of the grid this becomes 8:5:8. These numbers will be recognised as that system of proportion used by the ancient Greeks, the Romans and by medieval and Renaissance architects and referred to nowadays as the Golden Section.

Once it is realised that all the walls of the keep conform to the rules of the Golden Section, in other words are established by lines which conform to the proportional relationship of 2:3:5:8:13:21 (etc.), then it will be seen that every wall and every width in the keep is deliberate (with one or two exceptions where work on site has departed slightly from the plan). It can also be seen that tower and lantern *together* lie at the heart of this proportional exercise.

The unexpected factor and the reason why the cross-arms do not seem at first to break 'regularly' from the keep's main square, is the way in which the building's walls have been laid out. Once he had set up his 'Golden Section grid', the architect, in devising his plan, set his walls, not immediately over the lines demarking the divisions between squares and cross arms, but on either side of them. This allows much greater freedom in arranging the internal spaces of the keep. There is nothing arbitrary or pragmatic about the positions where the four cross-arms break from the sides of the square keep, and it is not 'somewhat irregularly set out', as described by H.L. Honeyman in 1954; the design is deliberate and constitutes an intellectual exercise on a high scale.

---

[3] This was suggested by Honeyman op. cit., in 1954 and accepted by Pevsner.

Two conclusions result from this study of the keep's plan. The first is that it cannot, as had previously been believed, be the result of two building periods. Every wall in the building, extending to the upper courses of the tower, is dependent on supporting walls provided on the ground floor which fall within an overall rule. The second conclusion concerns the keep's architect. Here is a mind which was highly educated in the system of mathematical proportion, certainly beyond the experience of a local mason. At the same time the use to which this education was put was highly original and reveals a love of the complex and the unexpected which we might more likely have met in the designer of a maze.

In the absence of documents, the date of the keep can only be established by an examination of its architectural features (vaulting, door heads, window mouldings) and by looking for similar buildings elsewhere. The ground floor of the building is very plain: windows are simple slits, doors covered by unmoulded pointed arches, and the whole interior covered by rather crude stone tunnel vaulting. In this area of England such details need not suggest an early date. Whoever the architect of the keep was, he would still be dependent on a local workforce and pointed arches and barrel vaulting were being used in 1549 in the construction of the castle on Lindisfarne and even into the seventeenth century in the cellars of country houses.[4] On the first and second floors, features such as the chapel's sedilia (Plate 56a) must be at least early fifteenth-century and, again in the north-east of England, can be very considerably later. One feature is distinctive: the keep is constructed on a great sloping ramp. Although such ramps were used in castle construction in the twelfth and thirteenth centuries to prevent undermining, their use became less common in the fourteenth century. They appear at the French royal chateau of Vincennes in the 1370s but only came into more common use in the later fifteenth century as a protection against cannon fire. Monteul (Ain) was one of the earliest buildings to be so protected, in 1443.

Another feature which should be considered is the keep's main staircase. Situated in the south cross-arm, it was described by Honeyman as 'a wide and easy flight of steps ... where all pretence of military character is abandoned'. Such a staircase is totally unexpected in a late fourteenth- or even earlier fifteenth-century castle however grand; the royal tower-house at Vincennes, Tattershall Tower in Lincolnshire and Lord Hasting's Tower at Ashby-de-la-Zouche (after 1461) are all still constricted to the newel staircase. The wide, state staircase was a feature which was used by Henry VIII's masons, for instance at Hampton Court or at Thornbury Castle (Gloucestershire) in the early sixteenth century.

The arch form which is used on the first floor of the keep must also be taken into consideration. The openings into the great hall minstrel

---

[4] E.g. Capheaton Hall, 1668.

56a Warkworth Castle keep: south wall of chapel.

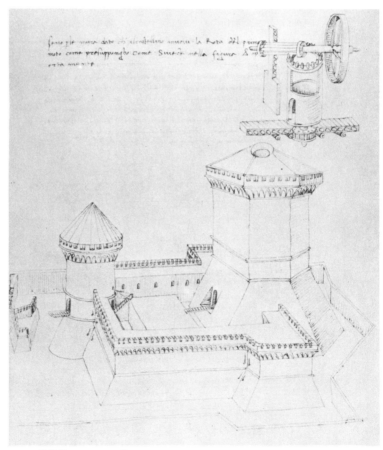

56b Francesco di Giorgio Martini, design for a fortress 1480–90.

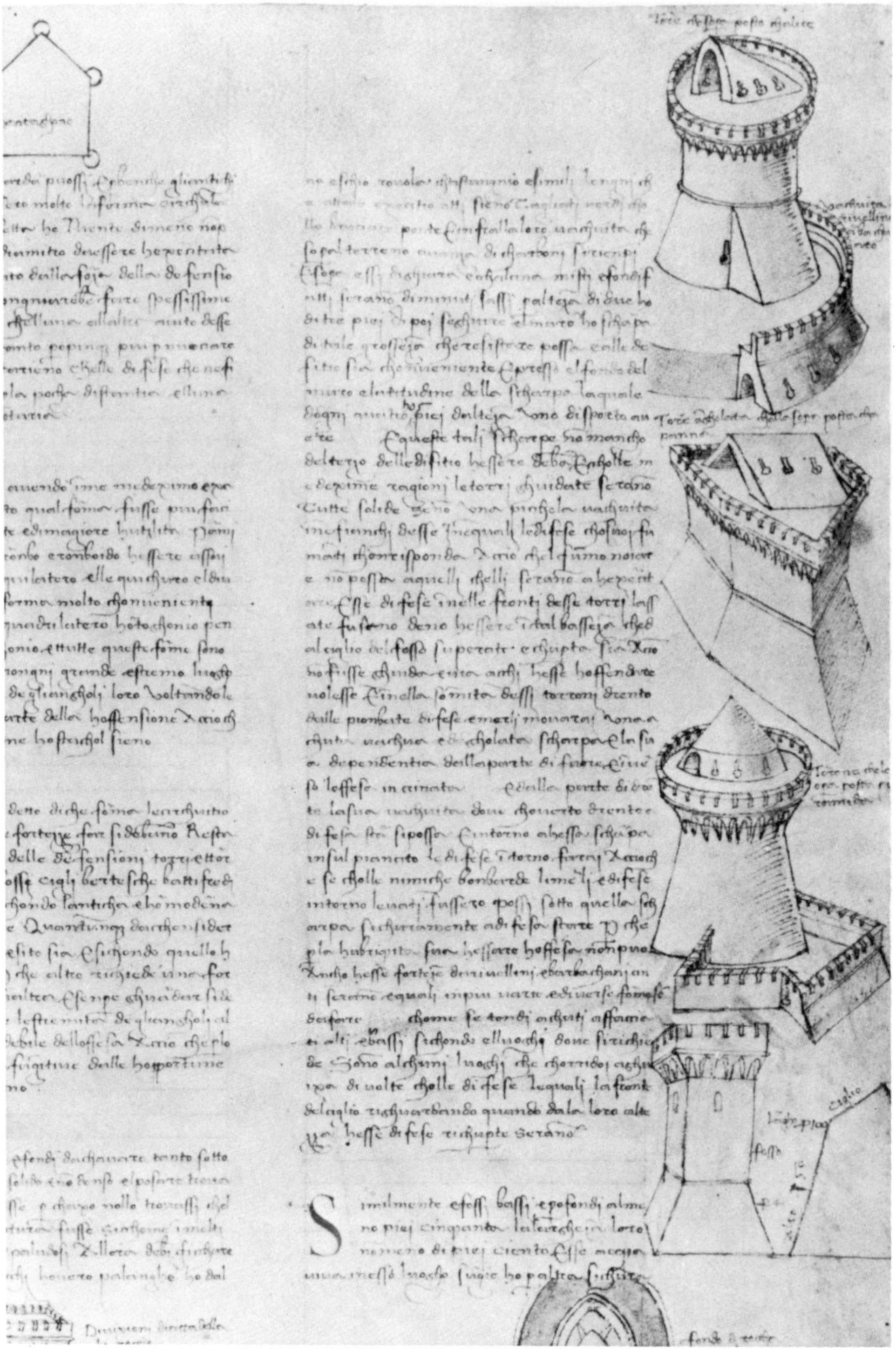

57 Francesco di Giorgio Martini, design showing the exits of ventilation shafts 1480-90.

gallery, the doors that lead from great hall into the buttery, the window in the great hall into the lantern and the sedilia of the chapel (Plate 56a) are all covered by depressed four-centred arches. Such arches characterise the Perpendicular architecture of the Tudor period. Those most similar in form to the Warkworth Keep ones are in the south aisle of Warkworth church, dated by Nikolaus Pevsner to 1500.

If such architectural features suggest a later date for Warkworth keep than has previously been accepted, the problem still remains of finding other buildings which, resembling it in any way at all, can point towards an architect or date. Grand domestic architecture in the north of England and Scotland of the late fourteenth and the fifteenth centuries was characterised by the rectangular tower house. With such buildings Warkworth keep has little in common. Although the most sophisticated examples, Belsay (Northumberland) of the late fourteenth century, or Borthwick (Midlothian) of 1430 for example, do use the Golden Section to establish the proportions of rooms, their plans are totally different from Warkworth. Indeed it has already been suggested that Warkworth cannot really be termed a tower-house.[5] The lantern changes its character to that of four ranges of buildings set around a central courtyard. Example of late fourteenth-century keep buildings constructed around a courtyard do appear, such as Wardour Castle (Wiltshire) or the keep at Durham Castle. But both these are polygonal buildings whose plans and character are quite different to Warkworth's. Where superficially similar plans to that of Warkworth keep do occur, as for instance at Trim Castle (Co. Meath), dated 1212 or at the castle of Grugnac, Sousceyrac (Lot) of about 1400, the resemblance must be attributed to chance.

One group of buildings do call to mind some aspects, at least, of Warkworth keep. These are the designs for fortresses by the Florentine architect Francesco di Giorgio Martini in *Trattati* of the early 1490s.[6] Plates 56b and 57 show examples of these buildings, thick-walled towers based on a rigidly geometric design whose characteristics were dictated by the need to resist cannon fire, and which were described by the architect in his accompanying text. Most evident is the sloping ramp on which the tower is constructed, bringing the lower walls of the tower to a very great thickness indeed, but this is a feature common to many late fifteenth-century European buildings. The feature that Francesco di Giorgio takes care to describe, and provides many illustrations of, runs down the centre of the tower: it is an open space, circular in this

[5] By W.D. Simpson, op. cit., 1941.

[6] Francesco di Giorgio Martini's designs for fortresses were dependent on those by Alberti, published in *De re aedificatorea* in 1485. Francesco di Giorgio produced his *Tratatti* in manuscript for the Duke of Urbino, 1480–90. Familiarity with these ideas, therefore, was restricted to those able to see Alberti's published work (unillustrated) or to visit the court of Urbino. Francesco di Giorgio Martini, *Trattati di architettura, ingegneria e arte militare*, Milano, 1967.

instance, whose function is to act as an air vent. The architect suggests that, in the event of cannon being used inside the building on the ground floor, their smoke can be channelled away up through the building by its means. Its secondary use would also be to take air and light to internal rooms, especially as this tower is so ill-provided with external windows. In none of Francesco di Giorgio's fortresses is the square or the cross chosen as a plan, but he and his contemporaries certainly experimented a great deal with combining them in another branch of architecture, the church. Someone who had the opportunity to study the *Trattati* would therefore find inspiration for using a 'lantern' and for designing a building on the format of a square combined with a Greek cross: both these elements are unusual enough in late medieval architecture to prompt the belief that there is some connection between Warkworth Keep and this late fifteenth-century Italian text.

If an early sixteenth-century date is accepted for Warkworth keep then one of the documents associated with it makes sense. The wood in the vicinity was felled in 1523 for centring, not to repair the chapel windows, but to construct them.[7] On the other hand the reference to cleaning the 'donjon' of 1472 has to be explained. I suggest that the twelfth-century motte did indeed carry a building on it, probably a shell-keep such as the one built at Alnwick, and that this is the building referred to in 1472 as the 'donjon', but that the walls of this were entirely levelled in the late fifteenth century to make way for the splendid new keep.

In 1489 the fourth Earl of Northumberland was murdered. He was succeeded by the fifth Earl who lived until 1527 and whose life-style earned him the title of 'the Magnificent'. His life was based on the court of Henry VIII, where a revival of interest in chivalry, pageant and tournaments prompted the building of palatial country seats that were also given the characteristics of the castle, for instance Thornbury Castle, built for the Duke of Buckingham in 1516. At Henry VIII's court a potential patron would have the opportunity to find a man who combined a scholarly knowledge of mathematics with a familiarity with much-admired Italian texts, a man capable of producing the masterpiece which is the plan of Warkworth keep.

For above all it is this plan that is the glory of Warkworth keep. Practical considerations, the suitability of the lantern for this geographical site, for instance, or the fact that the great hall was originally built without any form of fireplace, are entirely subordinate to this intellectual creation. It is a plan created to satisfy, not the patron, nor the people who would have to live in the building, but the mind of the master architect from which it was born.

---

[7] In 1523 also 2000 thousand stones, quoins and ashlar, were brought to Warkworth from Billing Quarry.

23

A Beginner's Guide to the Study of Architectural Proportions and Systems of Length

Eric Fernie

'Who dares to measure the fabric of yonder Temple shall
learn to blush for his misdeeds'.
Ezechiel 43:10 (Knox translation)

Proportions

When confronted with having to listen to a paper on architectural proportions, most architectural historians (let alone other mortals less closely associated with the divine mysteries) find their critical faculties retreating into a fog.

There are a number of reasons for this. The most immediate is the fact that large numbers of different dimensions are almost impossible to digest in the context of a lecture. Secondly, so much of what has been written on the subject is nonsense (a nonsense which unfortunately lends itself to the use of the computer), consisting of webs of literally unbelievable complexity and corresponding intellectual nullity which are clearly not worth the effort required to unravel them.

We are here in a sphere related to the almost pathological condition once described as pyramidiocy, exemplified by the sad figure of Piazzi Smythe who in the nineteenth century visited Egypt as a respected Astronomer Royal and returned a convinced exponent of the biblical truths embedded in the layout of the Great Pyramid.

Thirdly, there is the propensity which things in reality have for coincidence, such as the fact that the interior of the Pantheon is 147 Roman feet in diameter and the floor a little over 1470 square metres in area.

And fourthly, noone has written a simple guide to the subject. This essay is therefore offered to Peter Kidson as a means of increasing an appreciation of some of his most significant and interesting contributions to the history of the Classical world and the Middle Ages, and in the hope that it may contain a few items which are new to him.

The most important thing which such a guide needs to stress is that, while aspects of the subject can be dauntingly complicated (such as the geometry of cones arising from some of the diagrams in Villard de Honnecourt's sketchbook), the calculations required for large parts of the subject are childishly simple and no more difficult to grasp than the principles behind adding up a shopping bill.

Next, since the majority of pre-modern architectural designs in the western world appear to have been laid out geometrically, one can if one wishes restrict oneself to coming to terms with the diagrams of the argument, and only face the calculations when wishing to check the writer's information. The investigator on the other hand should always conduct the exercise by means of calculations using measurements derived from the building itself, and not by the inaccurate if more romantic method of drawing lines on plans.

Simpler still, even though many proportional systems may have been used in the Middle Ages, the investigator should restrict the exercise to one or two such systems at a time. Authors who pick and choose between a myriad of proportions to explain the dimensions of any particular structure may dazzle by their footwork, but they convince in inverse ratio to the complexity in which they indulge. In addition, one proportion appears to have been overwhelmingly more popular than any other in the designing of buildings, namely the ratio of the side of a square to its diagonal, which is one to the square root of two, or 1:1.4142.

Readers should, then, put themselves in the position of the designer at his desk with parchment, compasses and rule, or on site with rope, pegs and rod. For a two-cell building such as a church with chancel and nave he might have chosen the following common sequence:

> Lay out a square of convenient size to provide the interior of the chancel;
> Take the diagonal of this square and place it at right angles to the square (e.g. by rotating the square 45 degrees) to provide the internal width of the nave (Plate 48a illustrates the rotating of the square);
> Use the same diagonal length two or three times to establish the internal length of the nave.

The final stage of this sequence describes the plans of simple buildings like the eighth-century Anglo-Saxon church at Escomb, but exactly the same principle underlies many of the more complex structures of the later Middle Ages.

The drawing of one of the towers of Laon Cathedral on folio 18 of Villard's Sketchbook, for example (Plate 37a), appears to have been designed on the rotated square. This was proposed by Ueberwasser as long ago as 1935 (Plate 58), but Branner cast doubt on the theory because of the presence of contradictory construction lines which he claimed to have seen on the parchment but which he never described. Bucher in turn saw no reason to reject the original analysis.[1]

---

[1] W. Ueberwasser, 'Nach rechtem Mass', *Jahrbuch der Preuszichen Kunstsammlungen*, 56, 1935, p. 254, fig. 7; R. Branner, review of P. Booz, *Die Baumeister der Gotik* 1956, *Art Bulletin*, 40, 1958, p. 267; F. Bucher, *Architector*, i, New York, 1979, pp. 76, 181.

There are two surprising things about this brief historiography: the first is that both sides, the believers and the sceptics, are right, and the second is that none of them applied the beginner's rule mentioned above which would have demonstrated this, that is by measuring the drawing instead of drawing geometrical patterns on it.

The fact is, not to mix words, that Ueberwasser fudged his diagram: the shape in the centre of Villard's tower is not a regular octagon as the diagram requires, and the walls are thicker than those provided by the rotated square (compare Plate 37a with Plate 58). Ueberwasser only manages a correspondence by drawing very thick lines on a faint reproduction of the original. The use of the rotated square would produce a figure in which the inner side of the octagon multiplied by root-two equals the outer, but, as the figures in section 1 of Figure 2 indicate, the average length of the inner sides is 23.5 mm and of the outer 35.87 mm, while 23.5 mm multiplied by root-two equals 33.23 mm. This makes it look as if Branner was right to be sceptical, but the figures also reveal the fact that the sides of Villard's octagon are of two different lengths, the main sides being substantially longer than those on the corners, 24.25 mm against 22.75 mm, and 38.75 mm against 33 mm.[2] If one assumes that the intended form was octagonal and the sides were therefore supposed to be the same length, then the informal nature of the drawing becomes clear: the main sides are longer because visually they are more important.

The major and minor buttresses, where the proportions are more compact and hence would have been more immediately evident to the eye, support this conclusion: as indicated in sections 2 and 3 of the table they fit the requirements of the diagram very closely. Thus the rectangles forming the corner buttresses have sides which average 32.81 x 23.56 mm, and where the diagonal of a square is 32.81 mm the side will be 23.2 mm. Similarly the smaller buttresses divide up the sides of these rectangles so as to produce the figures shown in section 3, where the averages of the two lengths in question are 13.48 and 9.43 mm, and where the diagonal of a square is 13.48 mm the side will be 9.53 mm.

We can say, then, that Villard drew the larger outlines of his plan inaccurately because of the temptations of the unaided eye, Ueberwasser applied the right diagram to Villard's drawing but disguised those parts which did not coincide, and Branner and Bucher announced their respective rejection and acceptance of Ueberwasser's proposal, all in a situation where the act of measuring would have provided the information required. This exercise I hope illustrates not only the indispensability

[2] They have been taken from the reproduction in H. Hahnlohser, ed., *Villard de Honnecourt*, Graz, 1972, pl. 18. Since most of the dimensions given in this essay either do not exceed an inch and a half in length or vary from one another by very small fractions of an inch, Imperial equivalents have not been given.

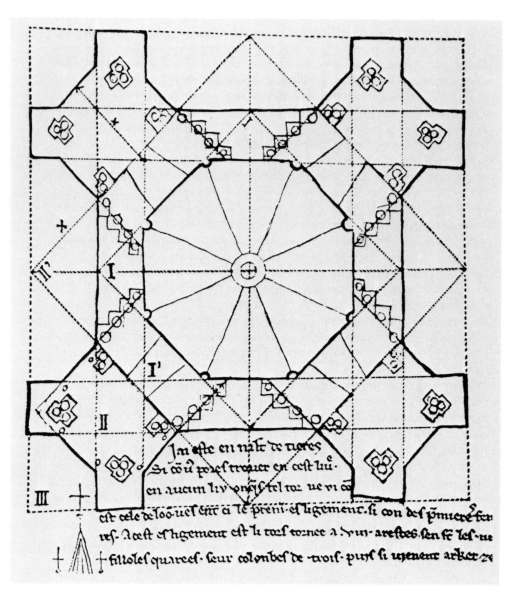

58 Villard de Honnecourt, Sketchbook, fo. 18. Plan of one of the towers of
Laon Cathedral with a diagram based on the rotated square imposed by W.
Ueberwasser.

Table 3

Table of Dimensions in Millimetres of the Plan on Folio 18 of Villard's Sketchbook.

1. *The Octagon: Inner Face*   *The Octagon: Outer Face*

	All sides	Main sides	Corner sides	All sides	Main sides	Corner sides
	24	24	22	39	39	33
	22	25	23	33	39	33
	25	24	23	39	38	33
	23	24	23	33	39	33
	24	—	—	38	—	—
	23	97	91	33	155	
	24			39		
	23			33		
	—			—		
	188			287		
Average	23.5	24.25	22.75	35.87	38.75	33

2. *The Corner Buttresses*

Top right:	33	23
	32	22.5
Bottom right:	33	22.5
	33	23
Bottom left:	33	26
	33.5	22.5
Top left:	32	24
	33	25
Average:	32.81	23.56

3. *The Corner Buttresses Divided in Preparation for the Minor Buttresses*
(The figures are given as if read in a clockwise direction)

Top right:	14	8.5	9.5	13.5	9.5	12	11
Bottom right:	12	10	9	14	10	9	14
Bottom left:	14.5	7.5	10	15	9	10	13
Top left:	14	9	9.5	14	7.5	11	13
Average:	13.6	8.75	9.5	14.1	9	10.5	12.75
Ideal:	13.5	9.5	9.5	13.5	9.5	9.5	13.5

of measurement in the analysis of proportion, but also the necessity of presenting such material in written rather than spoken form.

Why was it used? Nobody knows, but an educated guess suggests it was because it combined simplicity of operation with elevated intellectual status, a combination irresistible to any professional. The status was provided by the mystique attaching to geometry, which can be traced back from the fifteenth century, as with the bishop of Eichstaett to whom Roriczer dedicated his *Buechlein* as 'a lover and patron of the liberal art of geometry', through the thirteenth century with its portrayals of God creating the world with compasses in hand, to Plato, whose imprimatur applied not only to geometry in general but to the square root of two in particular.[3]

This last point is evident from an extraordinary passage in which Vitruvius (Book IX, Introduction, 3 and 4) ascribes to Plato the invention of a technique using the square root of two for doubling the area of a square field so as to produce a larger shape which is still square, and says that for this contribution 'honours ought of necessity to be bestowed upon <him for his part in> the development of human life'. Why was this little puzzle so important? The answer lies in the fact that the Pythagorean system required that everything be reducible to whole numbers, while the ratio of the side to the diagonal of a square cannot be reduced to such numbers: if the side is 10 then the diagonal will be 14+, if 100 then 141+, if 1000 then 1414+, and so on *ad infinitum*. There is a story to the effect that this embarrassing fact was pointed out to Pythagoras ('original chief of wranglers', according to Heraclitus) by an incautious disciple who was subsequently lost at sea.[4] Plato succeeded in relating side to diagonal via whole numbers by using geometry, as described in the *Meno* and exemplified in the exercise with the field; in so doing he gave the universe back its structure and hence deserved the gratitude of mankind.[5]

It may be in place to note that this triumph of the intellect, while mathematically and philosophically brilliant, seriously misled scientific investigation for nearly 2000 years, though happily the architects and builders of the Middle Ages can be said to have helped recoup some of the loss by playing a prominent part in the technical and economic revolutions of the twelfth and thirteenth centuries, which eventually made a re-evaluation of Platonism possible.

[3] M. Roriczer, *Buechlein von der Fialen Gerechtigkeit*, 1486; facsimile edition, Wiesbaden, 1965, and in L. Shelby, *Gothic Design Techniques*, Carbondale, 1977, p. 83.

[4] For Heraclitus' remark see K. Freeman, *Ancilla to the Pre-Socratic Philosophers*, Oxford, 1948, p. 30, no. 81. On the shipwreck see A. Wasserstein, 'Theaetetus and the History of the Theory of Numbers', *Classical Quarterly*, 8, 1958, pp. 165–66, nn. 2 and 3.

[5] Plato, *Meno*, 82a7–85b6, trans R.W. Sharples, 1985, pp. 67-77; Euclid, Bk 10, proposition 2, for the proof of the incommensurable nature of extreme and mean ratios, in T.L. Heath, *The Thirteen Books of Euclid's Elements*, Cambridge, 1908, iii, pp. 17–20, where the proposition is also related to root-two; concerning the discovery of incommensurables see also K.R. Popper, *Conjectures and Refutations*, London, 1972, chapter 2, esp pp. 83–87.

The attractiveness of the proportion is also illustrated at the other end of the chronological scale by its use as the basis of the new set of metric paper sizes of the twentieth century: the A system, adopted in 1922 as one of the *Deutsche Industrie Normen*, or DIN, standards.[6] In this each sheet has sides relating as one to root-two, which means that when a sheet is doubled or halved the new shape retains the same proportions, a result which is *only* produced by this ratio. The absolute sizes selected are, however, rather odd: A4 measures 210 x 297 mm; A3 297 x 420 mm; A2 420 x 594 mm; A1 594 x 841 mm; and A0 841 x 1189 mm. These apparently arbitrary lengths all derive from the fact that sheet A0 has an *area* of a square metre, surely an absurd way of establishing a metric scale of paper sizes. Given the elegance of the square root of two it may not be surprising that the proportion was selected, but it is less clear why it was decided to relate it to the metric system, other than the feeling that anything else would simply not have been modern enough.

Thus the system is 'metric' only in a rather rarified sense. It was accepted as the British standard in 1959, long before metrication in other spheres, possibly because it so patently has nothing to do with the metric system in any practical terms.[7]

Length

While planning on a geometrical basis may have predominated in the Middle Ages, some designs were undoubtedly laid out using dimensions; this is clear both from contemporary descriptions and from the existence of buildings in which the dimensions are in whole and in many cases round numbers of a particular unit (for example the Roman foot in the Pantheon, including the height of the column shafts and the size of the paving slabs).[8] It is therefore necessary to confront historical metrology, a study which provides what one might call a worm's eye view of both civilisation and scholarly endeavour. In this it is the reverse of proportion: far from being simple it is a nightmare world of conflicting indications received through channels which are more likely than not unreliable, and indeed which tend in many respects to be less reliable the closer one gets to the present day; in the words of Attilio Stazio, 'La metrologia non è una scienza, è un incubo'.[9]

This state of affairs should perhaps not surprise us given the assessment of the subject implicit in Josephus's claim (*Antiquities*, I, 59–64) that Cain 'increased his substance with wealth amassed by rapine and violence;

---

[6] *Brockhaus Enzyklopaedie*, Wiesbaden, 1972: *s.v.* 'Papierformate'.

[7] G.G. Glaister, *Glaister's Glossary of the Book*, 1979, p. 364.

[8] P. Davies, D. Hemsoll, M. Wilson Jones, 'The Pantheon: Triumph of Rome or Triumph of Compromise?', *Art History*, 10, 1987, pp. 133–53.

[9] A. Stazio, 'La Metrologia', *Enciclopedia Classica*, 1959, p. 535.

he incited to luxury and pillage all whom he met, and became their instructor in wicked practices. He put an end to that simplicity in which men had lived before, <and he did this> by the invention of weights and measures: the guileless and generous existence which they had enjoyed in ignorance of these things he converted into a life of craftiness'. In consequence, rather than an attempt at a systematic introduction, all that is offered here is four examples illustrating the character of the subject.[10]

i)   *The Greek Foot.*   There is a widespread belief in the current literature that the Greek foot was 308 mm long. This figure is based on Pliny's statement in discussing the measures of the Greeks that their stade, which was 600 feet long, equalled 125 Roman paces or 625 Roman feet (*NH*, Bk 2, 21, 85: 'stadium centum viginti quinque nostros efficat passus, hoc est pedes sexcentos viginti quinque'), and since the Roman foot is known to have been 296 mm long, the Greek must therefore have been 296 x 625/600 = 308.6 mm. This reasoning however takes as a comparison of *lengths* what was surely intended as a comparison of *systems*, since in the Greek system 6 feet = 1 fathom, and 100 fathoms = 1 stade of 600 feet, and in the Roman 5 feet = 1 pace, and 125 paces = 1 stade of 625 feet.

The question 'How long was the Greek foot?' is itself misconceived, as there was no such thing as 'the' Greek foot in the sense in which there certainly was a standard Egyptian cubit and a standard Roman foot. Because of the lack of standardisation, pre-Hellenistic Greece probably saw the use of dozens of feet, reflecting the lack of political unity.

ii)   *The 'pertica ad manus'.* The addition of the phrase *ad manus* to the name of a length tends to presage confusion, but not always as bluntly as in the statement in one twelfth-century English manuscript that the 'pertica ad manus xv pedes habet; quod per extensionem brachiorum verius esse demonstratur'.[11]

iii)   *The Palm.* The term 'palm' is unusual in having been applied to two entirely different lengths. In Antiquity its standard use was as a quarter of a foot, or about 75 mm depending on the length of the foot. On the other hand there are one or two references to it as the unit of three-quarters of a foot or *c.* 225 mm normally called a *dodrans* or, in Greek, *spithame.* Thus Jerome in his commentary on Ezechiel makes the following distinction: 'palmo, qui rectius graece dicitur palaestes, et est sexta pars

[10] See E. Fernie, 'Historical Metrology and Architectural History', *Art History*, 1, 1978, pp. 383–99.

[11] H. Hall and F.J. Nicholas, 'Select Tracts and Table Books Relating to English Weights and Measures (1100–1742)', *Camden Miscellany*, third series, 41, 1929, p. 4, BM manuscript Reg 13A XI, f141.

cubiti; alioquin "palmus" *spithame* sonat quam nonnulli pro distinctione "palma", porro "palaesten" "palmum" appellare consuerunt'.[12]

Such references however appear to be largely literary and lacking any indication that the use was common currency. In the course of the first millennium the old short palm ceased to be used, and the term was applied to the longer measure. The twelfth-century *Liber Sancti Jacopi* gives a man's stature as eight palms, or between 210 mm and 225 mm to the palm for a height between 1.68 m and 1.81 m, and the long palm is common in the cloth lengths of the thirteenth and fourteenth centuries.[13] The earliest exact dimension for it is the 223.2 mm which can be calculated from Philander's foot of 297.6 mm on Luca Peto's slab of 1535 in Rome.[14]

It is unlikely that the change can be ascribed to a switch from the width of the human palm to its length, as this seldom exceeds 200 mm. What we have here seems to be the odd occurrence of the shadowy and bookish secondary meaning of a name supplanting the original names of its host, the 225 mm length, while the standard unit to which the main meaning of the name had applied, that of 75 mm, dropped out of use.

iv) *The Metric System.* Finally, for an extreme manifestation of the obsession which measures can engender, there is the American periodical of the 1880s innocently entitled *The International Standard*, which proclaimed 'a ceaseless antagonism to that great evil, the French metric system', decrying it as nothing short of 'atheistic', and stiffening subscribers' resolve with a stirring song: [15]

> Then down with every 'metric' scheme
> Taught by the foreign school,
> We'll worship still our Father's God
> and keep our Father's rule!
> A perfect inch, a perfect pint,
> The Anglo's honest pound,
> Shall hold their place upon the earth,
> Till time's last trump shall sound!

In August 1988 the United States government formally required federal agencies to begin adopting the metric system.[16]

---

[12] *Corpus Christianorum, series latina*, lxxv, *S. Hieronymi Presbyteri Opera*, I, 4, 1964, pp. 558–59, lines 301–4. For a standard use of *spithame* see for example Pliny, *NH*, Bk. 7, part 2, section 26, where the author describes pygmies as 'ternas spithamas longitudine, hoc est ternos dodrantes'.

[13] E. Fernie, 'Pegolotti's Cloth Lengths', *The Vanishing Past: Studies of Medieval Art, Liturgy and Metrology Presented to Christopher Hohler*, British Archaeological Reports, International Series, 111, 1981, pp. 15–16.

[41] L. Paetus, *De Mensuris et Ponderibus Romanis et Graecis*, Venice, 1573, pp. 9–10, 12–13.

[15] M. Gardner, *Fads and Fallacies in the Name of Science*, New York, 1957, p. 180.

[16] *The Times*, 25 August, 1988.

24

Mouldings and the Analysis of Medieval Style

Richard K. Morris

Peter Kidson's teaching at Cambridge fired my enthusiasm for the medieval great churches of 'the west country', and instilled in me a belief that much could still be learnt about the process of history from a detailed study of their fabric. Too much faith had been placed in documentary evidence, too little time had been spent closely examining the buildings. This was the scenario for the research which I commenced at the Courtauld Institute in 1966 under Peter's supervision. Initially the subject was Decorated ballflower ornament (actually a wily suggestion of Christopher Hohler), though very soon this was expanded into a study of the worked stones on which the ballflowers were carved (Plate 59). So my now well known association with mouldings was born, although the fragrance of ballflower has never quite washed away.[1]

The absence of any modern survey of English medieval mouldings was highlighted by my doctoral research, although selected examples had been published by authorities such as W.R. Lethaby and John Harvey to justify attributions to particular craftsmen. As a result, my contextual study of English mouldings in the Decorated period appeared in the late 1970s.[2] In the same decade, the Warwick Mouldings Archive (a computerised archive of profile drawings) was established at Warwick University,[3] with a view to producing and coordinating archaeological surveys of other periods of British mouldings between the twelfth and sixteenth centuries, a project which is still under way. Since the 1970s I have become the 'agony aunt' of the mouldings world, responding to so many individual enquiries that a published report on the analysis of moulding

---

[1] See, for example, R.K. Morris, 'Ballflower work in Gloucester and its Vicinity', *Medieval Art and Architecture at Gloucester and Tewkesbury*, British Archaeological Association Conference Transactions, 1985, pp. 93–115.

[2] R.K. Morris, 'The Development of Later Gothic Mouldings in England, Part I', *Architectural History*, 21, 1978, pp. 18–57; 'Part II', ibid., 22, 1979, pp. 1–48. The encouragement of Peter Kidson, as well as John Newman, did much to facilitate the publication of this survey.

[3] The computer project is described most recently in *Scuola Normale/Getty Report on Data Processing Projects in Art*, Pisa, 1988, pp. 399–400.

profiles is long overdue.[4] As Peter sent me down this long, dusty road, it is appropriate that it should appear in this series of essays dedicated to him; the more so because it is based on a talk which I gave at a Courtauld 'research in progress' seminar in 1983, which I think he missed.

What constitutes 'proof' when interpreting medieval architectural detail? This is the issue to be considered here, to be seen in the current context of a general bias against stylistically based art history, a bias which misrepresents the important place of such methodology in the study of medieval and other pre-modern periods. More specifically, how far can the form of moulding profiles be used as valid evidence for dating, attribution, and other such judgements?

When I started out in the 1960s, it was generally assumed that the reuse of templates, or the virtual repetition of profile designs, would provide the proof necessary to distinguish one craftsman from another. In fact, it soon became apparent that such circumstances prevailed relatively infrequently in the Decorated period. It is rare to find the same template reused at two different sites, especially in direct conjunction with other identical features in both places (e.g. window tracery patterns). In the west midland area surveyed for my thesis, I encountered such parallels only three times: at Ludlow and Marden, and in two other instances.[5] Subsequent studies by other researchers in other areas and periods have drawn the same conclusion.[6] So this preferred, incontrovertible form of 'proof' is seldom afforded to the researcher.

The evidence for postulating the reuse of a template is that the carved profile is both the same size and design, but more frequently one encounters examples where the design is similar but the scale differs. This is no more than one would expect, as the physical size of the work varied from job to job and the dimensions of the mouldings were adjusted accordingly. The majority of these parallels turn out to be commonplace designs in their period, so that only limited significance can usually be attached to them, especially in matters of attribution. Typical examples occur amongst standard components like bases, moulded capitals, stringcourses and, to a certain extent, ribs and mullions (e.g. the Early English 'water-holding' base, or the typical Decorated base).[7] It is a common pitfall to place too much importance on such

---

[4] For advice on drawing and recording moulding profiles, see my contribution in *Recording Worked Stone*, Council for British Archaeology, Practical Handbook 1, London, 1987, pp. 23–28, 33-39.

[5] See R.K. Morris, 'The Local Influence of Hereford Cathedral in the Decorated Period', *Transactions Woolhope Naturalists' Field Club*, 41, Part 1, 1973, pp. 59–61.

[6] E.g. E. Roberts, 'Moulding Analysis and Architectural Research: The Late Middle Ages', *Architectural History*, 20, 1977, p. 8; R. Fawcett, 'St Mary at Wiveton in Norfolk, and a Group of Churches Attributed to its Mason', *Antiquaries Journal*, 62, Part 1, 1982, p. 35.

[7] Morris, 1979, op. cit., in note 2, pp. 26ff.; distinctive types are also noted, pp. 29ff.

59 Richard Morris with the 12-inch Warwick template former.

parallels, and for this purpose my research since the 1970s has moved towards establishing a context (a database) to differentiate the usual from the unusual.

Some commonplace mouldings deserve further study, for not all examples are as similar and characterless as may first appear. The chamfer moulding is a typical example, so frequently met with in arches and jambs of the later Gothic period that it tends to be neglected. I have read in one doctoral thesis of window jambs being 'unmoulded', when actually they consisted of plain chamfer mouldings. The geometry of the angles employed in designing common profiles can be of assistance even in the relatively simple stonework of medieval secular architecture, as in the case of the fourteenth-century work at Warwick Castle.[8]

So the comparison of moulding profiles is not a straightforward process, and keen observation and an aptitude for lateral thinking are useful personal attributes. The researcher is looking for similar mouldings or similar groups of mouldings, but should not expect to be presented with profiles repeated verbatim or with the same combination of mouldings at each site. The basis of the method has been clearly expounded by Eileen Roberts,[9] and applied in the published case studies of various authorities as well as in my own.[10] It cannot be overstressed that a sense of context must be retained in assessing the validity of observed parallels, from such general considerations as historical and geographical probability to more specific factors affecting artistic production. Is the style of mouldings likely to have been influenced by previous work in the same building? Such archaism is graphically illustrated at Exeter Cathedral, where many of the mouldings employed for the fourteenth-century nave follow closely those created for the new east end almost fifty years earlier.[11] Alternatively, is the artistic milieu of the period in question noted for stagnation or revivalism? Both of these can be found, for example, in fifteenth-century Perpendicular. Or is it an 'age of invention', typically 'transitional', as in the second half of the twelfth century, the Decorated period and the early Tudor period? There is little doubt that times of fast changing fashion provide the most favourable situation for close dating and personal attributions, and these are judgements which now warrant closer scrutiny.

---

[8] R.K. Morris, 'The Architecture of the Earls of Warwick in the 14th century', in W.M. Ormrod (ed.), *England in the Fourteenth Century*, Woodbridge, 1986. See also Morris, op.cit., 1973, in note 5, for the application of geometrical and arithmetical modules.

[9] Roberts, op.cit., in note 6.

[10] E.g. J.M. Maddison, 'Master Masons in the Diocese of Lichfield; A Study of 14th-century Architecture at the Time of the Black Death', *Transactions Lancashire and Cheshire Antiquarian Society*, 85, 1988; and Fawcett, op. cit., in note 6.

[11] See R.K. Morris, 'Thomas of Witney at Exeter, Wells and Winchester', *Medieval Art and Architecture at Exeter*, British Archaeological Association Conference Transactions, (forthcoming).

What is the potential of information derived from moulding comparisons? What should we be trying to achieve with it? First, to provide a date for the moulding. Sophisticated scientific methods of dating now exist for organic materials like timber, and progress is also reported on applications to man-made materials like brick, but no such tests have any validity for stone. The need arises, therefore, for a series of guidelines to be devised for worked stones, based upon close scrutiny of all their external features: most obviously mouldings and ornamental embellishments, but also masons' marks, assembly marks and tooling. It is incidentally highly desirable to do the same for mouldings in other materials such as timber, as one of several checks on dates arrived at by more scientific methods.[12]

Of course the main framework for the stylistic dating of medieval stonework was established by antiquarians like Rickman, Paley and Sharpe in the first half of the nineteenth century, but modern scholarship demands a more rigorous typology.[13] Samples of different moulding profiles are collected from a wide geographical distribution of buildings both nationally and in Europe which, crucially, have dates established by independent criteria such as documents or archaeological excavation. In a fortuitous example at Exeter, famous for its extensive surviving fabric accounts, we are told the exact year, 1318, when stonework carved with the sunk chamfer moulding was introduced into the cathedral.[14] On this basis, a date-span of twenty to thirty years (i.e. plus or minus ten to fifteen years) can often be given to a group of mouldings, and sometimes to an individual moulding, which compares well with results achieved by scientific methods for other materials. Local circumstances are not always favourable: Oxfordshire, for example, is notoriously devoid of documentary dates for its medieval churches (eg. dedications). Nonetheless, in most areas this typology is useful, and frequently invaluable where no other precise evidence for dating is available. Many parish churches fall into this category, and this method is also becoming more generally applied to stonework from archaeological excavations, and collections of loose stones which have been detached from their archaeological context, with useful results.[15] In addition to providing absolute dates, the typology

---

[12] Research into moulding profiles in timber is currently being undertaken by Anthony Drew Edwards, under the supervision of David Parsons at the University of Leicester.

[13] For a brief critique of earlier publications on mouldings, see Morris, 1978, op. cit. in note 2, pp. 18–19 and notes.

[14] Ibid., p. 31; and see also A. Erskine, *The Accounts of the Fabric of Exeter Cathedral, 1279–1353*, Part 1, Devon and Cornwall Record Society, new series, 24, Torquay, 1981, p. 98.

[15] See, for example, R.A. Stalley, 'Mellifont Abbey: A Study of its Architectural History', *Proceedings of the Royal Irish Academy*, 80C, 1980, pp. 263–354; and R.K. Morris, 'Architectural Fragments at Lichfield Cathedral', *Medieval Art and Architecture at Lichfield*, British Archaeological Association Conference Transactions, (forthcoming).

of mouldings can often supply the evidence for a sequence of phases; for example, stages of construction revealed by changing base profiles.[16]

The second expectation is that the study of mouldings will provide a guide for the connoisseur to distinguish one craftsman's work from another's. Indeed, for some authorities, this has been the only avowed purpose of mouldings analysis.[17] The designing of profiles is a human activity, and less likely to be influenced by external factors than the designing of more general architectural features such as ground plans or window tracery. There is much potential validity in John Harvey's famous dictum that mouldings can reveal the hand of the architect much as brushwork does that of the painter.[18] The question is whether one can prove it from a study of mouldings and related minutiae. Apart from the well known studies by Lethaby, Oswald and Harvey, one can cite publications by younger scholars which have argued at length for particular attributions.[19] I have recently presented a paper proposing that we would know from the mouldings that Thomas of Witney had worked at Exeter Cathedral, even if the documentation in the fabric rolls had not survived.[20]

It must be admitted that often the circumstances do not permit a firm attribution to an individual master, anonymous or named. The sort of difficulties encountered can be illustrated by an experiment I ran a few years ago on the Warwick Archive's computerised database, concerning the above-mentioned Thomas of Witney. Following the case made by Harvey [21] that, both on archival and stylistic evidence, Witney not only worked at Exeter but also at other great churches such as Wells (Lady chapel and retrochoir) and Malmesbury (nave vault and clerestory), I arranged for the computer to compare all the relevant moulding profiles from these sites; to produce a 'concordance'. The result was deadening. The print-out revealed only four parallels between the different sites, out of a total 'vocabulary' of 160 profiles; all four were mouldings in common use.[22] Surprisingly, the highly ornate bases of the Exeter pulpitum and the Wells retrochoir, considered to be the most distinctive of the mouldings attributed to Witney, failed to register among the concordances. Why not? Because they are not identical designs, despite their apparent similarity, and the computer programme used to compile the con-

[16] E.g. S.E. Rigold, 'Romanesque Bases in and South-East of the Limestone Belt', in M. Apted, et al. (eds.), *Ancient Monuments and their Interpretation*, Chichester, 1977, pp. 99–137.

[17] E.g. Roberts, op. cit. in note 6, p. 10.

[18] J.H. Harvey, 'The origin of the Perpendicular Style', in E.M. Jope (ed.), *Studies in Building History*, London, 1961, p. 155.

[19] E.g. Roberts, and Fawcett, op. cit. in note 6 (though note the slightly quizzical tone of Fawcett's conclusion, p. 54); and Maddison, op, cit. in note 10.

[20] Morris, op. cit. in note 11.

[21] Most recently in J.H. Harvey, *English Mediaeval Architects: a Biographical Dictionary down to 1550*, 2nd ed., Gloucester, 1984, pp. 338–41.

[22] In total, there were twenty-six concordances, but only four incorporated mouldings from more than one site.

cordance recognised exact parallels only.

This example therefore serves in part to warn against the potential pitfalls of some kinds of computer-generated data. Taken at face value, this print-out could be used to demonstrate that there is nothing in the style of the mouldings to corroborate the attribution of Wells and Malmesbury to Witney. In fact a more judicious manual search of the profile drawings has suggested some comparisons between these works, though not entirely straightforward in interpretation.[23] The Archive database is actually very successful in operation when a search for a specific moulding design (or for two or three mouldings in conjunction) is conducted, as a parallel for a feature discovered at another site; but produces less meaningful results when an open-ended concordance programme is run.[24]

The real moral of this tale is that connoisseurship in the field of historic architecture can seldom, if ever, be conducted on a machine. The concordance of mouldings emphasises the crucial point made earlier, that exactly repeated designs which are not commonplace are rarely encountered. Some might regard this as an inevitable consequence of artistic creativity, but the general validity of this concept is questionable in the craft-based economy of medieval England. It is at least doubtful that artistic creativity would produce such inconsistencies as to make it impossible to distinguish master masons from such evidence.

We need therefore to consider alternative explanations for variety, and one of these could be that not all mouldings were invariably designed by the master mason. Ever since Willis published Gervase's account of Master William of Sens ordering the works at Canterbury, including the words 'he delivered the molds for shaping the stones to the sculptors',[25] there has been a tendency to envisage the master mason as running a sort of centralised drawing office, with all the details emanating from his hand.[26] However, recent researchers, of the generation of students taught by Peter Kidson, have drawn attention to the more incoherent and fragmented aspects of later Gothic building programmes (both in terms of manpower and design), as in the well documented case of Troyes Cathedral nave.[27] In England, the fourteenth-century fabric accounts of

[23] See further Morris, op. cit. in note 11.

[24] The Archive database currently runs on the Oxford Concordance Program, designed particularly for the production of concordances; but the particular form of the mouldings data makes the other facilities of this software more appropriate for the Archive's purposes.

[25] R. Willis, 'The Architectural History of Canterbury Cathedral', reprinted in idem, *The Architectural History of Some English Cathedrals 1842–1863*, Chicheley, 1972, i, p. 36.

[26] E.g. L.F. Salzman, *Building in England down to 1540: a Documentary History*, Oxford, rev. ed. 1967, chapter 1.

[27] S. Murray, *Building Troyes Cathedral: The Late Gothic Campaigns*, Bloomington, 1987, chapter. IV; and idem, 'Bleuet and Anthoine Colas, Master Masons of Troyes Cathedral: Artistic Personality in Late Gothic Design', *Journal Society of Architectural Historians*, 41, 1982, pp.7–14.

Exeter Cathedral reveal several masons of important status beneath the master mason, with occasional changes from year to year. Two of them, John of Banbury (Oxfordshire) and Robert Attebox (Box near Bath, Wiltshire) arrived at about the same time as the new master, Thomas of Witney, and appear to be members of his team, to whom he could confidently assign some matters of design. Their presence may provide the explanation for the variety of moulding details in the stone furnishings of the cathedral, within an overall scheme of profiles which is generally coherent.[28] This is not to deny the body of documentary evidence that shows that design was officially the responsibility of the master, but rather to suggest that in practice some aspects concerning detail might often be delegated.

Such developments may be expected in an historical situation in which major masters were supervising two or more jobs simultaneously; and in a practical environment, almost inconceivable today, in which a skilled craftsman could carve a moulding by hand from memory, without reference to a drawing or a template. More research is needed to understand the effect of such factors on the appearance of the fabric, the visual evidence for the archaeologist and the architectural historian. But it must be admitted at the outset that in such circumstances personal attribution on the basis of moulding profiles is likely to be convincing only in a minority of cases.

On the other hand, it cannot be stated too strongly that there is a much better chance of providing a regional attribution for a moulding or, preferably, a series of mouldings. The design of mouldings in a particular area tends to be dominated by the established practice of one or more workshops centred on a city or great church, providing continuous employment over several decades or more. Against such a background it is possible to detect the appearance of new profiles, usually heralding the arrival of a mason from another region. This principle was demonstrated in my survey of English mouldings, *c.* 1250–1400, as for example in the case of the blatant south-eastern origin of the mouldings of Edward II's tomb at Gloucester.[30] Its use in an archaeological context was dramatically demonstrated in the 1978 excavations of the chapter house site at St. Albans Abbey, where just one particular moulding profile permitted connections to be made with the Divinity School work at Oxford (probably with Master Richard Winchcombe) and ultimately with Gloucester.[31]

[28] See further Morris, op. cit., in note 11.

[29] Morris, op. cit. in note 2, especially Introduction and Summary.

[30] Ibid., 1979, e.g. pp. 22–23, 28.

[31] R.K. Morris, 'The 15th-century Chapter House of St Albans Abbey', report submitted to Martin Biddle, St Albans Research Committee, 1988, intended for publication as part of the report on the 1978 excavations by the St Albans and Hertfordshire Architectural and Archaeological Society.

I hope this essay has demonstrated the continuing validity of stylistic analysis for the details of Gothic architecture. It is a methodology which can provide significant sources of information in a period seriously lacking in more conventional primary sources of evidence. It is therefore important that its reputation should be guarded against too high expectation of what it can achieve, especially in the field of individual attribution. It should be seen as a research tool, and not an end in itself, enabling a wider understanding of architectural history of the period. Although I have been recently flattered with the title of 'le père ... de la modénature en Grande-Bretagne',[32] I trust that this will not give the impression that the field has been sewn up by my contemporaries and myself. A vast amount of recording and interpretation remains to be undertaken, not only in the British Isles but in many parts of Europe. The exhortations of F.A. Paley (the real father of English Gothic mouldings) to nineteenth-century students are still appropriate today:

> looking at every ancient building with a more searching eye
> ... regarding every shattered arch with a new attention ...
> finding the same satisfaction in examining it which a
> botanist finds in a rare plant.[33]

[32] N. Coldstream, 'Le "decorated style": recherches récentes', *Bulletin Monumental*, 147, 1989, p. 74.

[33] F.A. Paley, *Manual of Gothic Mouldings*, 3rd ed., London, 1865, p. 7 (slightly adapted).

25

'Gothique Moderne': The Use of Gothic in Seventeenth-Century France

T.H. Cocke

The aim of this essay is to examine some aspects of the Gothic, medieval in essence but often Renaissance in detail, which flourished in sixteenth- and seventeenth-century France: the 'gothique moderne' of the title. Studies of French theoretical attitudes to Gothic in this period have had as their prime concern the origins of neo-classical and later architecture, rather than the continuing use of the style between the Reformation and the Revolution.[1]

French Gothic did not die with the Middle Ages, but as in England, lived on, not as the wan shadow of past glories which the English 'survival' or, worse still, the German *Nachleben* (after-life) suggest, but as a style capable of monumental and vigorous works. Neither was it the antiquarian choice of an eccentric few. Every French province can boast scores of sixteenth- and seventeenth-century buildings, especially for the Church, which are in some sense Gothic.[2] Yet in the standard work by Anthony Blunt on French art of this period, only a few such sixteenth-century buildings are discussed in any detail; all later examples are relegated to a footnote as 'retardataire'.[3]

The subject's relative neglect is probably because it does not fit the accepted account of French architecture, in which there are two major themes (the emergence of Gothic in the twelfth and thirteenth centuries and the development of classicism from Philibert de l'Orme in the 1540s to François Mansart in the seventeenth century and Ange-Jacques Gabriel in the eighteenth) both concentrated on Paris and the Ile de France and intimately connected with the royal court. French architecture, seen thus from the centre, is a history of progress, wherein new architectural ideals are expressed with ever-increasing perfection. By contrast post-

---

[1] See especially R. Middleton, 'The Abbé de Cordemoy and the Graeco-Gothic Ideal', *Journal of the Warburg and Courtauld Institutes*, 25, 1962, pp. 278–320; 26, 1963, pp. 90–123; and W. Herrmann, *Laugier and Eighteenth-century French Theory*, London, 1962.

[2] Many French classical churches reveal vestigial Gothic influence, especially in their tall proportions and their style of vaulting, eg St-Pierre, Richelieu of *c.* 1631 by Lemercier or St-Paul, St-Louis, Paris by Derand of 1634.

[3] A.F. Blunt, *Art and Architecture in France, 1500–1700*, revised edition, Harmondsworth, 1973, p. 421 (n. 28 to chapter 5).

Renaissance Gothic, largely favoured by autonomous provincial bodies, could ignore or defy metropolitan taste.

What was this 'Gothique moderne' and why should it have developed in France? The word most often used by Vasari and his contemporaries for medieval architecture was *moderno* and it was only in the early seventeenth century that 'Gothic' began to be accepted both north and south of the Alps as a stylistic term.[4] So it is not surprising that the medievalising design of 1626 for the north transept of Orléans Cathedral was described as 'à la Moderne et d'ordre gotique' [5] and again, in 1643 rib vaults were described as 'voûtes modernes ou Gotiques'.[6]

French late medieval art, as in England and Germany, put up a resistance to the Renaissance forms introduced largely as a result of the Italian wars of Charles VIII, Louis XII and Francis I.[7] They were adopted as a new repertoire of ornament, to be applied to existing building types. This Renaissance vocabulary, however, owed little to the chaste Florentine forms devised by Brunelleschi and Alberti. Its models lay in the areas of Italy with which the French were most concerned at this period, Liguria and Lombardy, and in particular the Certosa of Pavia which Commynes thought the 'most beautiful that I have ever seen',[8] with its lavish detailing of twisted balusters and candelabra pinnacles.

This mixed style was confidently employed on a series of major churches all over France. The best known is perhaps St-Eustache in Paris, begun in 1532, which retained the Gothic proportions and elevation of tall arcade, triforium and traceried clerestory, but translated into a relatively correct Renaissance. St-Pierre at Caen, designed by Hector Sohier and built 1528–45, similarly has a Gothic plan of ambulatory and radiating chapels but with inventive contemporary detailing.

Variations on the theme are found in the Burgundian churches of St-Michel in Dijon and St-Florentin (Yonne). St-Florentin, of *c.* 1525–39, consists only of a choir and transepts, the height of which is accentuated by the absence of a nave. The handling of Renaissance detailing here has developed away from direct Italian precedents. The capitals of the arcade piers are formed by a broad band of egg-and-dart moulding and the tracery of each Lady chapel window is drawn into a giant fleur-de-lys. At St-Michel, Dijon, the body of the church, built 1499–1529, is in a straightforward Flamboyant but the west front, begun in 1537, is of a very

---

[4] See E.S. de Beer, 'Gothic: Origin and Diffusion of the Term. The Idea of Style in Architecture', *Journal of the Warburg and Courtauld Institutes*, 9, 1948, pp. 143–62, and T.H. Cocke, 'The Wheel of Fortune' in J.J.G. Alexander and P. Binski (ed), *The Age of Chivalry*, London, 1987, pp. 183–84.

[5] G. Chenesseau, *Sainte Croix d'Orléans: Histoire d'une Cathédrale Gothique Reédifiée par les Bourbons, 1599–1829*, 3 vols Paris, 1921, i, p. 95.

[6] F. Derand, *L'Architecture des Voûtes*, Paris, 1643, p. 9.

[7] A.F. Blunt, *Philibert de l'Orme*, London, 1958, p. 1.

[8] S. Kinser (ed), *The Memoirs of Philippe de Commynes*, trans. I. Cazeaux, 2 vols, Columbia, South Carolina, 1973, ii, p. 465.

different nature. The basic conception is medieval, a massive twin-towered 'westwork', with three deeply recessed portals, perhaps to give St-Michel the status of a great church. Gothic details were, however, limited in the rich ornament and sculpture of the portals to the flanking niches and pinnacles and replaced on the towers by four tiers of super-imposed orders.

By the middle of the sixteenth century the hybrid style was becoming somewhat provincial. Philibert de l'Orme and Lescot were producing for the Court buildings clearly French and truly classical. Machicolation, towers and crenellation continued to be added to chateaux throughout the seventeenth century for conservatism or feudal pride as much as for security, but in secular architecture it was largely the technical aspects of Gothic masonry, rather than its detailing, which remained of significance. Stone vaulting continued to be a major interest of French architects. In 1643 François Derand published *L'Architecture des voûtes ou l'art des traits et coupes des voûtes*, which included all the traditional forms of vaulting, with barrel, groin and rib, and illustrated how to build them.[9]

Gothic could play a more prominent role in ecclesiastical buildings which, hardly recovered from the ravages of the Hundred Years War and the decadence of traditional religious institutions, suffered grievously from the bitter violence of the Wars of Religion. After Henry IV's reconciliation with Rome in 1595 had ensured the future of cathedrals and monastic houses, a large number of great churches were in need of major repair or even total rebuilding.[10] The Huguenots' iconoclasm had extended beyond the destruction of images, monuments and liturgical furnishings to the demolition of the offending Catholic buildings themselves. It took most of the seventeenth century to repair the damage, especially as there were constant interruptions by wars, both at home and aboard.

The major monument of this 'Bourbon reconstruction' is Orléans Cathedral. The gradual rebuilding of the Romanesque church, begun at the east end in the fourteenth century, had been rudely halted west of the crossing by the assaults of the Huguenots in 1568, who battered down all except the apsidal chapels at the east end.[11] Henry IV on a visit to the city in 1598 expressed a pious wish for the reconstruction and completion of the cathedral, which the chapter successfully converted into a royal pledge to finance all the building works.[12] Work began on

[9] Derand, the Jesuit architect of, among other buildings, St-Paul, St-Louis in Paris, makes no polemical distinction between Renaissance and Gothic styles of architecture.

[10] The sculptures of the west front of Reims Cathedral were extensively restored in 1611–12: P. Kurmann, *La Façade de la Cathédrale de Reims*, 2 vols, Lausanne, 1987, 1, p. 35.

[11] For a detailed account of how the assault was conducted, see Chenesseau, op. cit., i, p.vi.

[12] The commitment only died with the dynasty. The western towers were finally completed in 1829, a year before the last legitimate Bourbon king, Charles X, was forced to abdicate.

60a Orléans Cathedral, south transept: south front.

60b Saintes Cathedral, south aisle of nave: vault.

61 St-Maixent Abbey Church, interior looking east.

the east end and choir in 1600. By the 1620s a start could be made on the transepts and crossing but it took the rest of the century to complete the body of the church and then the whole of the eighteenth century to erect the vast west front.

In 1600 the commissioners in charge of the rebuilding and, more important, their masons, had no qualms about embarking on the construction of a major Gothic cathedral with all the sophistications of late Flamboyant design, including pierced *clair-voies* in the apse vaulting and complex flying buttresses and pinnacles around the east end. However, when twenty-five years later it came to building the transepts, still Romanesque in the pre-1568 building, a conscious decision had to be made whether to follow the classical designs submitted under the auspices of Salomon de Brosse, the leading architect of the day, or to commission new Gothic designs. In 1626 the distinguished Jesuit architect Etienne Martellange had his design for the north transept, 'ung desseing à la gotique' accepted.[13] Its treatment of gable and rose window and the geometrical panelling of the wall surface owed more to Italian facades, such as Orvieto or Siena, than to French. Martellange had spent several years in Rome in the mid 1580s.[14] When the south transept was built in the 1670s, the commissioners still preferred to match the design of Martellange, rather than yield to a classical alternative proposed by François le Vau, brother of the great Louis le Vau, and protégé of Colbert. Royal patronage was marked by the incorporation of the head and motto of the *Roi Soleil* himself as the centre of the rose (Plate 60a). Other Gothic facades of the mid century owed more to French tradition; those of the Augustinian priory of St-Père-en-Vallée at Auxerre (1630–58) and of the cathedral of St-Louis at Blois (from 1628) are vertiginously steep, with bulky superimposed orders flanking large traceried windows.

There are certain recurring characteristics in this seventeenth-century Gothic. Where churches had been damaged in the Wars of Religion, it was usually the upper parts, gables, pinnacles, flying buttresses, roofs and vaulting, which most needed restoration. Their detailing was simplified and their mouldings were also made less complex and more classical, with cornices replacing string courses. At Luçon (Vendée) Cathedral the top of the Romanesque north transept was reconstructed with a plain pediment-like gable, while at St-Maixent (Deux-Sèvres) the staircase tower, again in the north transept, was crowned not by pinnacles but by a strong cornice with brackets, resembling machicolation. The fifteenth-century flèche of Saintes Cathedral (Charente-Maritime) was transformed abruptly into an ogee cupola; the vertical mouldings dividing the facets of the spire were converted into ribs to the little dome. Gables retained

---

[13] Chenesseau, op. cit., i, p. 83.
[14] P. Moisy, 'Martellange, Derand et le conflit du Baroque', *Bulletin Monumental*, 110, 1952, p. 238.

their steep medieval proportions, even when the roof behind them was reduced in pitch. The result, as seen at Notre-Dame, Niort (Deux-Sèvres) or the priory church at Celles-sur-Belle (Deux-Sèvres) is impressive, if rather gaunt.

Ribs were the most usual form of vaulting. They could replace original groin vaults, as probably in the chancel at Chancelade (Dordogne), or even the domed vaults, typical of the Romanesque in central France, at both Ste-Marie-des-Dames, Saintes and St-Etienne, Périgueux (Dordogne) (though their original form has been restored in this century).[15] Rib vaults could be either quadripartite or octopartite. The first type was popular even where such a vault was the only concession to medievalism, as in the priory refectory at Celles-sur-Belle which is in a totally new construction of the 1670s with an ambitious rusticated facade. St-Sauveur in La Rochelle (Charente- Maritime), an essentially classical rebuilding, has a simple quadripartite vault over the chancel. Octopartite vaults appear in scores of churches, especially in aisles, for example in the nave aisles of Saintes Cathedral where they are dated 1618 on a keystone (Plate 60b). More elaborate versions such as star vaults were also attempted in crossings and chancels. The Poitevin master-mason and architect François le Duc continued at Celles-sur-Belle and St-Maixent the Flamboyant practice of enriching such places with pendants (Plate 61).[16]

The more usual area wherein medieval fantasy was still appreciated and imitated was in window tracery. The mixed style of the sixteenth century had smoothed foils and cusping into 'tear-drops' or round-headed lights topped by a tracery of circlets as at St-Eustache in Paris, St-Michel in Dijon or St-Père-en-Vallée in Auxerre. In the seventeenth century the more elaborate Flamboyant forms returned to favour, with certain exotic variations. The tall two-light windows in the chapel of the Abbey of Chancelade (1630), just outside Périgueux, enclosed in their traceried heads not conventional quatrefoils but hearts and fleurs-de-lys.

Why did Gothic building continue in France throughout the *Grand Siècle* of the rich but restrained classicism of Mansart and Le Vau?[17] Conservatism and the dislocation due to religious war may account for its survival around 1600, but, as Orléans Cathedral shows, Gothic could continue to triumph over classical challenges even in a building directly under the royal eye.

Local pride and conservatism must have played an important part, especially in cities such as Rouen or Reims where the great medieval

[15] P. Héliot, 'L'Heritage Mediéval dans l'Architecture de l'Anjou et de l'Aquitaine', *Annales du Midi*, 67, 1955, pp. 143-44.

[16] R. Crozet, 'François et Pierre le Duc, Architectes en Poitou, et leurs Oeuvres', *Bulletin de la Société de l'Histoire de l'Art Français*, 1949, pp. 48–54.

[17] For a comparison with equivalent building in contemporary England see T.H. Cocke, 'Le Gothique anglais sous Charles I', *Revue de l'Art*, 20, 1975, pp. 21–30.

churches formed the focus of local patriotism.[18] This was surely the motivation of Nicholas de Son when he published his meticulous engraving of the 'somptueux frontispice <sic> de l'église Nre dame de Reims' in 1625. Cathedral chapters and monasteries fostered an interest in their own history. The Benedictine order in particular was keenly aware of its glorious past, especially after the success of the Maurist reformers.[19] Their headquarters at St-Germain-des-Prés in Paris pioneered the study of French medieval history, although their voluminous writings admittedly made little mention of architecture. The Augustinians' reform movement, called the Génofévain, was similarly interested in the maintenance and recording of their medieval inheritance. Yet it was not only the ancient religious orders who were prepared to build in Gothic. The Jesuits, not established in France until the reign of Henry IV, erected several of their early chapels, such as that at Poitiers, in a spacious 'gothique moderne', just as they did, on a larger scale, in Flanders and the Rhineland.[20]

This conservatism was due to the strength of tradition rather than to confessional propaganda. There was little need to stress Catholic continuity with the medieval church since the Calvinist Huguenots, unlike the Anglicans or the Lutherans, rejoiced in Protestantism's complete break with the past. They distrusted all traditional ecclesiastical building as potentially superstitious, since consecration implied 'a conceit of holiness in the walls'.[21]

Another reason is that Gothic presented an omnipresent and potent image. The great churches of France are still nearly all medieval, and to those surviving today must be added the scores destroyed during and after the Revolution. Even Palladio's pupil Vincenzo Scamozzi had been impressed by them on his journey to France in 1599.[22] It is significant that when Colbert wanted to investigate the quality of different building materials, he sent the Academy of Architecture not to contemporary models but to the medieval churches of the Paris region and to the cathedrals of Rouen and Chartres.[23]

---

[18] P. Héliot, op. cit., pp. 157–58. Even in the papal Comtat Venaissin, de la Valfenière rebuilt Notre-Dame des Anges at L'Isle-sur-Sorgue in 1645–70 in accord with local tradition as a spacious rib-vaulted *nef-unique* with chapels between the internal buttresses: R. Amiet, *La Collégiale Notre-Dame des Anges*, L'Isle-sur-Sorgue, 1969, p. 6.

[19] N. Edelman, *Attitudes of Seventeenth-Century France toward the Middle Ages*, New York, 1946, pp. 55–59.

[20] P. Héliot, 'La Fin de l'Architecture Gothique dans le Nord de la France aux XVIIe et XVIIIe siècles', *Bulletin de la Commission Royale des Monuments et des Sites*, viii, Brussels, 1957, pp. 9–13.

[21] See K. Thomas, *Religion and the Decline of Magic*, London, 1971, p. 59.

[22] R. Wittkower, *Gothic versus Classic: Architectural Projects in Seventeenth-Century Italy*, London, 1974, pp. 86–87.

[23] *Le Gothique Retrouvé avant Viollet-le-Duc*, Caisse Nationale des Monuments Historiques et des Sites, Hotel de Sully, Paris, 1979, p. 47.

There were two other important reasons why major building in Gothic should have continued: the problem of raising money and the principle of conformity. Even in the prosperous early years of Louis XIV funds could fail. At St-Maixent in the 1660s plans for a new classical church had to be dropped because rebuilding in Gothic meant that the foundations and surviving piers and external walls could be reused, even if the vaulting system had to be changed from barrel to rib vaults. To build a 'modernised' i.e. simplified medieval structure, rather than a classical one, also economised on fine masonry and carving. At St-Jean-d'Angely (Charente-Maritime) a fragment of the medieval abbey church was patched up in the early seventeenth century for immediate use and remains, underneath a nineteenth-century clothing, to this day: the vast new classical church begun in 1741 never progressed beyond the west front which still stands eerily alone with its carved details abandoned while only blocked out.

If money was available, grand modernisation schemes were often directed towards the conventual buildings rather than to the church. At Cluny the vast Romanesque church was left undisturbed when the monastery was rebuilt after 1750 on a Bavarian scale.[24] Ironically, it was the latter which survived the Revolution. The monks' concern for their domestic quarters should not be attributed to mere self-interest. Their life had changed away from the communal pattern to a more Carthusian ideal of brethren living in self-contained cells and only coming together for worship.

On a more theoretical level it was ironically the classical principle of conformity that sanctioned the continuing use of Gothic. At Orléans the desire for conformity with the rebuilt apse had led the commissioners to ignore the classical designs submitted for the transepts first in the 1620s and then in the 1660s, despite powerful backing for both projects. It was for the same cause that in 1707 Louis XIV himself quashed all thoughts of a classical spire to replace the hexagonal obelisk erected by Jacques Lemercier over the crossing. The next year the king equally rejected a classical west front for the cathedral by pronouncing that it would not be *convenable* with the rest.[25] Better unity in an outmoded style than confusion.

[24] J. Evans, *Monastic Architecture in France from the Renaissance to the Revolution*, Cambridge, 1964, pp. 51–52.
[25] Chenesseau, op. cit., i, pp. 236–37. *Acknowledgements* This paper is dedicated in respect and affection to Peter Kidson, who first showed me how to understand a medieval building.

26

A Carolingian Lesson in Vitruvius

Anat Tcherikover

The two architectural configurations in a drawing of the tenth century (Plate 62) (contained in a manuscript of the Vatican Library) remain something of a riddle despite repeated scholarly attention.[1] Described by one scholar as reliquaries[2] and by another as towers[3], their nature is clearly disputed. The present essay will approach this problem from the point of view of possible models, suggesting Carolingian sources connected with a study of Vitruvius's *De Architectura*. This is not to say that the model, or indeed the Rome drawing itself, was in any way related to real architectural practices.[4] Quite on the contrary, it reflects an intellectual rather than practical interest in the text of Vitruvius.

The drawing was added to an originally blank page of a Carolingian manuscript, along with some ornamental and figural designs of other pages. These additions have been seen by successive scholars as a sort of model-book, executed in some centre in the Loire Valley.[5] Eliane Vergnolle has recently attributed them more specifically to St-Benoît-sur-Loire, and showed the figural and ornamental motifs to derive, now from Carolingian minor arts, now from Antique architectural decorations.[6] The evidence concerning the drawing in question is of mixed kind. In addition to Vergnolle's observations on this matter, it may be noted that the structure on the left is stylistically consistent in itself, in

---

[1] The greater part of the manuscript is in Paris, Bibl. Nat. lat. 8318, fols. 49–64. Two pages are in Rome, Bibl. Vat., Reg. Lat. 596, fols. 26–7, of which 27r carries the drawing discussed here.

[2] B. Bischoff, 'Die Ueberlieferung der technischen Literatur' (first published in 1971), in this author's collection of papers under the title *Mittelalterliche Studien*, 3, Stuttgart, 1981, pp. 277–97, esp. 296.

[3] E. Vergnolle, 'Un Carnet de modèles de l'an mil originaire de St-Benoît-sur-Loire', *Arte Medievale*, 2, 1985, pp. 23–56, esp. 40–42; idem, *St-Benoît-sur-Loire et la sculpture du XIe siècle*, Paris, 1985, pp. 121.

[4] This is contrary to Vergnolle's opinion that the drawing is, in a sense, an architectural one. She thus suggests that the draughtsman haphazardly combined disparate details drawn from Antique architecture in a process which resembles the indiscriminate reuse of Antique elements in Carolingian buildings. See the previous note.

[5] R.W. Scheller, *A Survey of Medieval Model Books*, Haarlem, 1963, pp. 49–51, with references to earlier literature; Bischoff, op. cit., p. 293.

[6] Vergnolle, op. cit.

that all the capitals belong with a foliate type known from manuscript illuminations of the ninth and especially the tenth centuries.[7] It thus conforms with the style of the draughtsman's own period, in direct line from Carolingian art. Conversely, the structure on the right partly deviates from this stylistic standard by interpolating capitals and fluted columns of Antique inspiration. It is this deviation that provides the clue for a new appreciation of the drawing.

One capital, at the second level of that structure, is almost a true Corinthian, comprising long and short volutes above the foliage and a curved abacus with a flower. In this, it differs from the other foliate capitals in the drawing. At the first level, the capital on the right resembles the classical Ionic, portrayed in a side view. The cushion is striated and tied in the middle, as on a Carolingian Ionic in the crypt of St-Germain at Auxerre.[8] The volutes, which would not normally show in a representation from this angle, are nevertheless present, inverted and oddly extended sideways. They are very prominent, as indeed they should be for the capital to qualify as Ionic. The draughtsman thus conflated two views of the Ionic capital in order to include all its essential features.

A third capital, also at the lower level, has a pattern of egg-and-dart usually associated with the Ionic, but which can be found also on some Roman capitals of a structure resembling the Doric.[9] A comparison to a drawing in a manuscript at Sélestat (perhaps coming from St Gall and variably dated by scholars between the eighth and the tenth centuries) suggests that the draughtsman indeed understood this form as Doric (Plate 63a).[10] The Sélestat drawing represents two capitals, inscribed as Ionic (top) and Doric (bottom),[11] and the latter closely resembles the capital in the Rome drawing: both consist of an abacus with a flower, an ornate echinus, and a double-astragal. Both draughtsmen clearly had no idea of the true form of the Doric capital, but the Sélestat inscription

[7] Eg. St Gall, Stiftsbibl. Cod. 390–91, illustrated ibid., fig. 28; or the celebrated painting by the Magister Gregorii in the Musée Condé at Chantilly, see C.R. Dodwell, *Painting in Europe, 800–1200*, Harmondsworth, 1971, plate 62.

[8] Illustrated in J. Hubert and others, *Carolingian Art*, London, 1970, plate 253. Ionic or composite capitals are rare in the Middle Ages north of the Alps, but they nevertheless occur in a number of Carolingian buildings; see R. Buechler and H. Zeilinger, 'Reste einer karolingischen Elfenbeinarbeit in Seligenstadt', *Kunst in Hessen und am Mittelrhein* (Schriften der Hessischen Museen), Darmstadt, 11, 1971, pp. 19–31, esp. 26–27.

[9] Illustrated in E. Nash, *Pictorial Dictionary of Ancient Rome*, revised edition, London, 1968, 1, fig. 99.

[10] Sélestat, Bibliothèque et Archives Municipales, MS 360 (1153 bis), fol. 36r. For the early dating see G. Scaglia, 'A Translation of Vitruvius and Copies of Late Antique Drawings in Buonaccorso Ghiberti's *Zibaldone*', *Transactions of the American Philosophical Society*, 69, Philadelphia, 1979, pp. 13–15. For the later dating see K.A. Wirth, 'Bemerkungen zum Nachleben Vitruvs im 9. und 10. Jahrhundert und zu dem Schlettstaedter Vitruvcodex', *Kunstchronik*, 20/9, 1967, pp. 281–91, esp. 283 and 288; and Bischoff, op. cit., pp. 280–82, where an attribution to St Gall is suggested in n. 20.

[11] Wirth transcribes: *ionicum <capitulum>* and *dorica <columna?>*; see op. cit., p. 290.

proves that this is what they thought it looked like. What stands behind this strange notion is apparently an erroneous reading of Vitruvius's text. Vitruvius says that the Doric echinus is enriched with annulets, undoubtedly refering to the encircling fillets of the true Doric capital, but the Sélestat draughtsman drew a row of rings.[12] Vitruvius says that the Doric capital possesses a necking, using the same word as for the astragal at the top of the column, and the result is a double astragal.[13] The interpretation of the text is thus revealed as strictly literal in a manner evoking Carolingian Bible illustrations like those in the Utrecht Psalter, except that the draughtsman did not always understand the words he was illustrating. Where Vitruvius does not elaborate, for instance on the shape of the Doric abacus, the draughtsman adopted the flower from other types of abaci.

One problem arising from the above analysis concerns access to the text of Vitruvius. The Rome manuscript provides no evidence on that matter. The one in Sélestat contains various writings on technical matters, including substantial parts from Vitruvius's *De Architectura*, besides several drawings of Antique-inspired architectural motifs including the one in question. The drawings are, however, apparently unrelated to the text. They occupy a separate double-leaf, and the inscriptions which accompany them are Vitruvian only in part. Scholars have proposed the intervention of other, unknown, textual sources.[14] Considering that extant late Antique and early medieval texts on architecture are usually related in some way to Vitruvius, we can assume a mixed tradition to account for the Vitruvian reading of the drawing as offered above.[15]

Another problem involves a shifting balance between textual and artistic requirements. The Sélestat drawing emerged above as a sort of diagram aimed at clarifying a textual notion, and is clearly little related to real art or architecture. Conversely the Rome drawing belongs with a collection of models copied from works of art, presumably with the purpose of incorporating them in other works of art. In other words the Sélestat draughtman was interested in texts, whereas the Rome draughts-

---

[12] 'Crassitudo capituli dividatur in partes tres, e quibus una plinthus cum cymatio fiat, altera echinus cum anulis, tertia hypotrachelion', *De Architectura*, IV, 3, 4. In this essay quotations from Vitruvius are taken from: *Vitruvii de architectura libri decem*, ed. C. Fensterbusch, Darmstadt, 1964. English translations are based on: Vitruvius, *The Ten Books on Architecture*, trans. by M.H. Morgan, New York, 1960.

[13] Ibid., lower down the same passage, concerning the architrave: 'Item epistylii latitudo ima respondeat hypotrachelio summae columnae'.

[14] Wirth, op.cit., pp. 288–89; Bischoff, op.cit., pp. 283–84.

[15] Ibid. p. 282. On Vitruvius manuscripts and on derivative excerpts see C.H. Krinsky, 'Seventy-Eight Vitruvius Manuscripts', *Journal of the Warburg and Courtauld Institutes*, 30, 1967, pp. 36–70. On medieval architecture and Vitruvius see C. Heitz, 'Vitruve et l'architecture du haut moyen-ages', *Cultura antica nell'Occidente latino dal VII all' XI secolo* (Settimane di Studi, 22), Spoleto, 1975, pp. 725–57; also Vergnolle, op. cit., *St-Benoît*, p. 65.

62 Rome, Bibl. Vat. Reg. Lat. 596, fo. 27r.

63b Bookcover, Munich, Bayerische
Staatsbibliothek, MS Clm. 4452
(detail).

63a Sélestat, Bibliothéque et Archives
Municipales, MS 360 (1153 bis), fo. 36r.

63c Chadenac (Charente-Maritime), church, capital on the west front.

man was interested in art or architecture or both. His capitals therefore look relatively real despite a preconception of the Sélestat type, so that the diagrammatic rings of the Sélestat 'Doric' were transformed into the egg-and-dart motif, familiar from real art and architecture. He also departed from textual accuracy for the sake of formal symmetry. In variance with the Sélestat drawing, the Ionic capital thus received an extra necking and the 'Doric' rudimentary volutes.

The Rome drawing is not a complete work of art. Only some columns are fluted, and the rest are plain. Only some capitals are fully detailed, and in particular the 'Doric', Ionic and Corinthian described above. The care taken, for instance, to include all the main features of the Ionic, resulting in the strange conflation of two viewpoints, stands in sharp contradiction to the casual treatment of the capital above it and of those in the superstructure, which are either blank or conform with the more usual style of this drawing. Many other motifs in the same corpus, on other pages, are likewise incomplete, though details suffice for clarifying the principles of each design, as befits a model-book.[16] Similarly the three unusually elaborated capitals sufficed to express a principle of design, which therefore emerges as the one saying that the Antique styles of capitals, indeed of architecture, are three: Doric, Ionic and Corinthian. This principle derives, of course, from Antique architectural theory as expressed by Vitruvius. He specifically states that the other forms of capitals are variations on these three, as are the very terms used to describe them.[17] The significance that a medieval reader must have attached to the terminological aspect of Vitruvius's argument will become clear further down.[18]

[16] Cf. Bischoff's explanation for the inconsistent finish in the Rome drawing as a result of its nature as a *Lehrbild*; op. cit., p. 294. For examples from the other pages see e.g. in the Paris fragment, fol. 64v; illustrated in Vergnolle, op. cit., *St-Benoît*, fig. 103.

[17] 'Sunt autem, quae isdem columnis imponuntur, capitulorum genera variis vocabulis nominata, quorum nec proprietates symmetriarum nec columnarum genus aliud nominare possumus, sed ipsorum vocabula traducta et commutata ex corinthiis et pulvinatis <Ionic> et doricis videmus, quorum symmetriae sunt in novarum scalpturarum translatae subtilitatem'; *De Architectura*, IV, 1, 12.

[18] In an object involving references to Vitruvius, one expects some preoccupation with proportions. Nothing certain can, however, be said about this matter, and this for several reasons. First, there is some difficulty in taking measurements, because the execution of the drawing is casual and the building as a whole is lopsided, partly because the vellum appears to have shrunk on the right side (the leaf measures 214/205 x 174 mm). Secondly, proportions may well become distorted in copying, and the Rome drawing, as will be shown shortly, probably copies a model. Thirdly, any Vitruvian proportions which might have been used in non-classical architectural configurations, such as medieval ones, are bound to have undergone some adaptations, and therefore the relationship can never be proven beyond doubt. Bearing these reservations in mind, some suggestions may be made about the 'building' in question. The proportions of the main part, excluding the superstructure, resemble those prescribed by Vitruvius for the round temple. According to Vitruvius, the height of the columns should equal the diameter taken between the outer edges of the stylobate walls ('Insuper stylobatam columnae constituuntur tam altae, quanta ab extremis

It may be asked whether the iconographical originality noted above should be attributed to the Rome draughtsman himself or to some lost model. If such a model existed, it is likely to have been Carolingian, and of a minor rather than monumental nature. The structure discussed above is thus topped by jewels characteristic of sacred objects, and has been convincingly described, by several scholars, as a variation on something similar to the celebrated Arnulf ciborium.[19] Concerning the other structure, the identification of shapes is more complicated because two hands were involved in the drawing, apparently at different times. The first two storeys and, separately, the domed structure at the top are executed in the delicate and confident line of the original draughtsman but not so the connecting storey (which is also displaced), the soldiers, and the side turrets. The differences in the quality of line show even in the photograph, and are striking in the original. The most satisfactory explanation to this muddle was given by Bischoff, who suggested that the lower two storeys and the domed structure were intended as separate objects, and then joined together with the aim of turning them into a representation of the Holy Sepulchre, complete with swooning guards.[20] Bischoff thought that a later hand was responsible for this adaptation, but the original draughtsman must have already indicated the idea since, as noted by Vergnolle, some of the crude connecting lines were drawn over original ones.[21] Both the lower and the upper structures are traditionally associated with the Holy Sepulchre. The upper is inscribed *Rotund<um>*, which may refer to any round building but in particular to the rotunda of the Holy Sepulchre, and a variation on the lower structure appears in a representation of the Visit to the Sepulchre on a

parietibus est diametros stylobatarum...', *De Architectura*, IV, 8, 1.). In the drawing, the height of the column on the non-distorted left hand side (inclusive of the base and the capital with its abacus, as indeed meant by Vitruvius), is 51.5 mm (the opposite column measures 51 mm), which is practically the same as the distance of 52 mm between the outer faces of the plinths. Vitruvius prescribes that the height of the dome should equal half the diameter of the whole work ('In medio tecti ratio ita habeatur, uti, quanta diametros totius operis erit futura, dimidia altitudo fiat tholi praeter florem', *De Architectura*, IV, 8, 3.) In the drawing, the total width of the platform measures 63 mm, near enough to double the 31 mm of the height of the second level, which encloses the arch (30 mm on the distorted right-hand side, and both measurements to the line of the entablature which is blurred by later paint). The arch is not drawn by compasses, and therefore its height must have been determined by this rectilinear measurement of 31 mm. It was even made stilted, in order to reach the required level. It seems, therefore, that the arch thus substitutes the dome; not as a cross section, which cannot be expected in the tenth century (see Vergnolle, op. cit., 'Un Carnet', note 56)), but rather as conflated interior and exterior views, like some representations of the Holy Sepulchre (e.g. ibid., fig. 28).

[19] Scheller, op. cit., p. 51; A. Boeckler, 'Das Erhardbild im Utacodex', *Studies in Art and Literature for Belle da Costa Greene*, ed. D. Miner, Princeton, 1954, pp. 219–30, esp. 230; Bischoff, op. cit., p. 294. For an illustration of the Arnulf ciborium see P. Lasko, *Ars Sacra*, Harmondsworth 1972, plate 58.

[20] Bischoff, op. cit., pp. 293–94.

[21] Vergnolle, op. cit., 'Un Carnet', p. 40, n. 45.

Carolingian ivory, now in Munich (Plate 63b).[22] The three-storey sepulchre here possesses, on each storey, corner colonnettes with bases and capitals, and, on the upper two, the wall is divided by horizontal lines at the base of the windows, as in the Rome drawing. The dividing line makes no sense in the drawing except by comparison with the ivory, where it also marks the upper edge of a pattern of coursed masonry. The formal relationship is so close that one can imagine the Carolingian sculptor freely combining elements from a forerunner of the Rome model-book, and rearranging them to suit his purpose.[23] Similar models must have propagated far and wide without losing their original meaning, so that, centuries later, the Romanesque sculptor of Chadenac (Charente-Maritime) produced another combination of architectural motifs like those in the drawing, limiting his choice to an arched building with a superstructure alongside a two-window structure; here too the context is the Biblical narrative of the Visit to the Sepulchre. The women approach from the right, and an angel is seated in the midst of the various structures which together represent the Holy Sepulchre (Plate 63c).

This sepulchre iconography deserves close attention in its own right, but what concerns us here is its reflection on the models of the Rome drawing. They clearly belonged in the domain of Carolingian minor arts, and were relevant not only for the design of objects like the Arnulf ciborium, but also for representations of sepulchral monuments in ivory carvings.[24] Real architectural practices do not come into this. On the other hand the Carolingian preoccupation with miniaturised architecture, like the Arnulf ciborium, is of particular interest here. Examples include at least one Antique-inspired object, namely the lost arch of Charlemagne's councillor Einhard.[25] It may be noted that the same Einhard is the probable author of a well known letter dealing, among other topics, with the 'obscure words and names' in the books of Vitruvius.[26] Just how obscure were these words and names for the Carolingians is amply illustrated by the Sélestat 'Doric' capital. The letter also implies

[22] Reused on the cover of the Pericopes of Emperor Henry II; Munich, Bayerische Staatsbibliothek, Clm. 4452.

[23] For reasons of this comparison, I believe the left hand structure in the Rome drawing to derive entirely from minor arts and biblical illustrations, in preference to Vergnolle's suggestion that it represents a veritable tower, albeit endowed with biblical symbolism. See Vergnolle, op. cit., 'Un Carnet', p. 40. In the drawing there are some inscriptions on the second storey and on the cornice of the first storey, but these are almost completely faded. An attempt to decipher a few words in connection with Easter iconography (ibid., note 46), tempting as it is in connection with either interpretation, has very little to go by.

[24] Or perhaps various reliquaries, as suggested by Bischoff, see note 2.

[25] The arch served as a base for an altar cross; see Lasko, op. cit., p. 21 and pl. 20.

[26] '<N>isi igitur tibi verba et nomina obscura ex libris Vitruvi, quae ad praesens occurrere poterant, ut eorum notitiam ibidem perquireres. Et credo, quod eorum maxima pars tibi demonstrari possit in capsella, quam domnus E columnis eburneis ad instar antiquorum operum fabricavit', *Bibliotheca rerum germanicarum*, ed. P. Jaffe, 4: *Monumenta carolina*, 478.

that the Carolingians were interested in the text partly for its own sake, and approached it like grammarians rather than like men of praxis.[27] Einhard, however, was not satisfied with abstract textual interpretation, and he refers also to an *objet d'art* which, like his arch, was probably a miniature building. He thus observes that most of the 'words and names' in question could be found illustrated in a little casket which '*domnus E* made with ivory columns in imitation of Antique works'.[28] Such objects indeed existed in Einhard's circle, witness the exceptionally classicising miniature columns in ivory, coming from a ruined reliquary and found in Einhard's abbey at Seligenstadt.[29] By Einhard's own testimony, the design of the casket thus combined imitation of Antique models with illustration of Vitruvian terms. The two need not always go hand in hand, but in this case they did.

The analogies with the right hand structure in the Rome drawing are striking. In its triple relationship to Carolingian minor arts, to Antique architectural details and to Vitruvius, it clearly goes back to the same tradition. Could it possibly represent the very casket mentioned by Einhard? [30]

[27] The only Vitruvian term actually mentioned in the letter is '*scenographia*', and the writer suggests a course of inquiry by checking what Virgil, in *Georgica*, iii, means by '*scena*'. See Wirth, op. cit., p. 282.

[28] See note 26.

[29] There has been an attempt to identify the Seligenstadt reliquary with the casket mentioned in Einhard's letter, but this implies Einhard himself was '*domnus E*' of the letter, in which case he could not have been the writer; see Buechler and Zeilinger, op. cit., p. 28. '*Domnus E*' is traditionally identified with Eigil, Abbot of Fulda (818–22); see *Bibliotheca rerum germanicarum* (as in note 26), p. 478, nn. 2 and 3. The fragments from two miniature columns survive at Seligenstadt. They are slender and fluted, and their capitals are Ionic.

[30] Carolingian miniature objects were indeed represented in later medieval painting, see Boeckler, op. cit., for a representation of an object similar to the Arnulf ciborium in the Uta Codex from Regensburg, early eleventh century.

27

Images of Higher Education in Fourteenth-Century Bologna

Robert Gibbs

This essay considers the formal characteristics and layout of representations of Bolognese teachers and their students, the personal characterisation of the leading doctor of law, Giovanni d'Andrea, the depiction of debates and of two distinguished young women who took part in them.

In 1352 Tomaso da Modena completed, signed and dated the redecoration of the chapter house of the Dominicans in Treviso which featured forty portraits of leading members of the order as scholars in their cells (Plate 64a, b, 65a).[1] Most of them are no doubt imaginary, but several appear to be reconstructed from tombs.[2] Tomaso retained a fresco of the *Crucifixion* dating, perhaps, from the rebuilding programme of 1304.[3] To the left, as one views it, were the three canonised members of the order sitting behind frontally placed desks, while the other thirty-seven friars are shown sitting at an angle inclined towards the *Crucifixion* and the three saints. The three saints, already damaged by damp, were reduced to rubble by bombing in 1944.

For Zuliani the saints are 'images offered for a conventional devotional relationship' and 'the weakest of the whole cycle'.[4] Yet quite different compositional relationships were readily intelligible to those friars who had visited or studied in Bologna; for in the course of the fourteenth century there evolved in Bologna a commemorative imagery that celebrated in a distinctive way the successful teachers of law and medicine

---

[1] R. Gibbs, *L'Occhio di Tomaso*, Treviso, 1981, pp. 61–103, 123–26, pls. IV-XX, figs. 62–100, and idem, *Tomaso da Modena: Painting in Emilia and the March of Treviso, 1340–1380*, Cambridge, 1989, pp. 63–87, pls, A, 11–44, figs. 41–61.

[2] See Gibbs, op. cit., 1981, p. 83, figs. 95–100; Gibbs, op. cit., 1989, pp. 77, 79–80. figs. 57–60.

[3] Muraro, however, considers it to date from around 1250: M. Muraro, 'Aspetti dell'arte gotica nel Veneto dal Duecento fino a Tomaso da Modena', in Gibbs, op. cit., 1981, pp. 371–415. The rest of the decoration dates from around 1304 (Gibbs, op. cit., 1981, pp. 123–26).

[4] F. Zuliani, 'Tomaso da Modena', *Tomaso da Modena*, ed. L. Menegazzi, Treviso, 1979, pp. 87–88. The frescoes were ruinous even before their destruction, but their fragments are deposited in Santa Caterina, Treviso. Coletti did not illustrate them in his fundamental monograph on Tomaso, *L'arte di Tomaso da Modena*, Bologna, 1933, 2nd edn., Venice, 1962–63.

upon whom the celebrity of the university and a substantial part of Bologna's prosperity depended.[5] This imagery is marked both by a richness of detail descriptive of academic life and by an immediately recognisable formal structure.

The three saints are not, in fact, frontal themselves, but slightly inwardly inclined behind frontal desks, so that they have a similar relationship to the *Crucifixion* as the other friars have to the saints. They are seated in an arrangement which signifies an assembly around a central authority, an authority that may be either intellectual or legal, or indeed both. It may represent an imperial court, a papal or ecclesiastical council or any other kind of legal tribunal. In fourteenth-century Bologna, it frequently represents an assembly of students around their *doctor*.

The evolution of this imagery can be traced in the tombs that form by far the most important aspect of medieval Bolognese sculpture, as Renzo Grandi has shown.[6] The earliest Bolognese tomb representation of a teacher and pupils commemorates Rolandino dei Passaggeri (d. 1300), who was not, in fact, a doctor of laws at all but a notary (Plate 66). He was, however, the greatest of all Bolognese notaries, author of the standard source book for his profession, the *Summa artis notarie*, and Bologna's political leader for much of the later thirteenth century. He was responsible for the city's defiant refusal to free Frederick II's son, King Enzo, captured at Fossalta. He also played a large part in the triumph of the Guelf (Geremei) faction in Bologna and its extremely democratic constitution (by pre-twentieth-century standards) which survived many vicissitudes through the course of the fourteenth century. This ensured continuity for both the reputation of Rolandino and the imagery in which it was celebrated. On one side of the sarcophagus under the canopy which gives Rolandino quasi-imperial status he is shown facing an emblematic series of students, each probably representing a row of similar figures following his commentary in their texts.[7]

The essential ingredient of this composition, and one which suits well its subject, is the author portrait, well known from countless examples in all kinds of text (but above all Gospel books).[8] In Bolognese law manu-

[5] For the Bolognese tombs see Renzo Grandi: *I monumenti dei dottori e la sculptura a Bologna, 1267–48*, Bologna, 1982. Comparable tombs are found in Verona (Grandi, op. cit., 1982, fig. 187); and Pistoia, Cino dei Sighibuldi (1337–39); and in Modena (Gibbs, op. cit., 1989, figs. 50–51).

[6] R. Grandi, op. cit., and for a brief overview of wider scope, 'Le tombe dei dottori bolognesi: ideologia e cultura' *Atti e Memorie della Deputazione di storia patria per le provincie di Romagna*, n.s., 29–30, 1978–79, pp. 163–81, pls. I-IV.

[7] Grandi, op.cit., 1982, pp. 57–59, 118–21; J. Deer, *The Dynastic Porphyry Tombs of the Norman Period in Sicily*, Cambridge, Mass., 1959. For Rolandino's political career see G. Tamba, *I documenti del Governo del Comune di Bologna*, Quaderni culturali bolognesi 6, Bologna, 1978, pp. 11–13.

[8] The 6th-century *Dioscorides*, the images of Jerome in the Vulgate Bible, and 14th-century copies of Gratian's *Decretum*.

64a Treviso, chapter house, general view.

64b Treviso, chapter house, the three canonised members of the Dominican Order.

65a Treviso, chapter house, Dominican friars.

65b Bologna, Museo Civico, Tomb of Giovanni d'Andrea, from San Domenico.

scripts they are usually reduced to small though full-length figures in the initial letter of the text, set below a more formal composition the full width of the text.

Author portraits are normally in profile, like Rolandino, or in three-quarter view, but the formal Bolognese composition set above such initials (showing Justice or Justinian in Civil Law texts, God granting the two powers to Pope and Emperor in the *Decretum Gratiani*, the Pope in Council at the head of the various volumes of *Decretals*) is symmetrical. These images of authority are as old as official Christian art.[9] The Gratian Distribution of Powers itself derives from an early ninth-century image on the Triclinium of Leo III, still partially preserved, and is probably cognate with, and not derived from, the Last Judgement with which its derivations are sometimes confused.[10]

There are other ancient traditions of representation, for both the teacher and the author. Grandi has drawn attention to the Roman sarcophagus in Trier which shows a teaching scene foreshadowing in content and the near-symmetry of the arrangement several stages of the Bologna tombs and their evolution.[11]

The author or teacher seated with a (portable) desk, on the other hand, is represented at the base of the voussoirs of the Virgin Portal of Chartres' *Portail Royal* and taken up in Italy by Benedetto Antelami and his school. The splendid monumental carving in the Palazzo Ducale, Mantua, *c.* 1215, by Antelami or his pupil and believed to represent Virgil, is a fine example which undoubtedly inspired a later carving of inferior quality but considerable prominence upon the Tower of the Broletto (Palazzo Communale) as well as the Virgil on Mantua's 1257 *grosso* coinage.[12]. A similar representation of Livy in Padua from the mid fourteenth century confirms the enduring impact of these images of literary authority: they undoubtedly influenced the development of Bolognese tomb design despite limited influence in Mantua and Padua themselves.[13] The establishment of the cult of the Doctors of the Church in 1297 confirmed the associations of the figure at a desk with learned authority, but their representations more commonly share with the Evangelists the three-quarter view of the author portrait.[14]

[9] E.g. Constantine addressing his troops on his Arch, D. Strong, *Roman Imperial Sculpture*, London, 1961, pp. 75–79, figs. 136–37; or Christ as philosopher and judge, ibid., p. 69, fig. 125; or the Theodosius *missorium*, ibid., p. 79, fig. 143.

[10] A. Melnikas, *The Corpus of the Miniatures in the Manuscripts of Decretum Gratiani*, *Studia Gratiana*, 16–18, Rome, 1975, i, pp. 29–104.

[11] Grandi, op. cit., 1978–79, pp. 178–79, pl. 1.

[12] Grandi, op. cit., 1978–79, pp. 180–81, and op. cit., 1982, pp. 61–62. pls. 161–62.

[13] W. Wolters, 'Appunti per una storia della scultura padovana del Trecento', *Da Giotto a Mantegna*, Catalogue of the exhibition in Padua, ed. L. Grossato, Milan, 1974, pp. 37–38.

[14] Boniface VIII officially promulgated the cult of the Doctors of the Church in 1297. See e.g. H. Belting, *Die Oberkirche von San Francesco in Assisi*, Berlin, 1977, p. 96.

In our visual culture frontal and symmetrical images are considered formal, rigid, hieratic, iconic, devotional (as in Zuliani's negative reading of the Treviso saints). Yet they possess other qualities: in the laws of physics the simplest balance is symmetrical, and balance is embodied in our image of Justice by the simplest of variants of straight symmetry in the sword and scales. Balance is an aspect of harmony and dignity. The role of symmetry, therefore, in the evolution of picture compositions can represent an achievement arising from artistic development rather than an elementary structure to be escaped from. It also has other pictorial advantages. In 1318 the symmetrical option began to be explored for the visualisation of the doctors and their students in Bologna. Perhaps it owed something to Giotto's development of this format during the same years for his frescoes in the Lower Church at Assisi and the Bardi Chapel in Santa Croce, Florence, as well the *Stefaneschi Altarpiece* on the high altar of St Peter's: Bologna was self-consciously the second city of the papal domain.[15] In any case we need to be aware of the essentially visual possibilities of the format and not take for granted either the traditional aesthetic response or the possibility of a social reading of such images as reflections of a growing centralisation in fourteenth-century politics.

In 1318 the tomb of the lecturer in medicine, Lucio dei Liuzzi, and his celebrated nephew Mondino (d. 1326), who wrote the standard treatise on *Anatomia*, was carved by Roso da Parma with a more imposing and expressive version of the Rolandino composition.[16] In the same year the doctor of laws, Bartoluzzo de' Preti, died and was represented on his tomb enthroned between his students, seated frontally like him, three on either side behind desks.[17] Only the mysteriously opened oak terminal on the right side of his throne breaks the symmetry. This tomb or its prototype did not have a spectacular immediate success against the lateral design, but it made steady inroads, partly no doubt because of the possibilities of developing the characterisation of the master and particularly the students, who testify by their varied costume, academic dress and character to the international celebrity of the doctor (literally *ubique doctor*), licensed by his degree to teach anywhere in the world where imperial and papal writ prevailed, except (because of the closed shop created by the native lawyers) Bologna itself (legal restrictive practices have long outstripped those of less remunerative trades).

Giovanni d'Andrea (d. 1348) was the outstanding commentator upon the later Canon Law texts of fourteenth-century Bologna, and he played a major part in the cultural and religious life of the city, corresponding

[15] For a discussion of the similarities between the Stefaneschi Altarpiece and the Assisi frescoes, see G. Previtali, *Giotto e la sua bottega*, Milan, 1967, pp. 94–105, and my paper, 'The Three-bay Interior from Giotto to Van Eyck', University of Warwick Giotto Conference, 1987, forthcoming.

[16] Grandi, op. cit., 1982, pp. 78–79, 138–39, pls. 52–56.

[17] Idem, pp. 77–78, 134–35, pls. 42–45.

66 Bologna, Tomb of Rolandino dei Passaggeri.

67a 'The Illustrator': frontispiece to
Giovanni d'Andrea, *Novella super Libro
Sexto Decretalium*, Biblioteca Apostolica
Vaticana, Vat. Lat. 2233, fo. 1r.

67b 'The Illustrator': Giovanni d'Andrea,
Novella super Libro Sexto Decretalium,
Biblioteca Apostolica Vaticana, Vat.
Lat. 2233, fo. 1r, detail.

67c Niccolò da Bologna: Giovanni
d'Andrea, *Novella super Decretalibus*
(detail). Biblioteca Apostolica
Vaticana, vat. lat. 1456, fo. 1r.

67d Assisi, San Francesco, Alborñoz Chapel.
Andrea de' Bartoli: St Catherine's
Disputation with the Philosophers.

with Petrarch and perpetuating his influence through his adopted son Giovanni d'Andrea Calderini, as well as through his daughters. On his tomb he is shown wearing a typical gown and an open hood over his head rather than across his shoulders (Plate 65b).[18] Noticeable to the left is a face of distinctly oriental character, conceivably a Tartar belonging to the Hungarian nation well represented at Bologna.[19]

This tomb represents the culmination of a development in the frontal symmetrical composition from the 1318 de' Preti tomb and the Cerniti tomb of 1338, where both master and pupils face the viewer in an obviously stilted fashion, to the tombs of Michele da Bertalia (1328) and Bonandrea de' Bonandrei (1333) with the students converging from the sides.[20] On the tomb of Bonifacio Galluzzi (1346) an illusionistic interior is attempted.[21] The viewer looks over the shoulders of the students seated on diagonally converging benches and desks, an awkward visual effect which, however, leads to the classic solution of Giovanni d'Andrea's own. This implies a circle through space by setting the diagonal benches frontally on either side, but giving the impression of the audience converging on and attentively facing the master. The resulting formula was clearly considered successful since it remained the standard formula for ninety years and was used by technically greater artists such as the dalle Masegne (the tomb of Giovanni da Legnano, 1328)[22] and Jacopo della Quercia (Antonio Galeazzo Bentivoglio, 1436).[23]

This design was probably derived from illumination, which had long shown, for many subjects, a figure of authority flanked by councillors, in particular the Consistory Court which this arrangement of the lecture closely resembles. The debates and trials held in the consistory court form the normal subject for the *Decretals*, the second volume of the Canon Law, issued by Gregory IX, as well as for the sequel, the *Liber Sextus* of Boniface VIII. Here the councillors are shown on flanking benches, all essentially frontal: one might see these converging benches as being comparable to the seating of a chapter around the walls of a chapter house, like those of the Dominicans held in Treviso and elsewhere.[24]

---

[18] Grandi, op. cit., 1982, pp. 82–84, 163–67, pls. 139–57; Gibbs, op. cit., 1989, pp. 37–38, 74–76. For Giovanni d' Andrea see F.C. von Savigny, *Geschichte des Roemischen Rechts im Mittelalter*, Heidelberg, 2nd edn., 1850, vi, pp. 98–125; S. Stelling Michaud, 'Jean d' André', *Dictionnaire de droit canonique*, 6, Paris, 1957, pp. 89–92.

[19] It was a Hungarian rector who led the exodus in 1321: Grandi, op. cit., 1982, pp. 133–34.

[20] Idem, 1982, pp. 79–82, 146–47, 153–54, pls. 88–96.

[21] Ibid., pls. 104–9; *Introduzione al Museo Civico Medievale, Palazzo Ghisilardi-Fava*, Bologna, 1985, pp. 48–49.

[I] Ibid., pp. 53–55.

[23] A.M. Matteucci, 'Le Sculture', *Il Tempio di San Giacomo Maggiore in Bologna*, ed. C. Volpe, Bologna, 1976, pp. 74–77, figs. 25–31.

[24] Gibbs, op. cit., 1989, esp. pp. 63–66.

Giovanni d'Andrea's own glosses and commentaries on the Canon Law dominate the illuminated output of the Bologna workshops from the 1340s. In the illustrations to these manuscripts a design resembling that of the Consistory Court is used quite specifically to represent a lecture given by Giovanni himself in progress. The frontispiece of Giovanni's *Novella super Sexto Decretalium* (Vat. MS lat. 2233, fol. 1r)(Plates 67, a, b) shows such a lecture alongside the presentation of the text to the Pope.[25] It is not symmetrical, since it is paired with the presentation, but the 'Illustrator', the outstanding Bolognese illuminator who painted it, was able to complete the picture space with the students seated in the foreground like the front desks of scribes in the Consistory Court. This the tomb sculptor had to renounce because of his shallow surface and relief space. Judging from the tight-cut dress and extended sleeves (*manicottoli*) of Novella, a young lady who represents Giovanni's daughter as well as his title,[26] this is a late work of the 'Illustrator' from the mid 1340s and an important dating source for the end of his career.

A young rival of the 'Illustrator', the '1346 Master', had developed this design as the frontispiece to Giovanni's *Hieronymianus*, the first major study of St Jerome, who Giovanni saw as the neglected patron of scholars and Bologna and to whose cult he devoted much patronage.[27] It introduces the earliest known copy, in the Collegio di Spagna (MS. 273), Bologna, written in a perfect Bolognese hand by Stanislas of Cracow. It might will be the direct model for Giovanni's tomb itself. The chronological convergence of the 1346 *Hieronymianus*, the 1348 tomb, and Tomaso's chapter house frescoes of 1351–52 surely represents the climax of a compositional development spanning the various visual arts practised around the university and derived from the most brilliant work of both the first and second generations of Bologna's fourteenth-century illuminators and painters.[28]

By 1353 Niccolò da Bologna had evolved a crowded composition for the longer *Novella super Decretalibus* (Plate 67c) in which the lecture itself is merely one of three scenes and shown from the side again. The range of native and foreign students' dress even includes a turban, an unambiguous indication of non-Indo-European and possibly non-Christian

[25] Grandi, op. cit., 1982, pl. 212; Gibbs, op. cit., 1989, pp. 75–76, fig. 54.

[26] For Novella see in particular G. Rossi, 'Contributi alla biografia del canonista Giovanni d' Andrea (L'insegnamento di Novella e Bettina, sue figlie, ed i prisunti responsa di Milancia, sua moglie)', *Rivista Trimestrale di Diritto e Procedura Civile*, 1957, pp. 1451–1503.

[27] M. Meiss, 'French and Italian Variations on an Early Fifteenth-century Theme: St Jerome and his Study', *Gazette des Beaux Arts*, 62, 1963, pp. 147–70; O. Paecht, 'Zur Entstehung des "Hieronymus in Gehaeus"', *Pantheon*, 21, 1963, pp. 131–42: Gibbs, op. cit., 1989, pp. 38, 101–2.

[28] For the 1346 Master, F. Arcangeli, *Pittura bolognese del Trecento*, Bologna, 1978, ibid., pp. 92–95.

origins.[29] But Niccolò includes two frontal images of Giovanni studying, the latter recalling the images of St Jerome himself.

It is striking that the high-cheekboned hook-nosed face of Giovanni, a standard type of the 'Illustrator', corresponds both to his portraits on his tomb and to Niccolò's pictures of him, although it is *not* a standard type of Niccolò's. It is therefore very likely to be a genuine portrait of Giovanni and recognisable to his contemporaries. In this case, it was also a natural source for one of the 'Illustrator''s most typical characterisations of venerable and learned figures, repeated many times in his illustrations to legal texts.[30] From this example Tomaso probably took his own interest in the individual characterisation of the Dominicans which is such a celebrated aspect of his Treviso chapter house frescoes (Plate 64b, 65a), and in particular the idea of creating a historical representation of those whose tombs might furnish a recognisable or at least an official likeness.[31]

A notable feature of both Giovanni's tomb and Tomaso's frescoes is the range of attitude expressed among the audience, not youthful beginners but men of experience and knowledge, often questioning or critical in attitude and enhancing their teacher's status by their own. The figures sharpening and clearing a pen of its shavings, checking in an open volume or reflecting upon it with chin in hand recur in Tomaso's work.[32] They gain in visibility from the frontal composition, and their relevance to the Treviso frescoes is heightened by the fact that the tomb was originally in the Dominican church in Bologna along with those of Bonifacio Galluzzi, Giovanni da Legnano (1383) and Bartolomeo da Saliceto (1411).[33] These burials (and those in San Francesco and San Giacomo) reflect the close association of the mendicant orders with the main university as well as the *studia* for their own members alongside it.

Student life in all ages is coloured, of course, by romance and fair maidens, in the all-male world of the fourteenth-century Bolognese schools as much as in the altogether more feminine classes of the Courtauld Institute. It was a niece of Giovanni d'Andrea who was abducted by a Spanish student; his subsequent execution led to the student revolt and exodus of 1321.[34] Giovanni's daughter, Novella, is one of the heroines

[29] For Niccolò's illumination see Gibbs, op. cit., 1981, fig. 148. A general introduction to the presence and representation of Asian and Middle Eastern peoples in Italy is provided by L. Olschki, 'Asiatic Exoticism in Italian Art of the Early Renaissance', *Art Bulletin*, 26, 1944, pp. 95–106.

[30] Conti, op. cit., pls. XXVIII, upper and lower right, pls. 260, first and second left, 271, centre, 273–74, centre, 275, second left; Melnikas, op. cit. Causa II, fig. 40, bishop, Causa V, fig. 40, first right.

[31] Gibbs, op. cit., 1981, pp. 81–84, 1989, pp. 79–80, for Tomaso's representation of St Dominic, Benedict XI and Jacopo Salomone in this way.

[32] Gibbs, op. cit., 1989, pls. 20, 39, 23, 18, 25, 36, 21, 34, 35b, 41.

[33] Grandi, op. cit., 1982, pp. 150–51, 163–67; *Introduzione al Museo Civico Medievale*, pp. 53–55, 58–60.

[34] See above, n. 19.

of Christine de Pisan's *Livre de la Cité des Dames*, standing in for her father at lectures and hiding her beauty behind a curtain to avoid distracting the students.[35] Novella and her sister Bettina, their mother and their husbands are all supposed to have been lawyers. Christine was herself the daughter of the Bolognese doctor of medicine and professor of astrology, Tommaso da Pizzano.

Yet the young lady who represents most vividly the academic life of fourteenth-century Bologna in art was no historical native of the city but the legendary virgin martyr, St Catherine of Alexandria. Her cult was encouraged, like so many, by the Dominican Jacobus de Voragine's *Golden Legend*.[36] Not only her conventional beauty but her conversion by an icon made her a natural subject for the painter and patron of religious painting. Her particular interest for the Bolognese and the Dominicans of the fourteenth century was surely the dispute in which St Catherine converted pagan philosophers to Christianity.

Christ arguing with the Doctors was a natural subject to substitute for contemporary debates and an authoritative prototype for them, some-times shown as the frontispiece to Part Two of the *Decretum Gratiani* and clearly of particular interest to Bolognese artists and their patrons. It appears regularly in New Testament cycles and notably in one of the Pseudo-Jacopino's polyptychs, where its relevance to academic debate is emphasised by the prominence of the relevant texts, in this case those of the Bible, and flung round by Christ's frustrated opponents, while above Christ is enthroned precisely in the manner of a university master.[37] St Catherine clearly provided another equally colourful variation on this theme which became popular both in Bologna and elsewhere. It was visualised by the Bolognese painter Andrea de' Bartoli in the frescoes commemorating Cardinal Albornoz at Assisi, 1362–69: his philosophers employ the optical instruments that Tomaso had just introduced into the Treviso Dominican portraits (Plate 67d).[38] Albornoz founded the first college in Bologna, in whose library the earliest copy of Giovanni d'Andrea's life of St Jerome, illustrated by the 1346 Master, is preserved.[39]

Catherine's disputation is usually shown in a less symmetrical arrange-ment than Christ's, governed by narrative immediacy rather then formal structural logic. Here it is the subject, the local colour of the details of her dress and her beauty, of the academic dress and aged features of the philosophers, that typify the scenes, not a predictable layout of social

[35] See n. 26; Christine de Pisan, *The Book of the City of Ladies*, transl. by E.J. Richards, London, 1983, esp. II, 36, 3.

[36] Jacobus de Voragine, *Legenda Aurea*, edn. Leipzig, 1850, pp. 789–97.

[37] For the polyptych panel (Bologna, Pinacoteca Nazionale, inv. 217, cat. 159) see Arcangeli, op. cit., p. 126, pl. 17.

[38] Gibbs op. cit., 1989, pp. 83–84, fig. 61, pls. 19, 27.

[39] For the *Hieronymianus* see n. 27.

and visual relationships.[40] But these scenes also provide an image of Bologna's school life in action, seen from the perspective of the Dominicans, men of the church but also academics, with their own schools in Bologna, aiming their teaching at a wider audience than the legal and medical professions. The dedication of their important church in Pisa to Catherine of Alexandria, the choice of name of their new self-martyring saint, Catherine of Siena, suggest a crossing of currents that is perhaps more than mere coincidence.

It is rarely appreciated how important this university set in territory fought for by Alborñoz and the Church, where the leading administrators of Europe acquired their training, was for European culture. Yet pictures like Tomaso's in Treviso and Andrea de' Bartoli's at Assisi used a formal language and imagery that no visually-sensitive pupil of the universities could have failed to understand.

Acknowledgement: I should like to pay tribute in this essay to the insights into the significance of the architectural setting of figurative representations provided by Peter Kidson's lectures, as well as to his entertaining reflections upon the changing demography of the specific micro-educational context within which his lectures were presented. This essay also benefited from discussion at the University of Toronto's Medievalists' seminar.

[40] Catherine is often dressed in regal features such as trailing oversleeves and miniver or ermine trimmings (Florentine examples at Santa Caterina all' Antella; Altichiero's frescoes in the Oratorio di San Giorgio, Padua).

28

Simone Martini and the Problem of Retirement

Andrew Martindale

'(1344) Magister Simon mortuus est in Curia;
cuius exequias fecimus
in conventu die iiij mensis augusti'.[1]

It may seem bad taste to start off a contribution to a Festschrift with an obituary notice. This essay is, however, not so much concerned with the manner of Simone's passing as the manner of his survival during the last ten years of his life. It concerns his life from *c.* 1335, at which date he was over fifty. This was fairly advanced by medieval (and indeed post-medieval) standards; and in modern times retirement would have been under discussion. Retirement can be a melancholy business and fortunately little is heard of it in the Middle Ages, this for the obvious reason that retirement in its modern sense hardly existed. Working people, if they survived into old age, worked till they dropped; or if they were fortunate, until they could with dignity retreat into the bosom of their family. The uncertainties, inherent in this, account for the competition for the relatively small number of appointments which carried with them both emoluments and life-tenure. In an age when even the Arch-bishop of Canterbury retires on a pension and only Field-Marshals are left to carry the banner of life-appointment, this world has almost vanished. But at any period before the twentieth century it had a sharp reality. In the Middle Ages, the church certainly possessed the greatest number of such positions. Men of international repute, such as Petrarch, were sustained by them. In the world of arts and crafts, however, the opportunities were sadly diminished. It seems clear that at least from the thirteenth century, senior masons might enjoy the expectation of gaining a position which, either de facto or even contractually, they might expect

---

[1] This quotation is from the necrology of S Domenico, Siena, to be found printed in P. Bacci, *Fonti e commenti per la storia dell'arte senese*, Siena, 1944, p. 188. A résumé of the documentary evidence for Simone's life is to be found in A. Martindale, *Simone Martini*, Oxford, 1988, pp. 216–18. This monograph will subsequently be referred to as Martindale/Simone.

to hold till death.[2] Painters, however, were in a different welfare league. Giotto (unusually) died as the (salaried) senior mason of the commune of Florence.[3] Clement VI's painter, Matteo Giovanetti, held three posts of ecclesiastical preferment.[4] But, for most people, the onset of the *Troisième Age* meant the uncertainties of independence, the uncertainties of family support, entry in some form into a religious institution, or indeed destitution.

All of this lends some interest to the career of Simone Martini. His life has been often described and there is no need here to recount it in detail.[5] Between *c.* 1315 and 1335 he was the principal painter in Siena. He enjoyed a near monopoly of official commissions; he built up a flourishing practice; he enjoyed relative affluence; and he owned two houses and counted as a substantial property holder. Though married, he had no children of his own; he had, however, other immediate kin and many nephews and nieces. He, of all people, might have enjoyed a dignified old age in Siena, fading gently from view and ultimately being buried in his parish church.[6]

Instead, as indicated in the earlier quotation, he went with his wife and brother to the papal court at Avignon, the *curia*.[7] Most accounts of

[2] A sample of the English evidence is to be found in D. Knoop and G.P. Jones, *The Medieval Mason*, Manchester, 1933, reprint 1949, pp. 95–96. Also L.F. Salzman, *Building in England down to 1540*, Oxford, 1952, pp. 585–94. Emoluments might be reduced in case of incapacity or ill-health. From the small amount of published evidence, it seems likely that long-term maintenance and long term contracts went together. The only long-term maintenance job for painters known to me is reflected in the decision made in Venice in 1422 to employ a salaried painter, whose sole job was to make good the ravages of salt and sea air on the 14th-century frescoes in the *sala del gran consiglio* in the ducal palace ('ut est manifestum cadunt in dies picture ipsius sale cum magna deformitate eius.' See G.-B. Lorenzi, *Monumenti per servire alla storia del Palazzo Ducale di Venezia*, Venice, 1868, Doc.148). But though the source of the finance was identified and the salary was good (100 ducats p.a.) nothing further is heard about this and it is not clear whether it was ever implemented.

[3] The decree of 12 April 1334 made Giotto *magister et gubernator* of the *Opera del Duomo* with responsibilities for the walls, fortifications and bridges. The document does not specify life-tenure but most of the holders of this position seem to have died in post.

[4] For information about Matteo Giovanetti, see M. Laclotte and D. Thiebaut, *L'école d'Avignon*, Tours, 1983, p. 155. Matteo held three ecclesiastical posts while at Avignon, a prebend at the church of S Luca, Viterbo (from 1328), the priorate of S Martino, Viterbo (from 1336) and the position of archpriest at Vercelli (from 1348). He survived til *c.* 1368/69.

[5] See Martindale/Simone pp. 5–8.

[6] Either S Donato or S Egidio (the evidence is ambiguous). He might also have sought burial in the church of the Dominicans, to whom he bequeathed 19 florins and who entered his name in their obituary book (see the start of this essay).

[7] Although Simone was in Avignon by the end of 1336, the date at which he was joined by Giovanna and Donato is not known. I assume that they either went with him or joined him very soon after. Donato's presence is not attested there until 1340; and Giovanna is known only to have returned to Siena after Simone's death and probably in 1347. See G. Milanesi, *Documenti per la storia dell'arte senese*, Siena, 1854, 1, p. 244.

this move proceed on the assumption that Simone had got either some form of promotion or something akin to a Hollywood contract. Yet it must be pointed out immediately that very little is known about his life there. Paradoxically, virtually everything that is known about Simone at Avignon is derived from the archives at Siena.[8] From one point of view this is understandable. Very little in the way of public archives survives from the city of Avignon during the period. In particular, there are no notarial archives at all; hence we have no information about property transactions and no wills. We shall probably never have a full account of Simone's property in Avignon at the moment of his death. By contrast the papal archives are unusually well-preserved. There is an extraordinary amount of information about the personnel of the papal court. We know, for instance, that Clement VI, who had been Archbishop of Rouen, kept a Norman cook on his establishment.[9] Much is also known about the building of the papal palace.[10] Simone's name has never been found in either context; and it may be said with some confidence that he never served in the papal *familia* nor yet was employed by the office of works. Where then does this leave the 'Hollywood contract'?

The point is made more sharply if a contrast is made with the career of Giotto at the court of Naples. Giotto was invited to Naples by the king, Robert the Wise. He was employed to paint the royal palace, the Castel Nuovo. He became a member of the royal *familia*. As important, he left a clear presence behind in the city of Florence (the workshop of Taddeo Gaddi); and he was eventually invited back again to Florence.[11] The fact that none of this appears to have happened to Simone prompts questions about the professional basis of his presence in Avignon, especially since the Lorenzetti workshop seems to have moved in to fill the vacuum left by his departure and absence.

The clue to this may be found in the nature of the works which either certainly or probably come from this period. They include the Liverpool *Holy Family* and the Ambrosiana Virgil frontispiece. With one exception, all are small or very small. They are in fact tiny and private and can only be seen as a series of highly personal commissions for very discriminating patrons with idiosyncratic requirements. They include, for instance, the first recorded painted portraits.

---

[8] Martindale/Simone, p. 216, gives an account of the documentary situation.

[9] See B. Guillemain, *La cour pontificale d'Avignon, 1309–1376*, Paris, 1966, p. 404. He came from Rouen. This work gives the most comprehensive available account of the papal court.

[10] For the building of the palace, see L.H. Labande, *Le palais des papes et les monuments d'Avignon au XIVe siècle*, Aix-Marseille, 1925. For the decoration, see Laclotte-Thiebaut (note 4 above) and E. Castelnuovo, *Un pittore italiano alla corte di Avignone*, Turin, 1962.

[11] For a convenient summary of the outlines of Giotto's life, see G. Vigorelli and E. Baccheschi, *L'opera completa di Giotto*, Milan, 1966, pp. 83–84.

Even the exception, the fresco decoration of the porch of Avignon Cathedral for Jacopo Stefaneschi, has unusual imagery which is directly linked to the patron. There is one further peculiarity about these commissions. They are few in number. Adding together the certainties and the near-certainties, there are only seven.[12] Thus both in type and quantity, the work surrounding the name of Simone Martini *c.* 1335–44 hardly begins to sound like the normal output of a busy workshop. So what had happened?

There is a simple solution which may be suggested for this problem. It may reasonably be supposed that Simone acquired a private protector, perhaps a cardinal, perhaps a member of the Orsini or Stefaneschi families. With this might have gone membership of a princely, non-papal *familia* (of a cardinal, for instance) and, perhaps,a sinecure offering both emoluments and life-tenure. This is by no means impossible. Petrarch's first protectors were the Colonna family, who obtained for him a prebend in Lombez Cathedral;[13] and Petrarch's own evidence attests to the fact that Simone was an agreeable person.[14] It may be objected that the identity of such a person would surely be indicated, either by the paintings themselves or by some form of documentary evidence. Yet there are no relevant private household accounts for the period from Avignon; and the paintings themselves need not be very informative. If the Burgundian archives had been destroyed it would not be possible to tell from the surviving paintings that Jan van Eyck had been a close personal servant of Philip the Good of Burgundy. In that instance, indeed, the evidence suggests that Jan's personal and confidential value to the duke was as important as his ability to paint.[15]

[12] With reference to the catalogue in Martindale/Simone, the seven items are: the Altomonte St Ladislas (Cat. 1, uncertain); the Antwerp-Orsini polyptych (Cat. 2, uncertain); the Avignon Cathedral porch (Cat. 5, certain); the lost portrait of Laura (Cat. 6, certain); the lost portrait of Napoleone Orsini (Cat.7. uncertain); the Liverpool *Holy Family* (Cat. 14, certain); the Ambrosiana Virgil frontispiece (Cat. 15, certain).

[13] For Petrarch's life, see E.H. Wilkins, *Life of Petrarch*, Chicago, 1961. The canonry at Lombez was granted in 1335. Petrarch secured further preferments later in life.

[14] The reference is to his well-known marginal annotation attesting to Simone's qualities as a companion. See Martindale/Simone, p. 7.

[15] The evidence of Van Eyck's activity for the duke as a painter is very small. In 1428, he painted a portrait of Isabella of Portugal for Philip in advance of the ducal marriage. The only remaining near-contemporary evidence is Fazio's statement that he painted for the duke a 'circular representation of the world'. Otherwise the ducal accounts are silent on the subject, though Van Eyck was salaried and this may have precluded itemised payments for specific works. The accounts relate, however, the expenses for his famous confidential journeys (the 'secret voyages'), of the duke's visit to his workshop, of the duke apparently acting as godfather to Jan's son. The documents were printed by Le Comte de Laborde, *Les Ducs de Bourgogne*, Paris, 1849, 1. The account of the 1428 embassy is to be found in R. Vaughan, *Philip the Good*, London, 1970, pp. 178–84. A résumé of all the official archives is to be found in W.H.J. Weale and M.W. Brockwell, *The Van Eycks and their Art*, London-New York-Toronto, 1912.

Something similar, too, seems to emerge from the relationship of the Limbourg brothers to the Duke of Berry who, after ten years salaried employment by the duke had remarkably little to show for it in the matter of art.[16]

The protection of an affluent, powerful private patron might explain a further curiosity about the aftermath of Simone's life at Avignon. After his death his widow, Giovanna, stayed on for over two years until her brother, Lippo Memmi, came to bring her home in 1346–47.[17] Again, the examples of the families of Pol de Limbourg and Jan van Eyck may be instructive. The widow of Pol was still living in her late husband's house (provided originally by the duke) more than ten years after Pol's death;[18] and Jan van Eyck's widow, Margaret, received a pension.[19] In both cases, therefore, the protection afforded to the husband was extended to the widow. Was the same true of Giovanna, widow of Simone?

It may be remarked that, in terms of security, it was the position with emoluments and life tenure which really counted. Membership of a *familia*, for artists a relatively untested area of existence in the 1330s, offered no more than a salary and access to the prince.[20] A *valet* was, to use the medieval phrase, eminently *conductitius ac etiam remotivus*.[21] Moreover the later evidence is not entirely encouraging. Mantegna (well documented) survived two changes of marchese (and two changes of marchesa) to die (1506) still a court servant at the age of about seventy-five. Cosma Tura was not so fortunate. However, accessible positions with life-tenure were less than common, which explains the prominence achieved later by such posts as the Venetian *senseria* and the papal *piombo*.

---

[16] The three brothers probably entered the service of the Duc de Berry soon after the death of Philip of Burgundy in 1404. They died in 1416. During that period of about ten years they completed one manuscript (the *Belles Heures*) and started another (the *Très Riches Heures*). This hardly constitutes high productivity; and it is tempting to see the counterfeit book which they made as a new-year present for the duke in 1411 as an in-joke about this situation. The fact that the object was duly delivered to the librarian and entered in the inventory suggests that the joke, whatever its overtones, was well received. See M. Meiss, *French Painting in the Time of Jean de Berry*, London, 1974, p. 76.

[17] See note 7 above.

[18] See M. Meiss, op.cit., note 16, pp. 80–81. Pol's wife, Gillette la Mercière, seems, it is true, to have acquired limited tenure in unusual circumstances. The duke died in the same year as Pol; and it seems clear that nobody subsequently tried to turn her out. The situation remained thus up to her death (before 1434) and even after her second marriage. Thereafter, steps were taken by the king to retrieve the house from her second husband.

[19] See Weale and Brockwell in note 15. The duke also endowed his daughter so that she might enter a nunnery (1448–49). See Laborde, op.cit., note 15.

[20] See A. Martindale, *The Rise of the Artist in the Middle Ages and Early Renaissance*, London, 1972, where the access of artists to various household positions during the 14th century is discussed.

[21] Taken in this instance from the statutes of Eton College (1444), chapter 14, *De Magistro Informatore...*

   The purpose of this short essay has been to take the evidence for
Simone's presence in Avignon and to make some sense of it. The
evidence itself is very incomplete; and to some extent the silence of the
1330s has been filled with noise from the fifteenth century. If these are
the wrong conclusions, the interesting problems still remain: the small
output; its private nature; the total silence of the papal archives; the
character of the Avignonese patronage; the circumstances of Simone's
departure from Siena.

   It seems doubtful whether we really have a satisfactory answer to that
last issue.[22] It remains surprising that he left Siena; and, once at Avignon,
there is no surviving evidence of opportunities leading to works of the
quality and significance of the St-Louis altar or the Uffizi Annunciation.
One is therefore left in some uncertainty whether Avignon was really a
Promised Land, or whether it was, rather, a city of unfulfilled promises
and limited opportunities; an agreeable mistake, perhaps, but also an
irretrievable one. The other side of that picture is, indeed, the one
painted here; the sort of retirement which most people want for themselves and their friends, with good company, appreciative acquaintances,
adequate means, leisure and the obligation to do only those things
which one really wants to do. This essay may have started on the wrong
note; but the final thought, for a Festschrift, is an entirely appropriate
one.

---

[22] There was a 16th-century tradition that Simone was lured to Avignon by a French
cardinal who happened to be passing through Siena. In principle, this is entirely plausible
but it has never been substantiated. See Martindale/Simone p. 45.

Postscript: Peter Kidson as Tutor on the Courtauld Institute Summer Schools for the Study of Architecture, 1955–81

Barbara Robertson

Peter Kidson was a regular attender as one of the tutors on the long series of Architectural Summer Schools organised by me and my husband Charles. Every year for twenty-seven years we travelled on the roads of Europe thinking little of a day in a bus, and moving on each night, or two if we were lucky.

For eight years we were in England and the first trip abroad was the Pilgrimage route to Santiago de Compostela. Then followed Scandinavia, Sicily, Apulia, England and France, Poland, the Rhine, Western Turkey, Provence and Eastern Turkey. There was then a switch from medieval art and architecture to Baroque, visiting Bavaria, Austria, Rome, Normandy, Venice, Andalusia, France and Lombardy.

We set off always in the mid-summer days of July after the universities had come down: teaching, educating, encouraging and urging on the forty to fifty people from any country who had been rash enough to sign on. PK had a permanent place on the back seat of the bus which was an area of wine and laughter and a far cry from the nail-biting navigators in the front.

It was my job to steer the motley crew and I sometimes felt I was doing this in spite of the machinations of PK and his accomplice Christopher Hohler, a tempestuous pair of horses in any chariot. But when, for instance, we made it to Ani in Eastern Turkey and looked over the border into betanked Russian territory, there was no-one I would rather have had on board than PK.

Life on the road was not entirely smooth going and his predilection for Gothic edifices led us into some curious places. A lunch-time picnic at Schwaebisch-Gmuend on a sloping bank where everything slid downhill had, as a view, several immense gasometers surrounding a to-be-visited insignificant church enveloped in drizzle. At Cannae in Apulia I asked PK to give us a talk on the strategy of the battle. He replied that he could only do it with swords. Cursing his dodging the issue, I went out after supper, and, by a miracle, bought four plastic swords at a fair. It seemed a poor ration among forty civilians considering that Hannibal is said to have killed 50,000 Romans, but PK rose to the occasion with a weapon in his hand.

The word rubberneck comes to mind when studying Gothic vaulting from Aquitaine to Krakow and from Uppsala to Bari. With binoculars pressed painfully into the face, and squinting with our own inadequate eyes, we stood, heads flung firmly back, in growing agony while words like barrel, lierne, groin and rib, fan and tierceron flowed from PK with his whirling hands and his amazing knowledge. He had early learned that it was impossible to impart even one crumb of information if he stood near a monster church cleaner, such as the one in Hereford Cathedral with its output of decibels equalling a DC 10.

On the other hand, the dangers of having to listen, not to PK, but to some eager not-to-be-deterred curé in a French provincial church, with all the time in the world and no relevant information, led me to develop and perfect a method of silently diminishing a group of fidgeting summer-schoolers without being openly rude.

There were some dangers. Cyprus, for instance, was cancelled two days before departure because of the outbreak of war. One participant who had gone early had to be air-lifted off a beach by the R.A.F. A demented Ayatollah in Turkey gave us the evil eye and drove a crowd of children away from us. Poland, undertaken as an international venture, ended with Russian planes droning into Czechoslovakia over our heads. We were glad to get home. In Italy a large lorry loaded with earth stuck with spades crashed into the back of our bus. A suitcase containing several volumes from the London Library, ('it is strictly forbidden to take books abroad') received the full brunt of the collision. The driver, as is usual after lunch, was asleep at his wheel. PK was felled by hepatitis in Spain and had to be flown out to Madrid and on to a London Hospital. That taught me to be wary, especially in Turkey where hepatitis is endemic.

There is no doubt that PK was the champion tutor of the scholarship students, who numbered between sixteen and twenty each year from universities in Great Britain, Europe and the U.S.A. Some were wild, some serious: one had to be sent home because of love-sickness and one because of unsuitability. But all, in the end, became welded into the group at the back of the bus presided over by PK, surrounded by his bursting bag of reference books (from the Courtauld Library) and maps and bottles of wine. The wine was never spectacular or even very good. Indeed when in northern France we were happily picnicking on the battlements of the castle of Enguerrand de Coucy, a wedding party arrived on the usual post-nuptial walk. PK offered the bride and groom a glass of red: but the groom picked up a bottle and after a withering look said 'onze degrés seulement' and they whirled away in a flutter of white lace.

On a personal note, I am proud that so many of those scholarship students now turn up all over the place as museum curators, authors of articles and books, and university professors.

When from old age and a wish to finish while the going is going was good, Charles and I wrapped up the Summer Schools in 1981 on top of a mountain in Lombardy (since written about so memorably in *The Name of the Rose*), everyone by then was travelling about looking at buildings. We should have had to change the name to Home House Travel, booked in to luxury hotels and ordered a 'coach' with a loo. There was much to be said for our unsophisticated travels of the 1960s and 70s.

PK was a mainspring in this protracted venture. Dependable, amusing, a first-class teacher (who but he could spend half an hour on one stone?), a splendid companion and an ever-present help in any situation.

Index

Plate numbers are given in italics after page numbers

List of Subscribers

Abel Smith, Mrs L.
Alcock, Prof. Leslie
Alexander, Prof. J.J.G.
Anderberg, M. & S.
Andersen, Ingrid
Anderson, Dr. Freda
Andrew, Martin
Ashdown, John
Ayers, T.J.F.
Bascombe, Dr. K.N.
Batey, Angus R.
Bayle, Dr. Maylis
Beamish, G.M.
Bernasconi, John G.
Beston, Maria
Black, David W.
Blair, Dr. John
Blum, Dr. Pamela Z.
Bold, Dr. John
Bony, Prof. Jean
Borg, Alan
Bowness, Sir Alan
Boynton, Mrs. H.E.
Brodie, Allan
Brooke, Prof. C. & Dr. R.
Brown, O.F.
Brown, Sarah
Buckton, David
Bull, George
Burge, James
Bush, Paul
Caldwell, M.
Cambridge, Eric
Cannon, Dr. Joanna

Cazel, Prof. Fred A., Jr.
Chaney, Dr. Edward
Cherry, John and Bridget
Clanchy, Dr. M.T.
Claridge, Karyn
Clark, Prof. William W.
Cligman, Judith
Coales, John
Cocke, Dr. R.
Cocke, Dr. T.H.
Coldstream, Nicola
Colfox, Lady
Collingwood, Vera
Coope, Dr Rosalys
Cooper, Nicholas
Cooper-Hammond, John
Copplestone, Trewin
Corry-Smith, Miss E.C.
Courtney, Nora
Covert, Mary R.
Cowdrey, Rev. H.E.J.
Cox, Dr. D.C.
Croad, Stephen
Crossley, Dr. Paul
Crown, Ada
Culver, Jeannette
Cunningham, Miss J.A.
Curry, Ian
Da Cruz, Antonio
Davis, Prof. R.H.C.
Doran, P.M.
Downes, Prof. Kerry
Draper, Dr. Peter
Dyson, John

English, Dr. Barbara
Farr, Dr. Dennis
Feldman, Nina
Fergusson, Peter
Fernie, Prof. Eric
Flight, C.
Flood, Dr. John G.
Fowler, D.J.
Franklin, Jill A.
Froggatt, Paul
Fuglesang, Dr. Signe Horn
Gajewski, Alexandra
Garton, Dr. Tessa
Geddes, Dr. Jane
Gem, Richard
Getgood, Michael A.
Gibb, J.H.P.
Gibbs, R.J.
Givens, Dr. Jean A.
Glenn, C.V.
Grant, Lindy
Graves, C. Pamela
Green, Jane H.
Greenwood, Colin & Isabel
Gwynne, Robert T.
Hadden, Derek N.
Hall, Michael
Hall, Nicholas
Hardwick, Nora M.
Harker, K.M.
Harper-Bill, Dr. C.
Harris, Andrew
Harvey, Dr. Barbara
Hasloch, Elizabeth
Hawes, E.M.
Hearn, M.F.
Heffley, Sylvia P.
Heseltine, Mrs. M.
Heslop, T.A.
Heywood, Stephen
Higgins, Tim
Higgitt, John
Hilder, Ann
Hislop, Dr. Malcolm
Hoey, Prof. Lawrence

Hohler, Mr. C. & Mrs. E.
Holt, Sir James
House, Dr. John
Howell, P.G.
Hunt, J.
Jackson, Dr. E.P.
Jansen, Virginia
Jessiman, Dr. I.M.
Johnston, Graeme
Jones, Dr. M.C.E.
Jope, Prof. E.M.
Jundul, Stella
Kelly, Francis
Kelsall, Frank
Kennedy, B.J.
Kennish, Mrs. J.
Kidd, Peter
King, Heather A.
King, the Hon. Mrs.
Lacaze, Dr. Charlotte
Lankester, Philip J.
Lansdall-Welfare, R.
Law, Dr. John
Leach, Rosemary
Lee, Ronald A.
Leedy, Dr. Walter
Liden, Prof. Hans-Emil
Lockett, Richard
Loveland, Isabel
Lowden, Dr. John
Mainz, Miss V.S.
Marks, Dr. Richard
Markus, Mary
Martindale, Prof. A.H.R.
Massing, Dr. Jean Michel
Matthews, Mrs. P.K.
Maxwell, Robert
Mayor, Edward R.
McAleer, J. Philip
McEnery, John
McNab, Dr. Susanne
Meeson, R.A.
Mendelsson, W.
Mercer, Eric
Milburn, Catherine

Milner, Lesley
Minter, P.W.
Moore, N.J.
Morgan, Dr. Nigel
Morgan, Wendy
Morris, Richard K.
Morrison, Kathryn
Muratova, Dr. Xenia
Murray, Dr. Stephen
Murray, Prof. Peter
Myles, Dr. Janet
Neuenschwander, Dr. Brody
Newhall, R.
Nichols, Sarah C.
Norton, Dr. Christopher
Norton, Richard
O'Callaghan, Brian
O'Connor, David
O'Connor, Dr. T.P.
O'Keefe, Tadhg
O'Neill, Michael
Owen, Dr. D.M.
Palliser, Prof. D.M.
Park, David
Parker, Mrs. P.W.
Parsons, Dr. David
Passa, Anthony & Mary
Paul, Prof. Vivian
Pearson, Sarah
Pestell, Richard
Phythian-Adams, M.V.
Pillman, A.C.
Platt, Prof. Colin
Plumb, Rev. G.A.
Plumley, Chrys
Ponting, David A.
Powell, D.C.I.
Prache, Anne
Purchas, Anne
Reilly, Lisa
Reinke, Audrun
Renn, Dr. Derek
Roberts, Dr. Brian K.
Robertson, Eleanor C.
Robertson, Mrs. B.

Rodwell, Dr. Warwick
Rogers, Nicholas
Rosser, Dr. A.G.
Rowan, Genevieve
Russell, Francis
Saul, Dr. N.E.
Saunders, Andrew
Saunders, Dr. Ann
Schueler, Dr. Christian
Schwieso, Joshua J.
Scott, Jack G.
Sheppard, Peter
Simonson, Dr. Anne
Simpson, Dr. Amanda
Simpson, Dr. Grant G.
Singleton, Barrie
Spencer, Dr. John
Stalley, Prof. Roger
Steele, Mrs. J.C.
Stevens, Alan
Stocker, D.A.
Stratford, Mr. & Mrs. Neil
Sturgis, Alexander
Sutton, Ian
Tatton-Brown, Tim
Taylor, Dr. Arnold
Taylor, Robert
Tcherikover, Anat
Tolley, Dr. Thomas
Tomlins, Mrs. I.F.
Tredre, Angela
Trendall, Prof. A.D.
Tuohy, Dr,. Thomas J.
Underhill, Dr. Nancy H.
Waddington, Jane
Walker, Janet
Walker, Miss Lorna E.M.
Wayment, Dr. Hilary
Wedgwood, Prof. Pamela
Wei, Ian P.
Welander, Christopher
West, Dr. Jeffrey
West, Jeffrey James
Westerby, Ruth
Wilkinson, Kate

Wills, Dr. Catherine
Wilson, Dr. Christopher
Winkenbach, Gerald

Wood, Jason
Zarnecki, Prof. George